Fair Treatment of Persons in Police Custody

Ralf Alleweldt
Editor

Fair Treatment of Persons in Police Custody

Gefördert durch:
DSF Deutsche Stiftung Friedensforschung
german foundation for peace research

Springer

Editor
Ralf Alleweldt
Brandenburg State Police University
Oranienburg, Germany

ISBN 978-3-031-61736-2 ISBN 978-3-031-61737-9 (eBook)
https://doi.org/10.1007/978-3-031-61737-9

Gefördert durch die Deutsche Stiftung Friedensforschung (DSF)
Supported by the German Foundation for Peace Research

This Springer imprint is published by the registered company Springer Nature Switzerland AG
The registered company address is: Gewerbestrasse 11, 6330 Cham, Switzerland

Contents

Chapter 1
Fair Treatment of Persons in Police Custody: An Introduction

Ralf Alleweldt

Contents

Abstract Police authorities are entitled, if certain conditions are met, to deprive persons of their liberty. Such power brings with it the responsibility to treat the affected persons decently and with dignity. Although this is a requirement of international law, which, in addition, expressly prohibits any ill-treatment or torture, police forces in many countries do not always live up to their high responsibility. This presents a legal and ethical challenge: if a fundamental norm like the prohibition of torture is not implemented, the Rule of Law is undermined, and governments will lose their credibility and authority. The ability of victims to institute proceedings on the national or international level, while necessary, has proven insufficient to bridge the gap between law and reality.

Recognizing this challenge, the international community has established specific mechanisms for preventing torture and ill-treatment in recent decades. Experience shows that many activities may be successfully taken to improve the situation of detainees and preserve their dignity. The chapters of this book, which are outlined below, describe various problem areas as well as approaches how to ensure the fair treatment of persons in police custody.

R. Alleweldt (✉)
Brandenburg State Police University, Oranienburg, Germany
e-mail: ralf.alleweldt@hpolbb.de

R. Alleweldt (ed.), *Fair Treatment of Persons in Police Custody*,
https://doi.org/10.1007/978-3-031-61737-9_1

1.1 Police Custody: An Exceptional Measure

Human beings have the natural right to move around freely, and in particular, to leave any place they want to leave. Only under exceptional circumstances may they be deprived of this liberty by state authorities, including the police. They may usually only be arrested on a specific legal ground based on specific facts, for example, reasonable suspicion of having committed a particular criminal act. At the same time, everyone has the right to be presumed innocent until found guilty by a court.

In addition, when arresting a person, police often have to act quickly and based on a provisional assessment of the facts. A judge makes the final legal determination as to whether detention is lawful. Quite frequently, a person is released from custody when an initial suspicion has not materialized or other legal conditions for ordering detention are not met. Accordingly, police custody is always of a provisional, temporary character. Furthermore, while police authorities make an important contribution to ensure that criminal proceedings are conducted properly and offenders are punished, it is never their own task to pronounce guilt or to carry out any punishment.

In this context, and in any case, it is logical and imperative that all persons in police custody, regardless of whether they are guilty, dangerous, or innocent, whether detained lawfully or unlawfully, have to be treated decently and with dignity. In particular, their physical and mental integrity must be respected. Physical force can be used by the police only for overcoming unlawful resistance, and for countering any attacks or other dangers emanating from the detained person. Apart from that, even in cases where it appears that the detained person has committed a terrible crime, any punishment can only be ordered by the competent criminal court after the person has been given a fair trial. In particular, persons in police custody must not be forced to testify against themselves or to make any statement at all. This is guaranteed by the Rule of Law, by international human rights law, and, presumably, by any national legal order in the world. There is hardly any more apparent legal rule than the one laid down in Article 10 of the International Covenant on Civil and Political Rights:[1]

> All persons deprived of their liberty shall be treated with humanity and with respect for the inherent dignity of the human person.

1.2 The Prohibition of Torture

This rule is confirmed and reinforced by the absolute prohibition of torture and inhuman or degrading treatment or punishment, as laid down in Article 7 of the International Covenant on Civil and Political Rights, Article 3 of the European

[1] International Covenant on Civil and Political Rights of 16 December 1966, UNTS no. 999, p. 171.

Convention on Human Rights,[2] and many other international human rights instruments. The prohibition of torture and ill-treatment is also part of customary international law; it is generally considered to be a peremptory norm of international law and, we may say, a necessary component of any just and peaceful society.

In order to fight torture, governments agreed to conclude a specific convention in 1984.[3] The prohibition of torture and other ill-treatment is absolute; it does not allow for exceptions or restrictions in the interests of the community. Even in times of war or other emergency situations threatening the life of a nation, no derogation is possible.[4] Indeed, the laws of war have long contained specific rules requiring the humane treatment and excluding torture of prisoners of war and other protected persons.[5]

Accordingly, in terms of substantive law, it is a clear and imperative requirement that all persons deprived of their liberty must be treated fairly and adequately. This is especially true if they are detained by the police, an institution with a particularly high responsibility for ensuring that the law is respected by everyone.

1.3 The Practical Problem

In the real world, persons in police custody are not always treated lawfully, and with dignity. This may be seen from the findings of international monitoring mechanisms, international courts, and it is confirmed by reports issued by non-governmental human rights organizations.

With regard to the European continent, the Committee for the Prevention of Torture and Inhuman or Degrading Treatment or Punishment (CPT)[6] stated in 2019 that the infliction of ill-treatment during police interviews remained "a very serious problem." In particular, the Committee had received credible allegations of torture, supported by other evidence, in almost one-third of Council of Europe member states.[7] To give some examples, the CPT received in Romania "a large number of allegations of ill-treatment of detained persons by the police" (slaps,

---

[2] Convention for the Protection of Human Rights and Fundamental Freedoms of 4 November 1950, ETS no. 5.

[3] Convention against Torture and Other Cruel, Inhuman or Degrading Treatment of Punishment of 10 December 1984, UNTS no. 1465, p. 85.

[4] Cf. Article 4 of the International Covenant on Civil and Political Rights, Article 15 of the European Convention on Human Rights, Article 2 of the Convention against Torture.

[5] See the Convention (IV) respecting the Laws and Customs of War on Land and its annex: Regulations concerning the Law and Customs of War on Land, The Hague, 18 October 1907, Article 4; various articles of the four Geneva Conventions of 12 August 1949; Additional Protocol (I) to the Geneva Conventions, 8 June 1977, Article 75.

[6] See below, Section 1.5.

[7] See CPT, Preventing police torture and other forms of ill-treatment—reflections on good practices and emerging approaches, 28th General Report, 2019, CPT/Inf (2019) 9, para 65.

punches, kicks, and baton blows). The alleged ill-treatment occurred "at the moment of arrest (. . .), during transportation and at the police station, apparently for the purpose of forcing a confession to one or more criminal offences or for informal punishment."[8] Similarly, with regard to Slovakia, it was "a matter of serious concern for the CPT that a considerable number of persons who were or had recently been detained by the police – including juveniles – made credible allegations of deliberate physical ill-treatment by police officers."[9] In Turkey, the CPT delegation "received a considerable number of allegations of excessive use of force and/or physical ill-treatment by police/gendarmerie officers from persons who had recently been taken into custody (including women and juveniles). These allegations mainly consisted of slaps, kicks, punches (including to the head and/or face) and truncheon blows."[10] With regard to Portugal, the CPT emphasized that "the majority of persons met by the CPT's delegation stated that they had been correctly treated by law enforcement officials." However, at the same time, the delegation received "a considerable number of allegations of ill-treatment, inflicted as a means to force the suspects to sign certain documents, to confess to particular crimes or to punish them for the alleged crime committed."[11]

The European Court of Human Rights has found violations of the prohibition of torture when, for example, during the G8 summit in Genoa 2001, Italian police entered a school used by protesters as a night shelter and beat them up,[12] when two Moldovan nationals suffered injuries on their head, limbs, and feet during police custody,[13] or when Ukrainian police officers inflicted electric shocks on an arrestee in order to obtain a confession.[14]

Extensive insights into the human rights situation in Europe can be gained from the reports of the Committee of Ministers of the Council of Europe. This Committee is responsible, under Article 46 of the Convention, for supervising the execution of the Court's judgments, and in particular, for monitoring the general measures required for complying with such a judgment. In cases where human rights problems appear to be of a structural nature, the Committee may place the case, or a group of cases, under "enhanced supervision."[15] One of these human rights problems is "ill-treatment or torture in police custody and ineffective investigation into allegations of such acts." This issue is (in this or similar wording) under enhanced supervision

[8] CPT, Report on the visit to Romania in 2018, CPT/Inf (2019) 7, para 12.

[9] CPT, Report on the visit to the Slovak Republic in 2018, CPT/Inf (2019) 20, para 10.

[10] CPT, Report on the visit to Turkey in 2019, CPT/Inf (2020) 24, para 10.

[11] CPT, Report on the visit to Portugal in 2018, CPT/Inf (2020) 33, para 13.

[12] European Court of Human Rights, *Cestaro v. Italy* (2015), para 190; similarly, *Blair v. Italy* (2017) para 106, and *Azzolina v. Italy* (2017), para 137.

[13] European Court of Human Rights, *Levinta v. Moldova* (2008), para 71.

[14] European Court of Human Rights, *Nechiporuk and Yonkalo v. Ukraine* (2011), para 159.

[15] For details, see Council of Europe, Department for the Execution of Judgments of the European Court of Human Rights: The supervision process, https://www.coe.int/en/web/execution/the-supervision-process.

concerning twelve Council of Europe member states, namely, Armenia, Azerbaijan, Cyprus, Georgia, Greece, Hungary, Italy, Moldova, Romania, Slovakia, Turkey, Ukraine, and also, in addition, the former member state Russia.[16] In these countries, considerable efforts are clearly required to ensure the fair treatment of persons in police custody.

Outside of Europe, things do not appear to be any better. It can be seen from the published reports of the United Nations Subcommittee for the Prevention of Torture (SPT)[17] that, for example, the Committee heard "widespread and consistent allegations of police brutality" in Belize[18] and "numerous allegations concerning violent acts by the military police" in Brazil.[19] In Mongolia, the Committee heard "allegations from numerous sources of instances of torture and ill-treatment being inflicted during the initial phase of arrest and investigation by police, especially in remote and in small police stations."[20] With regard to Uruguay, the Committee reported that "several interviewees, in particular adolescents, claimed to have been subjected to torture and/or ill-treatment while in detention and/or during their stay in police facilities."[21]

It must be emphasized that the governments of these states, by consenting to the publication of SPT reports, show a degree of transparency which other governments do not. Many states visited by the SPT have not yet agreed to the publication of the visit reports. And many states do not agree to be visited by the SPT at all, since they are not contracting parties to OPCAT (see below Section 1.5). These include big states such as China, India, and the United States of America.

A number of years ago, Amnesty International reported incidences of torture and ill-treatment in 141 states.[22] Apparently, ensuring that all persons in police custody are treated fairly is a challenging task, and it is a task of civilization that has not yet been solved.

1.4 The Legal and Ethical Challenge

The considerable gap between the laws prohibiting torture and the real situation in the world constitutes a huge ethical and political challenge, and also a massive legal problem. Law does not exist without implementation and enforcement. If a

[16] See the respective Country Factsheets: Council of Europe, Department for the Execution of Judgments of the European Court of Human Rights: Country Factsheets, at: https://www.coe.int/en/web/execution/country-factsheets.

[17] See below, Section 1.5.

[18] SPT, Report on the visit to Belize in 2018, UN Doc. CAT/OP/BLZ/ROSP/1 (2022), para 58.

[19] SPT, Report on the visit to Brazil in 2015, UN Doc. CAT/OP/BRA/3 (2017), para 15.

[20] SPT, Report on the visit to Mongolia in 2017, UN Doc. CAT/OP/MNG/1 (2018), para 33.

[21] SPT, Report on the visit to Uruguay in 2018, UN Doc. CAT/OP/URY/1 (2019), para 24.

[22] See Amnesty International, Torture in 2014—30 years of broken promises (2014), p. 10.

fundamental rule of law, such as the prohibition of torture and the requirement to treat detained persons fairly, is disrespected in many cases, the authority and credibility of the law in general are called into question. The more state authorities disregard fundamental legal norms, the less citizens become inclined to recognize state-set rules as binding on them. Torture and other violations of human dignity therefore have the potential to undermine the idea of the law as a collection of binding rules regulating the relations between states and their citizens.

This is particularly true if human rights abuses are committed by police officers. The police is an institution closely connected to the Rule of Law, and is bearing a specific responsibility for upholding the law. If "law-enforcement" authorities break fundamental legal rules, if "security" forces attack the dignity and integrity of citizens, then they undermine and destroy the foundations of the very order they should protect, and they remove their own legitimacy. Their power may continue, but it will no longer be recognized as legitimate power.

In addition, serious human rights violations naturally trigger feelings of hate and frustration in their victims, and they may block the establishment of peaceful, cooperative relations within the state and society. Wherever human beings see their rights disrespected, they will think about how to defend themselves. Indeed, in severe cases, they may "be compelled to have recourse, as a last resort, to rebellion against tyranny and oppression" as the Preamble of the Universal Declaration of Human Rights states. Human rights abuses may threaten, and are threatening, public order as well as international peace and security; peaceful conflict resolution requires respect for human rights. Such respect, in particular treating persons in police custody fairly, thus supports peaceful relations between citizens and governments all over the world. Respect for human dignity contributes to world peace.

In sum, torture and ill-treatment in police custody make citizens lose their trust in the law, their government, and the legitimacy and usefulness of police forces. They put in danger the foundations of society. Treating persons in police custody fairly and adequately is a minimum requirement of a peaceful society where citizens trust their government, rely on the legal order, and accept the police as a protective, helpful, and valuable institution.

1.5 Domestic and International Legal Procedures: Preventive Approaches

How can the non-implementation of the legal rules prohibiting torture and ill-treatment be overcome? The traditional method of enforcing legal rules—namely, instituting court or complaint proceedings—has apparently not been sufficient so far to tackle the problem effectively. This is true for national court proceedings as well as for applications to international human rights bodies such as the European Court of Human Rights or the UN Human Rights Committee.

Of course, complaint proceedings are a necessary component of any effective system of human rights protection. They reflect a revolutionary development in international law: individuals have human rights and may enforce them in the international sphere, even against their own government. But it is now apparent that, for a variety of reasons, not all persons who have been ill-treated by state authorities complain about their treatment in any legal procedure.[23] They are typically shocked and in a state of fear; they may face reprisals or a counter-prosecution for libel or similar offenses; they may see no prospects of success for the lack of evidence; they may lack the energy or simply the money to pursue long court proceedings with an uncertain outcome. In addition, and most importantly, no legal proceedings and no compensation can remove the physical and psychological scars inflicted on the victims. In many cases, the damage done through torture may prove irreparable—at least not reparable by the outcome of any legal proceedings. As far as torture is concerned, the law is often either respected or irreversibly violated.

Accordingly, since recourse to legal remedies cannot compensate fully for torture and will not always be successful, governments have created—under some pressure from international human rights organizations—special bodies or mechanisms which aim to prevent violations of the prohibition of torture from the outset, and to secure the fair treatment of detained persons sustainably.[24] The first such mechanism is the European Committee for the Prevention of Torture (CPT), which took up its activities in 1990, based on the 1987 European Convention for the Prevention of Torture (ECPT).[25] In 2006 a similar institution was created at the universal level, namely, the Sub-Committee on Prevention of Torture (SPT). Its legal basis is the Optional Protocol to the United Nations Convention against Torture (OPCAT).[26] This Protocol requires State Parties, in addition, to create National Mechanisms for the Prevention of Torture (NPMs) which work parallel to the international mechanisms, but are, in principle, able to do a much more intense work since they may concentrate on one country only.

All preventive mechanisms are tasked with visiting all types of places of detention in their area and examining the situation of those detained. Following these visits, they prepare recommendations to the government aimed at improving the situation. Such recommendations are aimed at, for example, publicly acknowledging the existence of problems, limiting the time of police custody, videotaping police interrogations, allowing early access to a relative, to a doctor, and to a lawyer, effectively investigating and prosecuting alleged abuses, and, where appropriate, introducing new complaint procedures. Where appropriate, it is also recommended

[23] Cassese (1996), p. 17.

[24] In this context, "prevention is the key." See Cassese (1989), p. 128 (129).

[25] European Convention for the Prevention of Torture and Inhuman or Degrading Treatment or Punishment of 26 November 1987, ETS no. 152.

[26] Optional Protocol to the Convention against Torture and other Cruel, Inhuman or Degrading Treatment or Punishment of 18 December 2002, UNTS no. 2375, p. 237.

that police training and education be further developed and improved, for example with regard to modern methods of investigation.[27] The recommendations are summarized in detailed reports which are usually published sometime after the visit, together with a government response.

Government authorities are usually cooperating with preventive mechanisms, although the degree of cooperation varies greatly from state to state. In some states, quite measurable progress has been made—not always noticed by the public—in the treatment of detained persons, while in others there have been no significant changes. Preventive mechanisms depend on the cooperation from governments. They may repeat their recommendations, persistently if necessary; the ultimate measure in cases of insufficient cooperation is for the CPT and SPT to issue a public statement on the situation in a particular country (Article 10 ECPT, Article 16 OPCAT), an option of which they make rarely use. When preventive mechanisms work successfully, they have the potential to make a lasting contribution to the preservation of human rights.

1.6 This Book

The experiences of the last few decades—including those obtained by the work of preventive mechanisms—show that a multitude of activities may be taken to improve the treatment of persons in police custody. It is one of the aims of this book to identify and describe these activities, which may help, if necessary, to move a country from a torturing to a non-torturing state. The authors will define possible steps governments may take in this direction, often with support and pressure from civil society. Although these activities and steps aim to implement a basic legal rule, they are not all of a legal nature.

In Chapter 2 of this book, *Richard Carver* describes and evaluates the typical instruments, tools, and safeguards introduced by governments during the last decades, which aim to ensure the proper treatment of persons in police custody. First, acts of torture or other ill-treatment should be criminalized, investigated, and prosecuted. Second, detention places should be monitored by independent bodies. Third, independent complaint mechanisms should be available to all those who are not satisfied with their treatment in police detention. Finally, and very importantly, a number of fundamental safeguards should be available to all persons from the outset of their custody, namely, the rights of access to a lawyer, to notify a third party, and independent medical examinations. *Carver* presents the results of a study of 16 countries covering a 30-year period evaluating the effectiveness of these instruments. His findings indicate that the practical implementation of fundamental safeguards for persons in police custody is the most effective way of preventing torture. The

[27] See, in detail, for example the CPT "Standards and Tools" at https://www.coe.int/en/web/cpt/standards.

investigation and prosecution of torturers and the establishment of independent monitoring mechanisms also have an important impact in reducing the incidence of torture. In any case, and not surprisingly, torture prevention measures have proven ineffective as long as they remain merely as laws in the statute book. While legal reform is often a necessary precondition for protection against torture, it is never sufficient. It is only by ensuring *in practice* an end to unlawful detention, notification of a third party on arrest, prompt access to a lawyer, and independent medical examinations that people in police custody can be effectively protected. In other words: we need the right rules, and we need police forces abiding by these rules.

In Chapter 3, *Krassimir Kanev* examines the fundamental safeguards in more depth. He observes that the introduction and implementation of such safeguards does not guarantee that detained persons are treated correctly in reality. There are, in fact, a number of states where torture and other ill-treatment persist, although the responsible governments avail themselves of international scrutiny in all its forms. While the preventive approach taken by international visiting mechanisms—based, in essence, on constructive dialogue—apparently works reasonably well in many countries, there is a need to do more at the national level. Inter alia, he proposes to enhance civil society involvement in monitoring and legal assistance to victims of torture and other ill-treatment and, in particular, to create a firm legal basis in international law for NGO access to all places of detention.

Ensuring fair treatment of persons in police custody can be a challenge in any country, in particular in situations where a significant number of persons are likely to be arrested. In Chapter 4, *Christina Hof* addresses the practical challenges of respecting fundamental safeguards for detained persons during the G20 summit in Hamburg, Germany, in July 2017. After describing the specific situation and recalling international and national prevention standards, she takes a closer look at the practical challenges encountered in Hamburg with a focus on structural and material conditions of the mass detention center where the authorities did not always succeed in providing immediate access to a lawyer and conducting a prompt judicial hearing. She identifies some lessons learned in Hamburg with a view to contributing to better human rights protection in cases of mass detention in the future.

Police questioning is a situation where it is most important to preserve the dignity of the detained person. It is, as a rule, the objective of police officers during questioning to obtain information from the detainee, sometimes important information relating to a crime already committed or to an organization considered dangerous by the authorities. In such a situation, police officers may be tempted to exercise pressure on the detainee, and indeed some of the traditional methods of interrogation are based on the idea that detained persons—usually criminal suspects—should be brought under such intense pressure that they will confess to the crime. It is clear that such questioning may degenerate into exercising undue pressure on a person crossing the line from legitimate law enforcement action to degrading or inhuman treatment or even torture.

Investigative interviewing, in contrast, is a method of questioning based on non-coercive, cooperative communication, which has proven to be effective in obtaining the most accurate and reliable information from detained persons, including persons suspected of terrorist crimes, while at the same time fully preserving their dignity and autonomy. In Chapter 5, *Asbjørn Rachlew* describes in some detail, inter alia, how police officers may use this method in their practical work. In Chapter 6, *Frances Surmon-Böhr, Laurence Alison,* and *Emily Alison* report how the British authorities, when dealing with persons suspected of terrorism, moved from harsh interrogation methods to non-coercive interviewing. They give an overview of the ORBIT, an empirically based model of police interviewing based on counseling approaches and developed from the analysis of police interviews with terrorism suspects.

Human rights-oriented policing is better policing. When assessing the human rights situation in a given country, a critical, analytical look is usually necessary identifying violations and deficiencies. In contrast, additional tools and approaches must be included when looking for ways to change and improve the situation, enabling actors and institutions to move in a new, positive direction. In Chapter 7, *Walter Suntinger* and *Moritz Birk* propose a resource-oriented look at furthering human rights realization by the police, with a specific focus on the Appreciative Inquiry approach, a method designed to mobilize positive energy leading to desired change. Its use in police training may refocus attention on what already works well in police practice and how success stories can be harnessed to further strengthen police work in line with human rights standards.

The Optional Protocol to the United Nations Convention against Torture (OPCAT) requires contracting states to establish National Preventive Mechanisms (NPMs), and such mechanisms have been created in numerous countries since 2006. In Chapter 8, *Audrey Olivier Muralt* examines the powers of the NPMs under the OPCAT, including their right to access all places, persons, and information, and how these powers can be used to propose concrete changes to detention practices and laws. Based on the lessons learned during the last 15 years, the article highlights good practices, some successes, but also difficulties and problems that NPMs face in their daily work. In Chapter 9, *Nika Kvaratskhelia* gives an insight, based on first-hand experience, into the practical work of the NPM in the Republic of Georgia. While appreciating the progress made during the last few decades as regards the treatment of persons in police custody, he identifies a number of persisting shortcomings and challenges.

Fair treatment of persons in police custody is an important subject of development cooperation in the security sector. In Chapter 10, *Cristina Sganga* outlines some of the key steps to follow when designing and implementing effective capacity-building programs for law enforcement officials aiming at the prevention of torture and other ill-treatment.

The aim of ensuring appropriate treatment of detainees is a particular challenge for police forces in international peace missions. In the context of such a mission, i.e., in a post-conflict situation, the first and foremost objective is to re-establish a peace order in which public security is preserved as far as possible. Compared to the normal life of states, additional human rights problems arise. In Chapter 11, *Judith Thorn* describes a number of legal issues connected with detention in this context, while in Chapter 12, *William O'Neill* discusses practical problems related to detention and the rule of law during international peace missions.

In Chapter 13, *Wolfgang S. Heinz* takes stock of the efforts made so far to prevent torture effectively. He considers possible strategies for ensuring the fair treatment of persons in police custody in the future. Based on recent research, he proposes to tackle the problem by enhancing the competencies of police officers, making sure that ill-treatment is the subject of effective criminal investigation and prosecution, improving the interviewing process, and to fight corruption. Furthermore, he emphasizes the importance of the political country context since it may open or limit corridors for reform. It is also important to understand the self-image of relevant police actors, the way they think, and their informal rules and values. A good knowledge of the internal organization of police organizations and their inside police processes is necessary to understand them better, and develop strategies for change and reform even in the face of considerable resistance.

Based on the contributions in this book, I will then, in Chapter 14, summarize important findings, draw some conclusions, and develop further ideas about steps for ensuring the fair treatment of persons in police custody. In particular, in order to strengthen protection against ill-treatment during the first hours of detention, I will propose to reconsider the permissible length of police custody and develop arguments in favor of an immediate judicial intervention within hours after arrest. This could be achieved by introducing new national laws to this effect or by re-interpreting the norms of international human rights law by the European Court of Human Rights and other relevant bodies. In addition, I will also highlight once more investigative interviewing as a particularly important and immensely practical approach to ensuring the proper treatment of detainees in real life. Investigative interviewing could well provide the key to improving the human rights performance and, at the same time, enhancing the effectiveness of police forces throughout the world in the twenty-first century.

This book is based on the contributions given during the second Oranienburg international human rights conference, "Fair Treatment of Persons in Police Custody," which took place at the Brandenburg State Police University—Hochschule der Polizei des Landes Brandenburg—on 16 and 17 October 2018. The delay in publication lies entirely within the responsibility of the editor. Speakers and participants reflected a variety of perspectives, inter alia from the police force, other government authorities, international organizations, academics, and the human rights movement. The authors of this book naturally reflect this fruitful diversity.

As indicated above, treating persons in police custody fairly is an important element of human rights protection, and in this way, contributes to peaceful relations within society and in the world. The German Foundation for Peace Research—Deutsche Stiftung Friedensforschung—generously supported the conference financially. I am grateful for the extraordinary support given by my university, including by (former) President Rainer Grieger and Vice-President Jochen Christe-Zeyse, and the organizing team, in particular Jochen Matthaeus, Claudia Schimek, Dagmar

Heintze, and Stephanie Hopp. Dagmar also contributed greatly to the editorial revision of this book. Special thanks go to Walter Suntinger whose valuable input influenced the design and preparation of the conference considerably, and, indeed, made this event possible. Feedback is welcome at ralf.alleweldt@hpolbb.de.

Reports

Amnesty International, Torture in 2014—30 years of broken promises (2014), p. 10.

Council of Europe, Department for the Execution of Judgments of the European Court of Human Rights: Country Factsheets, https://www.coe.int/en/web/execution/country-factsheets.

- The supervision process, https://www.coe.int/en/web/execution/the-supervision-process.

European Committee for the Prevention of Torture and Inhuman or Degrading Treatment or Punishment (CPT): Preventing police torture and other forms of ill-treatment—reflections on good practices and emerging approaches, 28th General Report, 2019, CPT/Inf (2019) 9, paras 61–85.

- Report on the visit to Portugal in 2018, CPT/Inf (2020) 33.
- Report on the visit to Romania in 2018, CPT/Inf (2019) 7.
- Report on the visit to the Slovak Republic in 2018, CPT/Inf (2019) 20.
- Report on the visit to Turkey in 2019, CPT/Inf (2020) 24.
- Standards and Tools, https://www.coe.int/en/web/cpt/standards.

Sub-Committee on Prevention of Torture and other Cruel, Inhuman or Degrading Treatment or Punishment (SPT): Report on the visit to Belize in 2018, UN Doc. CAT/OP/BLZ/ROSP/1 (2022);

- Report on the visit to Brazil in 2015, UN Doc. CAT/OP/BRA/3 (2017);
- Report on the visit to Mongolia in 2017, UN Doc. CAT/OP/MNG/1 (2018);
- Report on the visit to Uruguay in 2018, UN Doc. CAT/OP/URY/1 (2019).

References

Cassese A (1989) A new approach to human rights. The European Convention for the Prevention of Torture. American Journal of International Law 83:128

Cassese A (1996) Inhuman states. Imprisonment, detention and torture in Europe today. Blackwell et al, Oxford etc

Ralf Alleweldt teaches constitutional law, EU law and international human rights law at the Brandenburg State Police University in Oranienburg. He holds an LLM from the European University Institute and a PhD from the University of Heidelberg. Since 2005 he has worked as a law teacher at the Yeditepe University Istanbul and the Universities of Constance, Potsdam and Munich as well as at the Catholic University of Eichstätt-Ingolstadt. He was also involved in long-term projects of the Council of Europe and the European Union dealing with justice reform in Ukraine and the legal education in EU law in Armenia. He has participated in human rights training and consulting activities in Eastern Europe and West Africa. From 2007 to 2012, he was an international scholar in the Academic Fellowship Program of the Open Society Institute.

His research interests include constitutional justice, refugee law and European human rights law including the prevention of torture. Important publications: Preamble to the 1951 Convention Relating to the Status of Refugees. In: Andreas Zimmermann (ed.), 1951 Convention Relating to the Status of Refugees and its 1967 Protocol (2nd ed. 2024); Avoiding another Brexit: the subsidiarity principle, the European Convention on Human Rights and the United Kingdom. Commonwealth and Comparative Studies 57 (2019), pp. 223-241; The police and international human rights law (ed., with Guido Fickenscher) (2018); Prevention of torture in the Black Sea region: progress or stagnation? In: Ralf Alleweldt, Raphaël Callsen, Jeanne Dupendant (eds.), Human rights abuses in the contemporary world (2012), pp. 27-45; Bundesverfassungsgericht und Fachgerichtsbarkeit (2006).

Chapter 2
Ensuring Fair Treatment of Persons in Police Custody: Theory and Reality

Richard Carver

Contents

Abstract A study of 16 countries over a 30-year period shows that practical implementation of safeguards for persons in police custody is the most effective way of preventing torture. The investigation and prosecution of torturers, along with the establishment of independent monitoring mechanisms, also has an important impact in reducing the incidence of torture. Independent complaints mechanisms, often advocated as a torture prevention tool, appear to have little effect. In all instances, torture prevention mechanisms are ineffective so long as they remain merely as laws on the statute book. While legal reform is often a necessary precondition for protection against torture, it is never sufficient. Practice very often falls short of legal provisions. It is only by ensuring *in practice* an end to unlawful detention, notification of a third party on arrest, prompt access to a lawyer, and independent medical examinations, that people in police custody can be effectively protected.

This chapter is based upon research conducted with Dr Lisa Handley, Visiting Research Academic at Oxford Brookes University. The author is very grateful for Dr Handley's collaboration and that of the entire research team.

R. Carver (✉)
Oxford Brookes University, Oxford, UK
e-mail: rcarver@brookes.ac.uk

R. Alleweldt (ed.), *Fair Treatment of Persons in Police Custody*,
https://doi.org/10.1007/978-3-031-61737-9_2

2.1 Research Question and Methodology

The research I shall describe in this chapter was commissioned by the Association for the Prevention of Torture (APT) and published in 2016 in a book entitled *Does Torture Prevention Work?*[1] The book title accurately represents the research question that guided the project. We were concerned to discover whether the array of torture prevention measures contained in binding international and regional instruments, national laws, soft international law, and recommendations of human rights organizations actually have a positive impact—that is, that they actually reduce the incidence of torture.[2] There is some existing literature on the impact of ratification of international human rights instruments,[3] as well as some individual case study research on torture prevention.[4] What was entirely lacking, however, was any comparative study of the impact of torture prevention. This is what we—myself, Lisa Handley, and a team of more than 20 researchers—set out to do.

It is important to stress the narrowness of the approach that we took. There are a number of associated questions that we did not directly address, such as what are the root causes of torture, or whether higher levels of torture are associated with different political systems or levels of conflict or economic development. We made sure to *control* for the effects of these other factors, in order to determine the efficacy of the measures that were our focus. It is also necessary to underline that we addressed only the impact of preventive measures upon the incidence of *torture*, not upon other forms of cruel, inhuman, or degrading treatment that might not rise to the level of torture.

Figure 2.1 illustrates the focus of our study. While of course acknowledging the important impact of the political environment—on law, on practice, and on the incidence of torture itself—this was not what we sought to measure. Political contexts varied widely across the 16 countries in our study; our interest, however, was in identifying any preventive factors that might operate across these different contexts and irrespective of political environment.

As noted, the literature that existed on torture prevention, aside from legal/normative studies, consisted almost entirely of qualitative case studies. Our choice of a comparative, quantitative method was aimed at reaching findings that were potentially generalizable. We combined this with a qualitative case-study approach, looking in depth at the experience of 16 countries from a broad range of geopolitical contexts over a 30-year period.[5] The same 16 countries were coded, year-by-year over that same period, making a total of 480 data points for the statistical analysis.

---

[1] Carver and Handley (2016).

[2] For a shorter summary of this research, see Carver and Handley (2021).

[3] For example, Hathaway (2002), p. 1935; Hollyer and Rosendorff (2012), p. 791.

[4] A particularly strong example is Sharma et al. (2012), p. 18.

[5] The countries were Argentina, Chile, Ethiopia, Georgia, Hungary, India, Indonesia, Israel, Kyrgyzstan, Norway, Peru, Philippines, South Africa, Tunisia, Turkey, and the United Kingdom. The period covered was 1985–2014.

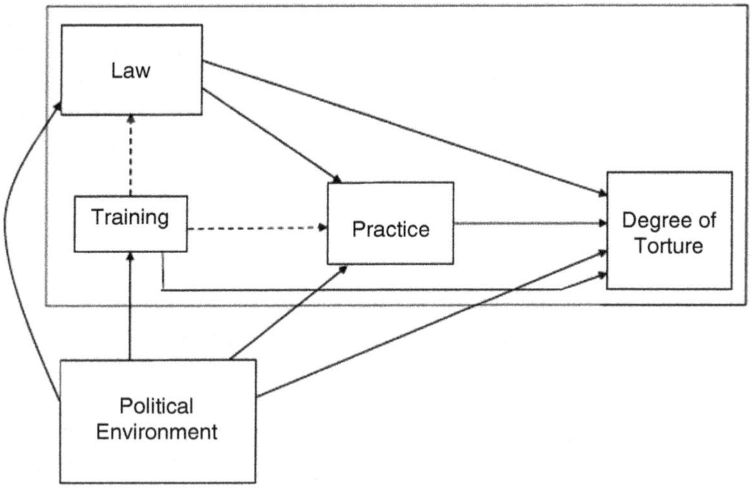

Fig. 2.1 Model of factors affecting the incidence of torture

Having initially considered using existing indices of the incidence of torture, such as the Political Terror Scale[6] or the Cingranelli-Richards scale,[7] we decided that being based on a content analysis of the texts of human rights reports rather than upon actual empirical data these were not sufficiently accurate for our purposes.[8] Instead we devised our own method of scoring—the Carver-Handley Torture Score (CHATS)—which was compiled for each country year in our study on the basis of primary and secondary research data. Three elements were taken into account when assigning a score: the frequency of torture; its geographical spread; and the severity of the methods used.[9] The CHATS per country year constituted the independent or outcome variable: the incidence of torture.

The independent variables were the different preventive measures set out in international and national law and in various authoritative policy recommendations. Unfortunately (from a methodological point of view), we identified rather a lot of these—66 in total. Therefore, for many of the analyses we conducted, we had to group these under four main headings.

[6] Wood and Gibney (2010), p. 367.

[7] Cingranelli and Richards (1999), p. 407.

[8] Both PTS and CIRI use content analysis of annual human rights reports to assign scores. This rests upon the choice of words by the authors of the reports (US State Department or Amnesty International) rather than directly reflecting the incidence of torture in the real world.

[9] It is important to underline that severity is not the same as visibility. We did not assume that "stealth" torture that leaves little or no visible marks on the victim was less severe than "classical" torture methods. We used a variety of criteria to assess severity, including duration and combinations of torture methods.

The first set of preventive measures was those deriving primarily from the United Nations Convention Against Torture and Other Cruel, Inhuman or Degrading Treatment or Punishment.[10] These are primarily aimed at criminalizing, investigating and prosecuting acts of torture. The second set of measures are to do with independent monitoring of places of imprisonment and detention with the aim of preventing torture. While this corresponds to the aim of the Optional Protocol to the UN Convention Against Torture (OPCAT),[11] the historical scope of our study long predated the OPCAT and included many countries that were not party to the protocol. We were interested in the impact of preventive monitoring, international, regional, or national, whatever the precise legal basis of the monitoring body.

Thirdly, we investigated the preventive impact of independent complaints mechanisms of the type provided by general or specialized ombudsman-type bodies or by some national human rights institutions. The importance of complaints procedures as preventive mechanisms has been advocated by the European Committee for the Prevention of Torture (CPT).[12] Finally, we were interested in the preventive impact of legal safeguards available to people at the time when they are deprived of their liberty. Although such safeguards are relatively weak in international law, their impact in torture prevention has been consistently advocated by non-governmental groups such as Amnesty International, as well as by the CPT.[13]

In addition, however, it seemed reasonable to hypothesize that the impact of any of these preventive mechanisms would generally be positive in the event that they are effectively implemented in practice. Hence, we scored them not only for their presence on the statute book, but also to the extent that they functioned in the real world. In most instances, these variables were scored on a three-point scale (0–2), roughly corresponding to total absence, partial presence, and complete presence. Hence, for example, the right to prompt access to a lawyer after arrest would score 0 if no such right existed (or only existed after a long delay). It would score 1 if the right existed but was circumscribed in some way (for example, if it could be suspended for certain categories of prisoner, such as in security or terrorism cases). It would score 2 if the right was present in all cases. There are two corresponding practice variables for the right of access to a lawyer: being informed of the right and exercising the right. These scores are on the same three-point scale and are based not upon the content of the law but upon actual practice as determined by empirical research: are detainees informed of their right to a lawyer—no (0), sometimes (1) or always (2)? Then, do detainees exercise that right? It should be stressed that this is a factual, not a normative finding. The purpose is not to assign "blame" if detainees do not consult lawyers. There may be many potential explanations for this. One may be obstruction by the police. Another may be poverty and the lack of a legal aid scheme. A third may be a shortage of lawyers. Our interest was

---

[10] United Nations (1987).

[11] United Nations (2006).

[12] Council of Europe (1989).

[13] Council of Europe (2015).

Table 2.1 Examples of preventive measures

	Law	Practice
Detention	• Unofficial detention illegal • Notification of family required • Right to lawyer • Prompt presentation before judge required • Medical exam required	• Is unofficial detention employed? • Are families notified promptly? • Is right to lawyer conveyed and exercised? • Is presentation before judge prompt?
Prosecution	• Criminalization of torture • Substantial penalties for torture • Independent authority to investigate allegations	• Are allegations of torture brought? • Are allegations thoroughly investigated? • Are charges being brought in court? • Are conviction rates comparable to other serious crimes?
Complaints	• Independent complaints mechanism • Power to compel evidence and witnesses • Power to refer complaint to investigative authority	• Are complaints investigated effectively? • Are complaints referred to investigative authority (e.g., prosecution)? • Are redress recommendations made?
Monitoring	• Domestic monitoring mechanism • Power to make unannounced visits • Power to conduct interviews with detainees	• Does monitor conduct regular and unannounced visits? • Does monitor interview detainees? • Are monitors sanctioned for their activities?

solely in determining whether the presence (or absence) of a lawyer made a difference to the risk of torture. Table 2.1 shows examples (not the complete list) of independent variables in each of these categories.

2.2 Main Findings

Our first finding may come as a surprise. It is commonly observed among those working in human rights that torture is "getting worse," a conclusion perhaps prompted by the challenges over the past two decades to the absolute prohibition of torture in international law. Yet in the 16 countries that we studied, between 1985 and 2014 the incidence of torture declined. This decline was not dramatic, nor was it consistent across the board: India had a very serious level of torture at both the beginning and end of that period, while Norway saw no torture at all. But the mean decline in CHATS (see Fig. 2.2) reflects a general reduction in the incidence of torture. How far this can be directly attributed to torture prevention mechanisms is clearly a separate question, as is the issue of whether this improvement might be indicative of a broader global trend.

Our second finding, by contrast, is unsurprising (except possibly to the most dogmatic of black-letter lawyers) and was anticipated in our decision to code the law

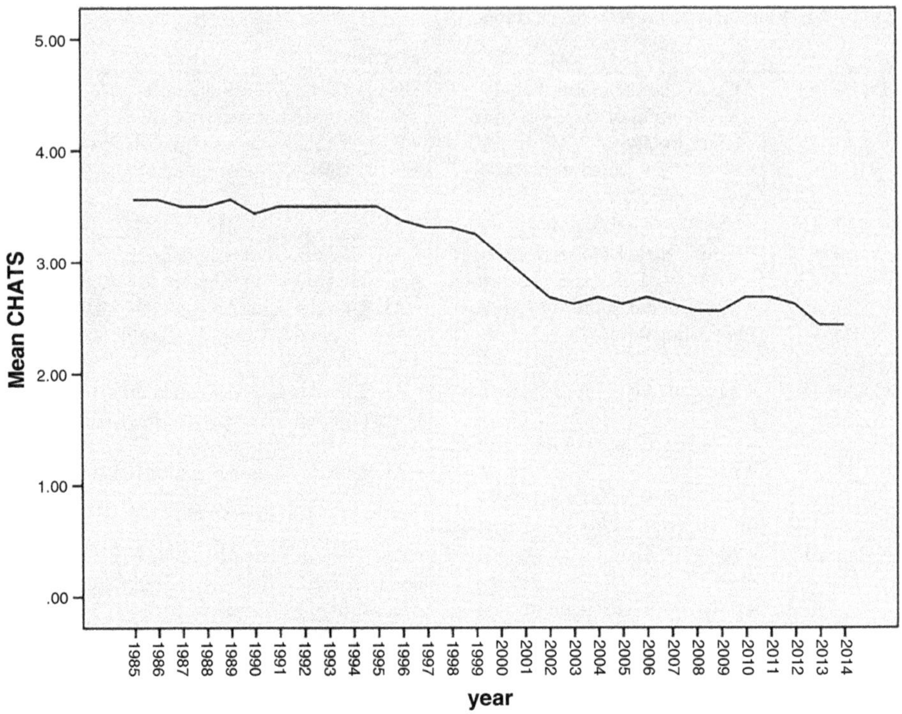

Fig. 2.2 Mean CHATS over time

and practice of preventive measures separately. It emerged very clearly that for most types of preventive measures there is a considerable gap between law and practice, with practice correlating much more strongly with a reduction in the incidence of torture (Fig. 2.3).

The starkest difference between law and practice is clearly visible in relation to the investigation and prosecution of torturers. The explanation for this appears simple: almost every country in the world criminalizes torture (even if not necessarily in the exact terms required in the UN Convention), yet the actual investigation and prosecution of crimes of torture is conducted reluctantly and ineffectively in most instances. The other area where this law-practice gap is striking is in relation to detention safeguards. Here too the explanation seems reasonably clear: there are going to be multiple reasons why arrested persons are not going to avail themselves of the legal protections that are available—in addition to the most obvious explanation that police will often not comply with the law.

For the other sets of variables, the distance between law and practice is less noticeable. In the case of complaints bodies, the law and practice lines on the graph are tangled together, suggesting that, by and large, these institutions carry out what they were legally established to do: investigate complaints. The graph for monitoring bodies starts similarly, but in recent years diverges. Presumably the explanation for

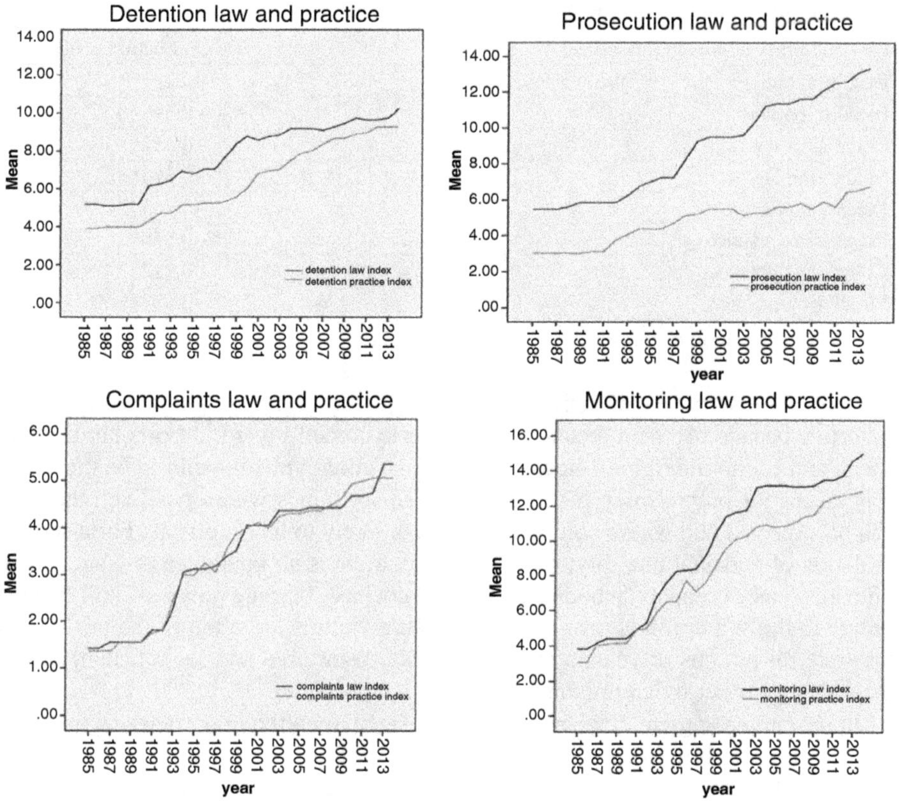

Fig. 2.3 The gap between law and practice

this is the proliferation of monitoring bodies in recent years, not all of which comply with the best legal standards.

Following from this gap between law and practice, emerges the most important finding of the research. Table 2.2 shows the bivariate correlations between CHATS and each of the law and practice indices. It is apparent from this that *none* of the law indices have a meaningful correlation with CHATS, while three of the practice indices do have a negative correlation (indicating that they are associated with a reduction in the incidence of torture). Complaints mechanisms appear to have no significant preventive impact at all. To be clear, this does not mean that complaints bodies, such as ombudsman institutions, "don't work." On an individual basis, it may be that a complaints procedure will provide adequate redress for an individual complainant. The point is that such a procedure will have no future deterrent effect, or otherwise prevent torture in the future. (We made a similar finding in relation to the impact of civil suits for reparation against governments that torture. Even civil remedies that worked effectively on an individual basis had no lasting preventive effect.) In fact, my own previous research strongly suggests that complaints

Table 2.2 Correlation of law and practice indices with CHATS

Law and practice prevention indices	Correlation coefficient
Detention law	−0.227**
Prosecution law	−0.198**
Complaints law	−0.352**
Monitoring law	−0.276**
Detention practice	−0.763**
Prosecution practice	−0.558**
Complaints practice	−0.312**
Monitoring practice	−0.457**

Pearson's r correlation coefficients, $^{*}p < 0.05$; $^{**}p < 0.01$

mechanisms tend to be ineffective in addressing serious human rights violations such as torture because of the reluctance of victims to come forward.[14] Complaints about social and economic rights—housing, pensions, employment—tend to be the mainstay issues for ombudsman institutions. These are topics where positive outcomes can be expected and where complainants are unlikely to fear reprisals. For a serious violation of personal integrity, such as torture, there is no guarantee of a successful outcome (since complaints bodies usually do not have binding powers—still less the power to bring a criminal prosecution). Torture victims are often in the custody of the state for months or years after they have been tortured and are reluctant to risk their safety further by complaining.

In recent years, great emphasis has been placed upon the importance of independent monitoring bodies as effective torture prevention mechanisms. This has been the particular emphasis of the APT—who commissioned our research—dating back to its genesis as the Swiss Committee Against Torture. The APT/SCAT has drawn its approach from the work of the International Committee of the Red Cross, which has long emphasized the positive impact of a neutral external presence in places of detention and imprisonment. This has found its way into international human rights law through the European Convention for the Prevention of Torture, which created the CPT as a pan-European monitoring mechanism, and through the OPCAT. The latter treaty creates a global monitoring mechanism, the Sub-Committee for Prevention of Torture, alongside national preventive mechanisms established in national law with various powers designated in the OPCAT. From our research it is clear that monitoring bodies that observe the basic standards of independence and effectiveness—making unannounced visits, conducting individual confidential interviews, protecting staff and inmates from reprisal—do indeed have a positive impact in reducing the incidence of torture. However, the findings in our 16 countries do not provide quite the ringing endorsement of monitoring as the most important element in any preventive strategy.

The criminalization of the act of torture, followed by its impartial investigation and the prosecution of its perpetrators, has been at the center of the international

[14]Carver (2012).

anti-torture approach for decades. The UN Convention Against Torture is framed not in the language of the typical human rights instrument, but along the lines of a treaty for the suppression of crime. As a consequence, it offers a level of detail in the obligations upon states that is unparalleled elsewhere in the international human rights legal canon. It is also, as made clear in Article 2, entirely directed towards the *prevention* of torture. Has this been the correct emphasis? Our findings strongly suggest that it has. The lack of success of the Convention lies in its non-implementation rather than in any seriously misconceived aims. The 16 countries in our study of course covered a range of varied experiences, but it is fair to summarize these as falling down every step of the way. Even when torture is criminalized in the terms required by the Convention and the supervising Committee Against Torture, charges are seldom brought against police and custodial personnel accused of serious ill-treatment. Rather, lesser charges carrying lesser penalties are brought. Investigations are often conducted by bodies that are not fully independent of those under investigation. Evidence is hard to come by and cases are seldom brought to court. When they are, conviction rates tend to be low. And, even when convicted, torturers are likely to face penalties that are not at all comparable with those faced by common criminals who commit similar offences against the person. So, our conclusion is based upon an extrapolation from a relatively small number of good examples; nevertheless, it was a clear finding that the time-worn call to "end the cycle of impunity" would indeed have a major and positive impact on the incidence of torture.

The most important factor in reducing torture, according to our research, was none of the above preventive mechanisms, however. What emerged clearly was that the safeguards applicable to people when they are first taken into police custody—the focus of this book—were by far the most important in preventing torture, with the important proviso that these must be implemented in practice, not merely written in law. This corresponds precisely to a commonly held view among some human rights activists, best articulated by Sir Nigel Rodley, one of the architects of the international legal regime for torture prohibition: "torture is a crime and, like many other crimes, is a crime of opportunity." Recalling his work at Amnesty International in the 1970s and 1980s he stated:

> We were aware that torture happened to people when they were held at the sole mercy of their captors and interrogators (incommunicado detention). The longer they were denied access to and from the outside world (i.e., to families, lawyers, doctors, courts) the more they were vulnerable to abuse by those wishing to obtain information or confessions from them.[15]

The most effective strategy to prevent torture, according to this reasoning, is to eliminate the times when the suspect is in the sole custody of the police without any form of external observation or supervision—from lawyers, medical personnel, family or friends, or judges. It is apparent from Table 2.2 that these safeguards are quite significantly the most highly correlated with a reduction in the incidence of

[15] Rodley (2009), pp. 15–21.

Table 2.3 Effects of preventive mechanisms on incidence of torture: Model 3

	Model 3a Random effects			Model 3b Fixed effects		
Explanatory variables	Coefficient	(Std. error)	*p*-value	Coefficient	(Std. error)	*p*-value
Detention law	0.026	(0.035)	0.454	0.016	(0.038)	0.681
Prosecution law	0.010	(0.033)	0.773	−0.006	(0.036)	0.862
Complaints law	0.042	(0.042)	0.319	0.088	(0.046)	0.059
Monitoring law	0.000	(0.015)	0.994	−0.011	(0.017)	0.523
Detention practice	−0.174	(0.027)	0.000	−0.182	(0.031)	0.000
Prosecution practice	0.024	(0.029)	0.400	−0.024	(0.034)	0.465
Complaints practice	−0.024	(0.036)	0.503	−0.018	(0.039)	0.643
Monitoring practice	0.001	(0.014)	0.917	−0.004	(0.015)	0.769
Democracy	−0.057	(0.021)	0.007	−0.064	(0.028)	0.021
Conflict	0.060	(0.025)	0.016	0.036	(0.027)	0.188
GDP_{ln}	−0.074	(0.086)	0.389	0.080	(0.121)	0.508
$Population_{ln}$	0.028	(0.116)	0.807	0.429	(0.132)	0.001
Africa	−0.299	(0.463)	0.518			
Europe	−1.75	(0.567)	0.002			
South America	−0.471	(0.463)	0.308			
West & Central Asia	−0.063	(0.510)	0.900			
	$N = 431$ $R^2 = 0.771$ Wald $Chi^2 = 240.89$**			$N = 415$ $R^2 = 0.537$ F (12, 387) = 5.59**		

torture. The same finding emerges just as clearly in the various multivariate correlation models that we tested.

The multivariate analyses included a series of control variables to isolate the independent variables from the various factors in the political environment that might have an effect on the incidence of torture: level of democracy, conflict, economic development, and population size. Table 2.3 shows the results from only one of these models, a GLS regression using random or fixed effects. This shows that detention practice—that is, safeguards on arrest and in police custody—are the only statistically significant independent variable, with a coefficient of −0.174 or −0.182. Two control variables are significant in each model, democracy and conflict or democracy and population.[16]

Whatever statistical approach we used, the finding was the same. Detention practice constituted the single most important set of preventive measures. It was consistently statistically significant, the sign of the coefficient was always in the expected direction, and the correlation between detention practice and CHATS was

[16]For a detailed discussion of the multivariate regression, see Carver and Handley (2016), pp. 57–66.

consistently stronger than that between CHATS and any other set of preventive measures.

2.3 Treatment of Persons in Police Custody

The reason that safeguards for people in police custody are crucial to the elimination of torture relates, clearly, to the circumstances in which torture most often takes place (and, by inference, the aims and purposes behind it). It is true that some of the most infamous instances of torture have taken place entirely outside the criminal justice system, for example by Latin American military regimes of the 1970s, or the US military and intelligence agencies in the "war on terror." In both these examples, individuals were "disappeared"—forcibly and arbitrarily removed from society in order to evade the protections that ordinary criminal procedure, or remedies such as *habeas corpus*, would afford. It is striking that states that have adhered to a criminal justice paradigm, rather than adopting the idea of the terrorist or communist as "enemy," had far greater success in avoiding the use of torture.

However, this "state of exception," although academically modish, does not accurately describe the circumstances in which most torture takes place. Most of the cases in our study confirmed my own observation, born out of more than three decades of working against torture, that the root cause of most torture is to be found in dysfunctional criminal justice systems. This dysfunction may manifest itself in different ways and may have varying proximate causes, but there are a number of characteristics that are recurrent. Police tend to be under-resourced and poorly trained. They have low status in society, are badly paid, and are consequently often corrupt. Prosecutors also lack the necessary skills. They too are under pressure to secure convictions—in one country in our study, prosecutors had monthly quotas for cases initiated, with the result that suspects were more likely to be tortured if they were arrested towards the end of the month. Confession evidence is often the only available basis for securing a conviction, so criminal investigations—whether led by police or prosecutors—usually have this as their sole aim. Courts are overburdened and not able effectively to process cases. This may lead to failures to convict, resulting in widespread social resentment. In these situations, which we saw in several of our case studies, the public supports police torture of alleged criminals because this may be the only punishment that they receive. Alternatively, courts fail to scrutinize evidence properly and convict on the basis of tainted confessions. Judges repeatedly fall short in investigating the provenance of evidence and often evince strong bias in favor of the prosecutors or police. *These* are the circumstances in which torture flourishes, not the hypothetical moral philosophy problems of "ticking bombs" so beloved in the literature.

Of course, in countries where torture is endemic, it tends to be worse in situations of political conflict, precisely because normal procedural protections may be suspended. As it was put to us, one is at greater risk of torture in Kashmir than in Bangalore. But underpinning this was the fact that torture is endemic throughout the

Table 2.4 Correlation of detention law and practice measures with CHATS

Detention measures	Correlation coefficient
Detention law	
Unofficial detention illegal	−0.112*
Family notification	−0.155**
Access to lawyer	−0.016
Presentation before judge	−0.042
Medical exam	−0.089
Recording of interrogations	−0.346**
Video monitors	−0.085
Detention practice	
Unofficial detention not practiced	−0.720**
Family notified	−0.720**
Informed of right to lawyer	−0.696**
Exercise right to lawyer	−0.651**
Presentation before judge promptly	−0.453**
Medical exam	−0.610**
Recording of interrogations	−0.481**
Video monitors used and available	−0.421**
Training of police and custodial personnel	−0.400**
Less reliance on confessions	−0.503**

Pearson's r correlation coefficients, $^{*}p < 0.05$; $^{**}p < 0.01$

Indian criminal justice system—and has been throughout the colonial and post-colonial period. Israel was an unusual example in that torture takes place exclusively in political cases. These are almost always geographically located within the occupied Palestinian territories, where the procedural protections available in Israeli law do not function. The United Kingdom was another of our case studies where torture flourished in the context of political conflict, in Northern Ireland (and latterly in occupied Iraq). But even in this example, what was striking was that the (ill) treatment of political suspects borrowed directly from techniques already used by police in common criminal cases. The notorious case of the "Birmingham Six"—who falsely confessed to planting an Irish Republican bomb that killed civilians in a bar—was investigated by a police unit, the West Midlands Serious Crime Squad, that systematically used torture as a method to extract confessions. The UK tackled its torture problem in part by arriving at a political solution to the conflict in Northern Ireland, but more profoundly by addressing a number of important issues of criminal procedure.

Table 2.4 shows the bivariate correlations between CHATS and all the different independent variables under the detention safeguard category. It is apparent that all the practice variables are more highly correlated with reduced incidence of torture than all the law variables. Indeed, the only law variable that appears to have any importance is when it is legally required that police or prosecutorial interviews with suspects be electronically recorded. In the instance of this particular provision, there is not a particularly wide gap between law and practice. In other words, when the law requires recordings, this usually takes place (as might be expected). For some of the other variables, the gap is vast. Most strikingly of all, the legal entitlement to prompt access to a lawyer has almost zero correlation with the incidence of torture. Yet, if suspects are informed of their right to a lawyer and then exercise the right, it appears that the risk of torture diminishes significantly. In this, as with most of the variables, it cannot be concluded that the contents of the law are irrelevant. Often legal reform will be a precondition for improved practice (although this was not always the case in our study). The point is rather that while good laws are usually necessary for the proper treatment of suspects, they are never sufficient. The challenge in preventing torture and ill-treatment of detainees lies in bridging the gap between law and practice.

The potentially protective impact of a lawyer being present is largely separate from access to a lawyer as a function of the right to a fair trial, which is how the issue is generally expressed in both national and international law. This has allowed national legal systems to limit lawyers' access to their clients in order not to impede the investigation. This was, for example, enshrined as a central principle of French criminal procedure until very recently. The jurisprudence of the European Court of Human Rights has recently begun to tackle this issue. The United Kingdom is in advance of most others on this issue, with the Police and Criminal Evidence Act having introduced a publicly-funded duty solicitor scheme that assigned lawyers to every police station. Defense lawyers regard this as the single most important step in eliminating police torture in the UK because even when an individual suspect does not avail herself of the right to a duty solicitor, she still benefits from the lawyers' presence.

The obstacles to realizing the right of access to a lawyer have already been discussed. A very similar set of problems surrounds the right to an independent medical examination, which our research suggests is also very important. Sometimes the problem is direct interference with the independence of the examination by police—for example, by officers remaining in the room for the exam or demanding that the results be presented to the police, not the detainee, unsealed. However, often there is a structural problem of the lack of independence of medical staff from the police. In the UK, medical staff are from the National Health Service, which, while it is a state body, functions quite independently. In, for example, South Africa a system of district surgeons offers relevant medical expertise but not independence (as has been seen in a number of high-profile cases involving deaths in custody). In India, a separate problem was noted—although surely not unique to that country—which was the medical profession's general lack of sympathy for criminal suspects. In Turkey, home of the Istanbul Protocol governing investigation of allegations of torture, a section of the medical profession has been very active in promoting independent supervision and examinations in order to prevent torture. This has included extensive training of doctors. Yet the doctors trained have often gone into other specializations and the impact on the quality of examinations in custody has been much less than expected.

Again, the protections offered by independent medical examinations are self-evident. The presence of a professional providing oversight of police conduct is likely to be beneficial in itself. When there are claims that a detainee has been ill-treated, independent medical evidence is of great significance. One of the reasons why convictions of the crime of torture are so low is the lack of independent evidence to corroborate a victim's allegation. The colleagues of accused officers are seldom willing to testify against them. Reliable and contemporaneous medical evidence can be vital.

The European CPT talks about a "trinity" of essential procedural safeguards against torture.[17] Along with access to a lawyer and independent medical examinations, the CPT sees notification of a third party when someone is arrested as being of great importance. Our findings wholly reinforce this belief. Notifying a family member or friend is also often delayed or suspended on the grounds that it will impede the investigation—perhaps tipping off accomplices so that evidence can be destroyed. Yet the importance of this for the prevention of torture is essentially the principle that no one should be in unacknowledged, incommunicado or (still worse) unofficial detention. Notification of the outside world is vital and should have none of the practical obstacles that often exist in engaging a lawyer, for example. We observed that practice in this area seemed to have improved with time, which some evidence suggested was to do with technological advances. Widespread cellphone use, in particular, makes it much easier to contact people. The right to notify a third party manifests itself in two distinct ways in different legal systems: it may be framed as a right of the detainee to notify someone, or it may be an obligation on the detaining authorities to do the notifying. Although the former may appear to offer the stronger protection, we observed no practical difference.

The CPT's "trinity" is ultimately directed at ensuring the lawfulness of detention. Not surprisingly, we found that taking a person into a lawful place of detention and recording the arrest properly and in accordance with lawful procedure provided one of the most important protections against torture. Outside the system, essentially there are no protections at all. Medical examinations, legal consultation, and notification of the outside world will only be triggered by someone being taken into custody lawfully—not to mention other protections such as presentation before a judicial authority. The use of unlawful places of detention may increasingly be used as means of evading efforts to tighten other procedural protections. Our researchers on Kyrgyzstan, for example, reported a significant increase in the use of informal (and unlawful) detention places in response to official attempts to tighten safeguards for detainees. In several countries we noted that suspects were increasingly ill-treated out of formal custody—in vehicles, in police station car parks, or simply on the streets. Closed circuit television cameras or body cameras do not seem to have been very effective in monitoring or deterring such behavior, because in large part of the uncanny tendency of such technology to fail (or for recordings to be lost), when evidence of abuse is required. The international legal norm requiring judicial

[17] See, for example, Kozma and Rachlew (2018).

supervision of arrest and detention is stronger than many of the other procedural safeguards we researched. All of the countries we studied required relatively prompt presentation of a detainee before a judge, with one exception (Indonesia). Not all require presentation within a 48-hours period (Norway and Hungary allowing up to 72 hours). Several countries allow extensions or exceptions for certain types of case, usually under emergency or anti-terrorism provisions. Most of the countries in our study do generally comply with their own laws on presentation before a judge. Although this does indeed constitute an important part of the protection against unlawful detention, it did not occupy quite the central position that we had expected. This may be because judges do not always discharge their oversight responsibilities with full commitment. In some polarized situations—for example in Turkey in the 1990s—judges may be strongly hostile to the prisoners brought before them, particularly in political cases. Sometimes "presentation" does not even mean that the detainee is physically in the same room as the judge. The connection may be made by video link, which is usually not an adequate means for the judge to assess either the demeanor or the physical state of the detainee. We heard a number of accounts of detainees in different countries showing physical wounds to judges, which they claimed were inflicted in custody, only to have the claims waved aside without investigation. A procedure is only as good as the people responsible for implementing it.

A final point should be made in this discussion of the most important safeguards. The conduct of interviews or interrogations is central to the protection of suspects against torture and other ill-treatment. The electronic recording of interviews has been shown to be highly effective in those systems where it is used as a routine procedure. Several countries in our study used recordings as an optional extra, at the request of either prosecution or defense, which does not provide the systematic protection required.

More fundamentally, the *purpose* of police or prosecutorial interviewing is crucial to the protection of the suspect. We found that legal systems that placed less weight upon confession evidence were less likely to torture. This reduced weight of confessions is not always, or even primarily, driven by conscious anti-torture efforts. Electronic surveillance evidence assumes great importance in many countries because of the widespread use of cellphones. Generally speaking, the greater the skill and sophistication of investigators, the less likely they are to torture because they have several other avenues of approach aside from seeking a confession. Two of the countries in our study, both post-Soviet, illustrate this point. After the collapse of the Soviet Union in 1991, both Georgia and Kyrgyzstan lost many of their most experienced police investigators. While the Soviet Union was hardly a watchword for the protection of detainees' rights, what followed was much, much worse. Rapidly promoted investigators simply did not know how to approach cases and resorted to beating confessions out of suspects. Things have improved—Georgia in the mid-2000s taking the radical step of simply dissolving and then reconstituting its police force. The United Kingdom was the first country to reconceptualize the purpose of police interviewing away from the notion of the interrogation towards the "investigative interview." Where the traditional police interview is usually aimed at getting the suspect to confirm (or repudiate) the hypothetical explanation of the crime that the police have formed, the investigative interview is much more open-ended. Asbjorn Rachlew, the Norwegian police superintendent who has become a global advocate for investigative interviewing, describes this as "operationalizing the presumption of innocence."[18] Respect, rapport-building and an open-ended, open-minded approach make investigative interviewing a much more effective tool for the police in discovering the truth, as compared to the outmoded search for confessions. In addition, of course, this approach minimizes the risk of a suspect being ill-treated, either before or during an interview. One of the most encouraging developments since we completed our research has been the formulation and launch in 2021 of the Méndez Principles for Effective Interviewing (named for former UN Special Rapporteur on Torture, Juan Méndez) and their endorsement by various United Nations bodies, as well as regional human rights mechanisms.[19] These embody the principles of investigative interviewing and the protection of the suspect against ill-treatment.

2.4 Reforming the Police: Some General Observations

It was noted above that the root cause of torture in most situations is generalized dysfunction in the criminal justice system. The specific safeguards that protect detainees from torture, if effectively implemented, go some considerable way towards correcting that dysfunction—or at least are premised upon improvements in its functioning. Hence, for example, a move away from confession evidence assumes a police force that is more professionally competent and able to discharge its core responsibilities. The implication is that reforms need to be tackled at a more systemic level. Preventing torture means developing stronger safeguards for people in custody, which in turn implies a system that fosters the necessary skills and accountability mechanisms.

Much energy in recent years has been directed towards the issue of transitional justice, aimed at creating accountability for those who have carried out gross violations of human rights, including torture. Transitional justice measures may include prosecutions of those responsible or, as a "softer" option, truth processes in which past violations are fully documented and the perpetrators identified. Our research clearly shows that prosecution of torturers is an effective preventive measure. However, in our quantitative analysis we did not specifically distinguish "transitional" from regular justice processes. The understanding is normally that transitional justice has a greater symbolic value and very explicitly asserts the notion that no one is beyond the rule of law. While we did not quantify our findings on

[18] Cf. the contribution in this book by Asbjorn Rachlew, Section 5.1.1.

[19] Association for the Prevention of Torture, Washington College of Law, Norwegian Institute for Human Rights (2021).

transitional justice, many of our case studies were nevertheless revealing. The overwhelming majority of the countries that we studied had undergone some sort of transition during our 30-year period, whether from conflict to peace or from authoritarian to more democratic. The only real exceptions were India, Israel, and Norway. Argentina made its transition from military dictatorship to democracy just before the beginning of our study period, so is still relevant. These countries displayed a variety of different transitional justice mechanisms from truth commissions (for example, South Africa, Argentina, Chile, and Peru), to criminal prosecutions (for example, Argentina, Chile, Ethiopia, and Indonesia), to nothing at all (for example, Turkey and Northern Ireland). From these cases, it was difficult to detect any particular positive impact from transitional justice mechanisms, although most have not regressed back into the pattern of gross violations seen under previous regimes. The experience of Argentina may illustrate why. Often held up as an example of the positive impact of prosecuting human rights violators, the country has indeed consolidated its democracy and held top officials of the old military regime accountable for the unlawful arrest, torture, and disappearance of thousands of political opponents. Yet torture persists, if not at the level experienced in the 1970s. While good detention safeguards have been enacted into law, these are largely ignored in practice. Torture is a crime—and torturers from the 1970s and 1980s continue to be prosecuted, but not those from the 2000s or 2010s. No one draws any strong connection between accountability for the crimes of the military dictatorship—clearly understood to be human rights violations—and the crimes of the police today, which are understood in quite different terms. As in several countries that we studied, rising crime is seen as a serious social problem and politicians explicitly and repeatedly advocate tough policies against criminals. If a Buenos Aires cop beats up a street child, probably outside any lawful custodial process and with fair clear public endorsement from politicians, then neither the police hierarchy nor much of the public are much concerned.

By contrast, in Northern Ireland the long, low-level armed conflict known as "the Troubles" was ended in 1998 by the Belfast Agreement, a treaty between the United Kingdom and the Republic of Ireland. Many have criticized the fact that the Irish settlement contained no transitional justice provisions. Although some historic cases involving human rights violations continue to be investigated, there has been no systematic attempt at securing accountability. Yet, in Northern Ireland torture has been entirely eliminated—in the part of the United Kingdom where it was systematic and fairly widespread from the 1970s to the 1990s. The explanation probably lies in another difference between Argentina and Northern Ireland: whereas the Argentinian police were left structurally intact after the fall of the dictatorship, a root-and-branch reform of the Northern Ireland police was an essential part of the peace agreement. In Argentina, the police were not seen as the main culprits for human rights violations and energy was rather devoted to reform of the military. Power structures in Argentina are decentralized through the federal system and even at the provincial and local level chains of command are weak. So, the police basically continue to evade accountability. In Northern Ireland, the old Royal Ulster Constabulary was dissolved, to be replaced by the Police Service of Northern Ireland.

Although many old personnel were reintegrated into the new police service, the worst were got rid of and a conscious effort was made to recruit new police from the minority community. Equally importantly, a new civilian oversight system was established, consisting primarily of the Northern Ireland Policing Board and the Police Ombudsman. The former has an explicit human rights mandate. The latter is a well-resourced and independent mechanism for investigating complaints against the police. Unlike typical ombudsman bodies, the Northern Ireland Police Ombudsman has the power to forward cases directly to the prosecutorial authorities, so is exempt from the general shortcomings of complaints mechanisms that we identified in this study. The upshot of all this has been not a single case of torture by the police since 1998.[20]

The contrast between Argentina and Northern Ireland is a stark one. Several other cases sit at less dramatic points of the spectrum. South Africa conducted a full truth process, but limited prosecutions. It implemented a partial police reform that was halted because of public and political concern about rising crime. Its success in protecting detainees from torture has been mixed. Georgia, as noted above, carried out a thoroughgoing police reform, combined with a number of other preventive measures, including legal reform and an effective monitoring mechanism. It has had considerable success in reducing torture.[21] Indonesia has failed to implement many crucial protections of detainees' rights, but it did demilitarize the police after the democratization of the late 1990s. Torture has declined. Transitional moments seem, then, to present potentially important opportunities to put in place the architecture of torture prevention. Of course, this is not to suggest that it is necessary to wait for moment of dramatic historical rupture. While there are obvious legal and procedural improvements that are implied by our findings, one of the most important may be at a rather modest level. For all our four sets of independent variables we also asked about the impact of training—whether of police, prosecutors, judges, prison personnel, monitors, or complaints handlers. In the model shown at the beginning of this chapter (see Fig. 2.1), it can be seen that we hypothesize that training may present a possible link between law and practice. Our statistical finding is that training is indeed correlated with a reduction in CHATS—often more modestly than the practice variables but always more strongly than the law variables. Training of prosecutors and judges and of arresting, interrogating and custodial personnel seem to be of particular importance.

We did not investigate statistically the particular form that this training should take. Our case studies, however, provided some clear examples of where training had a positive impact, or where lack of training presented problems. Several of these have already been discussed: medical personnel who lack the forensic skills to

[20]Of course, positive reforms are always reversible. A substantial section of the British political class is not in favour of unilaterally renouncing the treaty commitments made under the Belfast Agreement in order to facilitate the UK's withdrawal from the European Union. At the time of writing, the final outcome is unclear.

[21]For a detailed discussion of the Georgia example, see Carver and Handley (2020).

identify torture (and indeed judges with the same lack); police investigators who know no way to solve a case other than beating a confession out of a suspect; police interviewers who acquired the skills to conduct investigative interviews, and so on. Anecdotally, it seemed that training that was integrated into the curriculums of police academies, law schools or medical schools was likely to more enthusiastically received (and hence more impactful) than stand-alone human rights training. However, this is not a firm finding and further research would be useful.

2.5 Conclusion

The clear finding of our research is that, in the 16 countries that we studied, the implementation of safeguards for those held in police custody was clearly the most important factor in protecting them from torture (and quite possibly from other forms of deliberate ill-treatment). This suggests that at an international level there may need to be a recalibration of priorities in the anti-torture movement. The point, however, is not to downgrade the importance of current priorities, such as the work of independent monitoring bodies. Rather it is to suggest that detention safeguards should be at the front and center of the work of monitoring agencies. This is already the case in the work of the European CPT, for example, as well as some national level oversight bodies, such as the Public Defender in Georgia. Overall, however, bodies that visit closed institutions have made prisons their main focus, since this offers a logistically more straightforward task, with a relatively small number of places to visit and a much more stable population. So, more concentrated monitoring of police custody could be an effective way of determining whether legal safeguards for detainees are being observed in practice. Prison visits, using confidential interviews with inmates, can be used to probe their earlier experiences in police custody to determine whether ill-treatment took place and whether safeguards are implemented.

References

Association for the Prevention of Torture, Washington College of Law, Norwegian Institute for Human Rights (2021) Principles on effective interviewing for investigations and information gathering. https://www.apt.ch/sites/default/files/publications/apt_PoEI_EN_11.pdf

Carver R (2012) Central and Eastern Europe: the Ombudsman as agent of international law. In: Goodman R, Pegram T (eds) Human rights, state compliance, and social change: assessing national human rights institutions. Cambridge University Press, New York

Carver R, Handley L (2016) Does torture prevention work? Liverpool University Press, Liverpool

Carver R, Handley L (2020) Evaluating national preventive mechanisms: a conceptual model. J Hum Rights Pract 12(2):387–408. https://doi.org/10.1093/jhuman/huaa030

Carver R, Handley L (2021) Effective torture prevention. In: Evans SM, Modvig J (eds) Research handbook on torture. Edward Elgar

Cingranelli DL, Richards DL (1999) Measuring the level, pattern, and sequence of government respect for physical integrity rights. Int Stud Q 43:407

Council of Europe (1989) European Convention for the prevention of torture and inhuman or degrading treatment or punishment (adopted 26 November 1987, entered into force 1 February 1989) ETS 126

Council of Europe (2015) European Committee for the prevention of torture and inhuman or degrading treatment or punishment, CPT Standards, Strasbourg 2015, CPT/Inf/E (2002) 1 - Rev. 2015

Hathaway OA (2002) Do human rights treaties make a difference? Yale Law J 111:1935

Hollyer JR, Rosendorff BP (2012) Do human rights agreements prolong the tenure of autocratic ratifiers? N Y Univ J Int Law Polit 44:791

Kozma J, Rachlew A (2018) Combating torture during police custody and pre-trial detention. In: Conference hosted by the Danish chairmanship of the CoE Council of Ministers, Copenhagen, March 2018

Rodley NS (2009) Reflections on working for the prevention of torture. Essex Hum Rights Rev 6: 15–21

Sharma M, Massagé I, McDonald K (2012) Lawyers' intervention at pretrial stage helps to prevent torture, illegal detention and other human rights violations: experiences of advocacy forum - Nepal. J Hum Rights Pract 4:18

United Nations (1987) Convention against torture and other cruel, inhuman or degrading treatment or punishment (adopted 10 December 1984, entered into force 26 June 1987) 1465 UNTS 85

United Nations (2006) Optional protocol to the convention against torture and other cruel, inhuman or degrading treatment or punishment (adopted 18 December 2002, entered into force 22 June 2006), UNGA Res 57/199

Wood RM, Gibney M (2010) The Political Terror Scale (PTS): a re-introduction and a comparison to CIRI. Hum Rights Q 32:367

Richard Carver was Reader in Human Rights and Governance at Oxford Brookes University, until his retirement in 2022, and co-editor of the *Journal of Human Rights Practice* (Oxford). He holds an LLM in international law and a PhD in human rights. Before joining Oxford Brookes in 2008, Dr Carver had a long career as a human rights researcher with Amnesty International, Human Rights Watch, ARTICLE 19, and various United Nations agencies. His area of geographic specialisation is southern Africa.

Dr Carver's research focuses on mechanisms for the protection of human rights, especially national human rights institutions, and has particularly addressed the rights of people deprived of their liberty. He directed a multi-country study on torture prevention funded by the Association for the Prevention of Torture, resulting in the book *Does Torture Prevention Work?* (Liverpool University Press, 2016), co-authored with Dr Lisa Handley. He is also the author of *A Mission for Justice: the International Ombudsman Institute 1978-2018* (Verlag Österreich, 2018) and many journal articles and book chapters on torture prevention, national human rights institutions and other human rights issues.

Chapter 3
Fundamental Safeguards Against Ill-Treatment: Good Practices and Challenges

Krassimir Kanev

Contents

Abstract This contribution is a critical review of fundamental safeguards against torture and other ill-treatment. It focuses on the concept of prevention as developed through the work of the CPT and the OPCAT mechanisms and explores its meaning at the international and at the domestic level. The preventive approach, based on visits to places of detention and followed up by constructive dialogue with authorities, translated into norms of international law the work of the ICRC. This works well and effectively at the level of international visiting mechanisms. However, the adoption of a purely preventive approach at the national level into the work of the national preventive mechanisms may create problems with the synchronisation of this approach with other positive obligations of the states. While the existing mechanisms for punishment and prevention of torture and other ill-treatment contributed to the reduction of their incidence, they are still widespread in many parts of the world, including in states which availed themselves of international scrutiny in all its different forms. There is therefore a need to do more. It is suggested that civil society involvement in monitoring and legal assistance to victims of torture and other ill-treatment may contribute further to their eradication. The contribution

K. Kanev (✉)
Bulgarian Helsinki Committee, Sofia, Bulgaria
e-mail: krassimir@bghelsinki.org

R. Alleweldt (ed.), *Fair Treatment of Persons in Police Custody*,
https://doi.org/10.1007/978-3-031-61737-9_3

reviews the current state of international standards in that regard and proposes the establishment of a firm legal basis for NGO access to all places of detention.

3.1 Introduction

International standards on the prohibition and prevention of torture, inhuman and degrading treatment and punishment developed over the past three decades in a variety of directions. The overall direction of these developments has been positive and they have brought some reduction in the incidence of torture and other ill-treatment, as well as improvements of the material conditions of detention.[1] Yet, even in countries that have adopted in law or in practice most of the commonly recommended mechanisms for punishment or prevention of torture, its incidence continues to be relatively high. According to the latest statistics of the European Court of Human Rights (ECtHR), more than 19% of the violations of the European Convention of Human Rights (ECHR), which it found in 2021, were of Article 3 (prohibition of torture and inhuman and degrading treatment).[2] While more than two thirds of these violations originate from one Member State (the Russian Federation), the remaining are spread among many others.[3] On its part, the European Committee for the Prevention of Torture (CPT) continues to make observations on police ill-treatment upon detention and inside police custody in a number of both Eastern European and Western European states,[4] as well as on prison overcrowding.[5] In Bulgaria, an EU Member State which has adopted all international mechanisms for combating and preventing torture, every third prisoner who has been arrested by the police and subsequently sentenced to deprivation of liberty, complains of having been ill-treated by the police.[6]

This is a serious challenge to the European and global systems of combating torture. While on the basis of current research we can assume that the established safeguards against torture/ill-treatment contribute towards reducing these practices, it has also been pointed out that they exhibit some shortcomings and tend to work mostly under certain political and social conditions.[7] The current systems for combating torture perhaps needs to be supplemented by some further steps and

[1] Carver and Handley (2016), pp. 629–633.

[2] ECtHR (2021) Annual Report 2021. Council of Europe, Strasbourg, p. 183.

[3] Ibid., pp. 186–187.

[4] CPT (2018), pp. 16–23.

[5] CPT (2019), pp. 25–29.

[6] Kanev (2022), p. 14, available at: https://bghelsinki.org/web/files/reports/158/files/2022-kanev%2D%2Dproblems-with-the-equal-treatment-of-accused-persons-in-pre-trial-proceedings-in-bulgaria.pdf.

[7] Cf. Carver and Handley (2016), p. 24.

mechanisms in order to strengthen its preventive capacity. While, on the one hand, recent developments at the level of the ECtHR case law are by no means encouraging,[8] on the other hand, a parallel process of the implementation of the EU Roadmap Directives, adopted after 2009, although aiming at strengthening fairness of the criminal procedure, especially at the pre-trial stage, is expected to strengthen also the safeguards against torture and other ill-treatment. Empowerment and effective involvement of non-governmental actors in monitoring places of detention and in legal assistance of victims is another promising practice that needs to be expanded and supported by more determined standard-setting at the international level.

3.2 Types of Safeguards Against Torture/Ill-Treatment

Article 2.1 of the UN Convention against Torture (UNCAT) obliges state parties to adopt effective legislative, administrative, judicial or other measures to prevent acts of torture anywhere under their jurisdiction. Article 16.1 expands this obligation to acts of cruel, inhuman or degrading treatment or punishment which do not amount to torture. These are general provisions with unclear meaning, yet, at least in theory, they are supposed to include all types of safeguards, which both the convention and the other legal and non-legal mechanisms for combating torture include. This has been the way they were interpreted by the Committee against Torture (CAT) in its review of state parties' reports.

The UNCAT itself specifies measures which states parties are obliged to adopt, like, as a minimum, the criminalisation of acts of torture and complicity in torture (Article 4). The case law of international bodies, such as the European Court of Human Rights (ECtHR), adds to this duty also the criminalisation of other deliberate ill-treatment which does not constitute torture.[9] The convention requires that law enforcement officials are properly trained regarding the prohibition of torture and ill-treatment (Article 10); that the states parties ensure periodic review of interrogation rules and arrangements for the custody and treatment of persons subjected to detention (Article 11); prompt and impartial investigation in cases of torture and deliberate ill-treatment (Article 12); effective investigation into complaints of torture and ill-treatment (Article 13); and an enforceable right to fair and adequate compensation (Article 14). It also requires the establishment of proper jurisdiction on the crime of torture, taking into account its serious nature, including universal jurisdiction (Article 5), and prohibits the use of statements obtained under torture in any proceedings (Article 15). The latter prohibition was extended by the ECtHR to cover

[8] Over the past 2 years in a series of judgments the Grand Chamber of the ECtHR, unlike some previous chamber judgments, refused to recognize the right of access to a lawyer in criminal proceedings as in independent right under Article 6 of the Convention. Instead, it declared that it will find violations only where the "overall fairness of the proceedings" is negatively affected by the lack of access.

[9] See e.g.: ECtHR, *Krastanov v. Bulgaria*, No. 50222/99, Judgment of 30 September 2004, § 60.

also other ill-treatment,[10] as well as the use of derivative evidence, albeit to a limited extent.[11]

All of the above measures, including those that would subsequently be deemed "judicial,"[12] are legitimate prevention measures.[13] What is missing among them is preventive monitoring through visits to places for deprivation of liberty. In reality, this was something that the drafters of the UNCAT did consider. A draft optional protocol to the convention, which envisaged detention monitoring through visits by an international body, had been in existence since 1980, but Costa Rica, which made the initial proposal, withdrew it in order to allow a smoother adoption of the convention. When the UNCAT was adopted in December 1984, efforts to renew negotiations on the optional protocol started again. However, the process was divisive and protracted, with two major "camps" forming around the issue of the degree to which member states would be allowed to control the monitoring powers of the international body in exercising what they considered to be the fundamental principles of the UN Charter—non-intervention and state sovereignty.[14] Meanwhile, the Council of Europe adopted the European Convention for the Prevention of Torture and Inhuman or Degrading Treatment or Punishment (ECPT), which establishes such an international monitoring mechanism through the European Committee for the Prevention of Torture (CPT). In 1998 the International Criminal Tribunal for the former Yugoslavia (ICTY) delivered its judgment in the case of *Prosecutor v. Furundžija*. In it the ICTY held that the states are not only obliged to punish torture when it occurs but are also "[. . .] bound to put in place all those measures that may pre-empt the perpetration of torture".[15]

The divisions among the drafters of the OPCAT were ultimately overcome with the so-called "Mexican draft" of 2001 which aimed to establish a two-pillar system of visits by an international body, the Subcommittee for the Prevention of Torture (SPT) and by bodies established at the national level, national preventive mechanisms (NPM). This draft, with subsequent amendments, became the kernel of the Optional Protocol to the Convention against Torture and Other Cruel, Inhuman and Degrading Treatment and Punishment, adopted by the UN General Assembly on 18 December 2002. Its Preamble proclaims, just as the Preamble of the ECPT does, that the protection of persons against torture and other ill-treatment "[. . .] can be strengthened by non-judicial means of a preventive nature." It is in the framework of

[10] See e.g.: CEDH, *Göçmen c. Turquie*, no. 72000/01, Arrêt du 17 octobre 2006, § 74.

[11] ECtHR, *Gäfgen v. Germany*, No. 22978/05, Grand Chamber judgment of 1 June 2010, § 167.

[12] See e.g. the Preamble to the Optional Protocol to the Convention against Torture and Other Cruel, Inhuman and Degrading Treatment and Punishment (OPCAT).

[13] "[. . .] many of these measures could be said to have a 'preventive' effect. Criminalising torture, eliminating impunity, providing rehabilitation and redress to victims – these things will, it is to be hoped, not only deal with past abuses but also deter their recurrence." (Rodley and Pollard 2009, p. 228).

[14] Nowak and McArthur (2008), pp. 901–905.

[15] ICTY, *Prosecutor v. Furundžija*, No. IT-95-17/1, Trial chamber judgment, 10 December 1998, § 148.

the discussions around the drafting of the OPCAT, along with those in the framework of the CPT with its established working methods, where another concept of prevention was announced in both the international documents and in the scholarly literature.

Thus, we have now two concepts of prevention—a broader one in the UNCAT and a narrower one in the ECPT and the OPCAT. Over the past two decades the latter concept started to prevail.[16] Similarly, we have two types of safeguards against torture and other ill-treatment:

- *Those under the UNCAT. They* include criminalisation, investigation and prosecution, education/training, review of interrogation rules, prohibition of evidence obtained through torture/ill-treatment, right to compensation, etc.
- *Those under the "non-judicial" preventive mechanisms*. The major one among them are the visits, which themselves have a preventive effect. In addition, both the CPT and the SPT developed specific safeguards: the so-called "three rights" (notification of a third party about the detention, access to a lawyer from the moment of detention and medical examination by a doctor of detainee's choice); legal regulation of custody records; keeping of a single custody record;[17] electronic recording of the police questioning; information about rights; judicial review of detention; establishment of an independent inspection authority, etc.[18]

The concept of prevention that will be used below will be of the latter, narrower type. Before we examine its meaning in more detail however, we will have to make another important distinction. Some of the safeguards devised under the "non-judicial" preventive mechanisms became in fact legally binding in many countries, as well as through the Roadmap Directives of the EU. These include the secondary legislation in the framework of the *Roadmap for strengthening the procedural rights of suspected or accused persons in criminal proceedings*, adopted by Resolution of the European Council on 30 November 2009.[19] In December 2009, the Council included the Roadmap in its programme: *An open and secure Europe serving and protecting the citizens* (the Stockholm Programme).[20]

[16]Cf. Rodley and Pollard (2009), pp. 228–229: "At the same time, certain measures against torture and other ill-treatment have come to be seen as especially associated with the concept of 'prevention'; chief among these is the idea of repeated and systematic visits by independent experts to all places of detention, applying the methodology of the International Committee of the Red Cross not only in times of armed conflict, but all the time."

[17]CPT (1992), § 36–43.

[18]CPT (2002), § 32–50.

[19]Council of the European Union, Resolution on a Roadmap for strengthening procedural rights of suspected or accused persons in criminal proceedings of 30 November 2009, (OJ 2009 C 295/1), 4.12.2009.

[20]The Roadmap Directives include: Directive 2010/64/EU of 20 October 2010 on the right to interpretation and translation in criminal proceedings (OJ 2010 L 280/1); Directive 2012/13/EU of 22 May 2012 on the right to information in criminal proceedings (OJ 2012 L 142/1); Directive 2013/48/EU of 22 October 2013 on the right of access to a lawyer and the right to have a third party and consular authorities informed upon deprivation of liberty (OJ 2013 L 294/1); Directive EU

The Roadmap Directives specifically provide, among other things, for the right of access to a lawyer, as well as to legal aid, the right to notify a third party about the detention, information about rights, electronic recording (in some cases) of the police questioning for everybody who is suspected and accused of having committed a criminal offense. The respective obligations of the state authorities would normally be triggered from the moment of detention in the framework of criminal proceedings.[21] The primary purpose of these safeguards, which must have become national law in all EU Member States by now, is to ensure the fairness of these proceedings. But they serve to prevent also other human rights violations, including the right not to be subjected to torture and other ill-treatment.[22]

3.3 The Meaning of Prevention at the European and at the UN Level

The idea of prevention of torture and other ill-treatment through visits to places of detention has its clear origin—the approach of the International Committee of the Red Cross (ICRC) in times of armed conflicts. This was the inspiration of the Swiss banker Jean-Jacques Gautier and of the other persons and institutions who played an important role in triggering developments in international standard-setting in that sphere.[23] The ICRC approach developed *vis-à-vis* situations in which the rule of law is substantially undermined or made to play a subordinate role (often nominal) to the exigencies of "exceptional circumstances." Detainees in those circumstances are, if not in law, often in practice, at the mercy of the combatants. It is only the constructive dialogue with those in command that can alleviate their situation and prevent abuses.

Historically, the situation of prisoners sentenced for having committed criminal offences at times of peace has often been similar to that of prisoners of war (POWs).

2016/800 of 11 May 2016 on procedural safeguards for children who are suspects or accused persons in criminal proceedings (OJ 2016 L 132/1); Directive (EU) 2016/1919 of 26 October 2016 on legal aid for suspects and accused persons in criminal proceedings and for requested persons in European arrest warrant proceedings (OJ 2016 L 297/1); Directive (EU) 2016/343 of 9 March 2016 on the strengthening of certain aspects of the presumption of innocence and of the right to be present at the trial in criminal proceedings (OJ 2016 L 65/1) . To these, the Commission Recommendation of 27 November 2013 on procedural safeguards for vulnerable persons suspected or accused in criminal proceedings, which is not legally binding, should be added (OJ 2013 C 378/2) (European Commission 2013).

[21] Bulgaria is perhaps the only EU Member State that refuses to accept that police detention based on data that the affected person has committed a criminal offense makes that person a "suspect" within the meaning of the Roadmap Directives.

[22] Recital 52 of Directive 2013/48/EU refers, in addition to fair trial rights, also to the prohibition of torture and inhuman and degrading treatment, the right to liberty and security and the right to respect for private and family life.

[23] Cf.: APT (2007), pp. 2–3.

The very idea of imprisonment as punishment originated with the belief that prisoners are persons who have no rights and are at the mercy of the prison governor. Even where the idea of "prisoner law" had some constitutional roots or legal backing, "hands-off" doctrines in the judiciary prevailed, in some countries until the 1960s and 1970s.[24] Reliance on confessions and on other information extracted, often through different types of coercion during the early stage of the criminal investigation, prompted legislators and law enforcement authorities to build in law and in practice an atmosphere of secrecy around that stage and to restrict communication between the detainee and the outside world in order to achieve their aim.

Jean-Jacques Gautier and his associates from the Swiss Committee against Torture advocated a system of visits by international experts, with the agreement of the government, to all places of detention, similar to those carried out by the ICRC. The major tool of such mechanism was to be the constructive dialogue with authorities, aiming at the improvement of the treatment and the conditions of detention. In addition, the very existence of such a mechanism with the possibility for an external eye to potentially target every place of detention, was considered to have a preventive effect by itself. Neither at the time of its origin, nor subsequently, when the idea was implemented in practice, were there any doubts that such mechanisms would be useful in protecting detainees.[25] Indeed, it proved to be so, first in Europe after the establishment of the CPT visiting mechanism in 1989, and elsewhere in the world with the work of the OPCAT mechanisms.

Already with its first general report the CPT made it clear that it bases its work on the concept of cooperation with Member States as provided for by Article 3 of the ECPT. Thus, "[t]he CPT's task is not to publicly criticize States, but rather to assist them in finding ways to strengthen the 'cordon sanitaire' that separates acceptable and unacceptable treatment and behavior."[26] In this process "the best way [for the CPT] of attaining its objectives is through a constructive dialogue with States."[27] Moreover, in the view of Silvia Casale, former president of the CPT and, subsequently, of the SPT, the international visitors have a "common interest in, and shared sense of, what prisons should be like."[28] The CPT is thus "[. . .] an important ally for prison personnel who are striving, often against the odds, to run a safe and decent prison."[29] Such statements are hard to justify as a general approach, however. Those who run detention facilities where torture is routine, as is its covering-up, will find it difficult to see some common interest with an international monitoring team whose mandate is to prevent and eradicate torture. But they are revealing of what "constructive dialogue" might sometimes mean, as well as of the reasons why, for all the problems with the lack of follow up on the CPT recommendations by a number of

[24] See: Sigler and Shook (1995), pp. 245–254.

[25] Rodley and Pollard (2009), p. 231.

[26] CPT (1991), § 3.

[27] Ibid., § 99.

[28] Casale (2010), p. 1499.

[29] Ibid., p. 1496.

European governments, the Committee has used its powers to issue public statements so sparingly.

Closely related to the constructive dialogue is the duty of confidentiality in-built into the ECPT mechanism, as well as, to a limited extent, into the OPCAT mechanism of prevention.[30] This duty obliges the international monitoring body to keep confidential any information gathered in relation to the visit; to publish its report, together with any comments of the party concerned only when requested to do so by the state party; to refrain from publishing personal data without the express consent of the person concerned (Article 11 of the ECPT). CPT members and experts are obliged to maintain the confidentiality of the information of which they have become aware during and after their terms of office (Article 13 of the ECPT). Reasonable as it is with regard to publication of personal data, the obligation of confidentiality, which allows governments to control the release of information gathered during the visits, even where it concerns severe cases of torture, is hard to justify. It has its roots in concerns relating to state sovereignty, which have historically stood behind many efforts to cover up all types of repulsive practices and human rights abuses.[31]

Discussions in the working group on the OPCAT at the UN also focused very much on the meaning of prevention, cooperation and confidentiality. Elizabeth Odio-Benito of Costa Rica, the Chairperson-Rapporteur and the key trigger behind the adoption of the OPCAT, proposed that reference to confidentiality and cooperation is made in its preamble.[32] Representatives of Cuba, Algeria, China, Egypt, Saudi Arabia, the Sudan and Syria made a joint statement that, starting from the preamble, the content of the treaty should reflect its cooperative, preventive, confidential, non-duplicative and advisory nature.[33] Interestingly, these countries have neither signed, nor ratified the OPCAT after its adoption. But such calls were made repeatedly in the working group. At the end of the day, the OPCAT was provided with some teeth—the possibility of the Committee against Torture to make a public statement at the request of the SPT in cases of failure of the state party to cooperate with the Subcommittee (Article 16.4 of the OPCAT); the exemption of the national preventive mechanisms from the duty of confidentiality and their possibility to publish their reports and recommendations without any obligation to seek the consent of the governments (Article 19 of the OPCAT). The OPCAT also imposes a modest obligation on the governments to "examine the recommendations of the national preventive mechanism and enter into a dialogue with it" (Article 22 of the OPCAT).

The approach of the SPT since the beginning of its operation was influenced by the work and practice of the CPT.[34] This was quite natural, given the similarities of the purpose and of the provisions in the respective treaties. Explaining its approach

[30] The NPMs, the second pillar of the OPCAT, have no duty of confidentiality.

[31] Bicknell et al. (2018), p. 33.

[32] Nowak and McArthur (2008), p. 889.

[33] Ibid.

[34] Bicknell et al. (2018), p. 12.

on prevention in a key document from 2010, the SPT refused to devise a comprehensive statement of what the obligation of states to prevent should mean *in abstracto*. Instead, it formulated ten principles that were to guide its approach to prevention. These principles inform the focus of the inquiry and the working methods of the SPT. They include the general framework for the guaranteeing and enjoyment of human rights; the specific framework related to deprivation of liberty and the extent to which the procedural safeguards against torture and other ill-treatment are in place; detention conditions; proper conduct of the visits and subsequent reporting on the findings; domestic mechanisms of oversight; openness of places for deprivation of liberty to external scrutiny and attending to the plight of the specific vulnerable groups in them.[35] The same year, in its Third Annual Report the SPT underlined the importance of constructive dialogue with authorities:

> The main objectives of the mechanisms are to formulate recommendations on the basis of observations made and information obtained and to enter into a dialogue with the competent authorities with a view to improving the situation of persons deprived of their liberty and proposing ways of implementing the recommendations.[36]

The CPT approach to prevention limits its actions *vis-à-vis* specific cases of torture, which its delegations encounter during their visits. There is no question of referring these cases to the competent national authorities for investigation or for testifying in national proceedings of whatever type. Nor is there any possibility to participate in such proceedings in one way or another if they are initiated. Such actions go against the principle of confidentiality under Article 13 of the ECAT. On the other hand, any compulsion on the part of the national authorities to that effect would contravene provisions on the privileges and immunities from the Annex to the convention.

While the CPT mechanism contributed substantially to the significant reduction of torture and other ill-treatment in Europe, it is unclear whether we can make a similar conclusion as to the work of the SPT. Because of the SPT's much wider territorial scope and its scarce resources, the Subcommittee's visits to Member States are very rare. Therefore, its possibilities for follow up on recommendations are fewer than those of the CPT. There is also another important difference—the ratification of the ECPT, though not in law, but in practice, is a condition for membership in the Council of Europe. As a result, both CoE member states with a good human rights record, as well as those with a poor one, are obliged to subject themselves to the CPT visits and to respond to its recommendations. The OPCAT pool of member states is different. Ratification is not a condition for anything and so far the UN member states, which have ratified this treaty, are predominantly those with a relatively good human rights record.

---

[35] SPT (2010a).

[36] SPT (2010b), § 50.

3.4 Prevention at the National Level

The OPCAT requires the states parties to maintain, designate or establish one or several national preventive mechanisms for the prevention of torture at the domestic level. They must be independent, well-resourced and able to exercise their tasks in a professional way. Their composition must have due regard to women, ethnic minorities and other vulnerable groups. Articles 19 and 20 provide for the powers of the NPM in the exercise of its preventive mandate: access to all places of detention and liberty to choose which ones to visit; possibility to interview detainees in private; access to official information on the number and location of the detention facilities and on the treatment of persons detained there; possibility to make recommendations to competent authorities with the aim of improving the treatment of detainees and the conditions of detention; possibility to submit proposals and observations concerning the existing or draft legislation. State authorities are prohibited under Article 21 to sanction persons or organisations that provide information to the NPMs.

The national preventive mechanisms are sometimes seen as "the prolonged hands of the SPT" and as "a small SPT on a national level."[37] According to the SPT:

> The Subcommittee is of the view that a national preventive mechanism should also be empowered and able to deliver the whole 'preventive package', including examining patterns of practices from which risks of torture may arise; advocacy, such as commenting on draft and implementing legislation; providing public education; undertaking capacity-building; and actively engaging with State authorities.[38]

Wide as it is, this scope of activities is in the framework of the constructive dialogue with authorities. It does not go beyond it. But is it possible for the national preventive mechanism, being a national institution deriving its mandate and powers from the law, on the basis of which it is established, to act only as a "small SPT on a national level"? The answer to this question seems to be a bit more complicated than what the drafters of the OPCAT envisaged.

Article 21.2 of the OPCAT provides that confidential information collected by the NPM shall be "privileged." This has been interpreted to mean that no state authority may compel the NPM to disclose such information and that the state has a legal duty to protect it against pressure from third parties.[39] This should eventually lead to the exemption of the members of the NPM and their experts to testify in court. They can thus avoid entering into contentious relations with state officials and authorities in order to protect their sources and to remain within the framework of the constructive dialogue. But is this always justified *vis-à-vis* the imperative of combating a serious international crime, such as torture? In fact, exemption from testifying in court is not universally accepted in the contemporary systems of prevention at the national level.

[37] Marija Definis Gojanovic, member of the SPT in: Murrey et al. (2011), p. 134.

[38] SPT (2018), § 54.

[39] Nowak and McArthur (2008), p. 1094.

The legal duty of a state body to act upon a complaint from the victim is even more challenging in relation to the NPM powers. Positive obligation to investigate torture and other ill-treatment should be triggered by a complaint from the victim as a matter of international obligation. Article 13 of the UNCAT imposes a requirement on the states parties to ensure that any individual who alleges to have been subjected to torture in any territory under their jurisdiction has the right to file a complaint before the competent authorities and have his/her case promptly and impartially examined by them. In accordance with Article 16, this obligation also covers cases of other prohibited treatment committed by, or at the instigation or with the consent or acquiescence of a public official. In both the UN system and the regional systems for human rights protection, violation of the obligation to investigate is a violation of the general obligation to prohibit torture, cruel, inhuman or degrading treatment or punishment, as well as of the obligations to ensure an effective domestic remedy for violations of the rights guaranteed in the respective treaties.

In its case law on individual complaints, the Committee against Torture has established violations of the obligation to investigate following a complaint from a victim in a number of cases. With the existence of special provisions in the UNCAT on the legal duty to investigate, the Committee has not put forward the question of violation of the general prohibitions due to a refusal to investigate. In the case of *Blanco Abad v. Spain* from 1998, CAT established violations of Articles 12 and 13 because of the refusal to investigate a complaint by the applicant, made orally before a local court, that she had been subjected to physical ill-treatment and threatened with rape while in detention. The Committee noted:

> [. . .] [A]rticle 13 of the Convention does not require either the formal lodging of a complaint of torture under the procedure laid down in national law or an express statement of intent to institute and sustain a criminal action arising from the offence, and that it is enough for the victim simply to bring the [information] to the attention of an authority of the State for the latter to be obliged to consider it as a tacit but unequivocal expression of the victim's wish that the facts should be promptly and impartially investigated, as prescribed by this provision of the Convention.[40]

The approach of the European Court of Human Rights is similar. The Court has held on numerous occasions that when an individual makes a credible assertion that he/she has suffered treatment infringing Article 3 of the Convention at the hands of the police or other similar agents of the state, that provision, read in conjunction with the State's general duty under Article 1 of the Convention to "secure to everyone within [its] jurisdiction the rights and freedoms defined in ... [the] Convention," requires by implication that there should be an effective official investigation. In *Ahmet Özkan and Others v. Turkey* of 2004, the Court specified this general obligation to investigate in response to a complaint from a victim of ill-treatment. The Court required that in cases where a public authority is not competent to investigate a complaint, it should bring this information to the attention of a

[40]CAT, *Blanco Abad v. Spain*, No. 59/1996, Decision of 14 May 1998, § 8.6. See also CAT, *Bouabdallah Ltaief v. Tunisia*, No. 189/2001, Decision of 14 November 2003, § 10.6.

competent body.[41] Elsewhere the Court held that once the facts of torture/ill-treatment have come to the attention of the authorities, an obligation to lodge a formal complaint to the appropriate body cannot be left exclusively to the applicant's initiative.[42]

How should then a member of the NPM act when he/she is confronted with serious cases of torture and receives complaints from the victim in a place of detention during a visit? Is it and should it be legally possible in such circumstances to confine oneself to the framework of the constructive dialogue? These are questions and challenges that stem from the status of the NPM as a national institution, which the OPCAT does not address clearly. They need to be studied, discussed and addressed at both the national and international levels in the future.

3.5 The Role of Human Rights NGOs

The OPCAT was established with the presumption that further measures were necessary to achieve the purposes of the UNCAT.[43] International law sets very high standards of state action in combating and eradicating torture. Its prohibition is an absolute and non-derogable peremptory norm of customary international law.[44] The UNCAT requires the establishment of universal jurisdiction for the crime of torture. The torturer is nowadays not just an ordinary criminal within a national jurisdiction, but *hostis humani generis*.[45] Some courts and writers go as far as to view the prohibition of torture as an obligation *erga omnes*.[46]

Such a status of the prohibition of torture certainly justifies a variety of approaches to combat this serious crime. It is true that the ECPT and the OPCAT mechanisms are in this sense unique; no such mechanisms apply to the protection against other human rights violations. But they have their limitations, which are based, at least to some extent, on outdated perceptions of the relationships between human rights protection and national sovereignty. While there may be little doubt about their usefulness and their ability to reduce the incidence of torture and other ill-treatment, it is also true that the problems persist and that even in the most advanced countries, which have availed themselves of all contemporary mechanisms for protection, violations exist.

---

[41] ECtHR, *Ahmet Özkan and Others v. Turkey,* No. 21689/93, Judgment of 6 April 2004, § 359.

[42] ECtHR, *Muradova v. Azerbaijan*, No. 22684/05, Judgment of 2 April 2009, §§ 123–125; ECtHR, *Gjini v. Serbia*, No. 1128/16, Judgment of 15 January 2019, § 94.

[43] Nowak and McArthur (2008), p. 891.

[44] CAT, General Comment No. 2: Implementation of Article 2 by States Parties, CAT/C/GC/2, 24 January 2008, § 1.

[45] U.S. Court of Appeals, *Filártiga v. Peña-Irala*, 630 F. 2d 876, 2nd Cir. 1980.

[46] ICTY, *Prosecutor v. Furundžija*, Trial chamber judgment, § 151. See also: Shaw (2003), p. 116.

One further step in the fight against torture, although until now not recognised well enough at the international and at the national levels, has been the civil society involvement in combating torture through monitoring places of detention and through assistance of the victims. Visiting prisons and other places of detention by civil society organisations has been a long tradition in Europe and North America. The famous saying of Jesus "I was in prison, and you came to me" (Matthew 25:36) has inspired thousands of prison visitors for centuries. They had the right to meet prisoners in private long before the ECPT and the OPCAT were adopted. The twentieth century saw the formation of national associations of prison visitors in a number of countries. For the most part, the purposes of these groups are to offer support to those who seek contacts with the outside world. Visits by charitable organisations and non-profit entities organising rehabilitative and other services for prisoners have been another form of involvement by civil society in the life of the prison. Such an involvement was relatively easy to achieve, in so far as it did not challenge the sovereign power of the state to investigate and to punish the wrongdoers.

It is much more difficult for those who want to monitor and to assist detainees who become victims of the abuse of state power. Access of non-governmental organisations to places of detention for the purposes of human rights monitoring is a relatively recent development. At present, there is no legal obligation at the international level for states to allow such access, except for some specific purposes. There is however some "soft law" in that regard, as well as recommendations of some international bodies. There are also advocacy initiatives to that effect by human rights NGOs.[47] Some of these recommendations specify the purpose of the visits, i.e. monitoring. Others speak more generally about "visits."

Perhaps the first statement of an international body in that regard were the recommendations of the Supplementary Human Dimension Meeting of the OSCE on Prison Reform in Vienna of 8–9 July 2002. According to these recommendations:

- "OSCE participating States are encouraged to allow for comprehensive civil society monitoring of all places of custody.
- OSCE participating States should consider providing for a firm legal basis for NGO monitoring of places of custody, including pre-trial facilities and police detention facilities. In the absence of a clear legal basis authorities should use their discretionary powers to allow for civil society."[48]

A few months later, the African Commission of Human and Peoples' Rights adopted its Robben Island Guidelines for the Prohibition and Prevention of Torture in Africa, Guideline 42 of which states: "States should [. . .] encourage and facilitate visits by NGOs to places of detention."[49] At around the same time, the UN Committee against Torture also started recommending to the states parties, albeit

[47] See most recently: OMCT (2022).

[48] OSCE (2002).

[49] African Commission on Human and Peoples' Rights (2002).

on an occasional basis, to permit NGO visits to places of detention.[50] Subsequently, for some time such recommendations were abandoned; instead, the Committee recommended strengthening of the NPMs. Over the past 5 years it renewed its recommendations on NGO visits albeit not on a systematic basis.[51] In some of these recommendations the CAT would refer to NGO "visits" generally whereas in others it would refer to their specific purpose—monitoring.

This is an important distinction. NGO monitoring has a number of advantages: the genuine human rights NGOs are normally independent; they adopt a broader human rights approach; they are more flexible in their advocacy strategies and are not restricted in publishing their findings. In addition, NGO monitoring may be combined with other purposes, such as legal assistance to victims. The latter may sound odd, if not outrageous to the ears of the ardent believer in the unhindered sovereign power of states to investigate and punish. Allowing NGOs not only to monitor and engage in constructive dialogue, but also to offer legal assistance to victims of torture and other ill-treatment in the course of their monitoring is something which very few states nowadays would consider. Yet, it is hard to find rational reasons not to allow it. Moreover, it finds support in some "soft" international standards. Rule 78 of the UN Rules for the Protection of Juveniles Deprived of their Liberty (the Havana Rules) states:

> Every juvenile should have the right to request assistance from family members, legal counsellors, humanitarian groups or others where possible, in order to make a complaint. Illiterate juveniles should be provided with assistance should they need to use the services of public or private agencies and organisations which provide legal counsel or which are competent to receive complaints.[52]

This provision views the role of "humanitarian groups" and "organisations which provide legal counsel" in a much broader context than just monitoring. While it is restricted in its personal scope to juveniles deprived of their liberty, it nonetheless envisages a possibility for such groups to provide legal assistance on a broad scope of issues. Given the status of the prohibition of torture and other ill-treatment in international law, there is no reason why NGOs should not be allowed access and denied the possibility to assist victims of torture from the very moment of detention.

It has been observed that the rules relating to the legal standing of NGOs in the EU Member States are unreasonably narrow, which prevents civil society organisations from taking a more direct role in litigation over fundamental rights.[53] The EU Agency for Fundamental Rights (FRA) suggests that third parties should be offered

---

[50] See e.g.: CAT, Concluding observations on Cameroon, CAT/C/CR/31/6, 11 February 2004, § 8a.

[51] See: CAT, Concluding observations on Bulgaria, CAT/C/BGR/CO/6, 15 December 2017, § 20; CAT, Concluding observations on Italy, CAT/C/ITA/CO/5-6, 18 December 2017, § 27; CAT, Concluding observations on Tajikistan, CAT/C/TJK/CO/3, 18 June 2018, § 28; CAT, Concluding observations on the Russian Federation, CAT/C/RUS/CO/6, 28 August 2018, § 23; CAT, Concluding observations on Uzbekistan, CAT/C/UZB/CO/5, 14 January 2020, § 44.

[52] United Nations Rules for the Protection of Juveniles Deprived of their Liberty, General Assembly resolution 45/113 of 14 December 1990.

[53] FRA (2010), p. 11.

standing in hate crimes proceedings in order to unburden victims of reporting.[54] FRA points at the rules of standing in the EU anti-discrimination legislation where NGOs are allowed to act on behalf or in support of victims of discrimination. It also points at the obligation under the UNECE Convention on Access to Information, Public Participation in Decision-making and Access to Justice in Environmental Matters (Aarhus Convention), which allows for *actio popularis* in relation to environmental cases. FRA concludes that "[a]llowing associations to intervene on behalf of victims of discriminatory crimes could be a powerful instrument in enhancing access to justice."[55]

The above arguments on broadening of the rules of standing of NGOs are even more valid in regard to their access to detainees and their legal standing to act on behalf or in support of victims of torture. As shown above, torture is a human rights violation that has a special status in international law. This special status justifies the use of the widest variety of means for combating this serious crime. Victims of torture are usually much more scared and much more in need to be unburdened of reporting than victims of hate crimes. As practical experience by and large shows, the major reason of the underreporting of police misbehaviour is the fact that its victims are usually in the hands of the perpetrators and have pending criminal proceedings against themselves in which these same people who have abused them are involved on the prosecution side.

In another important development, the ECtHR established a legal obligation of the states to allow visits to places of detention of media representatives for some specific purposes. In the case of *Szurovecz v. Hungary* the Court found a violation of Article 10 of the Convention in a case of a journalist who was not allowed to carry out interviews and take photographs in a reception centre for asylum-seekers, thus preventing him from reporting on the living conditions there. The Court was not satisfied with the reasons which the Hungarian government provided to refuse his access and pointed out that the public interest in reporting from places of detention is especially relevant where the authorities' handling of vulnerable groups is at stake. According to the Court, "[t]he 'watchdog' role of the media assumes particular importance in such contexts since their presence is a guarantee that the authorities can be held to account for their conduct."[56] It can be assumed that the NGOs also have such a "watchdog" role and should therefore be entitled to exercise it through visits to places of detention and the possibility to conduct private interviews with detainees.

---

[54] FRA (2016), p. 34.

[55] Ibid., p. 35.

[56] ECtHR, *Szurovecz v. Hungary*, No. 15428/16, Judgment of 8 October 2019, § 61.

3.6 Conclusion

Over the past three decades there has been a marked progress in eradicating torture and other ill-treatment, at least in those states which have ratified the international instruments and adopted the mechanisms for combating and prevention which they envisage. Yet, problems remain and they are not found only in those states which have refrained from subjecting themselves to international scrutiny. Torture and other forms of ill-treatment by agents of the state, as well as inhuman and degrading conditions of detention, exist in many countries in Europe, as well as outside Europe. Their persistence is due to the specificity of these violations and the problems with their reporting and investigation. They are also due to the limited effectiveness of the preventive mechanisms at the international and at the national levels.

The status of the prohibition of torture in international law justifies the adoption of a wide variety of means for its eradication. The need to do more in that regard led to the establishment in law and in practice of the preventive mechanisms, which are based on visits to places of detention by independent expert bodies at the international and at the national levels. The work of the CPT in Europe, as well as of the SPT and the national preventive mechanisms provided for by the OPCAT, proved to be beneficial but insufficient. There is a need to go further in adopting other mechanisms.

One such mechanism is civil society monitoring and assistance to victims of torture. It has existed in many countries for decades and since the beginning of this millennium its usefulness has been recognised, albeit in the form of "soft law" and recommendations, also at the international level. Involvement of civil society and specifically of human rights NGOs in monitoring places of detention and in assisting victims from the very moment of their arrest or detention will contribute to further eradication of police torture and ill-treatment. This can become possible only through the establishment of a firm legal basis for NGO access to all places of detention and through broadening their legal standing to act on behalf or in support of the victims of torture and other ill-treatment.

Documents and Reports

CAT, *Blanco Abad v. Spain*, No. 59/1996, Decision of 14 May 1998

CAT, *Bouabdallah Ltaief v. Tunisia*, No. 189/2001, Decision of 14 November 2003

CAT, General Comment No. 2: Implementation of article 2 by States parties, CAT/C/GC/2, 24 January 2008

CAT, Concluding observations on Bulgaria, CAT/C/BGR/CO/6, 15 December 2017

CAT, Concluding observations on Italy, CAT/C/ITA/CO/5-6, 18 December 2017

CAT, Concluding observations on the Russian Federation, CAT/C/RUS/CO/6, 28 August 2018

CAT, Concluding observations on Tajikistan, CAT/C/TJK/CO/3, 18 June 2018

CAT, Concluding observations on Uzbekistan, CAT/C/UZB/CO/5, 14 January 2020
CPT (1991) 1st general report on the CPT's activities. CPT/INF (91) 3, Strasbourg, 20 February 1991
CPT (1992) 2nd general report. CPT/Inf (92) 3, Strasbourg
CPT (2002) 12th general report. CPT/Inf (2002) 15, Strasbourg
CPT (2018) 27th general report. Council of Europe, Strasbourg
CPT (2019) 31st general report. Council of Europe, Strasbourg
CEDH, *Göçmen c. Turquie*, no. 72000/01, Arrêt du 17 octobre 2006
Council of the European Union, Resolution on a Roadmap for strengthening procedural rights of suspected or accused persons in criminal proceedings of 30 November 2009, (OJ 2009 C 295/1), 4.12.2009
Directive 2010/64/EU of 20 October 2010 on the right to interpretation and translation in criminal proceedings (OJ 2010 L 280/1)
Directive 2012/13/EU of 22 May 2012 on the right to information in criminal proceedings (OJ 2012 L 142/1)
Directive 2013/48/EU of 22 October 2013 on the right of access to a lawyer and the right to have a third party and consular authorities informed upon deprivation of liberty (OJ 2013 L 294/1)
Directive (EU) 2016/343 of 9 March 2016 on the strengthening of certain aspects of the presumption of innocence and of the right to be present at the trial in criminal proceedings (OJ 2016 L 65/1)
Directive (EU) 2016/800 of 11 May 2016 on procedural safeguards for children who are suspects or accused persons in criminal proceedings (OJ 2016 L 132/1)
Directive (EU) 2016/1919 of 26 October 2016 on legal aid for suspects and accused persons in criminal proceedings and for requested persons in European arrest warrant proceedings (OJ 2016 L 297/1)
ECtHR (2021) Annual Report 2021. Council of Europe, Strasbourg
ECtHR, *Ahmet Özkan and Others v. Turkey,* No. 21689/93, Judgment of 6 April 2004
ECtHR, *Gäfgen v. Germany*, No. 22978/05, Grand Chamber judgment of 1 June 2010
ECtHR, *Gjini v. Serbia*, No. 1128/16, Judgment of 15 January 2019
ECtHR, *Krastanov v. Bulgaria*, No. 50222/99, Judgment of 30 September 2004
ECtHR, *Muradova v. Azerbaijan*, No. 22684/05, Judgment of 2 April 2009
ECtHR, *Szurovecz v. Hungary*, No. 15428/16, Judgment of 8 October 2019
ICTY, *Prosecutor v. Furundžija*, No. IT-95-17/1, Trial chamber judgment, 10 December 1998
SPT (2010a) The approach of the Subcommittee on Prevention of Torture to the concept of prevention of torture and other cruel, inhuman or degrading treatment or punishment under the optional protocol to the convention against torture and other cruel, inhuman or degrading treatment or punishment, CAT/OP/12/6, 30 December 2010
SPT (2010b) Third annual report of the Subcommittee on Prevention of Torture and Other Cruel, Inhuman or Degrading Treatment or Punishment, CAT/C/44/2, 25 March 2010

SPT (2018) Eleventh annual report of the Subcommittee on Prevention of Torture and Other Cruel, 630 Inhuman or Degrading Treatment or Punishment, CAT/C/64/4, 26 March 2018

U.S. Court of Appeals, *Filártiga v. Peña-Irala*, 630 F. 2d 876, 2nd Cir. 1980

United Nations Rules for the Protection of Juveniles Deprived of their Liberty, General Assembly resolution 45/113 of 14 December 1990

References

African Commission on Human and Peoples' Rights (2002) Resolution on guidelines and measures for the prohibition and prevention of torture, cruel, inhuman or degrading treatment or punishment in Africa, adopted at its 32nd ordinary session, held in Banjul, The Gambia, from 17th to 23rd October 2002

APT (2007) Letting the light: 30 years of torture prevention. APT, Geneva

Bicknell C, Evans M, Morgan R (2018) Preventing torture in Europe. Council of Europe Publishing, Strasbourg

Carver C, Handley L (2016) Does torture prevention work? Liverpool University Press, Liverpool

Casale S (2010) The importance of dialogue and cooperation in prison oversight. Peace Law Rev 5(5)

European Commission (2013) Recommendation of 27 November 2013 on procedural safeguards for vulnerable persons suspected or accused in criminal proceedings, which is not legally binding, should be added (OJ 2013 C 378/2)

FRA (2010) Access to justice in Europe: an overview of challenges and opportunities. FRA, Luxemburg

FRA (2016) Ensuring justice for hate crime victims: professional perspectives. FRA, Luxemburg

Kanev K (2022) Problems with the equal treatment of accused persons in pre-trial proceedings in Bulgaria. BHC, Sofia

Murrey R, Steinerte E, Evans M, de Wolf AH (2011) The optional protocol to the UN Convention against torture. Oxford University Press, Oxford

Nowak M, McArthur E (2008) The United Nations Convention against torture: a commentary. Oxford University Press, Oxford

OMCT (2022) (Re)opening prison doors to civil society: a catalyst for improving detention conditions, Geneva, December 2022. https://www.omct.org/en/resources/reports/new-guidance-note-urgent-need-to-open-prison-doors-to-civil-society

OSCE (2002) Supplementary human dimension meeting on prison reform. Final report, Vienna, 8–9 July 2002. https://www.osce.org/odihr/43115?download=true. Accessed 16 Apr 2023

Rodley N, Pollard M (2009) The treatment of prisoners under international law. Oxford University Press, Oxford

Shaw M (2003) International law, 5th edn. Cambridge University Press, Cambridge

Sigler R, Shook C (1995) The Federal Judiciary and corrections: breaking the "hands-off" doctrine. Crim Justice Policy Rev 7(3–4)

Krassimir Kanev is chairperson and acting director of the Bulgarian Helsinki Committee, the biggest human rights advocacy NGO in Bulgaria. He obtained his PhD in philosophy from Sofia University in 1986. Specialised on Human Rights and Religious Freedom at Columbia University in 1996-97. Taught courses in sociology, critical social theory, environmental studies, ethnic relations and human rights in a number of universities, including Sofia University, Plovdiv University, Central European University, the University of Sarajevo and the University of Oregon. Since 2003 teaches online courses for a US-based organisation Human Rights Education Associates (HREA) for human rights professionals. Dr Kanev published several books and dozens of articles on protection against torture, rights of the prisoners, freedom of expression, right to liberty and security of persons, hate speech, religious freedom, access to justice and violence against women. He served as member of the board of a number of international organisations, including the International Helsinki Federation for Human Rights, the Fundamental Rights Agency, the UN Voluntary Fund for Victims of Torture, the European Roma Rights Center, the Public Interest Law Network, the Association for the Prevention of Torture, the European Implementation Network and the International Partnership for Human Rights. At present, he is President of the Civil Liberties Union for Europe and Vice-President of the European Prison Litigation Network. Dr Kanev actively litigates before the European Court of Human Rights and has successfully represented more than 100 applicants before this court on a variety of human rights issues.

Chapter 4
The Practical Challenge of Respecting Fundamental Safeguards During the G20 Summit in Hamburg

Christina Hof

Contents

Abstract The following article addresses the practical challenges of respecting fundamental safeguards during the G20 summit in Hamburg, which took place in July 2017. It first addresses the specific situation and challenges a major event poses for the respect of fundamental rights of persons being arrested. Subsequently, relevant standards of the National Agency for the Prevention of Torture and the European Committee for the Prevention of Torture related to police custody will be presented. The article then takes a closer look at the challenges, which presented themselves in Hamburg with a focus on structural and material conditions of the mass detention centre, access to a lawyer as well as prompt judicial hearings. The case of Hamburg shows how practice differed from the theoretical concept the mass detention centre was based on and might contribute to a better protection of fundamental rights on the occasion of such events in the future.

C. Hof (✉)
Nationale Stelle zur Verhütung von Folter, Luisenstraße 7, Wiesbaden, Germany

R. Alleweldt (ed.), *Fair Treatment of Persons in Police Custody*,
https://doi.org/10.1007/978-3-031-61737-9_4

4.1 Introduction

“I presume that G20 will keep us busy until the end of 2019.”[1] This article focuses on the question how fundamental safeguards for persons who are arrested by the police can be respected during exceptional times, such as major events, taking the G20 summit in Hamburg in 2017 as an example. First, I want to address the specific situation and challenges a major event poses for the respect of fundamental rights of the persons being arrested. I will then briefly present the National Agency for the Prevention of Torture and give a short overview of the relevant standards of the National Agency and of the European Committee for the Prevention of Torture (CPT) related to police custody. Subsequently, I will elaborate how fundamental safeguards were challenged during the G20 summit and provide first-hand information about the background of the issues raised. Major political events like the G20 summit create serious challenges for the authorities in the host country regarding the handling of violent opponents and potentially high numbers of people being arrested within a short period of time. As local police stations usually do not have sufficient capacity for such large numbers of arrests, special facilities have to be provided for such events. The material conditions of detention of those facilities have to meet basic requirements and all processes related to the detention have to take place in a way that guarantees the respect of fundamental rights of people being arrested even in this exceptional situation. Therefore, proceedings also have to be very fast in order to limit detention to the shortest period of time possible and not to exceed the maximum period of time provided for by law. This also leads to organisational and logistical challenges regarding the contact to lawyers and judicial hearings. The fact that a considerable number of political activists from different countries might arrive for such an event is another challenge, as all processes have to run smoothly despite the fact that those persons will need translations for all communication that takes place, following their arrest.

However, when it comes to the arrest, there are fundamental requirements related to police custody, which also have their validity under these special circumstances. Before presenting those fundamental requirements, which are standards of the CPT and of the National Agency for the Prevention of Torture, the National Agency shall briefly be presented.

[1]Fröhlich (2018), non-literal translation.

4.2 The National Agency for the Prevention of Torture and Its Work Related to Arrests by the Police

The National Agency for the Prevention of Torture is Germany's National Preventive Mechanism in line with the Optional Protocol to the United Nations Convention against Torture and other Cruel, Inhuman and Degrading Treatment or Punishment (OPCAT). It is its principal task to prevent torture and ill-treatment by regularly visiting and inspecting places of deprivation of liberty and monitoring the detention conditions and treatment of the persons affected. The National Agency draws attention to deficits and makes recommendations and suggestions to the authorities for improvements of the situation of detainees. For this purpose, the National Agency has the following rights:

- Access to all information concerning the number of persons being deprived of their liberty at places of detention as defined in Article 4 of the OPCAT, as well as the number of places of detention and their location
- Access to all information concerning the treatment of these persons as well as their detention conditions
- Access to all places of detention, their installations and facilities
- The opportunity to hold private interviews with persons deprived of their liberty

Under Article 4 (1) of the Optional Protocol, a place of detention is any place under a state party's jurisdiction and control where persons are or may be deprived of their liberty, either by virtue of an order given by a public authority or at its instigation or with its explicit consent or acquiescence. These are, amongst others, police stations.

Since the National Agency took up work in 2009, visits of several hundred police stations of the Federal—and the Länder Police have been conducted, observing the treatment of persons in police custody. Every year, the National Agency has set itself an annual topic for its activities. In 2017 the Agency had a special focus on deprivation of liberty by the police and conducted monitoring visits on the occasion of major events like the Oktoberfest and the G20 summit in Hamburg.[2] Against its background and the gained experience of hundreds of monitoring visits, the National Agency translates recurring recommendations into standards. These standards are developed on a continual basis and are intended to provide the supervisory authorities and facilities with benchmarks for humane detention conditions and humane treatment of persons who are deprived of their liberty. Therefore, especially the standards of the CPT are taken into account. However, the CPT develops standards for all countries of the Council of Europe while the National Agency specifies and adopts its standards to the context in Germany.

[2]For detailed information about the mandate and work of the National Agency, see National Agency for the Prevention of Torture (2018), Annual Report 2017.

4.3 National and International Standards for the Treatment of Persons in Police Custody

Over a period of 25 years the CPT has developed standards regarding the treatment of persons in police custody. On the one hand, these standards are related to material conditions that have, amongst others, to meet the following basic requirements:

> All police cells should be of a reasonable size for the number of persons they are used to accommodate, and have adequate lighting (i.e. sufficient to read by, sleeping periods excluded) and ventilation; preferably, cells should enjoy natural light. Further, cells should be equipped with a means of rest (e.g. a fixed chair or bench), and persons obliged to stay overnight in custody should be provided with a clean mattress and blankets.[3]

On the other hand, the standards put emphasis on the following three basic rights:

> The right of the person concerned to have the fact of his detention notified to a third party of his choice (family member, friend, consulate), the right of access to a lawyer, and the right to request a medical examination by a doctor of his choice (in addition to any medical examination carried out by a doctor called by the police authorities).[4]

In the light of the CPT standards for police custody and based on its own experience of almost 10 years of monitoring the treatment of persons deprived of their liberty by the police, the National Agency set up its own standards adapted to the national context in Germany. It is important to note that there are no specific standards for mass detention centres until now. The period of time a person is held in regular police custody is relatively short (usually only a few hours). Consequently, also the conditions in a mass detention centre should meet the same requirements as they do in normal police stations. These standards shall be presented briefly as they are the fundamental basis on which deprivation of liberty during the G20 summit was assessed.

Regarding material conditions the National Agency states, that:

> Every custody cell should be equipped with a smoke detector, an emergency button, adjustable lighting, a non-flammable, washable mattress, a blanket, and a pillow. Where a custody cell is only equipped with a low bed, it must have additional seating at standard height.[5]
>
> It should be possible to adjust the lighting in custody cells to ensure that persons taken into custody are able to sleep, while at the same time reducing the risk of injury and enabling detainees to find their way in the dark. Every custody cell should receive natural light, including those intended for short-term custody. Furthermore, a suitable room temperature should be ensured in custody cells.[6]

Additionally, the National Agency demands the following minimum standard to be fulfilled regarding the cell size in police custody:

---

[3] CPT (2002), CPT/Inf/E (2002) 1—Rev. 2013, para 42.

[4] CPT (2002), CPT/Inf/E (2002) 1—Rev. 2013, para 36.

[5] National Agency for the Prevention of Torture (2018), Annual Report 2017, p. 23.

[6] Ibid.

> Police custody cells must be designed in a way that ensures humane detention conditions. A single-occupancy custody cell must have a floor space of at least 4.5 square metres. Multiple-occupancy custody cells must have a floor space of at least 3.5 square metres per person. Facing walls must be separated by a distance of at least two metres, and the ceiling must be considerably higher than two metres.[7]

Finally, concerning the reading of rights, the National Agency states among others:

> Each and every person deprived of their liberty must be informed of their rights, immediately and without exception. Forms containing all the relevant information should therefore be available in various languages. They should at the very least include information about the fact that anyone who is taken into police custody has the right to be examined by a doctor, to consult a lawyer, to notify a trusted third party and, where applicable, inform the consulate of their home country.[8]

Against this background the practical challenges concerning the respect of fundamental safeguards which presented themselves during the G20 summit shall be presented in the following.

4.4 Practical Challenges During the G20 Summit in Hamburg

4.4.1 Preparation and Concept of the Mass Detention Centre

In preparation of the G20 summit, concerning the question of the detention facilities, authorities relied on the experiences of the G7 summit, which had taken place in Bavaria in 2015. However, it has to be mentioned that the mass detention centre built for the G7 summit never demonstrated that it would be feasible in practice, due to the fact that hardly any cases of people being arrested during that summit occurred. In Hamburg, authorities decided to convert an already existing container complex, which originally used to house refugees, into the mass detention centre. It was situated on the outskirts of Hamburg and thus away from the events around the summit venue in the city centre. The detention centre was only planned for short-term detention of merely a few hours and could accommodate up to 400 detainees at a time. Regarding material conditions, the detention centre consisted of single cells, which measured only 3.3 square metres. The multiple-occupancy cells for up to five persons measured 9 square metres. Given the fact that the cells were situated in a hall within the container complex, the cells had no windows and there was no natural light or fresh air but artificial light and ventilation. The cells consisted of a seat, smoke detector and an emergency button. There was an additional building next to the hall with sanitary facilities.

---

[7] National Agency for the Prevention of Torture (2018), Annual Report 2017, Wiesbaden, p. 22.

[8] Ibid. p. 23.

For legal support, there was a free emergency legal service, which ensured that lawyers could be contacted at all times throughout the duration of the summit. The telephone number of the emergency service as well as a list with additional numbers were posted next to the phone boxes in the detention centre. A coordinating group within the mass detention centre was responsible for assisting detainees in contacting a lawyer, and interpreters for many different languages were available the whole time. Several consultation rooms were provided where detainees could speak to their lawyers in private.

In order to speed up procedures and to limit detention to the shortest possible period, an outpost of Hamburg's Local Court was set up in a complex of containers right next to the detention centre. Judges and interpreters were present in this complex continuously throughout the entire duration of the Summit and the judges at the temporary court worked in three shifts to conduct hearings around the clock, if necessary.

The National Agency first visited the detention centre approximately 1 month before the G20 summit took place to conduct a visual inspection of the facilities and discuss the way they were intended to be used during the summit. During this initial visit the National Agency took a critical stance regarding the size of the cells, especially the multiple occupancy cells, in combination with the number of persons intended to be arrested together, and taking into account the possible duration of arrest. Furthermore, the National Agency recommended to consider the use of textile hand restraint belts, should shackling be necessary in the custody cells. During the on-going operations, which the National Agency observed at different moments during the summit, various problems related to the respect of fundamental safeguards in police custody presented themselves and shall be elaborated in the following.

4.4.2 Duration of Transfer to Custody at the Mass Detention Centre

As already mentioned above, the mass detention centre in Hamburg was situated outside the city in an industrial area. Due to the fact that various streets in the city centre and around the conference venue had been blocked, there were long traffic jams in the city area. Thus, the vehicles intended for the transfer of detainees to the detention centre needed a very long time to get through the traffic, as well. Therefore, in a large number of cases, persons were transferred to one of the local polices stations after having been arrested on the street and had to wait there for the transfer to the mass detention centre. According to the available documents, several hours (in many cases between 3 and 6 hours) passed between the moment the person was arrested on the street and the point when they were brought to the mass detention centre, where processes related to their arrest just started.

4.4.3 Material Conditions and Duration of Detention

For the persons taken into custody based on police law, the mass detention centre had 250 places in multiple-occupancy cells for up to five persons. For persons arrested under the Code of Criminal Procedure, there were another 150 places available in single cells. The single cells had a floor space of 3.3 m^2, while multiple-occupancy cells measured 9 m^2.

In assessing how humane detention conditions and treatment are, a decisive factor is the duration of detention in connection with the size of the custody cells. The documents and interviews conducted with detainees during the visit revealed that many people were detained in the mass detention centre for more than 20 hours, some even for several days. Some multiple-occupancy cells, which according to the National Agency's minimum standard were supposed to hold not more than two detainees, were used to detain three persons over an extensive period of time, some cells even four persons, though only for some hours. This clearly does not correspond with the short detention period of just a few hours that had been planned by the authorities. Additionally, in a number of cases it was found that detainees were held overnight without being given a mattress. Instead, they only received a thin blanket. It became apparent that these individuals had not been informed about the availability of mattresses. Especially with regards to the size of the cells and the material conditions in combination with the long period of time persons had been arrested, the conditions did not comply with the minimum standards of the National Agency and have to be considered as very problematic.

4.4.4 Access to a Lawyer

Taken the provisions made, in some cases it took several hours for detainees to get the chance to contact a lawyer after they had been arrested and taken to the detention centre. In the follow-up process, the competent authorities did not give any further explanations to clarify this issue but drew the attention to several complaints related to the circumstances of legal support, which were part of criminal investigations. As a result, authorities stated that at least some of the allegations made publicly and related to the circumstances of legal support were not found justified.

4.4.5 Prompt Judicial Hearings

The documents provided and interviews conducted revealed that in many cases it took several hours until detainees were brought before a judge without any clear reasons that would justify such a delay. This led to doubts as to whether persons detained in the mass detention centre were granted a prompt judicial hearing.

In the follow-up to the summit authorities confirmed that in several cases there were considerable delays of 15–40 hours between the moment a person had been arrested and the judicial hearing. In those cases, the Hamburg Local Court found that the right to a prompt judicial hearing had been violated. Additional cases had been brought before the Court, which have not yet been decided.

4.4.6 Length of Time Before Release

The evaluated documents showed that in a large number of cases several hours passed between the judicial hearing and a release. If the judicial hearing does not result in a detention order being issued, the person concerned would have to be released immediately. Authorities stated that "there were several cases where the reason for a prolonged arrest was expected to cease in the foreseeable future." In those cases, for reasons of proportionality, it was decided not to transfer the persons concerned to a prison for the short period of time until they had to be released but to keep them in the detention centre. However, this decision was not documented.

4.4.7 Documentation and Training of Staff

Originally, hand-held scanners were intended to be used for the comprehensive documentation of all aspects related to the arrest in the detention centre. However, the scanners proved to be error-prone and it was decided spontaneously to use an electronic documentation system well known within the police in Hamburg and completed by written documentation. However, written documentation was carried out incompletely at peak times when high numbers of people being arrested were brought to the detention centre. Additionally, police officers employed in the detention centre were partly not familiar with the application of the electronic documentation system, which finally resulted in poor documentation of the processes during the summit.

Apart from the uncertainty regarding the documentation system, police officers had no previous training for the processes in the detention centre at all due to the fact that their initial training took part only during on-going processes. This might be one explanation for the delayed processes described above.

4.5 Summary and Outlook

Bearing in mind that each major event has its very own challenges the conditions in mass detention centres might differ greatly depending on many factors. Thus, it is difficult to draw general conclusions from the case of detention during the G20 summit in Hamburg.

However, the examples elaborated above show that some factors that influenced the respect of fundamental safeguards were already an inherent part of the concept and planning of the detention centre, taking the cell size and intended number of people to be detained in them as examples. Other challenges like the difficulties regarding comprehensive documentation only turned up during on-going operations and hardly were brought under control after they surfaced. It is relying on existing standards of National Preventive Mechanisms and the CPT as well as on experiences of the past that will help to guarantee conditions, which meet basic standards and the respect of fundamental rights in the future. At least as important as the material conditions are the qualifying and adequate training of staff for this specific situation. Unquestionably, the case of Hamburg serves as a revealing example of how practice differed from the theoretical concept the mass detention centre was based on and it might contribute to a better protection of fundamental rights on the occasion of such events in the future.

References

European Committee for the Prevention of Torture and Inhuman or Degrading Treatment or Punishment (CPT) (2002) CPT Standards, CPT/Inf/E (2002) 1—Rev. 2013

Fröhlich J (22.01.2018) "Ein Polizist, der Gewalt anwendet, macht sich nicht automatisch strafbar," Interview von Ansgar Siemens, Der Spiegel,

National Agency for the Prevention of Torture (2018) Annual Report 2017, Wiesbaden

Dr Christina Hof studied political science and French at the Friedrich Alexander University Erlangen-Nürnberg and the Université Laval, Canada. From 2011 to 2019, she worked with the National Agency for the Prevention of Torture, Germany's National Preventive Mechanism established under the Optional Protocol to the UN Convention Against Torture. Her main fields of work covered human rights protection in places of deprivation of liberty, especially police custody, prisons, juvenile detention centres and detention pending deportation.

Her main research interests went beyond questions of inhuman or degrading treatment and include human rights protection at national and UN level with a special focus on the UN Human Rights Council. In 2020, her doctoral thesis about the impact of Non-Governmental Organisations on the Universal Periodic Review mechanism was published. Since 2019, Christina Hof has been working in the field of cross-border cooperation at the Parliament of Rhineland-Palatinate, Germany.

Relevant publications: Hof, Christina (2020), New framework—new dynamics? Partizipation und Einfluss von Nichtregierungsorganisationen im Universal Periodic Review des Menschenrechtsrats. FAU Studien zu Menschenrechten (4), FAU University Press. Hof, Christina (2018), Freiheitsentziehung—werden die Menschenrechte mit den Effekten abgegeben? In: Frevel,

Bernhardt/Schmidt, Peter, Empirische Polizeiforschung XXII Demokratie und Menschenrechte. Herausforderungen für und an die polizeiliche Bildungsarbeit, Band 25, Verlag für Polizeiwissenschaft, S. 108-116. Hof, Christina/Bartelt, Jennifer (2017), Ein Blick der Nationalen Stelle auf den Frauenvollzug. Die Bangkok-Rules—wichtige Leitlinien für den Frauenvollzug in Deutschland, in: Forum Strafvollzug Vol. 66 (5), S. 325-328.

Chapter 5
Investigative Interviewing: A Change of Mindset

Asbjørn Rachlew

Contents

A. Rachlew (✉)
Norwegian Centre for Human Rights, Oslo, Norway

R. Alleweldt (ed.), *Fair Treatment of Persons in Police Custody*,
https://doi.org/10.1007/978-3-031-61737-9_5

Abstract Interviewing victims, witnesses and suspects is a core task of law enforcement. Consequently, *how* the police conduct their interviews will have a profound impact on the outcome, fairness, efficiency, and reliability of any subsequent criminal proceedings, and ultimately, how citizens perceive the fairness of the criminal justice system. With limited positive guidance or assistance in formulating strategies to improve ethical and effective information retrieval, agencies have developed their own skills and practices. Traditionally, these practices have not benefitted from critical research, allowing outdated skills and beliefs, even myths, to direct a confession-orientated practice, intended to reinforce the assumptions already held by interviewers and their organizations. In contrast, the purpose of investigative interviewing is to collect accurate and reliable information, sufficiently detailed in order to disclose all relevant facts and diminish (reasonable) doubt about matters under investigation. Investigative interviewing is informed by 40 years of scientific research, developed in close cooperation with the police to guide detectives through a mental and practical procedure with an open-mind, preventing common pitfalls associated with relying on premature conclusions. Research has revealed that these rapport-based interviewing techniques stimulate the flow of accurate and reliable information from victims, witnesses, and suspects of crime, whilst preserving the interviewees' dignity and human rights. For some police officers, it requires a change of mindset.

5.1 Introduction

Interviewing victims, witnesses, and suspects is a core task of law enforcement. Information obtained through these interpersonal encounters between the power and the people typically founds the basis for subsequent decisions by the police, prosecutors, and judges. Consequently, *how* the police conduct their interviews will have a profound impact on the outcome, fairness, efficiency, and reliability of any subsequent criminal proceedings, and ultimately, how citizens perceive the fairness of the criminal justice system.[1] After 25 years as a reformer and trainer within the police in various parts of the world, I have never come across anyone that does not agree with the statement above: Interviewing is our most important tool. Yet, it

[1]Convention against torture initiative training tools 1/2017 (CTI 1/2017). Investigative interviewing for criminal cases. Available in several languages at: https://www.cti2024.org/en/cti-training-material/.

strikes me—again and again—that my colleagues around the world have hardly received any qualified training on how to actually conduct a professional interview. In areas where training has been offered, it is typically not in line with the available, scientific knowledge that has accumulated in the last three decades. The first part of this chapter is meant to provide the reader with an introduction to the history, research and ethos underpinning contemporary investigative interviewing techniques. The general descriptions are followed by a more detailed narrative of the interviewing techniques itself.

5.1.1 From Interrogation to Investigative Interviewing

Legal safeguards, laws and human rights conventions have been constructed to ensure that the powers vested in officers are exercised in line with national and international standards. Typically, these standards have not been accompanied by a methodological framework assisting officers on how to operationalize the principles underpinning them. With limited positive guidance or assistance in formulating strategies to improve ethical and effective information retrieval, agencies have developed their own skills and practices. Traditionally, these practices have not benefitted from critical research, allowing outdated skills and beliefs, even myths, to direct a confession-orientated practice, intended to reinforce the assumptions already held by interviewers and their organizations.[2]

If we want to learn from our mistakes and change our criminal justice system for the better, we need to teach police officers to think differently: The shift *from* confession orientated interrogations to information gathering Investigative Interviewing techniques requires a change of mindset.[3] Police and prosecutors must be provided with knowledge—and methodology—that stimulates them to generate alternative hypotheses *and* actively test them (beyond reasonable doubt), not pursuing information confirming their premature beliefs of guilt.[4]

Torture is a fundamental breach of the presumption of innocence and under all circumstances strictly forbidden. Psychological coercion and manipulative interrogation techniques may not be as brutal, but these psychological modifications are only different means to achieve the same end; to get the suspect to confess. The mindset of the detectives remains the same: they are trying to solve their (sometimes complex) task with a methodology, designed to confirm their belief of guilt.

The human tendency (cognitive predisposition) to seek confirmation—and criminal justice systems encouraging their agent to do so—is a perilous mixture, feeding

---

[2]Leo (2008).

[3]Bull (2014).

[4]Kassin et al. (2009), pp. 3–38.

the underlying cause of wrongful convictions[5] and planting the seeds of torture.[6] In contrast, the purpose of investigative interviewing is to collect accurate and reliable information, sufficiently detailed in order to disclose all relevant facts and diminish (reasonable) doubt about matters under investigation. Investigative interviewing is developed to guide detectives through a mental and practical procedure with an open mind, preventing common pitfalls associated with relying on premature conclusions.[7]

In its Standards for police interviewing, the Council of Europe has captured the essence under the heading "Investigative Interviewing – a paradigm shift" (Art. 78): Police interviewers with an open mindset are far more effective; they apply in practice the presumption of innocence by generating and actively testing alternative hypotheses through systematic preparation, empathic rapport-building, the use of open-ended questions, active listening, and strategic probing and disclosure of potential evidence.[8]As acknowledged by the UN Special Rapporteur against Torture in his interim report to the UN General Assembly (2016), investigative interviewing is: "helping to ensure that the presumption of innocence is respected while strengthening the case against a guilty suspect."[9]

The difference between *Interrogations* (questioning designed to get the suspect to confess) and *Investigative Interviewing* (questioning designed to gather accurate and reliable information) is fundamental and distinct and cannot be mixed up. The mindset of an Investigative Interviewer cannot be altered along the way. To start off with "informal" or administrative intimidation and then move on to "Investigative Interviewing" and ("if necessary") do a bit of interrogation at the end—or in between—has been a common, oppressive technique in confession orientated interrogations for decades.[10]

Although interviewing victims, witnesses and suspects is a core task in all investigations, it nevertheless remains a part of a bigger process. It will never reach its potential as an effective and ethical concept unless its underlying logic and principles are operationalized by police- and prosecution service in general, from the moment of arrest until the final decision is made.

As will be evident in the more detailed step-by-step description below, the investigative interviewing framework consists of flexible phases within three main stages: (1) before, (2) during, and (3) after the interview. A crucial point is that each phase has a profound impact upon the next.

[5]Zuckerman (1992) and Fahsing et al. (2021).

[6]Rejali (2007) and Barela et al. (2020).

[7]Ask and Fahsing (2018), pp. 52–73.

[8]European Committee for the Prevention of Torture and Inhuman or Degrading Treatment or Punishment (CPT). Extract from the 28th General Report of the CPT, published in 2019. https://rm.coe.int/1680942329. Accessed on 5 May 2023.

[9]Mendez (2016).

[10]Gudjonsson (2003) and Geijsen et al. (2023).

5.1.2 Investigative Interviewing—A Flexible Tool Based on Science and Experience

Following a number of judicial breakdowns that erupted in police interviews of suspects in the United Kingdom in the 1980s, police and scientists were requested to cooperate and find an alternative to contemporary, often oppressive interrogation techniques. The first discovery was that UK detectives had little or no training. Competence was (more or less) based on experience alone—a remarkable, yet common situation, unfortunately revealed in several countries, even today.[11]

Scientists studying recorded interviews also discovered that officers conveyed more pride and prestige in their interviews of suspects than in interviewing victims and witnesses. The latter was not regarded as "real detective work." Investigative interviewing recognizes that statements from victims and witnesses can be of great value, and particularly so when they are interviewed professionally and with empathy. The macho-culture that coexisted with confession focused interrogations was counterproductive. With the introduction of investigative interviewing, a fundamental change emerged.

Forty years of scientific research have now confirmed that respect for human dignity, regardless of the legal status the interviewee may have, trumps any other tactic.[12] Interpersonal communication skills, knowledge of human memory, questioning skills, combined with a prepared plan (including a strategy for when and how to introduce information in the interview), are skills not unique to male interviewers.

Furthermore, research demonstrates that these skills are equally effective, irrespective of the interviewees' legal status. As outlined in more detail below, investigative interviewing comprises different techniques depending on the situation at hand, but the overarching framework is the same.[13]

5.2 The Purpose of Investigative Interviewing

The purpose of investigative interviews with victims, witnesses, suspects, and other sources is to collect accurate, reliable, detailed, and actionable information to disclose all relevant facts about events through a progressive elimination of doubt about matters under investigation. It is not about obtaining information that reinforces the assumptions already held by officers. Officers with an open mindset are far more effective; they are applying abductive logic through the elimination of doubt about matters under investigation by generating and actively testing alternative

[11] Walsh et al. (2016).

[12] Alison et al. (2013), pp. 411–431.

[13] Association for the Prevention of Torture (2021).

hypotheses through systematic preparation, empathic rapport building, the use of open-ended questions, active listening, and strategic probing and disclosure of potential evidence.[14]

5.2.1 Accurate and Reliable Information

Information is the lifeblood of any fact-finding operation. It directs investigations and opens up new lines of inquiries. Police, military, and security agencies have numerous sources that may provide information, including forensic and digital evidence. Interviewing human sources remains nevertheless, officers' most important tool to gather information. Information provided by the police is the foundation for subsequent decisions made by prosecutors. It enables the defense to evaluate the case against their clients and may indeed be presented as core evidence in court. Consequently, police must take every step possible to ensure that the manner in which the information is obtained is consistent with standards of the law. Equally important for the *accuracy* and *reliability* of the information obtained through interviews is that officer's conduct their interviews in line with knowledge derived from cognitive and social psychology in general and the emerging field of forensic (legal) psychology in particular.[15] Research and inquiries into the causes of wrongful convictions confirm, with consensus, that interviewing techniques employed by the police can have a profound impact on the *accuracy* and *reliability* of the obtained statements and hence, the subsequent proceedings.[16] It is imperative to recognize that unreliable information tends to become even more difficult to detect and correct the further into the criminal system it travels.[17] In this sense, investigators are the gate keepers of fair trials and the delivery of justice. The majority of researchers that has cooperated with the police in the creation and development of investigative interviewing are scholars with special knowledge from social- and cognitive psychology with a particular interest in (a) human memory and (b) how interviewers can use this knowledge to enhance the amount of relevant, accurate and reliable information from victims, witnesses, and suspects.[18]

[14]Kozma and Rachlew (2018).

[15]The English terms "Forensic psychology," "Legal psychology," and "Psychology and Law" are all pointing to the same, globally emerging field, a field of research comprising more specific research fields, including eye-witness psychology, legal decision making, investigative psychology and others.

[16]Fisher and Geiselman (1992).

[17]Huff et al. (1996).

[18]Milne and Bull (1999).

5.2.2 *Complete and Detailed Information—Proven Beyond Reasonable Doubt*

Accurate and reliable information is fundamental for police, military, and security agencies to solve crime and to secure states. Accurate and reliable information is also an essential requisite for analytics, commanders, judges, and members of the jury. The precision of their decisions is interlinked with the quality of the evidence presented before them. However, accurate and reliable information is not enough to meet the common standard of proof "beyond reasonable doubt." In order to reach this threshold, investigators must strive to gather *complete* and sufficiently *detailed* information. To assist interviewers, investigative interviewing offers positive guidance and strategies by stimulating a mindset advocated by decision making experts, arguing that the normative, golden standard for good thinking is represented by a thorough search for an alternative without favorizing the one already on mind.[19]

Without a normative theory of what constitutes complete and sufficiently detailed information in a given case or situation, officers are often left with the demanding task to follow their intuition, leaving them vulnerable for cognitive limitations and bias. To meet the burden of proof, interviewers must search for information, complete and detailed enough to eliminate alternative explanations, leaving the prosecution and the courts with complete and sufficiently detailed information to explain, beyond reasonable doubt *what* happened, *when, where; who, why and how*. If a suspect is identified, these six, fundamental questions are best answered, i.e., in a complete and sufficiently detailed manner, by following a mental procedure of progressive elimination of explanations consistent with innocence.[20]

5.2.3 *Actionable Information*

Information that can be substantiated by external facts is of greater evidential value compared to information that cannot be validated by external sources of information. It is in this cross-check perspective that the level of details becomes relevant. *Actionable* information contains details that provide opportunities to test and validate the information, and hence a more informative and safer foundation for subsequent decisions. Often, and in particular in the early stages of an investigation, investigators do not know which details may become decisive for the evaluation of the evidence. In challenging cases, officers may have to gather information that might not have any other value (or purpose) than bringing the investigation forward. The load of information can become overwhelming, and the psychologically attractive idea of a "short cut to the truth" has diverted officers, even scientists to proclaim

[19] Canter and Alison (1999).

[20] Zuckerman and Roberts (1989).

they are in a possession of a unique skill (or apparatus) that will help them distinguish between true and false information by "reading" the interviewee's body language and/or physiological responses.

This alleged ability has been tested in numerous scientific studies. The conclusion is clear. These attempts to find a short cut are—and have always been—a myth.[21] Yet, lie-detection remains essential element of manipulative confession orientated interrogation techniques. The focus on lie-catching diverts focus away from the core principles of investigative interviewing; to collect accurate; reliable, detailed; complete; and; actionable information to disclose all relevant facts about events.

5.2.4 *Before the Interview—A Holistic and Practical Approach*

Once the police have identified a person they consider a suspect, fair trial principles apply. A "spontaneous confession" induced by violence or other kinds of coercion during the arrest or transportation to the police station, is a blunt breach of the presumption of innocence. Unprofessional behavior at early stages may, like every other attempt to "short cut" criminal procedures, impact the investigations negatively, sometimes with devastating effects. Errors of justice of this kind can be difficult to correct. Guilty suspects can go free and innocent suspects may end up convicted.[22]

On the other hand, professional and safe field work at early stages may advance investigations profoundly and bring out the potential for subsequent inquiries. Investigative interviewing is a concept that is intimately linked with the investigation as a whole. Scientific studies indicate that a large proportion of suspects—in some studies, around 50%—enter the police interview not yet having decided whether to deny or confess. There are several variables at play, but there are strong reasons to believe that if the police treat the suspect with dignity, and ensure that suspects enjoy the legal safeguards, designed to protect them and the integrity of the process; from the moment of arrest and beyond, a significantly higher proportion of suspects will cooperate, even provide an admission.[23]

Because memory can be altered and influenced (contaminated) by questions and discussions about events, it is best practice to keep questions and discussion outside the interview to an absolute minimum. A professional police will in that way also prevent subsequent claims by the defense that they may have contaminated the interviewee's statement by the means of coercion or leading questions prior to the interview. Substantiated evidence that the police may have initiated "informal talks" with victims, witnesses, or suspects prior to the official interview, may lead to errors

[21] Vrij (2008).

[22] Forst (2004).

[23] Bull and Rachlew (2020).

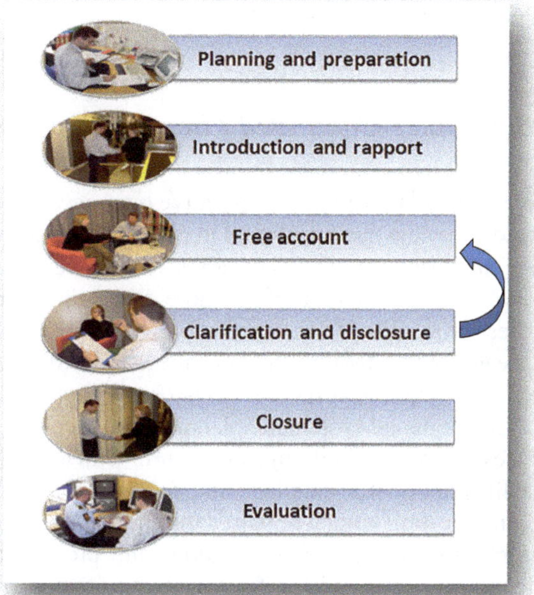

Fig. 5.1 The Norwegian investigative interviewing model (KREATIV, based on the "PEACE-model"—see Griffiths and Rachlew (2018), pp. 154–178)

of justice, including wrongful acquittals or worse, that innocent suspects are convicted based on unreliable evidence.

5.3 The Investigative Interviewing Methodology

As indicated in Fig. 5.1 (and described in more detail below), there are a number of flexible phases within a professional interview. The methodology emerged through cooperation between researchers and experienced officers in the UK. It has been developed and refined to fit officers' requirements in their daily work. It is informed by 30 years of research and is used by a growing number of police forces around the world.[24] It is practical, ethical, and proven to be effective.[25] It mitigates confirmation bias and tunnel vision,[26] and is designed to provide more accurate and reliable information than any other known interview technique. It prevents errors of

[24] Bull and Rachlew (2020).

[25] Meissner et al. (2012).

[26] Ask and Fahsing (2018), pp. 52–73.

justice,[27] and has been adopted by the UN[28], and advocated by the Council of Europe as best practice for Europe.[29]

5.3.1 *Inter-Connected Phases of the Interview*

An essential element of investigative interviewing is that each stage and every phase of the interview has a profound impact upon the next. One may think of the interview as a chain reaction. A lawful arrest where the arresting officers fulfill their professional obligations to use no more force than strictly necessary, followed by a professional and safe transportation to the police station where the arrested person is treated with dignity and informed about his fundamental rights, increases the likelihood that the suspect will choose to cooperate with the police.

Thorough and systematic planning and preparation will increase the likelihood of successful rapport building, and in turn, with a professional introduction and rapport, the likelihood of a detailed, first free recall also increases. If the first stage fails, communication will be impaired throughout the interview reducing the quality of the information obtained, and affecting the probing and strategic disclosure phases. Closing the interview professionally positively enhances the prospects for future successful communications. It also contributes to developing and maintaining good relations between the police and citizens. Carrying out professional evaluations of the evidence obtained will strengthen the possibility of a successful investigation. Evaluation of the interviewer's performance will stimulate professionalism, improve outputs in subsequent interviews, and even increase job satisfaction.

5.3.2 *Flexibility*

At first glance, the investigative interviewing model may look like a process that flows one way—from stage one, with interviewers rigidly working their way through the phases. This is not the case, rather on the contrary. Although there certainly are some key phases in which the organizations only get one chance to get it right the first time around, flexibility within the phases is an essential key to successful interviewing.[30]

The witness may have mentioned a particular car in her first, free recall of the event. Knowing that this car may be an important, evidential topic, the interviewer

---

[27] Kassin et al. (2009).

[28] UNPOL (2024).

[29] Boyle and Vullierme (2018). Council of Europe and European Committee for the Prevention of Torture and Inhuman or Degrading Treatment or Punishment (CPT) 28th General report of the CPT (2018), pp. 32–34.

[30] Shepherd and Griffiths (2013).

will take a note, and continue with active listening, allowing the witness to recall the sequences of events. Entering the next phase of the interview (Clarification and disclosure), the interviewer may invite the witness to provide a new, free account, this time about the specific topic: Please tell me, in detail, everything you can remember about the car. The very same questioning techniques, including active listening, will apply. The model has been found practical by officers, also because it is applicable for serious and more voluminous types of crime. In serious cases, the planning and preparation phase may take hours—even days. In a sustainable criminal justice system, it is neither possible nor desirable to spend hours on planning interviews when investigating volume crime. But every interview must be planned and prepared.

5.3.3 Rapport

An essential component in every phase within investigative interviews, is the building and maintaining of rapport with the interviewee. In order to master this, sometimes very difficult task, investigative interviewers need to understand and embrace the knowledge and principles underpinning investigative interviewing, as briefly introduced above. These principles do not only stimulate the operationalization of human rights and the rule of law, they also serve as a solid foundation for communicating empathy and respect for human dignity. Empathy and respect serve, in turn, as the most important elements for ethical and effective retrieval of information.

Thousands of hours of police interviews with suspects, including suspects of terror, have been carefully examined by scientists. Their conclusion is clear: Interviewers who manage to follow the principles and techniques imbedded in the framework of investigating interviewing communicate empathy and respect, and are likely to receive more information, including true confessions, than interviewers resorting to old habits of moral judgement, manipulation, and/or coercion.[31]

How to establish and maintain rapport is described in more detail in the different stages and phases of the framework described below.

5.3.4 Legal and Procedural Safeguards

Human rights and other procedural safeguards are natural components in all phases within the framework of investigative interviewing. It is simply not possible to establish and maintain rapport that brings out the full potential of effective investigative interviews if the interviewee does not know where she is, why she has been

[31] Alison et al. (2014), pp. 421–430; Meissner et al. (2012).

arrested, whether or not her family knows where she is, or if she does not fully understand the information and questions put before her. Nor is it possible to achieve optimal communication if the interviewee is not informed, and does not fully understand her fundamental human rights, including the right to have a lawyer present and the right that one cannot be compelled to testify against themselves. The mere fact that these safeguards are explained at the outskirts of the interview, are strong communicators of empathy and essential components in building rapport with the interviewee. The receiver of the information is more likely to sense a genuine feeling that the interviewer is indeed respecting his or her dignity and autonomi.

Successful investigative interviewers understand that these—and other—safeguards are essential to uphold human dignity, no matter what the interviewee may be suspected of. Successful interviewers embrace the fact that phases of the interview provide them with an excellent opportunity to check and ensure that interviewees have been protected by, provided with, and understood, the legal safeguards they are entitled to in the difficult situation they find themselves in. The related safeguards are so important that we cannot ignore any of them. They are, however complementary measures: The most important safeguard against torture and other ill-treatment is indeed the methodology employed by the police before, during and after the interview of the suspect.

5.4 Phase One: Planning and Preparation

Planning and preparation are the foundations to conducting a professional interview; without it, interviews may fail before they even begin. It has been argued by busy, sometimes overloaded officers, that they do not have time to plan and prepare. Following the implementation of investigative interviewing, officers have found that they in fact save time through proper planning. Solid preparations decrease the likelihood of having to re-interview victims, witnesses and/or suspects. Solid preparation as part of a professional interview also reduces the resource-draining endeavor of prosecuting cases—only to be dismissed by the courts—due to low evidential value or technicalities. If necessarily, supervisors must also be reminded of the fact that good planning is effective policing.

5.4.1 Dynamics and Flexibility

Professional planning will include (i) case-related, (ii) physical, and (iii) mental preparation. Like the framework, this phase is also flexible. In serious cases, officers may need to plan and prepare for hours, even days. This is impossible when investigating volume-crimes. Nevertheless, do *not* skip this phase. Interviewers should always take a few minutes and check that they have read the essential documents of the case and that they are physically and mentally prepared. The interview may feel trivial for the officers, but for the person they are about to meet, it can be just the opposite. Besides, being unprepared often generates an unpleasant feeling of always being one step behind, decreasing interviewers' chance of feeling confident and hence, making it harder to maintain rapport as it becomes evident for everyone involved that you are not prepared. Make sure you always come across as what you are; a professional.[32]

5.4.2 Case Related Preparations

It is essential that you know what you want to achieve from the interview—what your aims are. Knowledge of the crime you are investigating will increase your chance of retrieving the information you need from the interviewee. There may be a need to test certain information already in your possession. Assess what additional information is needed and how it can be best obtained.

Ensure that you know the legal definition of the crimes under investigation including the proof needed to support a prosecution. Make sure you know the legal rights and (when applicable) obligations that apply for the interviewee—and how you should present them. You should also obtain relevant information about the person you are about to interview, including any criminal records. Is there anything in that indicates that the interviewee is vulnerable?

Plan your disclosure of evidence. How this is strategically done will be described—in detail—in phase four below. In short, your strategy for disclosure must be based on the plan for the investigation as a whole, in which all relevant and competing hypotheses (i.e., the alternative explanations for the potential evidence you possess) is identified. It is crucial that you delay the disclosure of potential evidence until you have interviewed (asked about and exhausted) the alternative and plausible explanations, routinely including the possibility that the suspect is innocent.

It is taken for granted that police, military and intelligence officers are fully aware of legislation and associated guidelines. The standard of living for those who come into contact with its authorities are significantly affected to the extent the legislation is carried out in practice. Take pride in yourself and your organization. Make sure you are updated on the latest development, including jurisprudence from the courts related to interviewing and associated safeguards.

[32] Rachlew et al. (2022).

5.4.3 Physical Preparations

Prepare the technicalities of the interview (attending to exhibits, logistics, venue, equipment functioning, seating, and so on). Based on your case related preparation, you will know if the person to be interviewed will need an interpreter, legal guardian or be entitled to a lawyer if they wish. Make sure that these persons are present, or at reach (as required by law) before the interview starts. You will waste valuable time and resources if these legal (and other practical) requirements are dealt with too late. Is the printer working? Do you have enough ink in your pen? If not, fix it before the interview starts. Pay respect for everyone's time, including your own.

Make certain that there is nothing to distract the interview and—if possible—that the room is quiet, private, and free from unnecessary interruption. Turn off your phone and place a sign on the door. If this is not possible, remind your supervisor of the fact that the better physical conditions you have, the more effective you will become.

Access to a lawyer is one of the most fundamental, legal safeguards in place. Do all that is in your power to provide one according to law. Make sure that the evidence you are about to obtain does not get thrown out of court one the bases of legal technicalities. It is frustrating and extremely ineffective.

Defense lawyers have—in stark contrast—traditionally been seen as a "problem" by officers employing confession orientated interrogation by the means of manipulation and/or coercion. The belief has been that the presence of a defense lawyer reduces the chance of obtaining confessions. This may indeed—and rightly so—be true in some criminal justice systems, particularly in environments were the myth proclaiming that manipulative or coercive interrogations are necessary crime control devices and hence, are legally or silently accepted.

Professional investigative interviewers have a different mindset. Not only do they fundamentally understand and agree that an arrested person should have the right to a lawyer present if they wish. Investigative interviewers ensure that the opportunity to check and ensure that the suspect is (i) fully aware, and (ii) understands his right to have a lawyer present, *before* they move on to the information gathering phases of the interview. As described in more detail below, informing the suspect (as well as victims and witnesses) about their legal rights (and obligations according to law) is not only an integrated methodological step, but a vital part of the philosophy underpinning the concept of investigative interviewing.

Experienced investigative interviewers set up their interview room, looking similar to the illustrations in Figs. 5.2 and 5.3 below. This may not be possible in volume-crime interviews, but perhaps you can rearrange the seating, so that it resamples an optimal setting for communication?

Fig. 5.2 Illustration of an interview field set up

Fig. 5.3 Illustration of a designed interview room

5.4.4 Mental Preparations

Interviews can take a variety of directions. Research has established that a substantial proportion of guilty offenders are ready to provide an accurate account and even confess right away, while others are undecided when summoned for interviewing. Officers applying an aggressive, hostile, or insulting approach run the risk of making the suspect decide not to cooperate and not to provide any information; whereas it has been found that applying investigative interviewing techniques is more likely to encourage guilty offenders to cooperate and provide information or even confess.

You will need to be adaptable as something may occur spontaneously in the interview that requires you to think and act immediately, perhaps requiring a different tactic. You need to plan for how you will respond to the suspect when they deny guilt, admit guilt, or simply refuse to cooperate and remain silent. If the suspect denies being involved, is this because they claim to have been elsewhere at the time, or do they claim that they have been wrongly identified, or will they offer defenses (for example, the stolen property was theirs, their actions were in self-defense, they were acting reasonably but were misinformed)? You need to consider possible responses from the suspect and how you will deal with these in your search for the "truth."

Preparation also entails being psychologically ready for the interview. You need to be prepared to address the behaviors of the suspect positively, even where they may frustrate or challenge you. Your focus should be on maintaining rapport and promoting an environment that will be most conducive to allowing you to achieve your aims. You must also be aware of your own emotions and feelings and how you contain and control these in a way that does not impede the progress of the interview. Remember that the lead interviewer may give way to their colleague where personality or temperament appears to be impeding the building of rapport with the suspect.

5.5 Phase Two: Introduction and Rapport

The first step to encouraging a conversation is to establish rapport with the interviewee. In short, this is achieved by engaging the interviewee with respect, value their autonomi, and explaining the ground rules of the interview. To engage and explain is described as the most influential factor in ensuring productive interviews.

At the outset, the interviewee must be informed why they have been brought in for questioning and of the legal formalities that apply. Being interviewed can make people nervous and conversation that calms the interviewee may be needed. The aim is to engage the interviewee so that a cooperative and relaxed relationship—one that stimulates memory and communication—is sustained throughout the interview. However, interviewers shall not work towards a pretended "friendship" with interviewees. It is essential at this point that the interviewer communicates empathy. Interviewers must ensure that the interviewee experience a genuine feeling that they are respected as a person, equal in dignity, and that the interviewer understand the stress and problems associated with the situation in which interviewee may find themselves in.[33] Professional interviewers welcome the presence of defense lawyers as a legal resource, an eye witness to the fairness of the interview, and safeguard against misunderstandings. Police services where investigative interviewing has

[33] Alison and Alison (2020).

become standard practice report a significant decrease in disputes between lawyers and police—almost to the level of being non-existent.

Your goal is to create an empathetic and respectful relationship from the outset. This is best done by a respectful greeting of the interviewee and presenting yourselves. The interviewer should immediately follow up by explaining (i) what case the interview is meant to inform, (ii) the reasons why the interviewee is asked to provide a statement, (iii) their legal rights (according to national law), and (vi) how you have planned to conduct the interview. Inform in a comprehensive manner that if the interviewee is willing to provide a statement, they will be provided with an opportunity to tell their side of the story. Inform that you will listen and not interrupt. Inform that there is no rush, and that when they have told everything they know about the case under investigation, you will then follow up with questions that the police think are of importance. The meta-communication (communication about the communication) should always include an invitation that the interviewee should feel free to ask questions—at any stage—about any concern or question they may have. Respecting the intervieees autonomi is key. The initial opening should include information about audio/video recording and the possibility for breaks.

This phase lays the foundations for the interview, enabling the interviewer and the interviewee to develop a common understanding of the interview and its dynamics. It also allows the interviewer to assess the interviewee's communication abilities and modify language to make certain that the interviewee understands what has been conveyed. In interviews of suspects the interviewer has a particular responsibility to assess whether the suspect is vulnerable, and to explain the right to silence, the right to legal counsel, as well as other rights of the suspect, according to law in an understandable and candid way. The procedure outlined above increases the likelihood that rapport is established. If the suspect chooses not to talk, remains silent or appears hostile, never forget that you are the professional part. Nothing is personal. If you feel, or start to feel emotions you cannot control, you must ask yourself why you are struggling to remain professional. It you cannot resolve it, you should take a break and remind yourself that your role is not to judge, moralize, condemn, teach or advice. Your role is to gather as much accurate and reliable information as possible, and that this is best achieved through building and maintaining rapport.

5.6 Phase Three: The First, Uninterrupted Account

Having established rapport and explained the ground rules for the interview, interviewers should now allow the interviewee to present their uninterrupted (free) recall of the case (or event) under investigation. It is essential that the interviewee is provided with the opportunity to present "their side of the story," before more detailed questions are asked. It is well-documented that interviewers that ask closed,

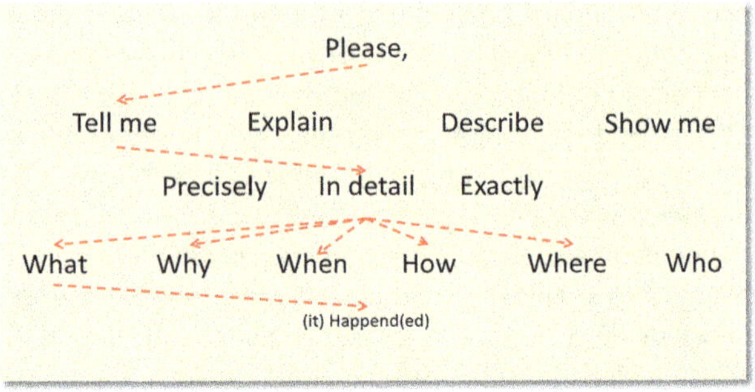

Fig. 5.4 Recommended questioning technique stimulating detailed, uncontaminated responses

or leading questions, run the risk of contaminating the interviewee's account.[34] Contamination refers both to distortion of genuine memories and unintentional leaking of details from the crime, which reduces the evidential value of the subsequent statements. The more open questions the interviewer asks, the more likely it is that the response contains details. Closed questions tend to evoke short responses and are more likely to contaminate the interviewees' memory of events. As illustrated in Fig. 5.4, the recommended questioning techniques are in fact not questions, but invitations to provide as much detail about matters under investigation as possible. It prevents contamination and stimulates communication and flow of information.

The interviewer may choose the combination of words that are most applicable to the given situation. For the first free recall, the combination: "Please tell me, in detail precisely what happened," may be an appropriate one. The technique allows flexibility and provides the interviewer with a variety of combinations when entering the next phase of the interview with detailed probing of relevant topics identified (i) in the case related preparation, or (ii) by listening to the interviewees' first uninterrupted recall.

5.6.1 *Memory Enhancing Interviewing Techniques*

When details are of particular importance, other memory enhancing interviewing techniques can provide additional details, for example from eye-witnesses. The apprehension of perpetrators and the prevention of future attacks may well rest on an interviewer succeeding in eliciting a detailed, accurate, reliable account from a witness. Extensive research demonstrates that interviewers that master these memory enhancing techniques (in the literature referred to as enhanced cognitive interview techniques), may provide approx. 40% more information than traditional, questioning techniques.[35]

---

[34] Milne and Bull (1999).

[35] Fisher and Geiselman (1992).

Before inviting the victim, witness or suspect to provide a free account with one of the combinations from Fig. 5.4 above, the interviewer—already having established and maintaining rapport with the interviewee—should inform the witness that the police are in need of details, and that no details should be left out. The witness should be asked to relax and concentrate. Then, when all distractions are mitigated, the interviewer may ask the witness[36] to think back and mentally reconstruct the environment where the observations were made. Some witnesses find it easier to do this with closed eyes and can be encouraged to do so, if they feel it will help them reinstate the context they were in when they made their observations. The interviewer should then calmly inform that it is ok if they do not remember, "but try as best as you can." Then calmly guide the witness mentally, by asking the witness to "picture themselves back at the crime scene." Allow the witness to do so. Then, continue the priming by assisting the witness to use all senses: "How did it look like? How did you feel at the time?. . . . . . . How was the temperature. . . . What did you see around you?....... Use all your senses. Was there any sound. . . .. Now, take your time, and when you are ready; please tell me in detail everything that happened."

Silence can be an effective tool, if used properly, to encourage the interviewee to expand on what has been said and to add extra detail or give a further account of events. You should listen actively; what is the interviewee telling me? Show that you are listening by a simple nodding of the head or commenting "I see" or "I understand." You may also reflect back key words "You said he looked threatening......?" You may make eye-contact, but do not stare when interviewees are thinking and retrieving details from their memory. It can be disruptive.

If you have doubts about the truthfulness or accuracy of the account, do not interrupt. You should allow the interviewees to give "their" version of events. Details from it will provide information that can later be checked and may strengthen or weaken the hypotheses you need to investigate to eliminate doubt about matters under investigation.

It is useful for a variety of reasons to summarize what the interview has said. It demonstrates that you are listening, and hence stimulating the communication. It may help the interviewee to remember more. Good summaries also prevent misunderstandings and provides the interviewee with an opportunity to agree with the summary or amend it as (they feel is) appropriate.

This interviewing approach will stimulate detailed accounts and consequently reduce the number of questions that may need to be asked. This is beneficial because each time a question is asked the interviewer runs the risk of leading the victim, witness, or suspect (contaminating the evidential value of their account). When you master the technique, it can be highly effective. Open ended invitations, with active and reflective listening combined with appropriate use of silence, serve as a pipeline for information, allowing the information to flow to you. Research have documented through hundreds of experiments that these interviewing techniques

[36]Memory enhancing, Cognitive interviewing techniques may of course also be used when appropriate in interviews of victims and suspects.

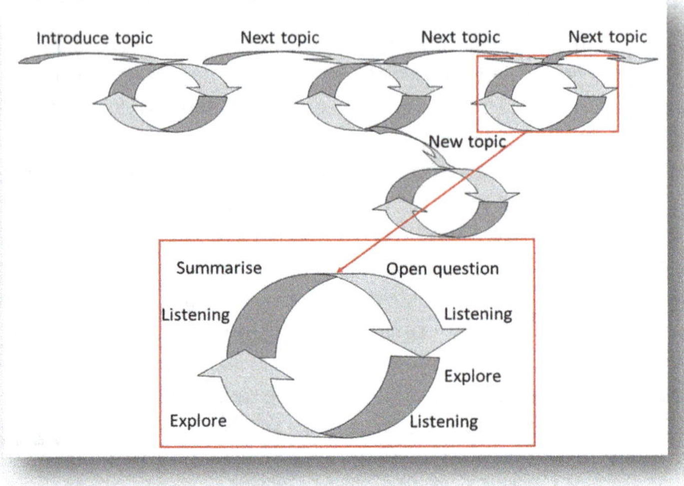

Fig. 5.5 The topic spiral

will allow the interviewer to "empty out" the witness's memory of events quicker and with less contamination (altering of the memory), than traditional interviews where interviewers typically ask (too) many closed (even leading) questions, all too often in a rapid manner.[37]

5.7 Phase Four: Clarification and Disclosure

Having actively listened to the first, free recall, it is time for the interviewer to expand and clarify all the relevant topics in the case; one topic at a time. The interviewer should introduce the relevant topics with a variety of invitations as illustrated in Fig. 5.4 above. When more details are needed about a certain topic, interviewers should encourage the interviewee to provide more information through open-ended, probing questions—What?, Why?, When?, How?, Where?, Who? Interviewers may vary their approach depending on the topic that needs to be explored. Again, use appropriate silence, listening activity and allowing the interviewee time to think and elaborate.

For each topic of interest, the interviewer should use the same techniques as described above regarding the first, uninterrupted account (phase three), allowing a structured interview as visualized in Fig. 5.5 below. Each topic should be introduced

[37]Memon (1998).

by an invitation as illustrated in Fig. 5.4 above (e.g., Please tell me, in detail, what happened next).

5.7.1 *Strategic Disclosure of Evidence: When and How to Disclose Evidence*

An essential part of the clarification and disclosure stage is how and when interviewers should disclose evidence during interviews.[38] If a suspect is arrested, clearly the police must have some information indicating guilt—otherwise, the arrest is unlawful and should never have been made.

Investigative interviewing necessitates the strategic disclosure of evidence. The strategy outlined below (Step 1 through 4) rests on a combination of practical experience from experienced detectives and a PhD study by the legal scholar Christian Diesen (1994). Having studied how judges in the Swedish Supreme Court evaluated evidence presented before them, Diesen concluded that all actors (police, prosecution, defense lawyers, and judges) should identify all plausible, alternative explanations to the evidence at hand, and then actively test them. As explained in more detail below, a tactical element was added to these ideas; namely to delay the disclosure of evidence until the alternative hypotheses are explored in detail. The model (Step 1 through 4) provides clear and positive instructions on *how*, *when* and—and all importantly—*why* interviewers should delay disclosure until the alternative hypotheses are explored. Early disclosure can either lead to innocent suspects being deprived of the opportunity to substantiate their innocence, or enable guilty perpetrators to tailor their explanation (statement) to the evidence presented by the police. Similar, early disclosure of evidence in witness interviews (e.g., informing what other witnesses may have seen) will run the risk of altering (contaminating) the witness memory.

When interviewing suspects, strategic probing and disclosure of potential evidence allows officers to explore the suspects account in depth before proceeding to the next topic, helping to ensure that the presumption of innocence is respected while strengthening the case against a guilty suspect by preventing the subsequent fabrication of an alibi.[39]

---

[38] Fahsing and Rachlew (2009).

[39] Mendez (2016).

5.7.2 *Interview Strategy—Step-by-Step*

5.7.3 *Step 1 (Identify All Potential Evidence Available in the Planning and Preparation Phase)*

Before the interviewer enters the interview room, he or she must be able to answer the question: What information am I planning to handle in a strategic way? (e.g., the fact that the suspect's fingerprint has been secured from the scene of the crime).

5.7.4 *Step 2 (Identify All Possible Explanations (Alternative Hypotheses) for the Potential Evidence in the Planning and Preparation Phase)*

In order to identify all possible explanations for the evidence at hand, interviewers are required to ask themselves the vital question: If the suspect is innocent, what are the possible (alternative) explanations to the evidence at hand? Let's continue with the potential evidence above: The suspect's fingerprint has been secured from the scene of the crime. Sure, it is potential evidence, indicating guilt. However, what are the plausible, *alternative* explanations? In other words, if the suspect is innocent; how may his fingerprint (legally) have ended up at the crime scene? Surely, if the suspect is innocent, there must be an (alternative) explanation.

On the other hand, if the suspect is guilty, and looks to avoid responsibility, he or she must come up with an alternative, deceitful explanation. Either way, the strategic interviewer must identify these alternatives before the interview starts. A useful approach at this crucial point is to think of explanations that—if they are not tested and eliminated—may cause reasonable doubt in the subsequent procedures, for example if the case is brought to court. With the legal threshold for evidence in mind, one may argue that the purpose of the interview is to eliminate or reduce doubt about matters under investigation. By attending alternative explanations (hypotheses), the police in general, and the interviewers in particular, are guided through a practical and mental process which will allow them to remain open-minded to all possibilities, rather than simply looking for information that is consistent with, or confirms, initial beliefs.

Having identified all, plausible, alternative explanations (hypotheses) before the interview start; it is time to test them.

5.7.5 Step 3 (Postpone Disclosure of Potential Evidence and Test the Alternative Explanations in the First Free Account and Clarification and Challenge Phase)

The interviewer will introduce and listen to the first free account and then probe for information that may prove or disprove the different possible explanations identified in Step 2. In Step 3 the interviewer is looking for information consistent with innocence, knowing that if such information cannot be found, the suspicion is strengthened. As pointed out above, a crucial element of the interview strategy is that the detailed probing of alternative explanations is carried out before the potential evidence (including inconsistencies within statements) is presented.

For example, in the case of the abovementioned fingerprint, the officer needs to ask questions such as: Did the suspect visit the crime scene (legal or illegal) before the crime was committed? Has s/he been there (legal or illegal) after the crime was committed? Did the suspect have legal access in any way? If the fingerprint is on a bottle or a pack of cigarettes, does s/he smoke or work in a nearby grocery store? (The suspect may have sold the victim a pack of cigarettes. . .). If such information is not found, the suspicion against the suspect is strengthened. This illustrates how important it is to gather this information before the potential evidence is disclosed.

In contrast, if the officer reveals the fingerprint too early, a guilty person may be provided with an opportunity to construct a deceitful, nevertheless plausible explanation that may be difficult—sometimes impossible—to disprove, and hence create doubt about matters under investigation. In order to avoid such a situation officers must meticulously complete these steps before presenting the evidence as described in Step 4. Any explanation (true or false) provided by the suspect before the disclosure of evidence (Step 4), must be explored in detail immediately using TED'S PIE and probing questions: When, What, How, Where, Who, Why. This will enable the police to obtain enough information to ensure that innocent suspects are cleared and strengthen evidence against guilty suspects that sometimes try to present plausible, yet deceitful explanations.

5.7.6 Step 4 (Disclosing the Potential Evidence in the Clarification and Challenge Phase)

When the interviewer is confident that every plausible alternative explanation has been explored and tested by the interviewee's own account (completed Step 3), the interviewer should present the potential evidence. Before disclosure, the interviewer should first summarize the suspects account, followed by an invitation, allowing the suspect to reconfirm, reject or correct the summary.

For example: "Have I understood you correctly when you said that you have never been at the crime scene at all?" "You do not smoke cigarettes. You have never met the deceased girl. You work as a psychologist and do not have any part time work," etc. By summarizing the suspect's account, misunderstandings are prevented and corrected if needed. This is of course of utmost importance if the suspect is innocent. It is simultaneously a strategically important step, inhibiting guilty suspects at a later stage to falsely claim that they were misunderstood. The interviewer is now in position to disclose the potential evidence they possess.

Whilst presenting the evidence, interviewers should maintain a calm and neutral tone of voice, followed by an invitation to the suspect to provide an explanation. Gloating or bravado should be avoided because it is likely to disrupt further communication regardless of the suspect's guilt or innocence.

When evidence is presented, the interviewer must be prepared to disclose how and when it was obtained, allowing the suspect and his/her lawyer to make a fair assessment as to the reliability of the interviewer's sources and possible biases and prejudices.

After posing the question, the interviewer should give the interviewee time to answer. If the suspect is innocent—and this was not revealed during Steps 2 and 3—the suspect must be given time to concentrate in order to explain and clarify. The same applies if the suspect is guilty. S/he is now considering available options. Should s/he now provide an honest account, or can s/he come up with an alternative explanation that has yet to be considered? A professional, well-planned and conducted strategic investigative interview will reduce the guilty suspect's opportunity to advance such a defense strategy. An example of a good presentation (disclosure) of evidence (after alternative explanations has been tested and summarized) may be formulated along these lines: "Our crime scene detectives have found your fingerprint at the crime scene. Please explain how your fingerprints may have ended up inside the apartment."

5.8 Phase Five: Closure of the Interview

Evaluations of police interviews show that officers tend to rush the closing of the interview, yet the closure is important and needs to be methodically conducted. Your aim for this phase is to ensure there is a mutual understanding of the interviewee's account by reviewing and summarizing it. You should verify that all aspects have been sufficiently covered by checking that interviewees have given all the information they are able and willing to provide.

As the interview comes to an end, the interviewing officer should explain what will happen next by giving the interviewee appropriate information about the next stages of the process: for example, inform suspects of potential pre-trial detention, tell witnesses whether or not they should expect to attend court, etc.

Finally, the interviewee should be asked if they have anything they would like to add to their account or if they have questions for the interviewing officer at this stage. This has little or no real effect if the communication has been coercive. However, if the interview has been conducted as outlined above, this question may add to the interviewee's perception of having been treated fairly and keep channels open for future communication. To provide the interviewee with a genuine opportunity to ask questions will help to ensure that the interview is concluded with a positive feeling about the whole process.

5.9 Phase Six: Evaluation

Investigative interviewing recognizes the fact that interviewing is a practical exercise, requiring a variety of skills, first and foremost, communication skills. An essential part of skills training is evaluation and feedback.

The evaluation is where the interviewer (and supervisor/senior officer) examines whether the aims and objectives of the interview have been achieved. Because the interview is closely interlinked with the investigation, information obtained during the interview must be reviewed. Professional interviewers (and organizations) may reflect upon how well the interview was conducted, identify the positives (such as good flow of information), and consider future improvements. If the interview is evaluated by a supervisor, senior officer, or colleague, make sure that the interviewing officers are given the opportunity to comment on their own performance, before the evaluator gives their points, starting with what was positive, moving on to what could be improved next time. With regard to evaluation, it is worth noting that research has found that officers are generally poor at evaluating their own interviewing abilities. Hence, conducting the evaluation with a colleague is useful. The colleague can be a partner, supervisor, or senior officer. The key is to review the interview with someone who is honest and frank, and treats the assessment confidentially. If the interview was recorded, as recommended by scientist and other experts, recording will obviously aid and professionalize the evaluation process.[40]

5.10 Benefits of Audio and/or Video Recording

Many States have found it effective to audio and/or video record interviews, both as a safeguard against abuse, but also as a way to improve evidence gathering, protect officers against false accusations, and for training and evaluation purposes. In fact, officers that initially expressed concern before the introduction of electronic recording of police interview, quickly become in favour of electronic recording. Today's technological advances, and access to easy-to-use and cheaper mobile technologies, means that recording is possible in many settings, and has many advantages, such as[41]:

[40] European Committee for the Prevention of Torture and Inhuman or Degrading Treatment or Punishment (CPT) Standard report CPT/Inf/E (2002) 1 - Rev. 2015, Art. 36.

[41] CTI training tools 1/2017.

- It reduces cognitive overload because it allows the interviewer to focus on the interview rather than typing all the information manually or taking notes.
- Recording permits the interviewer to employ active listening strategies and improves communication with the interviewee. Consequently, the interviewee can provide their account without constant interruptions.
- Recordings preserve the most important evidence—the oral evidence—in its original form. They produce a full and valid representation of the information provided and how the interview was conducted (they secure evidence and minimize miscarriages of justice).
- Failure to record interviews, or failing to record the entire interview, can increase the scope for abuse or speculation of abuse.
- Recordings can protect interviewers against false accusations of abuse, coercion or manipulation, or of failing to follow procedural rules.
- Recordings can help organize and thereby analyze the information provided. There are software solutions for the latter available.
- Recordings are great tools for evaluation and feedback on interviews, and for training and research, leading to a more professional police service Recordings opens up for research and development, and stimulates transpharency in general.

References

Alison E, Alison L (2020) Rapport. The four ways to read people. Vermilion, London

Alison L et al (2013) Why tough tactics fail and rapport gets results: observing rapport-based interpersonal techniques (ORBIT) to generate useful information from terrorists. Psychol Public Policy Law 19:411–431

Alison L et al (2014) The efficacy of rapport-based techniques for minimizing counter-interrogation tactics amongst a field sample of terrorists. Psychol Public Policy Law 20:421–430

Ask K, Fahsing I (2018) Investigative decision making. In: Griffiths A, Milne R (eds) The psychology of criminal investigation: theory into practice. Routledge, London, pp 52–73

Association for the Prevention of Torture (2021) Principles on effective interviewing for investigations and information gathering. (The Mendez Principles). Retrieved on 05 May 2023 from https://interviewingprinciples.com/The-Mendez-Principles

Barela SJ et al (2020) Interrogation and torture. Integrating efficiency with law and morality. Oxford, New York

Boyle M, Vullierme JC (2018) A brief introduction to investigative interviewing. A practitioner's guide. Council of Europe, Strasbourg

Bull R (2014) Foreword. In: Bull R (ed) Investigative interviewing. Springer, New York

Bull R, Rachlew A (2020) Investigative interviewing: from England to Norway and beyond. In: Barela S, Fallon M, Gaggioli G, Ohlin J (eds) Interrogation and torture: research on efficacy, and its integration with morality and legality. Oxford University Press, Oxford

Canter D, Alison LJ (1999) Offender Profiling Series Vol I: Interviewing and Deception (1–21)

Convention against torture initiative training tools 1/2017 (CTI 1/2017) Investigative interviewing for criminal cases. Available in several languages at: https://www.cti2024.org/en/cti-training-material/

Diesen C (1994) Bevisprövning i brottmål. Norstedts Juridik, Stocholm

European Committee for the Prevention of Torture and Inhuman or Degrading Treatment or Punishment (CPT). Extract from the 28th General Report of the CPT (2019), pp. 4–5 https://rm.coe.int/1680942329. Accessed on 5 May 2023

European Committee for the Prevention of Torture and Inhuman or Degrading Treatment or Punishment (CPT) 28th General report of the CPT (2018), pp. 32–34

European Committee for the Prevention of Torture and Inhuman or Degrading Treatment or Punishment (CPT) Standard report CPT/Inf/E (2002) 1 - Rev. 2015, Art. 36

Fahsing IA, Rachlew A (2009) Investigative Interviewing - The Nordic region. In: Milne B, Savage SP (eds) Williamson T. International developments in Investigative Interviewing, Devon, pp 39–65

Fahsing IA, Rachlew A, May L (2021). Have you considered the opposite? A debiasing strategy for judgement in criminal investigation. The Police Journal: Theory, Practice and Principles, published August 14th 2021.

Fisher RP, Geiselman RE (1992) Memory-enhancing techniques for investigative interviewing. The cognitive interview. Charles C. Thomas Publisher, Springfield

Forst B (2004) Error of justice. Nature, sources and remedies. Cambridge University Press, Cambridge

Geijsen K, Mergaerts L, Otgaar H, De Ruiter C (2023) Basisboek politie-interview: Voor de Nederlandse politie en andere opsporingsdiensten. Gompel & Svacina

Griffiths A, Rachlew A (2018) From interrogation to investigative interviewing. The application of psychology. In: Griffiths A, Milne R (eds) The psychology of criminal investigation: theory into practice. Routledge, London, pp 154–178

Gudjonsson GJ (2003) The psychology of interrogations and confessions. Wiley, Chichester

Huff CR, Rattner A, Sagagrin E (1996) Convicted but innocent. Wrongful conviction and public policy. Sage Publications, Inc, Thousand Oaks

Kassin S et al (2009) Police-induced confessions: risk factors and recommendations. Law Hum Behav 34(2):3–38

Kozma J, Rachlew A (2018) Combating Torture During Police Custody and Pre-Trial Detention. Discussion paper presented 22–23 March 2018 in Copenhagen, Denmark, at the international Conference hosted by the Danish Chairmanship of the Committee of Ministers of the Council of Europe

Leo RA (2008) Police interrogation and American justice. Harvard University Press, Cambridge

Meissner C et al (2012) Interview and interrogation methods and their effects on true and false confessions. Campbell Syst Rev 13

Memon A (1998). Telling it all: the cognitive interview. In: Memon, Vrij A, Bull R. Psychology and law. Truthfulness, accuracy and credibility. McGraw-Hill Publishing Company, London

Mendez JE (2016) Interim report to the general assembly (A/71/298). Submitted by the special rapporteur on torture, Juan E. Méndez, in accordance with Assembly resolution 70/146. United Nations, Geneva. https://digitallibrary.un.org/record/839995/files/A_71_298-EN.pdf. Accessed on 16 Apr 2023

Milne R, Bull R (1999) Investigative interviewing. Psychology and practice. Wiley, Chichester

Rachlew A et al (2022) A guide to the professional interview. A research-based interview methodology for people who Ask questions. Anthem Press, New York

Rejali D (2007) Torture and democracy. Princeton University Press

Shepherd E, Griffiths A (2013) Investigative interviewing, 2nd edn The conversation management approach. Oxford University press, Oxford

United Nations (2024) UN manual on Investigative Interviewing for Criminal Investigations. In: Department of Peace Operations, Office of the High Commissioner for Human Rights, Office on Drugs and Crime. United Nations

Vrij A (2008) Detecting lies and deceit: pitfalls and opportunities, 2nd edn. Wiley, New York
Walsh D et al (2016) International developments and practices in investigative interviewing and interrogation. Volume 2: suspects. Routledge, London
Zuckerman AA (1992) Miscarriage of justice—a root treatment. Criminal Law Review, May 1992
Zuckerman AA, Roberts P (1989) The principles of criminal evidence. Clarendon Press, Oxford

Asbjørn Rachlew (PhD) is a Detective Superintendent at Oslo Police District, Norway, and guest researcher at the Norwegian Centre for Human Rights, University of Oslo (UiO). He completed his MSc in Investigative psychology at the University of Liverpool in 1999 and his Ph.D. on *Errors of Justice in police investigations* at the Faculty of Law, University of Oslo in 2009. He won Politiforums' Prize of honour in 2018 for his longstanding reform and development work within the Norwegian Police.

Rachlew has published a wide range of texts on investigative interviewing, including the book; A Guide to professional interviewing (2022). He is recurrently used as an expert on investigative interviewing in Norwegian courts, governmental and international committees and panels, including the expert-driven Steering Committee assembled to develop a global protocol for the UN on effective and human rights compliant police interviewing, *The Mendez principles*. In December 2021, Rachlew was elected by the Council of Europe as Norway's representative in the European Committee for the Prevention of Torture (CPT).

Chapter 6
The Coercion and Counselling Approaches to Interrogation of High Value Detainees: Perspectives from the UK

Frances Surmon-Böhr, Laurence Alison, and Emily Alison

Contents

Abstract This contribution discusses the problems associated with using coercive interrogation methods and the benefits of utilising counselling approaches when interrogating high-value detainees (i.e. individuals suspected of terrorism). It focuses first on the context of terrorism and the use of harsh interrogation methods (including torture) by both US and UK interrogators. It then outlines the move from interrogation to interviewing in the UK and the adoption of non-coercive approaches. Lastly, it gives an overview of ORBIT—an empirically based model of police interviewing, based on counselling approaches, developed from analysis of real-world police interviews with terrorism suspects. Furthermore, it discusses research conducted over the last 12 years that provides empirical support for using the ORBIT model of interviewing.

F. Surmon-Böhr (✉) · L. Alison · E. Alison
University of Liverpool, Liverpool, UK
e-mail: f.surmon-bohr@liverpool.ac.uk; l.j.alison@liverpool.ac.uk; E.Alison@liverpool.ac.uk

R. Alleweldt (ed.), *Fair Treatment of Persons in Police Custody*,
https://doi.org/10.1007/978-3-031-61737-9_6

6.1 Introduction

The social context of terrorism is one of heightened emotion, fear and uncertainty (Sprang 2003). When the national security of liberal democracies is threatened by terrorism, states have employed alarmingly coercive tactics that are then justified by the presumed necessity to ensure national safety (Hajjar 2009). Despite such approaches violating international laws and conventions, when faced with international terrorism, the use of coercive practises that include torture can seem like an appealing quick and low-cost way to gather such intelligence (Conrad et al. 2016). Although a small number of individuals from various intelligence and policing agencies believe that the use of coercion or torture can be an effective interrogation technique (even if only for short-term tactical advantage), research has consistently found that it is ineffective and produces unreliable information (O'Mara 2015). In addition to its lack of efficacy, torture carries high political costs such as fuelling terrorist propaganda (Johnson et al. 2016) and increasing the likelihood of a subsequent terrorist attacks (Dreher et al. 2010). There is also evidence that coercive techniques produce false confessions. Within the criminal justice system, a worryingly high number of DNA exonerations have shed light on the issue of the verifiably false confessions that have resulted from coercive police interrogations (Costanzo and Leo 2007; Kassin et al. 2010; Kassin and Gudjonsson 2004).

In response to several miscarriages of justice against terrorism suspects in the UK, police interrogations have undergone significant legislative and organisational change to ensure the fair treatment of suspects. A great deal can be learned from the evolution of UK police interrogation and which may hold valuable lessons for military and intelligence interrogations. This paper will outline the history of coercive interrogation methods and their conceptual underpinnings and then outline the limitations of this approach. It will then provide an overview of the evolution of police interrogations in the UK and the development of an empirically based model of interviewing (ORBIT) developed from analysis of real-world police interviews with terrorism suspects and based on several disparate but well researched counselling methods.

6.2 The History of Harsh Interrogation

Torture has been widely used in both democratic and authoritarian societies throughout history (Rejali 2009). However, details of the CIA's interrogation and 'extraordinary rendition' programme, which relied on out-sourcing interrogational torture during the US's so-called 'war on terror', thrust the issue back into the spotlight. This contentious phrase, also known as the 'war on terrorism', was coined by the Bush Administration to describe the US-initiated hostilities following the 9–11 terrorist attacks. These attacks led to President George Bush declaring war on

Al-Qaeda (AQ) and all terrorists around world.[1] This heightened emotional and political context, led to reduced civil liberties and breaches of human rights. For example, President Bush suspended the Geneva conventions for detainees held as part of the 'War on Terror' (Bush 2010), an edict later overturned by the Supreme Court (*Hadman v. Rumsfeld*), which ruled that Article 3 of the Geneva Conventions *did* apply to America's war with Al Qaeda. Most notoriously though, the 'war on terror' was used to justify the CIA's use of 'Enhanced Interrogation' Techniques (EITs) on terrorism suspects (Bellamy 2006; Stritzke and Lewandowsky 2009). As listed in a 2005 Justice Department memo, the 13 enhanced interrogation techniques (EITs) used included:

1. Abdominal Slap
2. Attention Grasp
3. Cramped Confinement
4. Dietary Manipulation
5. The Facial Hold
6. The Facial Slap/Insult Slap
7. Nudity
8. Stress Positions
9. Sleep Deprivation
10. Wall Standing
11. Walling (slamming the detainee against a wall)
12. Waterboarding
13. Water Dousing

Although the recent spotlight of political shame has fallen on the US because of their use of these techniques, less well discussed is the UK's history of involvement in and reliance on torture for the purpose of interrogation. Indeed, Britain's use of coercive interrogation methods known as the 'five techniques' were used as part of the justification for the use of EITs.

6.2.1 The Five Techniques

The British developed the now notorious 'five techniques' in Kenya in 1953/1954. The five techniques included: hooding, sleep deprivation, food deprivation, white noise and stress positions. Details of these tactics emerged as part of the Lord Parker Inquiry which investigated claims of British torture and abuse of suspected Irish Republican Army (IRA) members (i.e. terrorism suspects) held without trial during the conflict in Northern Ireland in the 1970s. The resulting Parker report (1972) revealed that the British had been experimenting with these techniques since the

[1] See https://www.theguardian.com/world/2001/sep/21/september11.usa13 for President Bush's full speech to Congress and the American people.

second World War and had used them in Palestine, Malaya, Kenya, Aden, Malaysia, British Cameroons and other former British colonies, prior to their use in Northern Ireland. The purpose of the five techniques was allegedly twofold: firstly, for the safety and security of both the interrogators and those being interrogated (i.e. the use of hooding and white noise) and secondly, to make the detainee 'feel that he is in a hostile atmosphere' and that 'he is completely isolated so that he fears what may happen next' (Parker 1972, p. 3). The suggestion was that these techniques were designed to show the detainee who was in charge, that their situation was futile, that they were under the control of the interrogation facility and that they would not be assisted (Alison and Alison 2017).

The rationale was to establish control rather than to instil fear or distress. When the British's use of the five techniques came before the European Court of Human Rights (ECHR) in 1978, the court ruled that the techniques amounted to 'inhuman and degrading treatment' but did not constitute 'torture'. This ruling was utilised by President Bush and included in the Bybee memo (Greenberg and Dratel 2005) to justify the use of EITs, to argue that like the five techniques, although EITs may be dehumanizing, they fall short of 'torture'. The treatment of detainees and interrogation methods used by the British were brought to public attention once again following the death of Baha Mousa, a hotel receptionist who died whilst being questioned by British troops in Basra, Iraq, in 2003. A subsequent post mortem examination of his body found that he had sustained 93 surface injuries (Gage 2011). In 2010, High Court proceedings were brought on behalf of 222 former detainees who alleged that they had been mistreated by the British military interrogation team in Iraq (Cobain 2010). The allegations included being hooded, subject to electric shocks, sensory deprivation, food and sleep deprivation, forced into painful stress positions, enforced nakedness and threatened with execution (Cobain 2010). Video footage was released to accompany the court case, which evidences some of these allegation (Cobain 2010).[2] In addition to the use of the five techniques, the video released by the Guardian newspaper shows that British interrogators in Iraq were using standard operating procedures for tactical questioning (as shown by the similarities to a training exercise also played in the video).

The 'harsh approach' was a permitted method of questioning that could be deployed as the questioner considered necessary. Harsh techniques included: shouting as loudly as possible, with uncontrolled fury, or with cold menace and there could be personal abuse; making personal attacks on the detainee's physical and mental attitudes and capabilities via taunting or goading; attacking the detainee's pride and ego in order to generate insecurity or humiliation; using high speed questioning, interrupting or misquoting their replies to generate confusion (as described by Collins J. in the Divisional court in the case of *Hussein v. Secretary of State for Defence*). The report by Sir William Gage (2011) into the death of Baha Mousa extensively criticised the use of the harsh approach and recommended its use should be forbidden from tactical questioning since it could

[2] See https://www.theguardian.com/uk/2010/nov/06/iraq-prisoner-abuse-court.

not be sufficiently regulated or monitored. Gage also concluded that there was widespread ignorance and insufficient thought given to what was and was not permitted in the handling of prisoners of war in Iraq (including disregard for the 1972 ban imposed on the five techniques), in line with the Geneva conventions. Although the harsh approach in and of itself would not cause actual physical harm to a detainee, encouraging soldiers in the use of a technique that includes dehumanising language and threats designed to instil fear of physical harm, sexual assault or death arguably contributes to an atmosphere in which there is an increased risk of violence toward detainees. The Ministry of Defence (MoD) has since revised its policy for interrogation (May 2012), removing the harsh approach and replacing it with the more restrictive 'Challenge' Strategy. Authorised approaches included Neutral, Friendly, Firm and Challenging. Challenge can be indirect or direct, but '*neither approach is intended nor permitted to threaten, coerce, insult, humiliate, or degrade captured persons or place them in fear of violence*'. Rather, the aim is '*to refocus the detainee's attention on the reality of their situation and futility of intransigence*'. Furthermore, Challenge approaches are only to be used once all other alternative approaches have been proven unsuccessful and are never to be used against detainees who qualify as PoWs, or are assessed as vulnerable.

6.2.2 The Psychology of Coercive Interrogation

There are numerous potential theoretical underpinnings for the use of coercion and torture as interrogation methods. One suggestion by O'Donohue et al. (2014) is that its use resembles well-known scientific phenomena, such as avoidance and escape from aversive stimuli and operant conditioning (Skinner 1990). O'Donohue et al. (2014) argue that it is hard to claim that interrogations are so different that they would defy the basic regularities found in operant conditioning. They refer to several studies that have shown animals and humans engaging in escape and avoidance conditioning. They suggest that detainees are likely to provide information through positive reinforcement (i.e. a detainee is given something valued like a phone call home) and negative reinforcement (i.e. a detainee is subjected to aversive stimuli such as prolonged sleep deprivation or waterboarding and in an effort to escape repeated experience of this, when offered a 'get out' of giving up information, they might take that opportunity).

Regarding EITs specifically, the programme was designed by psychologists James Mitchell and Bruce Jessen, who 'reverse engineered' techniques used in the US Military's Survival, Evasion, Resistance and Escape (SERE) School, designed to expose military students to what they might face if captured (Feinstein 2014). Mitchell's logic is supposedly based on Seligman (1975) theory of 'learned helplessness' (McCoy 2007). This phenomenon refers to a mental state in which a subject (human or animal) repeatedly exposed to an inescapable stressor, develops a behavioural syndrome whereby they show reduced capacity to escape the stressor even when escape is possible. Mitchell argued that EITs were designed to break someone who is being uncooperative and resistant into being cooperative, at which point EITs stop being used and the detainee is permitted to talk. Hence, Mitchell does not claim that it was during waterboarding sessions that detainees would give up information. He states that information was given up after the sessions, in situations in which the detainee wanted to avoid being subjected to such techniques again (Mitchell and Harlow 2016). As such, it seems what Mitchell is referring to is a trade-off of information, in order to avoid aversive stimuli (i.e. 'You don't have to go through this awful process again—if you talk').

6.2.3 Cognitive Impact of Torture

The logic behind interrogational torture and coercive techniques—based on the idea that generating helplessness, humiliation and instilling fear in suspects is an effective strategy for eliciting information—directly contradicts research findings. O'Mara (2015) collated an extensive body of research on the independent effects of numerous torture techniques on the brain (including stress, pain, sleep deprivation and simulated drowning). In contrast to the assumption that torture will 'break' an individual's resistance, which in turn will result in compliance, O'Mara uses extensive neuroscientific literature to conclude the opposite. He found that torture fails as a device to extract truthful and accurate information. O'Mara shows how severe and sustained stressors severely impair the brain's capacity to appropriately regulate thoughts, emotions and behaviours. For example, sleep deprivation causes deficits in general cognitive function and profoundly impairs declarative memory. Likewise, near-drowning or suffocation causes oxygen restriction and a redistribution of blood flow away from brain areas involved in memory and direct recall of information from memory, which can impair its functioning. Other research has shown how food and sleep deprivation and extreme temperature variations, can impair soldiers' voluntary recall of information (Morgan III et al. 2006).

6.2.4 The Problem of False Confessions

In addition to causing cognitive deficits and impairments, it has been well documented that the use of coercion and torture can produce false information and confessions. It is often assumed that an innocent person would never confess to a crime they did not commit. However, unfortunately this can and does happen. There are numerous accounts from individuals who were held and tortured by the US government as part of their extraordinary rendition programme and the 'war on terror', who claim to have falsely confessed to the crimes of which their torturers accused them (e.g. *Arar v. Ashcroft*). The Senate State Committee on Intelligence (SSCI) report (Feinstein 2014) also states that numerous detainees subjected to EITs reportedly fabricated or retracted information during such interrogations.

Additionally, within the criminal justice system, a worryingly high number of DNA exonerations have shed light on the issue of verifiably false confessions that have resulted from police interrogations much less coercive than those that used EITs (Costanzo and Leo 2007; Kassin et al. 2010; Kassin and Gudjonsson 2004).

False information might not be problematic if it were possible to distinguish between true and false statements. However, research consistently shows that people are poor lie-detectors (Kassin and Gudjonsson 2004). More worryingly, research suggests that trained officers have a perceptual bias of believing others are lying to them (Masip et al. 2005; Meissner and Kassin 2002); that they are overconfident in their lie-detection skills (Kassin and Fong 1999; Meissner and Kassin 2002) but are not much better than chance at detecting lies (Vrij 2004). Thus, trained interrogators are *not* accurate at determining the truthfulness of suspects' accounts (Costanzo and Leo 2007; Vrij et al. 2010). Therefore, it is extremely problematic to use methods which increase the likelihood of false information and/or confessions.

6.2.5 Why Does Torture Continue To Be Used?

Given the detrimental costs of using interrogational torture, at least part of why it continues to be used lies in the belief that it is only used when there is no alternative and it is for the greater good (Alison and Alison 2017). Alison and Alison suggest that 'just-world' thinking can provide a template for people to believe that people get what they deserve (or not), which in turn can be used to justify the use of torture (see Lerner and Simmons 1966, 'just-world' cognitive distortion). This is particularly true in relation to the torture of terrorism suspects as the most sustained defence for the use of torture utilises the terrorism specific 'ticking-bomb' scenario. The scenario is often represented as follows: a terrorist has planted a bomb and said terrorist has been captured. The terrorist says they know where the bomb is but refuses to give the location. Should we contemplate torturing the terrorist to produce the information needed to stop the bomb going off, which would save many lives? Despite its prominence in scholarly and wider public discussion on the use of torture, it has received much criticism. For example, the scenario has been deemed both 'mythic' and 'manipulative', as it is based on a sequence of improbable assumptions, designed to pre-judge the moral outcome, and provoke the thought that torture might be acceptable or even necessary (Bloche 2016). Such a scenario also presumes that torture can and will have rapid effects, which even advocates such as James Mitchell, who assisted in the development of the EIT programme, do not claim (Bloche 2016). Thus, there is a profound inconsistency between the justification of torture in a time-critical 'ticking-bomb' situation and actual estimated times of effectiveness (O'Mara 2015). Nonetheless, the prominence of the scenario to defend the use of torture reflects the strong emotions terrorism creates and the limited sympathy for terrorists among some sections of society (Roberts 2011).

The torture of terrorists has also been linked to revenge. Alison and Alison (2017) highlight how interrogations regularly occur in high-conflict, high uncertainty situations and instances where the enemy is dehumanised. For example, the treatment and interrogation of prisoners held in Iraq by British soldiers and by US soldiers as part of the 'war on terror'. In line with this, McCauley (2009) provides an interesting analysis of how terrorism has been dealt with in recent years, the rhetoric of war that has surrounded it, and how this contradicts the notion of justice. He states that success against terrorism often comes from police work, in a criminal justice setting. Whereas failure has often stemmed from attempts to tackle the issue through a military/war approach in which torture is included. McCauley (2009) puts forward a convincing argument for putting an end to the war rhetoric surrounding terrorism, which justifies the counter-productive use of torture, and to move toward an entirely criminal-justice based approach. Importantly, this requires recognition that unlike war, which requires dehumanisation of the enemy, interrogation requires the opposite (i.e. humanisation of the enemy combatant). It is also important for interrogators to assess their goals—is it to seek revenge and punish? Or is it to secure reliable, actionable information/intelligence?

6.3 From Interrogation to Ethical Interviewing in the UK

In the United Kingdom (UK), terrorism suspects are interviewed by Counter-Terrorism police officers who work within the framework of strict legislation to ensure the fair treatment of those being interviewed (interrogation has been referred to as *interviewing* in the UK since 1992). Such legislation was brought about in response to a series of notorious wrongful convictions of individuals accused of terrorist offences (e.g. the 'Birmingham Six' and the 'Guilford Four'). Studies conducted around this time revealed that police viewed gaining a confession as the sole purpose of an interrogation (Softley et al. 1980) and that they often relied on threats, pressure, and fabrication of evidence to do this (Smith et al. 1983). Consequently, the Police and Criminal Evidence Act (PACE) (1984) was enacted to ensure fairness and transparency in the custodial questioning process. The subsequent development of the PEACE model (an acronym for 'Planning and preparation, Engage and explain, Account, Closure and Evaluation') provided a clear framework for interviewers to follow, in line with the new legislation (Milne et al. 2007).

With requirements including the tape-recording of all interviewers and permitting all suspects the right to communicate with solicitors (at no expense), police interviews of suspects in the UK are now some of the most strictly regulated and highly monitored in the world. In effect, a change occurred in how police viewed and conducted their questioning of suspects with a shift away from guilt presumptive and confession-orientated 'accusatorial methods' to a more objective, open-minded 'information-gathering' approach. This sparked similar changes in other countries; for example, Norway, Australia, and New Zealand (among others) have also adopted similar non-coercive, information-gathering approaches. These approaches are similar to military human intelligence (HUMINT) interrogations in that both aim to elicit reliable information from a source/suspect (Evans et al. 2010). A growing body of research provides support for information-gathering approaches over accusatorial ones, due to their diagnostic value—they elicit a greater proportion of true confessions, whilst reducing the likelihood of false confessions (Meissner et al. 2017).

6.3.1 Moving Towards a Rapport-Based Approach

The importance of developing rapport, a key component of information-gathering approaches, is also well documented within the literature (Abbe and Brandon 2013; Evans et al. 2010; Kelly et al. 2013; Walsh and Bull 2012; Gabbert et al. 2021). Interrogators, interpreters and analysts all report rapport to be a fundamental component of a successful interrogation (Goodman-Delahunty et al. 2014; Redlich et al. 2014; Russano et al. 2014a, b), and these findings have been found to hold true cross-culturally (Goodman-Delahunty 2015). Building rapport is assumed to enhance cooperation and elicit more accurate information when used in investigative interviews (Vanderhallen and Vervaeke 2014). However, despite such a clear consensus on its importance, within an interrogative context, rapport has proven difficult to both define and measure (for a comprehensive review see Vallano and Schreiber Compo 2015). Indeed, interviews with experienced interrogators, who unanimously emphasised the importance of rapport and relationship building, revealed a lack of consensus regarding its definition and relevant tactics (Russano et al. 2014b).

Rapport can broadly be considered the relationship established between interviewer and interviewee over the course of their interaction, based on trust, empathy, and a shared understanding of one another (Alison and Alison 2017; Evans et al. 2010; Kelly et al. 2013). Within the counselling domain, rapport has been measured using constructs such as being 'warm and caring' (Joe et al. 2001). However, within an investigative context, the relationship between interviewer and interviewee should be considered professional and respectful but is not to be confused with friendliness or affection (Vallano and Schreiber Compo 2015). Although efforts have been made to identify ways to build and maintain rapport in an investigative context, they are often either poorly defined or contain highly specific tasks lists such as: 'touch source in a friendly manner'; 'build a bond'; 'use immediacy behaviours' (e.g. lean forward); or 'disclose personal information' (Abbe and Brandon 2013; Kelly et al. 2013).

6.4 The ORBIT Model of Interviewing: Lessons from Counselling

In the UK, Alison et al. (2013) looked to the counselling arena where rapport is well established and developed a behavioural coding framework for reliably measuring interrogations in field operations. A coding framework known as 'ORBIT' (Observing Rapport Based Interpersonal Techniques) was developed based on analysis of the largest real-world dataset of police interviews with terrorism suspects in the world (secured by Professor Laurence Alison, working in cooperation with the UK Counter Terrorism Unit). ORBIT has since evolved from a research coding framework into a comprehensive interviewing model for practitioners and is now trained to UK/US law enforcement and military personnel, UK border force, war crimes as well as a range of other agencies and organisations (see Alison et al. 2020a). The theoretical underpinnings of ORBIT were drawn from over 70 years of research in two well-established therapeutic domains: (1) Personality and interpersonal relating (Leary 1958) and (2) Motivational Interviewing (Miller and Rollnick 1991).

6.4.1 Interpersonal Behaviour Circle

Based on Leary's (1958) interpersonal circumplex model and other interpersonal relating theories, ORBIT measures dyadic interactions between the interviewer and suspect using an interrogation specific model (referred to as the 'interpersonal behaviour circle'; IBC) as shown in Fig. 6.1. Communication is structured along a vertical dimension of 'agency/power', which ranges from dominance to submission, and a horizontal dimension of 'communion/intimacy' ranging from hostility to cooperation (Horowitz et al. 2006). As such, adjacent octants on the wheels are conceptually more similar than those on the opposing side. On the vertical axis, communication works on the rule of correspondence (i.e. dominant behaviours invite submissive ones in return and vice versa) whereas behaviours on the horizontal axis work reciprocally (i.e. confrontational behaviours invite confrontational behaviours in return and cooperation invites cooperation). Communication can also be done adaptively (likely to increase communication) or maladaptively (likely to hinder communication). For example, being *in charge, sets the agenda, advises* are examples of adaptive dominant behaviour, whereas being *demanding, dogmatic, or bossy* are examples of maladaptive dominant behaviours. Figure 6.1 shows the ORBIT interpersonal wheel with the inner circle representing adaptive behaviours and the outer circle representing the maladaptive variants.

Elite interviewers will avoid the use of maladaptive/outer wheel behaviours (i.e. interpersonally competent) and recognise that different individuals need to be dealt with differently (i.e. interpersonally sensitive). For example, a highly dominant terrorist leader will require a very different approach to a potentially frightened individual suspected of a minor offence. The most effective interviewers will also be

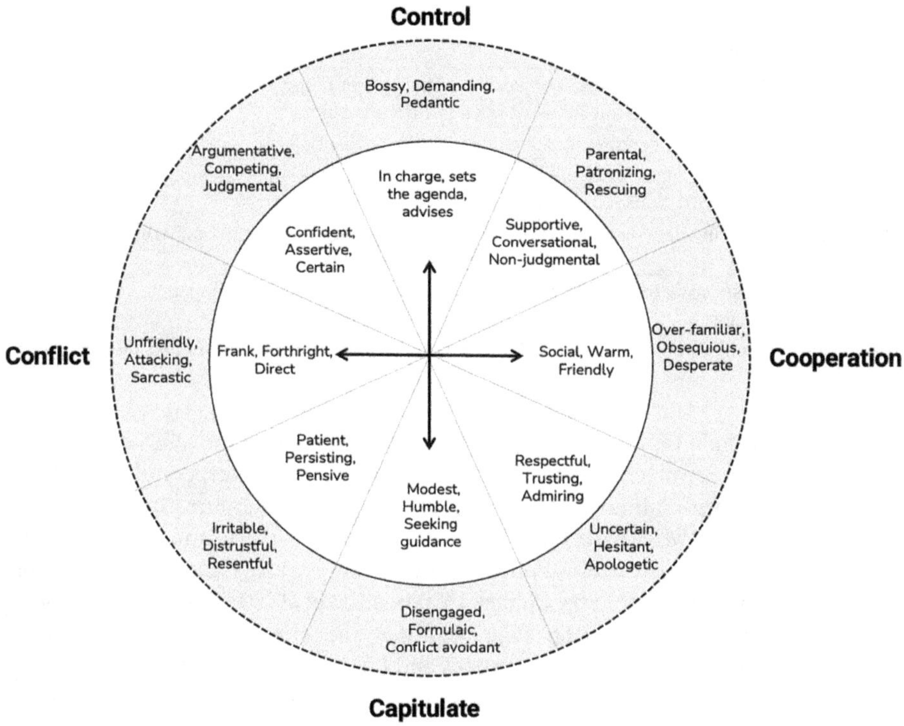

Fig. 6.1 Schematic representation of the ORBIT interpersonal wheel with adaptive and maladaptive variants of interpersonal behaviour

versatile, utilising a range of interpersonal approaches in response to different suspect behaviours. Interviews with experienced military and federal interrogators revealed that those who were interpersonally skilled and adaptive were perceived to be the most effective interrogators (Russano et al. 2014b).

6.4.2 Rapport-Building Strategies

The second component of ORBIT contains six global approaches to build rapport (honesty,[3] empathy, evocation, adaptation, autonomy and reflection—known as the 'H.E.E.A.A.R principles') adapted from the Motivational Interviewing literature (Miller et al. 2008) (see Table 6.1). ORBIT recognises that it is up to the interviewer

[3]The original ORBIT coding framework contained five global MI skills—Acceptance, Adaptation, Autonomy, Evocation and Empathy. More recently, Acceptance was replaced by 'Honesty' to ensure interviewers are being non-judgmental but also clear about the reasons for the interview; and reflection was added as it is a key rapport-based skill that helps achieve the other principles.

Table 6.1 ORBIT global rapport-based strategies (H.E.E.A.A.R)

Skill	Definition
Honesty	Being direct, clear and objective—That is, not being judgmental or avoidant of asking difficult questions or raising difficult topics
Empathy	Displaying genuine understanding of the suspect's actions or mindset
Evocation	Eliciting statements from the suspect about their thoughts, feelings and the underlying core values or beliefs
Adaptation	Altering agenda in response to the suspect rather than rigidly adhering to interview plan
Autonomy	Respecting or emphasizing the suspect's right to choose to cooperate, speak, engage or not
Reflection	Repeating back strategic elements of what has been said or implied by the suspect

to build and sustain rapport with a suspect. The HEEAAR approaches are intended to help an interviewer create an honest but supportive and respectful atmosphere conducive to open-communication without the use of pressure, intimidation or external influence. MI was originally developed as an intervention for substance misuse, but it has since been applied further afield to areas such as social work (Hohman 2015), with problem gamblers (Yakovenko et al. 2015) and with offenders (McMurran 2009). It has been suggested that the effectiveness of MI can be attributed to increasing client engagement and cooperation (Moyers et al. 2005), a finding that has been demonstrated in an interview/interrogation context (Surmon-Böhr et al. 2020).

Alison et al. (2013) have drawn several parallels between the principles of MI and police interviewing, namely that they both seek to establish a respectful, non-judgmental, and empathic atmosphere (i.e. 'search for the truth'), with an emphasis on autonomy (i.e. it is the suspect's right to choose to talk or not). As such, pressure to reveal information is not created by external pressure but is rather the result of internal conflict created within the individual, as they decide whether to reveal or withhold information (if they have any). This is a key difference between rapport based approaches and accusatorial approaches, as the latter relies on external pressure from the interrogator either through coercion, persuasion or manipulation. Thus, critically, as an investigative interviewing method, the use of MI consistent approaches is both legally compliant and ethically sound.

6.4.3 Using ORBIT in the Field

The ORBIT framework categorises (1) the interpersonal behaviours of the interviewers and suspect; (2) interviewers' rapport-based skills and behaviours counter to rapport-building; (3) suspect counter-interrogation/resistance strategies (used to resist cooperating); (4) engagement level of the suspect; and (5) information, evidence and intelligence (collectively referred to as 'yield'). Coding all these variables has allowed for complex analysis into the effects of different interviewer behaviours on suspect behaviours, suspect resistance strategies and ultimately how this effects the amount of yield produced.

Since the creation of the ORBIT framework in 2012, an extensive research programme has culminated in a series of publications in internationally recognised journals (e.g. Alison et al. 2013, 2014; Surmon-Böhr et al. 2020) as well as a book on the ORBIT model (Alison et al. 2020a). Specifically, research has examined how interviewer behaviours impact suspect behaviour and the subsequent amount of evidentially useful information disclosed in interviews with terrorism suspects, child sex offending suspects and victims of sexual offences. The ORBIT research team have now coded over 2000 hours of police interviews and a series of studies using the ORBIT framework have provided empirical support for adopting a rapport-based interpersonal approach.

The first study to systematically assess ORBIT in real operations was conducted by Alison et al. (2013). The study was based on analysis of 418 audio and video recordings of police interviews with 29 terrorist suspects. The study concluded that interviewer behaviours consistent with the principles of MI were positively associated with adaptive interpersonal behaviour from the suspect, which led to increased interview yield. Conversely, even minimal expression of maladaptive interpersonal interrogator behaviour increased maladaptive interviewee behaviour as well as directly reducing yield. Building on these initial findings, Alison et al. (2014) next study examined the impact of ORBIT's rapport-based strategies on suspect's use of Counter Interrogation Tactics (CITs) (based on the same dataset outlined in Alison et al.'s 2013 paper). The study found that interviewers' use of rapport-based strategies was directly associated with decreases in certain CITs, including silence and 'no comment' responses (Alison et al. 2014). A more recent study by Surmon-Böhr et al. (2020) which expanded the original data set and examined 804 interview tapes with 75 terrorist suspects, found that not only do MI skills encourage engagement but, comparatively, the use of approaches that are antithetical to MI significantly reduced suspect engagement and yield.

Although the initial ORBIT research programme focused on ORBIT and its application to samples of police interviews with terrorist suspects, the model has also been tested and validated within other samples. Recently, in partnership with the UK's National Crime Agency (NCA), ORBIT has been validated in police interviews with individuals suspected of child sex offences. Looking at 35 interviews with 25 individuals convicted of Child Sexual Abuse (CSA) offences, two studies replicated Alison et al. (2013) and Surmon-Böhr et al. (2020) findings in this context (Alison et al. 2022; Humann et al. 2023). ORBIT has also been shown to be effective within a victim interviewing context. Specifically, Kim et al. (2020) examined interviews with 86 victims of sexual offenses in South Korea and found that rapport-based approaches positively influenced adaptive communication between the interviewer and victim and resulted in more yield.

Based on these research findings, ORBIT sits at the heart of the UK Advanced CT police interviewer training programme known as 'Alcyone' (it is also a central model in the US High Value Detainee Interrogation Group's core training programme).

Alcyone is a comprehensive, six-day, specialist interviewer training course for police interviewers in the UK who work within the CT unit. The course begins with theoretical lectures outlining the key concepts and underlying philosophy of ORBIT. There is a strong focus on the interviewers' mindset and on understanding the approach before the more tactical elements are taught. Based on the research findings, there is also a strong emphasis on first stopping maladaptive behaviours before attempting to acquire new skills. Approximately 80% of the course involves immersive scenario-based role-play for participants to practice deploying the skills. Two studies have examined the efficacy of ORBIT training on the Alcyone course with very promising results. First, a study examined 29 officers' rapport-based interview performance on the first and last day of the course which found significant increases in the use of rapport-based strategies and decreases in approaches that may impede rapport by the end of the course (Alison et al. 2019).

A second study examined 31 sets of real-life CT interviews conducted between 2012 and 2017, of which, all interviewers had undertaken advanced interviewer training, but 16 interviewers had also undergone Alcyone training (Alison et al. 2020b). Alcyone trained officers were found to use significantly more rapport-based strategies than untrained officers and were significantly less likely to use maladaptive behaviours. Importantly, the findings showed that interviewers who were Alcyone trained yielded significantly more information from their interviews than those who were not trained. The Alcyone trained interviewers had received their training between 3 and 30 months prior to conducting the interviews included in the dataset which suggests that Alcyone training in ORBIT is not only effective but has an enduring impact.

Taken together, these findings provide empirical support for adopting a sophisticated interpersonal and rapport-based approach when interviewing suspects. As in counselling, it seems that being non-judgmental, listening to and showing genuine interest in trying to understand a suspect's perspective, can lead to a respectful, empathic atmosphere that facilitates cooperation. Such an approach is both ethically and legally compliant and in direct contrast with harsh approaches historically taken to interrogate terrorism suspects. Achieving this interpersonal rapport-based approach is no easy task though and it is much more than 'being nice'. It is hard for interviewers to consider the needs of the suspect and remain flexible and non-judgmental, especially in the face of aggressive and/or demanding behaviour. Furthermore, adaptive behaviour may include being direct, firm, and authoritative (but never degrading or cruel), as well as more reserved, humble strategies (but never weak and submissive). The key is for the interviewer to be adaptable and adopt the most appropriate set of behaviours in response to the specific context and the suspect with whom they are engaged. However, most importantly, the research highlights the negative effects of maladaptive interpersonal behaviours on the interpersonal relationship with the suspect and therefore the amount of information disclosed by the suspect.

6.5 Conclusions

The questioning of terrorism suspects is an incredibly demanding task. There are a minority of individuals from various intelligence and policing agencies who believe the use of coercion or torture can be an effective interrogation method. However, the use of such techniques run a number of risks from unreliable suspect accounts, to increasing the likelihood of further attacks and damaging international relationships with other countries. In contrast, a large body of research now exists to support the approach adopted by UK police, which is focused on building rapport and gathering information, to mitigate these risks. The science behind interrogation has improved greatly over the last 30 years and empirically supported techniques which maintain respect, dignity and the fair treatment of suspects now exists. One example is the development of ORBIT—an empirically grounded, psychological model of interrogation/interviewing. Research into ORBIT highlights how techniques that are both legally and ethically compliant with human rights acts, can successfully reduce suspect resistance, increase suspect engagement and ultimately increase the amount of evidentially useful information suspects are willing to disclose. The importance of these findings lies in its application to training interviewers in which skills to use and/or avoid, in order to give them the best chance of securing information. ORBIT forms the central approach for the UK National Counter Terrorism advanced police interviewer training course and academics and practitioners work closely to ensure the continuation of empirical research informing practice. Of course, the UK police system is not perfect and errors will still be made, but it is hoped that other interrogator communities can be encouraged by the ethical, evidence-based approaches being utilised in the UK and consider moving away from coercive interrogative practices altogether.

References

Abbe A, Brandon SE (2013) The role of rapport in investigative interviewing: a review. J Investig Psychol Offender Profiling 10:237–249. https://doi.org/10.1002/jip.1386

Alison L, Alison E (2017) Revenge versus rapport: interrogation, terrorism, and torture. Am Psychol 72:266–277. https://doi.org/10.1037/amp0000064

Alison L, Alison E, Noone G, Elntib S, Christiansen P (2013) Why tough tactics fail and rapport gets results: observing rapport-based interpersonal techniques (ORBIT) to generate useful information from terrorists psychology. Public Policy Law 19:411. https://doi.org/10.1037/a0034564

Alison L, Alison E, Noone G, Elntib S, Waring S, Christiansen P (2014) The efficacy of rapport-based techniques for minimizing counter-interrogation tactics amongst a field sample of terrorists. Psychol Public Policy Law 20:421. https://doi.org/10.1037/law0000021

Alison L, Plummer N, Humann M (2019) Motivational Interviewing training of practitioners who interview terrorists: assessing the effectiveness of ORBIT training on an advanced CT interviewer course. [unpublished manuscript]. University of Liverpool, Liverpool

Alison L, Alison E, Shortland N, Surmon-Bohr F (2020a) ORBIT: the science of rapport-based interviewing for law enforcement, security, and military. Oxford University Press, Oxford

Alison L, Barrett-Pink C, Surmon-Böhr F, Christiansen P, Alison E (2020b) Assessing the effectiveness of ORBIT training with police interviewers. In: Alison L, Alison E, Shortland N, Surmon-Böhr F (eds) ORBIT: The Science of Rapport Based Interviewing for Law Enforcement, Security, and Military. Oxford University Press, Oxford

Alison E, Humann M, Alison L, Tejeiro R, Ratcliff J, Christiansen P (2022) Observing rapport-based interpersonal techniques (ORBIT) to generate useful information from child sexual abuse suspects. Investig Interviewing Res Practice 12(1):22–39

Bellamy AJ (2006) No pain, no gain? Torture and ethics in the war on terror. Int Aff 82:121–148

Bloche MG (2016) Toward a science of torture. Tex Law Rev 95:1329

Bush GW (2010) Decision points. Crown.

Cobain I (2010) Iraqi Prisoners were abused at 'UK's Abu Ghraib', court hears The Guardian p.^pp. Retrieved from https://www.theguardian.com/uk/2010/nov/06/iraq-prisoner-abuse-court

Conrad CR, Conrad J, Walsh JI, Piazza JA (2016) Who tortures the terrorists?Transnational terrorism and military torture. Foreign Policy Analysis 13:761–786. https://doi.org/10.1111/fpa.12066

Costanzo M, Leo RA (2007) Research and expert testimony on interrogations and confessions Expert psychological testimony for the courts:69–98

Dreher A, Gassebner M, Siemers L-H (2010) Does terrorism threaten human rights? Evidence from panel data. J Law Econ 53:65–93

Evans JR, Meissner CA, Brandon SE, Russano MB, Kleinman SM (2010) Criminal versus HUMINT interrogations: the importance of psychological science to improving interrogative practice. J Psychiatr Law 38:215–249

Feinstein D (2014) The senate intelligence committee report on torture: committee study of the central intelligence Agency's detention and interrogation program. Melville House, Johannesburg

Gabbert F, Hope L, Luther K, Wright G, Ng M, Oxburgh G (2021) Exploring the use of rapport in professional information-gathering contexts by systematically mapping the evidence base. Appl Cogn Psychol 35(2):329–341

Gage W (2011) The Report of the Baha Mousa Inquiry. Retrieved from London

Goodman-Delahunty J (2015) Insights into investigative interviewing from practitioners and suspects in Indonesia, the Philippines and Sri Lanka International developments and practices in investigative interviewing and interrogation 2:18–33

Goodman-Delahunty J, Martschuk N, Dhami MK (2014) Interviewing high value detainees: securing cooperation and disclosures. Appl Cogn Psychol 28:883–897. https://doi.org/10.1002/acp.3087

Greenberg KJ, Dratel JL (2005) The torture papers The Road to Abu Ghraib

Hajjar L (2009) Does torture work? A sociolegal assessment of the practice in historical and global perspective. Ann Rev Law Soc Sci 5:311–345

Hohman M (2015) Motivational interviewing in social work practice. The Guilford Press, New York

Horowitz LM, Wilson KR, Turan B, Zolotsev P, Constantino MJ, Henderson L (2006) How interpersonal motives clarify the meaning of interpersonal behavior: a revised circumplex model. Personal Soc Psychol Rev 10:67–86

Humann M, Alison E, Alison L, Surmon-Böhr F, Ratcliff J, Christiansen P, Tejeiro R (2023) Motivational interviewing in child sexual abuse investigations: approaches shown to increase suspect engagement and information gathering during police interviews. Int J Police Sci Manag 14613557231167695

Joe GW, Simpson DD, Dansereau DF, Rowan-Szal GA (2001) Relationships between counseling rapport and drug abuse treatment outcomes. Psychiatr Serv 52:1223–1229. https://doi.org/10.1176/appi.ps.52.9.1223

Johnson DA, Mora A, Schmidt A (2016) The strategic costs of torture: how enhanced interrogation hurt America. Foreign Aff 95:121–132

Kassin SM, Fong CT (1999) "I'm innocent!": effects of training on judgments of truth and deception in the interrogation room. Law Hum Behav 23:499–516

Kassin SM, Gudjonsson GH (2004) The psychology of confessions: a review of the literature and issues psychological science in the. Public Interest 5:33–67

Kassin SM, Drizin SA, Grisso T, Gudjonsson GH, Leo RA, Redlich AD (2010) Police-induced confessions: risk factors and recommendations. Law Hum Behav 34:3–38

Kelly CE, Miller JC, Redlich AD, Kleinman SM (2013) A taxonomy of interrogation methods. Psychol Public Policy law 19:165–178. https://doi.org/10.1037/a0030310

Kim S, Alison L, Christiansen P (2020) Observing rapport-based interpersonal techniques to gather information from victims. Psychol Public Policy Law 26(2):166

Leary T (1958) Interpersonal diagnosis of personality. Am J Phys Med Rehabil 37:331

Lerner MJ, Simmons CH (1966) Observer's reaction to the "innocent victim": compassion or rejection? J Pers Soc Psychol 4:203–210

Masip J, Alonso H, Garrido E, Antón C (2005) Generalized communicative suspicion (GCS) among police officers: accounting for the investigator bias effect 1. J Appl Soc Psychol 35: 1046–1066

McCauley C (2009) War versus criminal justice in response to terrorism: the losing logic of torture. In: Stritzke WGK (ed) Terrorism and torture: an interdisciplinary perspective. Cambridge University Press, Cambridge

McCoy A (2007) A question of torture: CIA interrogation, from the cold war to the war on terror. Metropolitan Books

McMurran M (2009) Motivational interviewing with offenders: a systematic review. Leg Criminol Psychol 14:83–100

Meissner CA, Kassin SM (2002) "He's guilty!": investigator bias in judgments of truth and deception. Law Hum Behav 26:469–480

Meissner CA, Surmon-Böhr F, Oleszkiewicz S, Alison LJ (2017) Developing an evidence-based perspective on interrogation: a review of the US government's high-value detainee interrogation group research program. Psychol Public Policy Law 23:438–457

Miller WR, Rollnick S (1991) Motivational interviewing: preparing people to change addictive behavior. Guilford Press, New York

Miller WR, Moyers TB, Ernst D, Amrhein P (2008) Manual for the motivational interviewing skill code (misc), version 2.1 substance abuse and addiction (CASAA). Univ New Mexico 8:901–904

Milne B, Shaw G, Bull R (2007) Investigative interviewing: the role of research. John Wiley & Sons, Ltd, Sussex

Mitchell JE, Harlow B (2016) Enhanced interrogation: Inside the minds and motives of the Islamic terrorists trying to destroy America. Crown Forum,

Morgan CA III, Doran A, Steffian G, Hazlett G, Southwick SM (2006) Stress-induced deficits in working memory and visuo-constructive abilities in special operations soldiers. Biol Psychiatry 60:722–729. https://doi.org/10.1016/j.biopsych.2006.04.021

Moyers TB, Miller WR, Hendrickson SM (2005) How does motivational interviewing work? Therapist interpersonal skill predicts client involvement within motivational interviewing sessions. J Consult Clin Psychol 73:590. https://doi.org/10.1037/0022-006X.73.4.59

O'Donohue W, Snipes C, Dalto G, Soto C, Maragakis A, Im S (2014) The ethics of enhanced interrogations and torture: a reappraisal of the argument. Ethics Behav 24:109–125. https://doi.org/10.1080/10508422.2013.814088

O'Mara S (2015) Why torture Doesn't work. Harvard University Press

Parker L (1972) Report of the committee of Privy Counsellors appointed to consider authorized procedures for the interrogation of persons suspected of terrorism. Retrieved from London: https://www.ncjrs.gov/pdffiles1/Digitization/30012NCJRS.pdf

Redlich AD, Kelly CE, Miller JC (2014) The who, what, and why of human intelligence gathering: self-reported measures of interrogation methods. Appl Cogn Psychol 28:817–828. https://doi.org/10.1002/acp.3040

Rejali D (2009) Torture and democracy. Princeton University Press, Princeton
Roberts KA (2011) Police interviews with terrorist suspects: Risks, ethical interviewing and procedural justice. Br J Forensic Practice 13:124–134
Russano MB, Narchet FM, Kleinman SM (2014a) Analysts, interpreters, and intelligence interrogations. Percept Insights Appl Cognitive Psychol 28:829–846. https://doi.org/10.1002/acp.3070
Russano MB, Narchet FM, Kleinman SM, Meissner CA (2014b) Structured interviews of experienced HUMINT interrogators. Appl Cogn Psychol 28:847–859. https://doi.org/10.1002/acp.3069
Seligman ME (1975) Helplessness: on depression, development, and death. A series of books in psychology. WH Freeman/Times Books/Henry Holt & Co, New York
Skinner BF (1990) The behavior of organisms: an experimental analysis. BF Skinner Foundation
Smith DJ, Small S, Gray J (1983) Police and people in London: survey of Londoners, vol 1. Policy Studies Institute, Addis Ababa
Softley P, Brown D, Forde B, Mair G, Moxon D (1980) Police interrogation: an observational study in four police stations. HM Stationery Office
Sprang G (2003) The psychological impact of isolated acts of terrorism Terrorists, victims and society: Psychological perspectives on terrorism and its consequences, pp 130–133
Stritzke WGK, Lewandowsky S (2009) The terrorism–torture link: when evil begets evil. In: Stritzke WGK, Lewandowsky S, Denemark D, Clare J, Morgan F (eds) Terrorism and torture: an interdisciplinary perspective. Cambridge University Press, New York, pp 1–17. https://doi.org/10.1017/CBO9780511581199.002
Surmon-Böhr F, Alison L, Alison E, Christiansen P (2020) The right to silence and the permission to talk: motivational interviewing and high value detainees
Vallano JP, Schreiber Compo N (2015) Rapport-building with cooperative witnesses and criminal suspects: a theoretical and empirical review psychology. Public Policy Law 21:85
Vanderhallen M, Vervaeke G (2014) Between investigator and suspect: the role of the working alliance in investigative interviewing. In: Bull R (ed) Investigative interviewing. Springer Science + Business Media, New York, pp 63–90. https://doi.org/10.1007/978-1-4614-9642-7_4
Vrij A (2004) Why professionals fail to catch liars and how they can improve. Leg Criminol Psychol 9:159–181
Vrij A, Granhag PA, Porter S (2010) Pitfalls and opportunities in nonverbal and verbal lie detection. Psychol Sci Public Interest 11:89–121. https://doi.org/10.1177/1529100610390861
Walsh D, Bull R (2012) Examining rapport in investigative interviews with suspects: does its building and maintenance work? J Police Crim Psychol 27:73–84. https://doi.org/10.1007/s11896-011-9087-x
Yakovenko I, Quigley L, Hemmelgarn BR, Hodgins DC, Ronksley P (2015) The efficacy of motivational interviewing for disordered gambling: systematic review and meta-analysis. Addict Behav 43:72–82. https://doi.org/10.1016/j.addbeh.2014.12.011

Cases

Hadman v. Rumsfeld, Secretary of Defence, judgment 19 June 2006., https://supreme.justia.com/cases/federal/us/548/557/. Accessed 16 Apr 2023
Haidar Ali Hussein v. Secretary of State for Defence, judgment 1 February 2013. https://www.judiciary.uk/wp-content/uploads/JCO/Documents/Judgments/hussein-secretary-state-defence-judgment-01022013.pdf. Accessed 16 Apr 2023
Maher Arar v. Ashcroft et al, judgment 30 June 2008., https://law.justia.com/cases/federal/appellate-courts/ca2/06-4216/06-4216-cv-20w-20errata-2011-03-27.html Accessed 16 April 2023

Dr Frances Surmon-Böhr is a research associate at the University of Liverpool and a consultant psychologist and ORBIT trainer at Protagoras Forensic Services. Her primary research area is investigative interviewing/interrogation and rapport-based communication. Frances completed her PhD in 2020 which was supervised by Prof. Laurence Alison and examined rapport-based interviewing approaches with High Value Suspects. She has worked on numerous research projects funded by U.K. Ministry of Defense and the U.S. High Value Detainee Interrogation Group where she was involved in the design, development, analysis and write-up of research projects relating the application of the ORBIT model of interviewing in various interviewing/interrogation contexts. As part of this work, she has observed and coded large numbers of UK police interviews with terrorists, covering a range of ideologies including Al Qaeda, Right-wing and ISIS. She is actively involved in the development, planning, delivery and evaluation of training programs for a range of law enforcement and intelligence gathering contexts. She has provided interview training to FBI/CIA/DoD, The UK National Counter Terrorism interviewing cadre, UK Military Joint Forces Intelligence unit, UK Border Force and The International Committee for the Red Cross, in the ORBIT communication framework. Before starting her PhD, she worked in secure psychiatric settings.

Professor Laurence Alison MBE is Director of Critical and Major Incident (CAMI) Research at the Department of Psychology, University of Liverpool. CAMI focuses on high profile critical and major incidents (from disaster management to terrorism). Prof. Alison has over 28 years of experience working on applied projects for law enforcement and the security services. This has enabled him and his team to conduct high quality rigorous research that has made a difference to practitioners ‘at the coalface’ and that transfers to training. His work has helped change policy, practice and procedure at both a national and international level. He has an international reputation and several high-profile publications on the subject of investigation, decision making and the psychological processes relevant to critical incidents. He currently provides training to FBI/CIA/DoD, The UKs National CT interviewing cadre and the British Army in the ORBIT framework for rapport-based interrogation methods. He was key psychological advisor on over 450 critical and major incidents debriefs including the 7/7 bombings, the Sharm El Sheik attacks, the poisoning of Alexander Litvinenko and the preparations for the London Olympics. He has over 200 published articles, books, edited books and government and industry reports. Prof. Alison was awarded an MBE in the Queen’s New Year Honours list 2020 for services to critical incident handling and to the NHS during COVID-19.

Emily Alison is a research associate at the University of Liverpool and the managing director of Protagoras Forensic Services and Interventions Ltd. She has worked as a behavioural consultant psychologist for the last 20 years, providing treatment in both the criminal justice sector and in the community. Emily specialises in the assessment and treatment of violence and has worked with over 850 domestic violence perpetrators as well as designed therapeutic interventions for Domestic Abuse, Child to Parent Violence, Healthy Relationships for Children and Young People, Sexually Harmful Behaviour and Sexual Risk Taking in Adolescents, and Gang and Weapon linked offending. For the last 12 years, she has also been a research associate with the University of Liverpool and has been involved in the development of the Preventing Violent Extremism Tool for profiling potential extremism and the ORBIT framework for Advanced High Value Detainee Interviewing. As part of this research, she has observed over 500 hours of UK police interviews with terrorist suspects covering a range of ideologies including Al Qaeda, Right-wing, and ISIS as well as child sex offender suspects. She is the co-creator of the ORBIT interviewing model and lead ORBIT trainer, designing and delivering training for a range of organisations globally including FBI/CIA/DoD, The UK National Counter Terrorism interviewing cadre, National Crime Agency, UK Military Joint Forces Intelligence unit, UK Border Force and UK War Crimes teams.

Chapter 7
Appreciative Inquiry: Mobilising Potentials Within Police Organisations to Realise Human Rights

Walter Suntinger and Moritz Birk

Contents

Abstract Deficit-orientation is still the default mode used to analyse and seek change of the social world, including in police organisations and in human rights practice. This contribution outlines the basic elements of a strength and resource-oriented look at furthering human rights realisation by the police, with the specific focus on the approach and method of Appreciative Inquiry. In line with systemic thinking, Appreciative Inquiry is widely used for organisational research and development in different areas. Social scientific research has shown Appreciative Inquiry to be successful in mobilising positive energy leading to desired change. The examples of its use in police trainings described in this contribution clearly highlight its potential to refocus attention on what already works well in police practice and

W. Suntinger (✉)
University of Applied Arts Vienna, Wien, Austria
e-mail: walter.suntinger@uni-ak.ac.at

M. Birk
Amnesty International, Vienna, Austria
e-mail: moritz.birk@protonmail.com

R. Alleweldt (ed.), *Fair Treatment of Persons in Police Custody*,
https://doi.org/10.1007/978-3-031-61737-9_7

how success stories can be harnessed to further strengthen police work in line with human rights standards.

7.1 Introduction: Context and Objectives

It is nowadays a truism to state that the biggest challenge in human rights is the "implementation gap," the gulf between human rights norms standards and the reality on the ground. How do we translate the seemingly lofty human rights into concrete practice on a daily basis? This question has been accompanying us since we have started our work in the field of human rights. And it has led us to search for new ways of thinking and acting with a view to effectively closing this gap, again: with a view to translating human rights norms into reality.

Some of the results of this attempt are contained in our publication showing the benefits of "systemic approaches to human rights practice."[1] Systems thinking[2] has proved to be useful for increasing both effectiveness and proper functioning of many organisations, in particular in the business sector. It consists of a set of scientifically well-grounded concepts which help explain and shape the social world and—equally important for practical implementation purposes—it provides a practical tool box for intervention.

In which way can systemic thinking help human rights practice?

We argue that human rights practice is still dominated by traditional epistemic approaches, in particular law-centred, often legalistic ones. Human rights are laid down as laws and, thus, lawyers obviously (must) play a big role. Many direct duty-bearers come from the executive branch, located in bureaucratic and legally structured systems, such as the police. Legal thinking is strongly determined by linear causal thinking; rightly so, as acts or omissions must be imputable to a person in order to impose penalties and other measures; that is, the causal link between act and actor has to be established. This perspective is necessary, but not sufficient for coming to grips with the challenges involved in human rights practice. As trained lawyers we believe that it requires a complementary thinking which allows to understand the broader picture of human interaction and life.

Systems thinking, we argue, provides for this broader perspective. It offers, first, a plausible theory of the social world and, second, a variety of tools for effecting sustainable change.[3] Developed in systemic consulting practice, these concepts and tools can very successfully enhance the impact of any social activity, including human rights practice. Systemic thinking is a vast field, and we do not have the space to present it here. So we confine ourselves to some general remarks. Systems

[1] Birk and Suntinger (2019).

[2] We use the terms "systemic" and "systems" thinking interchangeably.

[3] Birk and Suntinger (2019).

thinking produces a true shift in mindset, view and attention. If you adopt a systemic lens, you will never see the world in the same way as before. What, then, is different when you apply systemic thinking?

1. You know that there is no objective knowledge, but that any knowledge is subjectively constructed. "*Everything said is said by someone.*"[4] Constructivism thereby rejects the commonly held idea of the ability of objective observation and, thus, separating things neatly into true or false. In practical terms, this constructivist outlook means that we have to accept one crucial thing: multi-perspectivity. One's position and perspective is only *one* among many perspectives.
2. You understand that complexity, circular causality and unpredictability characterise (social) life. We commonly think: "If I do A—B happens." Instead, cybernetics assumes that things always occur in a "*reciprocal feedback loop*"[5] where cause and effect become indistinguishable: cause is always effect and effect is always cause. Adapting *Watzlawick's* famous example of a relationship between partners: one says: "I withdraw because you nag" and the other: "I nag because you withdraw," their behaviour becoming both the trigger and feedback within the communication.[6]
3. You accept that living systems (individuals and organisations) have a life of their own. They are autonomous, autopoietic and self-determined systems, not machines.[7] Thus, they cannot be controlled and changed directly from the outside. However, in order to ensure a necessary degree of stability and efficiency, individuals learn to trivialise themselves to some degree in a system to become more predictable, by adhering to certain established rules, codes and agreements. In other words, systems develop patterns of communication to maintain stability and reduce complexity.

Box 7.1 Systemic thinking in a nutshell
The following "systemic principles"[8] can serve as guides for the practical application of systems thinking:

(continued)

[4] Maturana and Varela (1992), p. 27.

[5] Seliger (2014), pp. 54 et seq.

[6] Watzlawick et al. (1967), p. 56.

[7] For a summary, see Seliger (2014), pp. 59 et seq., building on the foundational work of Chilean biologists Maturana and Varela (1992).

[8] This version of the ten systemic principles is taken from Suntinger and Birk (2021), where they are applied to preventive monitoring of places of detention. For a first presentation in a broader form, see Birk and Suntinger (2019), pp. 659–663.

Box 7.1 (continued)

1. Begin with the end in mind, developing a concrete image of the desired future.
2. Look at the whole picture instead of focusing only on parts and elements.
3. See relations and connections instead of singular events.
4. Engage with complexity and circularity: causes as effects and effects as causes.
5. Seek actively and integrate different viewpoints and multiple perspectives.
6. Look at the "bottom of the iceberg" and understand underlying cultural patterns.
7. Look at failures in the system, not in persons.
8. Look at resources and strengths, not only deficits.
9. Look for entry points and connections, while recognising the limits of intervention.
10. Include ongoing reflection and self-reflection.

In this article we focus specifically on the slogan "Look at resources and strengths, not only deficits." The slogan builds on the idea that strengths and resources can be used to support and sustain desired change processes.

This refocusing, this shift of mind, constitutes a move away from a deficit-oriented view which still dominates much of contemporary thinking. Deficit-orientation is still the default mode of the social world, and this includes both police and human rights work.

In line with this assumption, the objective of this contribution is to outline the basic elements of a strength and resource-oriented look at human rights realisation by police, i.e. the method of "Appreciative Inquiry," and present some initial thoughts and possible ways forward for exploring and testing out of such an approach.

We start with a brief presentation of the approach of and basic principles underlying Appreciative Inquiry (Section 7.2), we then present—as the main part—how this approach can be applied in endeavours to strengthen human rights in the field of policing, with specific reference to the International Police conference—where we tried it out (Section 7.3), and end with some tentative conclusions as well as proposals for the way forward (Section 7.4).

It is important to bear in mind that this is our first attempt to develop this type of thinking and, thus, has its obvious limitations. It is informed by the lived experience of the authors, but is not based on explicit empirical research.

7.2 Appreciative Inquiry

"Appreciative Inquiry" (AI)[9] is one of the most popular approaches to organisational research and development that take resource-orientation seriously. AI is located within the broader context of the burgeoning field known as "positive organizational studies" and the "strength-based" movement.[10] Developed in the 1980s at the Case Western Reserve University in Cleveland, Ohio, as an action research method, its basic assumptions are simple:

1. Every organisation has something that works well.
2. Systems and organisations develop in the direction which is the focus of attention or "inquiry."
3. If strengths, resources and potentials are brought into the focus of attention and appreciatively identified, organisations will develop in this direction.
4. This benefits all and has great mobilising power, strongly needed in the face of obstacles and hindrances.

7.2.1 A Practice-Oriented Definition of Appreciative Inquiry

Appreciative Inquiry is both a very specific look at and a useful tool for transforming social reality, based on a firm social scientific grounding.[11] In the words of the pioneers of this approach:

> Appreciative Inquiry is the cooperative co-evolutionary search for the best in people, their organizations, and the world around them. It involves the discovery of what gives 'life' to a living system when it is most effective, alive, and constructively capable in economic, ecological, and human terms. AI involves the art and practice of asking questions that strengthen a system's capacity to apprehend, anticipate, and heighten positive potential. The inquiry is mobilized through the crafting of the 'unconditional positive question', often involving hundreds or thousands of people. AI interventions focus on the speed of imagination and innovation instead of the negative, critical, and spiralling diagnoses commonly used in organizations. The discovery, dream, design, and destiny model links the energy of the positive core to changes never thought possible.[12]

This is a very helpful description of AI and elements of it will be visible throughout the following parts of this paper.

---

[9] See Cooperrider and Whitney (2005), Cooperider et al. (2008), Whitney and Trosten-Bloom (2010).

[10] Bushe (2011), p. 87.

[11] See ibid. and Whitney and Trosten-Bloom (2010), pp. 49–51.

[12] Cooperider et al. (2008), p. 3.

7.2.2 Settings/Types of Use

Appreciative inquiry can take different forms, ranging from the use of the Appreciative Inquiry Interview to a whole-scale organisational change process.

The Appreciative Inquiry interview is at the heart of any AI application and therefore a natural starting point for showing its logic. It is a one-and-one interview, an exercise in story-telling, of positive experiences of the past, the identification of individual and collective strengths and potentials that we have in the present as well as a bold look at how these strengths can be used for achieving a positive future image. Two persons interview each other along some fairly standardised questions (that can be adapted to the concrete situation):[13]

1. Describe a time in your organisation that you consider a high point experience, a time when you were most engaged and felt alive and vibrant.
2. Without being modest, tell me what it is that you most value about yourself, your work, and your organisation.
3. What are the core factors that give life to your organisation when it is at its best?
4. Imagine your organisation ten years from now, when everything is just as you always wished it could be. What is different? How have you contributed to this dream organisation?

These interview questions structure a movement: from the positive past to the experience of strengths and life-giving core factors in the present on to concrete visions of a positive future.

Box 7.2 Appreciative Inquiry—4D Model

This basic movement (past-present-future) also guides broader designs of AI-based change processes. AI's standard whole-scale change process is known as the 4D Model, which is "now almost universally described as *the* AI method."[14] It consists of four stages:

1. Discovery: on the basis of an AI interview, participants identify the positive and the life-giving factors: "the best of what is."
2. Dream: Participants co-create a results-oriented concrete vision for a given social system: "What might be."

   In addition, and in order to make the vision concrete on the basis of existing resources and strengths, the movement moves back to present.
3. Design: Participants create concrete propositions/thinking guidelines for shaping the organisation: "What should be."

(continued)

[13] Cooperrider and Whitney (2005), p. 14.

[14] Bushe (2011), p. 88.

Box 7.2 (continued)

4. Destiny: Participants develop concrete action of implementation: "What will be."

Application of this 4D Model of AI obviously varies. Many formats include what is known as an AI-Summit, an ambitious whole-scale change design which might spread over several days and which brings the different stakeholders from all parts of the system in a forum for learning.

Of these two basic uses of AI, this contribution focuses on the basic form, the AI interview and its potentials for getting change going. It is the most flexible form of use found in a variety of contexts and probably often done in a superficial way.[15] We find this quality of easy and flexible adaptation of AI interviews to different settings a particular asset of the method, in particular when working in the bureaucratic government sector where broader reform and change processes are difficult to get going. On the other hand, in order to understand how to apply AI in a sound way, we agree that it is necessary to have a firm grasp of the underlying concepts and principles. If not, the application of AI might not work out. "A fool with a tool is still a fool." This saying used in systemic consulting circles encapsulates the danger of applying tools without proper grounding.

7.2.3 Principles of Appreciative Inquiry

In the following, we present five principles which are widely accepted as the conceptual basis of Appreciative Inquiry.[16] They are in line with the ideas and slogans of systemic thinking as outlined above.

The five principles are:

1. The constructionist principle:[17] AI grew out of social constructionism as developed by, i.e. Kenneth Gergen.[18] All social reality is constructed; human knowledge and social life are interwoven. "Words create worlds"[19] is often used as a slogan to succinctly express this principle. Reality is constructed through language and communication. This means that attention is shifted from the

---

[15] See the critique in Fry (2008), p. VIII.

[16] See Bushe (2011), pp. 89 et seq.

[17] A note on terminology: The term "social constructionism" is widely used in the US social science tradition, while the term "constructivism" is more generally employed in epistemology. There is convergence on basic points of practical relevance for our purpose.

[18] Gergen (2001).

[19] Whitney and Trosten-Bloom (2010), p. 51.

individual to relationships, connections and communication. "From cogito ergo sum to communicamos ergo sum."[20]

2. The simultaneity principle: Inquiry is at the same time intervention into a given system, in line with the constructionist perspective. Inquiry and intervention are inseparable and intertwined. What you ask about produces at the same time changes. Questions are the essential element of the inquiry. Good questions might bring to light new things and change your whole perspective (e.g. in so-called "Aha" moments). There is broad evidence of this in particular in therapeutic settings. In a broader sense, this principle says: whatever we do and say has an effect.
3. The poetic principle: Rather than being machines, organisations are dynamic living systems, they are like "open books."[21] Much of life in living systems is expressed in stories, told in the kitchen and on the corridors. These stories are co-authored. What kind of stories are told and shared is important. AI helps to unearth positive stories of achievement and high energy moments.
4. The anticipatory principle: Images of the future guide and inspire present-day actions.[22] "Much like a movie projector on a screen, human systems are forever projecting a horizon of expectations ahead of themselves."[23] Creating positive images, showing potentials and elaborating possibilities helps organisations achieve concrete results. It belongs to the most important aspects of any change process. Existing research, including image theory, clearly supports this.[24]
5. The positive principle: A search for the positive leads to positive change and better relations. As AI practitioners know from experience, the focus on the positive tends to produce positive affect and emotions and strengthens relationships and social bonding. It thus enhances energy and amplifies the positive core, the existing wisdom, successful strategies, positive attitudes and affect, skills, resources and capabilities.[25]

As experienced by AI practitioners and supported by scientific research, AI has clear benefits:

- It allows identification of new aspects of reality which have previously not been seen, the positive ones. Thus, it helps draw a more complete picture of the social reality.
- It helps create a positive self-image grounded in actual experience ("the high points").
- This, in turn, can lead to enhancing positive emotions and energy for effecting desired change.

[20] Cooperrider and Whitney (2005), p. 50.

[21] Ibid., 51.

[22] Whitney and Trosten-Bloom (2010), p. 60.

[23] Cooperrider and Whitney (2005), p. 52.

[24] For a discussion, see Whitney and Trosten-Bloom (2010), p. 49.

[25] Ibid., p. 64.

- More generally, research has found that AI works because it helps liberate positive power through a set of facilitating conditions which revolve around freedom, the so-called "Six Freedoms":[26] freedom to be known in relationship, freedom to be heard, freedom to dream in community, freedom to choose to contribute, freedom to act with support, freedom to be positive.

7.2.4 *Use of Appreciative Inquiry to Strengthen Human Rights*

Considering the immense potential benefits of Appreciative Inquiry, we have attempted to explore this tool to increase effectiveness in our human rights work. We are following in the steps of other actors. For example, the Office of High Commissioner for Human Rights (OHCHR) has recommended the method of Appreciative Inquiry to enhance knowledge sharing as a "a method of organizational development that engages all levels of an organization (and its stakeholders) in its renewal, change and improved performance."[27] Moreover, the former UN Secretary General Kofi Annan stated:

> I would like to commend you more particularly for your methodology of Appreciative Inquiry and to thank you for introducing it to the United Nations. Without this, it would have been very difficult, perhaps even impossible, to constructively engage so many leaders of business, civil society, and government.[28]

Appreciative inquiry has also been used in NGO-contexts and for community and societal projects, including the development field.[29]

Moreover, the method has been used in prison research in order to analyse the work of prison officers and the importance of staff-prisoner relationships. In their ground-breaking work, Liebling, Price and Elliot illustrate the use of AI to study relationships in a maximum-security prison in the UK. They used AI to move away from a "problem-centred" to an "empathetic approach" assuming that it "might have particular value in a sensitive and beleaguered organization in which staff often felt at the receiving end of sometimes vague criticism."[30] The approach seeks not to deny the problems in prisons but to specifically look at the positive realities, resources, imaginations of staff and prisoners shifting the focus from deficits to accomplishments and achievements. In this sense it was used as a method of action research, fostering at the same time self-confidence, energy and faith as a creative

[26] Ibid., pp. 270 et seq. The six freedoms are most clearly present in broader change processes, based on the AI 4D cycle.

[27] Office of the High Commissioner of Human Rights (2011) p. 22.

[28] Former United Nations Secretary General Kofi Annan, speaking to the United Nations Leaders' Summit in mid-2004. Ibid., p. 22.

[29] See examples in Cooperider et al. (2008) and Elliot (1999).

[30] Liebling et al. (1999), p. 75.

and future oriented process.[31] The tool used was a "lightly structured talk," conducted in a narrative form to induce storytelling. It was based on an appreciative protocol with generative questions that were not followed strictly but were "designed to move and hold the interviewee in appreciative mode while a particular topic is explored."[32]

The researchers found that prison staff interviewed responded enthusiastically to unconditional positive regard, and that the AI approach turned out to be very effective to earn trust, generate open communication and stimulate cooperation and interest.[33] Yet, although the researchers felt that they had "broken new ground," the method also had its restrictions. The strong tendency towards negativity and despair limited the imaginative horizons of the participants. Thus, within the limited frame of this research, the full transformative potential as a method of action research remained underexplored.[34] Nevertheless the researchers concluded that the method "opened doors to data and interpretations that may have remained firmly shut in other research environments, and it clearly made a significant difference to the way at least some prison officers conceived of their role." Considering the effects it had on prison officers they hold the opinion that "as an instrument for change, the possibilities are endless."[35]

Their other findings highlighted the importance of prisoner-staff relationships and pointed out that the important "*peacekeeping work*" ("negotiating peaceful co-existence") of prison staff is "under-valued, under-theorized and under-estimated."[36] They explained this, inter alia, with the fact that the work of a prison officer is usually considered as successful if it is quiet and nothing happens. However, the authors rightly emphasise that the work of resolving and avoiding conflict should not be seen as omissions but as acts requiring considerable skill.[37] There are clear parallels to the work of police officers who also hold an unusual amount of power which is most of the time held in reserve. Rather than their mere law enforcement, police work is about their peacekeeping function achieved through conversations, mediating and deescalating.[38] But this role is often overlooked, and police often complain about a lack of recognition or even hostile behaviour[39] by citizens as their work is often criticised by NGOs, the media and in the public discourse.

[31] Ibid., p. 76.

[32] Ibid., p. 79—with a copy of the protocol used.

[33] Ibid., p. 89.

[34] Ibid., pp. 91–92.

[35] Ibid., p. 92.

[36] Ibid., pp. 90–91.

[37] Ibid., p. 81.

[38] For an overview, see Reiner (2015).

[39] See, e.g. reports from Germany stating that attacks on police officers have risen by 22% from 2013 to 2017: FAZ, Gewalt gegen Polizisten nimmt zu, 24.08.2018, https://www.faz.net/aktuell/politik/inland/angriffe-auf-beamte-gewalt-gegen-polizisten-nimmt-zu-15754577.html (last accessed on 29 April 2023).

7.3 Application in Police Context

7.3.1 Trying It Out

Inspired by the promising potential and experiences in similar contexts we were eager to test the potential of this method to strengthen human rights performance of police organisations. Two experiences of application are shown in this section.

Since the conference and the drafting of this article highly interesting research has been published on the use and value of appreciative inquiry in police research, particularly in police ethnography, including in the Global South.[40] The subtitle of one publication "Appreciative Inquiry in ethnography for understanding and transforming policing" points to the double value of this methodological approach: First, it can contribute to knowledge production about policing at a global scale. Second, it can help "co-create positive changes in the policing field."[41]

7.3.1.1 The Berlin Conference

We are very grateful to the organisers of the International Conference "Fair Treatment of Persons in Police Custody" to have given us the opportunity to present the method and try it out in a workshop to "mobilise potentials within police organizations to realize human rights." The workshop brought together conference participants and police students of the Brandenburg State Police University who had already made practical experiences in police operations. After a short introduction to the method of Appreciative Inquiry and its benefits we separated the participants in groups. Police officers and police students were asked to interview each other and inquire in an appreciative, resource-oriented manner on their experiences in protecting fundamental rights during police work. They were asked to listen patiently without judging the answers or assuming than one already knew what the other person was about to say and adopt an open-minded attitude, curious to learn new things. The participants who were not police officers acted as observers and had to keep time of the interviews, listen and take notes. Four questions were asked (see guiding questions below).

The first one inquired about the students' past and the reason behind the decision to become a police officer. This was supposed to bring back the possible "magic of the beginning," the fascination for the job. Not surprisingly, but important to note, most students actually wanted to become police officers in order to serve and protect others and ensure a safe and secure society. The protection of the human rights of persons thus showed to be a key driver for the job choice of police officers. It was also precisely this close work with people and the feeling of serving society that was

[40] Jardine and van Dijk (2023); Jardine (2023), Jardine (2020) Skinns et al. (2022).

[41] Jardine and van Dijk (2023), p. 320.

described as a key element that "connects" the students to the job and the police organisation.

The second question aimed at specifically inquiring about the positive experience in police work to protect fundamental rights. The students were asked to recount a "highpoint experience" in their work. While the challenge in this part of the interview is the willingness of participants to get involved as well as to be concrete enough and not move into generalisations,[42] the participants all managed to find an example from their recent practical experience and describe why it was so valuable to them. The experiences referred to complex situations from intervening in a domestic violence case to handling a person with a mental impairment and showed the high sensitivity and professionalism police officers need to apply in their daily work.

With questions three and four, students were led to take closer look at their own value and strengths they bring to work as well as the greatest strength of their organisation in respecting and protecting human dignity.

Questions for the interview:

1. Please remember the start of your career as police officer:
   - What attracted you to select this profession?
   - What do still like the most about it nowadays?
2. Think about a situation in your work as police that you consider a highpoint experience/where you felt you did a truly good job (in respecting and/or protecting human dignity) of which you are still proud and feel positive about.
   - What was the situation?
   - Who was involved?
   - What was your role in it? What difference were you able to make?
   - What does this situation still make particularly valuable for you?
3. In the light of this experience and without modesty: describe what do you value most about yourself? What are your most salient strengths and gifts that you bring to your work?
4. Where is your organisation at its best in respecting and protecting human dignity?

In the plenary discussion many police students readily shared that they found the exercise not easy because they were not used to specifically focus on their resources and strengths. They stated that there was a general "complaint culture" in the police force with the focus on what works badly. Some said that they only received

[42] See Liebling (1999), p. 80.

feedback when they did something wrong and the coverage from the outside, e.g. by the media or from human rights organisations, is experienced as overwhelmingly negative. Therefore, they described the exercise as a very valuable new experience that generated positive energy and brought to light the many strengths and potentials of the police in protecting human dignity. The participants specifically mentioned their communication skills as a highlight, treating everyone as a human being with respect and empathy. Moreover, the motivation to protect others, the victim, the offender, their colleagues and themselves is always described as the priority. They also commended the strong comradery among their colleagues, working together, looking out for each other.

In the final discussions and the anonymous feedback forms the exercise was recognised as useful to identify what already works well and how to build on that. It showed that Appreciative Inquiry can motivate police officers to reflect on the issue of policing and human rights and promote positive attitudes and to see the work of the police as an organisation to protect human rights. The method makes visible that human rights are always a key issue in police work. The students recommended repeating the exercise with police officers that have served for longer time. While for new recruits the thought of having joined the police force to protect and secure (including the learnings from the human rights courses) is still present, this may fade out after decades of serving, and officers may become unaware of the possibilities and potentials they have to react to in their daily work. For longer serving police officers, the reminder of the "magic of the beginning" may be specifically powerful and the positive focus specifically energising and liberating. Some even recommended to consider doing such exercise with new and experienced officers to exchange different perspectives on work, learn from each other (across generations and fields) and strengthen the companionship/solidarity among "young and old" and across departments.

7.3.1.2 Trainings of Austrian Police Officers

The context of this case of application of Appreciative Inquiry is the following:[43] Austrian street police officers who get promoted to the first management rank undergo a six months classroom training, spread over a period of nine months, including intermittent practice phases. One of the modules is a two and a half days training workshop on human rights. Its broad objectives are: (1) A sound understanding of the role of police with regard to human rights, including its positive role as protector of human rights; (2) A sound understanding of basic concepts of human rights and structures/mechanisms to realise them; (3) Analytical skills in applying human rights to concrete cases of police practice; and (4) Self-critical reflection on basic assumptions, including stereotypes. The trainings are held by an experienced police trainer in tandem with an external person active in the human rights field,

[43] See https://www.bmi.gv.at/104/Beruf_und_Karriere/start.aspx#e2a (accessed on 29 April 2023).

including one of the authors, Walter Suntinger. Designs of the human rights module are in a constant state of development. Recently, and as a consequence of the above-described Berlin workshop, an AI interview exercise was introduced in the afternoon of the first day. Prior to this exercise, participants will have expressed their expectations, had a first discussion of relevant human rights issues, including on the basis of a discussion of articles in current newspapers, and an exposition of the basics of human rights. In particular, they will know that police work is essentially human rights work, if they take the state obligation to protect seriously and to its logical end. [44] The prime example for showing this is domestic violence. This first positive reframing of police in light of human rights sets a positive and—at the same time—a more complete frame for the training.

The exercise of Appreciative Inquiry is a continuation of this approach. The basic setting is similar to the one described above. (1) Participants (regularly around 30) are asked to interview each other in pairs along the questions above, slightly adapted; (2) In a subsequent discussion in groups of 6 (3 pairs), participants are asked to share their story if they want (participants are free not to do so) and choose 2 or 3 stories to share in the plenary; (3) In the final plenary discussion, participants listen to the stories, discuss their human rights implication and are asked to share their learning from the exercise.

The following is an anecdotal description of some major results that are related to the above characteristics of AI. It is based on our own observation of the process and persons involved, but also on oral and written feedback given by co-trainers and participants. The themes of the stories shared can be broadly categorised along the human rights obligations to respect, protect and fulfil the most basic rights, the rights to physical integrity and the right to life. Police officers expressed satisfaction about professionally carrying out an action involving the use of force and leading to the arrest of suspects, while strictly abiding by the principle of proportionality and caring for persons injured in a professional way. Often mentioned are stories where police intervened in situations of domestic violence: protecting the victims of domestic violence, while keeping calm and respecting the rights of the perpetrator, and at the same time caring for children present. Furthermore, stories about their action to prevent suicides through determined action and/or empathic communication appear frequently in the stories told.

The most important strengths of police officers that become visible in these interviews are: courage, determination, empathy, firm sense of humanity, professionalism and negotiation/communication skills.

Reflections on the exercise tend to highlight the following:

- New aspects of their work become visible. "Interesting, we have understood new things" or "wow, we had never seen this before."
- However, looking at the positive aspects constitutes a challenge for many people in a job that is so much concerned with the difficult aspects of social life.

[44] See, in detail, Suntinger (2018), pp. 297–298.

- The positive emotions that accompany telling their story and the subsequent discussion in the plenary are strongly felt.
- Discussions revolve around the way in which such positive story-telling[45] can be integrated in daily practice.

The positive image of police as a professional actor for protecting and respecting human rights seems to be clearly strengthened.

7.3.2 Possible Uses

Based on these experiences, we draw the conclusion that Appreciative Inquiry can be useful to strengthen police organisations in different ways. This conclusion is strongly supported by the recently published research mentioned above (see FN 40).

First, it bears great potential **for organisational development**. It can be used by leaders in staff talks and meetings to enquire about the resources and promising practices in the organisation in order to build on as well as to motivate staff to learn and grow. It can equally be a very helpful tool for external consultants to gather valuable information and develop options for organisational reform. It can be a helpful element of police training and an instrument for police engagement with the community.[46]

In a similar way it can be a strong tool of **research** to find out about the resources and strengths in police organisations—what actually works and really matters—and thus bring to light new elements otherwise uncovered. As mentioned, and in keeping with the above-mentioned principles of Appreciative Inquiry, in particular the simultaneity principles, the research can itself lead to positive change and thus has transformational potential.[47] Moreover, Appreciative Inquiry has proved to be helpful in getting access to the field[48] and to create an environment of trust between the researcher and those being involved in the research. Specifically in settings such as prisons or police organisations there exists a certain caution or resistance to cooperate with researchers out of fear of being criticised. This could be overcome by the consistent focus on resources and the positive offered by the Appreciative Inquiry method.

---

[45] On the fundamental importance of story-telling in police, see Waddington (1999).

[46] For example, the Appreciative Inquiry event in Cheetham Hill, UK brought together 130 persons to hear their positive experiences from living in the community, what is important from them and what they expect from policing. Reportedly it was a very successful way to learn from and engage with citizens while sending the message that the police cares about their views, problems and need. See: https://www.youtube.com/watch?time_continue=118&v=glSHbM2WxzI (last accessed on 29 April 2023).

[47] Jardine and van Dijk (2023), summarising existing research.

[48] Jardine (2020), pp. 191 et seq., Skinns et al. (2022), p. 4.

This trust-building can also be very useful for **monitoring** police institutions. Indeed, we specifically recommend Appreciative Inquiry as a useful tool for National Preventive Mechanisms mandated to monitor places of detention and prevent torture and ill-treatment.[49] Our own experience using it in monitoring have shown that a positive framing is positively received by the authorities who are showing an increasing "monitoring fatigue," being served the same findings and recommendations again and again.[50] Furthermore, the same conclusions as for research and organisational development apply for monitors who, with the help of Appreciative Inquiry, can identify strengths and resources in the system and make recommendations and support police organisations to achieve change.

7.4 Challenges in the Application of Appreciative Inquiry

Despite the great potential of Appreciative Inquiry one should not ignore the challenges in its application.[51] These challenges are partly intrinsic in the use of AI in general, partly they result from the specific field of application: human rights within police.

First, it is important to consider AI not as magic cure but just as a possible tool among many. We want to emphasise that we believe that it is most useful if it is strategically embedded in the given context and used as part of an overall systemic approach to human rights and police work.

One of the common critiques is that Appreciative Inquiry might invalidate negative experiences.[52] This would of course be particularly problematic in the area of human rights if it meant ignoring or not taking seriously human rights violations and its victims. In line with a strategic approach, the use of AI needs to be clearly and critically reflected and balanced with other tools.

This might also mean that it would not be feasible in certain circumstances, particularly in situation of crisis and massive human rights violations. It may simply be unsuitable, unjustified or send a wrong message to focus on the positive in such an environment. At the same time, in situations of despair, Appreciative Inquiry may be the only way out of the negative and to find solutions. Like with other interventions and methods, it is also important to consider the cultural setting in which AI is used.[53] Moreover, the benefit of this method presupposes a general willingness of

---

[49] Suntinger and Birk (2021), pp. 36–37; Birk and Suntinger (2019), p. 674.

[50] Birk et al. (2015), p 16; Suntinger and Birk (2021).

[51] For a discussion of the limitations of AI in policing ethnography, see Jardine and van Dijk (2023), p. 330. These points strongly overlap with ours.

[52] Bushe (2011), p. 96.

[53] For a Southern Policing perspective, see the highly interesting work of Jardine (2020) and Jardine (2023) on policing in Vietnam. She provides "a theoretical framework to understand how variations in police cultures, practices and socialization occur in a distinctly non-Western context." Jardine (2020), p. 188.

the authorities to improve and to undertake genuine efforts to strengthen human rights.

7.5 Conclusion

In conclusion, we strongly believe in the potential of Appreciative Inquiry for understanding and transforming police work. The anecdotal results of our practical training approach are supported by thorough empirical research of policing. AI can be used in in numerous ways and different contexts: internally and by external consultants, by trainers, researchers and monitors. It may not always be easy but if carefully reflected and skilfully embedded in the right context it will usually yield promising results and steer an organisation towards positive change. We believe it is worth for different actors and in different situations to have the courage to try it out, and we are committed to continue to explore it as a key tool for systemic change management in our human rights practice. The question of the founders of Appreciative Inquiry seems pertinent also in the field of police: "What would happen to our change practices if we began all our work with the positive presumption that organizations, as centers of human relatedness, are alive with infinite constructive capacity?"[54]

References

Birk M, Suntinger W (2019) A systemic approach to human rights practice. In: Hladschik P, Steinert F (eds) Making human rights work. Neuer Wissenschaftlicher Verlag, Vienna

Birk M, Zach G, Suntinger W, Long D, Murray R (2015) Enhancing impact of national preventive mechanisms. Ludwig Boltzmann Institute of Human Rights/University of Bristol, Vienna

Bushe G (2011) Appreciative inquiry. Theory and critique. In: Boje D, Burnes B, Hassard J (eds) The Routledge companion to organizational change. Routledge, Oxford, pp 87–103

Cooperider D, Whitney D, Stavros J (2008) Appreciative inquiry handbook. For leader of change, 2nd edn. Crown Custom Publisher, Brunswick

Cooperrider D, Whitney D (2005) Appreciative inquiry. A positive revolution in change. Berret-Koehler Publishers, San Francisco

Elliot C (1999) Locating the energy for change: an introduction to appreciative inquiry. International Institute for Sustainable Development, Winnipeg

Fry R (2008) Foreword. In: Cooperider D, Whitney D, Stavros J (eds) Appreciative inquiry handbook. For leader of change, 2nd edn. Crown Custom Publisher, Brunswick, pp VI–X

Gergen KJ (2001) Social construction in action. Sage Publications, London/Thousand Oaks/New Delhi

Jardine M (2020) A Southern policing perspective and appreciative inquiry: an ethnography of policing in Vietnam. Policing Soc 30(2):186–205. https://doi.org/10.1080/10439463.2019.1680673

[54] Cooperrider and Whitney (2005), p. 3.

Jardine M, (2023) Policing in a changing Vietnam. Towards a global account of policing. Routledge, Milton Park, Abingdon, Oxon; New York

Jardine M, van Dijk A (2023) Why do positive experiences matter? Appreciative inquiry in ethnography for understanding and transforming policing. In: Fleming J, Charman S (eds) Routledge international handbook of police ethnography. Routledge, pp 319–334

Liebling A, Price D, Elliot C (1999) Appreciative inquiry and prison relationships. Punishm Soc 1(1):71–98

Maturana H, Varela FJ (1992) The tree of knowledge. Shambhala, Boston

Office of the High Commissioner of Human Rights (2011) Share, learn, innovate! Methods and technologies to share human rights knowledge and ideas, New York/Geneva 2011

Reiner R (2015) Revisiting the classics: three seminal founders of the study of policing: Michael Banton, Jerome Skolnick and Egon Bittner. Policing Soc 25(3):308–327

Seliger R (2014) The Jungle book of leadership. A navigation system for leaders. Carl-Auer Verlag, Heidelberg

Skinns L, Wooff A, Sprawson A (2022) 'My best day will be my last day!': appreciating appreciative inquiry in police research. Policing Soc 32(6):731–747

Suntinger W (2018) Police training and international human rights standards. In: Alleweldt R, Fickenscher G (eds) The police and international human rights law. Springer, Leiden/Boston, pp 279–304

Suntinger W, Birk M (2021) Systemic thinking in preventive human rights monitoring - a Dossier for national preventive mechanisms. Ludwig Boltzmann Institute of Human Rights, Vienna, https://helsinki.hu/en/wp-content/uploads/sites/2/2021/04/dossier_systemic_thinking_lbi_gmr.pdf. Accessed 4 July 2023

Waddington PAJ (1999) Police (canteen) sub-culture. An appreciation. Br J Criminol 31(2): 287–309

Watzlawick P, Beavin J, Jackson D (1967) Pragmatics of human communication. A study of interactional patterns, pathologies and paradoxes. W.W. Norton & Company, New York

Whitney D, Trosten-Bloom A (2010) The power of appreciative inquiry. A practical guide to positive change. Berret-Koehler Publishers, San Francisco

Walter Suntinger is a human rights consultant, trainer and university lecturer. Since 2021, he is a Senior Lecturer and the Academic Programme Manager of the Vienna Master of Arts in Applied Human Rights at the University of Applied Arts. He holds a law degree from the University of Graz (1990), with a specialisation in human rights law, and a certificate in systemic change management from the Steinbeis University/Berlin (2019). His areas of specialisation are: preventing monitoring of places of detention, human rights reform and training in the police and the criminal justice system, consulting activities for business. He has produced academic work (on torture, asylum law, monitoring, training, systemic approaches to human rights) and several practical tools, e.g. police training manuals and guidance documents for preventive human rights monitoring. Furthermore, as a Managing Partner at HumanRightsConsulting Vienna (HRCV) he advises business enterprises on how to integrate human rights in their policies and operations. His training and consulting journeys took him, inter alia, to South Africa, Kosovo, Armenia, Brazil, Turkey, Tunisia, Mauritania, Morocco and other countries. He is currently a lecturer at the University of Applied Arts, FH Campus Wien and the University of Vienna. Previous teaching assignments were at: the John Hopkins University—Bologna Center, the University of Oregon (study abroad program in Vienna), the European Peace University in Stadschlaining and the University of Applied Sciences Wiener Neustadt (Security Studies).

Moritz Birk LL.M. is an independent consultant, trainer and lecturer. From 2020 to 2023 he was the Advocacy and Research Director at Amnesty International Austria where he focused specifically on policing and human rights. He was moreover member of the Human Rights Advisory Board of the Austrian Ombudsman Board as part of the National Preventive Mechanism.

Previously he worked as Senior Researcher (2010–2012) and Head of the Department 'Human Dignity and Public Security' (2012–2020) at the Ludwig Boltzmann Institute of Fundamental and Human Rights leading a team of experts researching, advocating, consulting and training on the prevention of torture and ill-treatment worldwide. He is the co-editor and author of the Oxford Commentary to the UN Convention against Torture. From 2009 to 2010, he served as the assistant of the UN Special Rapporteur on Torture, Manfred Nowak, and before that worked with human rights organisations in Sweden, Mexico, Senegal and Ghana. He lectures on human rights law and practice at the University of Vienna and Frankfurt (Oder), Germany.

He holds a German law degree (Humboldt University Berlin) and a degree in international human rights law (Lund University, Sweden) and is certified as systemic organisational consultant and coach.

Chapter 8
Torture in Police Custody and the Effectiveness of Preventive Measures: The Role of National Preventive Mechanisms (NPMs)

Audrey Olivier Muralt

Contents

Abstract This article focuses on the role of National Preventive Mechanisms (NPMs), established under the Optional Protocol to the United Nations Convention against Torture (OPCAT), in preventing torture and ill-treatment in police custody. It examines their powerful monitoring mandate, in particular their unfettered access to all places, persons, and information, and how these powers can be used to propose concrete changes to detention practices and laws. The article puts an emphasis on the most effective measures to prevent torture and ill-treatment in police custody and

A. O. Muralt (✉)
Association for the Prevention of Torture, Geneva, Switzerland

R. Alleweldt (ed.), *Fair Treatment of Persons in Police Custody*,
https://doi.org/10.1007/978-3-031-61737-9_8

specifically the implementation of detention safeguards: access to a lawyer, access to a doctor, a right to notification and information about these safeguards. It takes into consideration recent developments in particular the Principles on Effective Interviewing for Investigations and Information Gathering, also known as the Méndez Principles. Finally, the article highlights good practices, some successes but also challenges that NPMs face in their daily work, based on lessons learned in almost two decades of implementation of the OPCAT.

8.1 The OPCAT: An International Framework to Prevent Torture in Police Custody

The Optional Protocol to the UN Convention against Torture and other Cruel, Inhuman or Degrading Treatment or Punishment (OPCAT) stands out as a rather distinctive human rights treaty in the field of international human rights law. It adopts a complementary approach to its parent treaty, the United Nations Convention against Torture and other Cruel, Inhuman or Degrading Treatment or Punishment (UNCAT), providing practical means for states to implement to fulfil their obligations to prevent torture and ill-treatment.[1] Due to its innovative emphasis on prevention and dialogue, as well as its operational spirit, the OPCAT is often described as "breaking new grounds"[2] within the human rights system. The OPCAT's objective is clearly stated in its preamble: strengthening the protection of persons deprived of their liberty. These persons are most at risk of suffering potential abuses as they are kept outside of the public eye. The OPCAT is based on the premise that one of the most effective means to prevent these abuses from happening is through transparency and openness of places of detention. It establishes a system based on regular monitoring of places of detention, conducted by an international body (the UN Subcommittee for the Prevention of Torture), and national monitoring bodies, also known as National Preventive Mechanisms or NPMs. Both the SPT and NPMs have the mandate to prevent torture and ill-treatment through monitoring places of detention, providing recommendations to relevant authorities and entering into dialogue regarding possible solutions. Through their work, OPCAT bodies aim to prevent potential abuses from happening, or re-occurring. Thanks to their regular monitoring of places of detention, they are able "to analyse the overall functioning of places of detention and provide

[1] UNCAT Articles 2 and 16. For the purpose of this article, we use the term "torture and other forms of ill-treatment" throughout the article. The term "ill-treatment" covers both torture and other forms of abuse, including cruel, inhuman or degrading treatment or punishment.

[2] Association for the Prevention of Torture and Instituto Interamericano de Derechos Humanos (2010) Optional Protocol to the UN Convention against Torture Implementation Manual revised edition, p. 12.

constructive, systemic recommendations aimed at improving the conditions and treatment of detained persons."[3] Their focus is on enabling an environment where violations—including torture and other ill-treatment—are less likely to occur.

The OPCAT does not prescribe any model that NPMs should adopt. It leaves a great margin of flexibility to states parties to choose the model that best suits their national context and institutional landscape. However, states do have to ensure that their NPMs comply with the minimum guarantees and powers set out in the OPCAT[4] (Articles 18 to 22) so that they are able to bring about change in detention. In particular, NPMs have the power to visit any place of detention at any time and without prior notice, including—but not limited to—prisons, police detention centres, migrant detention centres, psychiatric institutions, etc.[5] NPM powers also include the right to access relevant records and documents—including medical records and detention registers—as well as to speak in private with any individual of their choosing. Furthermore, the OPCAT provides for clear safeguards in terms of NPMs' independence from those institutions they oversee.

At the time of the OPCAT's entry into force (2006), the then UN Special Rapporteur on Torture had already highlighted the great potential of the OPCAT bodies to prevent torture, as follows:

> The very fact that national or international experts have the power to inspect every place of detention at any time without prior announcement, have access to prison registers and other documents, [and] are entitled to speak with every detainee in private . . . has a strong deterrent effect. At the same time, such visits create the opportunity for independent experts to examine, at first hand, the treatment of prisoners and detainees and the general conditions of detention . . . Many problems stem from inadequate systems which can easily be improved through regular monitoring. By carrying out regular visits to places of detention, the visiting experts usually establish a constructive dialogue with the authorities concerned in order to help them resolve problems observed.[6]

Almost two decades after its entry into force, the assumptions on which the OPCAT was drafted have been confirmed, by both practice and academic research.

[3] Submission of the Association for the Prevention of Torture to the Questionnaire of the OHCHR to members states, national human rights institutions, civil society and other relevant stakeholders on the role of prevention in the promotion and protection of human rights (2011).

[4] OPCAT Articles 18 to 22. For further analysis on these articles, please refer to APT, OPCAT Implementation Manual & APT, NPM Designation Guide.

[5] OPCAT Article 4.2, for a definition of places of deprivation of liberty: "deprivation of liberty means any form of detention or imprisonment or the placement of a person in a public or private custodial setting which that person is not permitted to leave at will by order of any judicial, administrative or other authority." For a detailed commentary on the Article 4 of the OPCAT, see UN Subcommittee on Prevention of Torture, Draft general comment No. 1 on places of deprivation of liberty (Article 4) and Association for the Prevention of Torture and Instituto Interamericano de Derechos Humanos (2010) Optional Protocol to the UN Convention against Torture Implementation Manual revised edition, p. 49.

[6] UN Special Rapporteur on Torture and other cruel, inhuman or degrading treatment or punishment, Report to the 61st session of the UN General Assembly (2006), A/61/259, para 72.

On the one hand, with their emphasis on domestic implementation, NPMs contribute to real and concrete changes in the situation and treatment of persons deprived of their liberty. At the time of writing (July 2019 and last updates in July 2023),[7] 77 NPMs have been established worldwide: some problematic detention practices can be identified thanks to their regular monitoring of places of detention, in particular police custody.

On the other hand, NPMs first-hand experience reinforces the results of an independent academic research commissioned by the APT, *Does torture prevention work?*,[8] which looked at thirty years of torture prevention in 16 countries (hereinafter referred as Carver and Handley research). This research confirms for the first time in a global quantitative and qualitative study that torture prevention works, and provides a better understanding of which measures are the most effective in reducing the risks of torture. It further examines the effectiveness of more than sixty different measures for the prevention of torture. It found that the most important measures for preventing torture in practice are the implementation of procedural safeguards during the first hours and days of custody.[9] The research highlighted four safeguards which are particularly effective in preventing torture: the right of access to a lawyer, the right of access to a doctor and the right to have the fact of one's detention notified to a relative or another third party of one's choice. The Carver and Handley research thus endorses the conclusions reached by the European Committee for the Prevention of Torture (CPT) since the early 1990s,[10] which recommend the application of these detention safeguards from the very outset of deprivation of liberty, regardless of how it may be described under the legal system concerned (apprehension, arrest, etc). In addition to these key safeguards, the research highlighted the importance of reducing reliance on confession evidence in criminal proceedings through the development of non-coercive interviewing methods which will later be known as the Méndez Principles.[11] Audio or video recordings of interrogations are also essential safeguards, although less implemented.[12] Further,

[7]Ninety states have joined the OPCAT, of which 71 have established an NPM. The majority of OPCAT states parties (50) have chosen to grant the NPM mandate to existing institutions, in particular National Human Rights Institutions (Ombudsperson's Office or National Human Rights Commissions). Other states have created entirely new institutions exclusively dedicated to torture prevention work, while others have decided to designate several institutions to perform the NPM mandate. For an updated list of OPCAT states parties and designated NPMs, please refer to APT OPCAT Database, available at: http://www.apt.ch/opcat (accessed on 29 April 2029).

[8]Carver and Handley (2016).

[9]APT (2016) "Yes torture prevention works," Insights from a global research study on 30 years of torture, prevention, p. 8.

[10]European Committee for the prevention of Torture and inhuman or degrading treatment of punishment (1992) 2nd General Report on the CPT's activities covering the period 1 January to 31 December 1991, Ref: CPT/Inf(92) 3 [EN], as well as CPT, 28th General Report of the CPT, covering the period 1 January to 31 December 2018, para 66.

[11]See Principles on Effective Interviewing for Investigations and Information Gathering, May 2021. Retrieved from: www.interviewingprinciples.com. Also known as the "Méndez Principles."

[12]Association for the Prevention of Torture (2016) "Yes torture prevention works" Insight from a global research study on 30 years of torture prevention, p. 8.

detention monitoring is an effective measure, in particular if monitors are granted strong powers of access to places of detention by law and in practice—including announced visits, have the ability to conduct private interviews and can exercise their powers free from any interference.[13] The importance of procedural safeguards in preventing torture in the first hours of custody was reiterated and further reinforced by the Méndez Principles, in particular Principle 2 "On practice."[14]

The effectiveness of the NPMs in monitoring police custody or in reducing torture and ill-treatment will not be examined in this article. It will rather focus on the role of the NPMs in preventing torture and ill-treatment in police custody, highlighting good practices, some successes but also challenges that NPMs face in their daily work attempting to effectively monitor the treatment and conditions of persons detained.

8.2 The Méndez Principles: A Reference Framework to Prevent Torture in Police Custody

In May 2021, a new set of international standards were launched as the result of a four-year extensive expert-led process. Their release stem from the call from the then UN Special Rapporteur on Torture, Juan Méndez, in his last thematic report to the UN General Assembly.[15] He called on States to "spearhead the development of a universal protocol aiming to ensure that no person is subjected to torture, ill-treatment or coercion, including any forms of violence, duress or threat."[16] His call was based on his observation during his tenure as UN Special Rapporteur on Torture that "that the most frequent setting where torture and coercion takes place is in the course of the interrogation of suspects and for the purpose of obtaining confessions or declarations against others."[17] This is why he dedicated his last report to the UN General Assembly on analysing this issue and proposing concrete ways forward, which resulted in what are now known as the "Méndez Principles for Effective Interviewing."

The Méndez Principles are the latest reference framework for National Preventive Mechanisms and oversight body on police custody. They assemble a set of six Principles which are grounded in science, law and ethics. The Principles offer an

[13] Carver and Handley (2016), p. 95.

[14] See Principles on Effective Interviewing for Investigations and Information Gathering, May 2021, Principle 2, pp. 16–22. Retrieved from: www.interviewingprinciples.com.

[15] UN Special Rapporteur on Torture and other cruel, inhuman or degrading treatment or punishment, Report to the 71st session of the UN General Assembly (2016), UN A/71/298.

[16] UN Special Rapporteur on Torture and other cruel, inhuman or degrading treatment or punishment, Report to the 71st session of the UN General Assembly (2016), para 101, UN A/71/298.

[17] See Principles on Effective Interviewing for Investigations and Information Gathering, May 2021, Foreword.

alternative to interrogation methods that rely on coercion to extract confessions through non-coercive interviewing based on the establishment of trust and rapport-based relations between the interviewer and interviewee. They provide guidance on obtaining accurate and reliable information in full respect of the human rights and dignity of all, including through the implementation of legal and procedural safeguards in the first hours of police custody.

8.3 Main Risks of Torture and Ill-Treatment in Police Custody

Risks of ill-treatment and torture are highest in the first hours of detention, i.e. between the time of apprehension by the police and the presentation before a judge. These first moments (which may vary between a few minutes, hours to several days in some countries) are times when detainees are most vulnerable and when law enforcement officials are under most pressure to secure information from them. The Méndez Principles recognise these moments of heightened risks, in particular the "excessive use of force, misuse of restraints, impromptu coercive questioning, and prolonged periods of confinement in transport vehicles—all of which may amount to torture."[18]

When looking at the areas of risks of torture and ill-treatment in police custody, material and structural conditions, as well as detention practices, institutional culture and police training should be examined.

8.3.1 Material and Structural Conditions of Police Detention

Police custody should, in principle, be of the shortest possible duration as recommended by the CPT and SPT,[19] e.g. no longer than 24 to 48 hours. The European CPT recognised very early on that "physical conditions of detention cannot be expected to be as good in police establishments as in other places of detention where persons may be held for lengthy periods."[20] However, the European CPT insisted that some "elementary material requirements should be met," including a reasonable size of the cells; adequate lighting and ventilation; means of rest; a clean

[18] See Principles on Effective Interviewing for Investigations and Information Gathering, May 2021, para 67; and UN Special Rapporteur on Torture, (2017) A/72/178.

[19] UN Subcommittee on Prevention of Torture, Report on the Visit of the SPT to the Maldives, UN Doc. CAT/OP/MDV/1, 26 February 2009, §78.

[20] European Committee for the prevention of Torture and inhuman or degrading treatment of punishment (1992) 2nd General Report on the CPT's activities covering the period 1 January to 31 December 1991, Ref: CPT/Inf(92) 3 [EN], 13 April 1992, para 42.

mattress and blankets if necessary; adequate means of cleaning and washing facilities and daily provision of food. In practice, material conditions in most police stations remain basic, with the infrastructure limited to "a bare minimum."[21]

Material conditions and infrastructures of police stations have an impact on the dignity of detained persons, and a lack of basic requirements could sometimes amount to ill-treatment. On one hand, police stations are sometimes used to house detainees for much longer periods than the maximum duration contemplated in national legislation and internationals standards. Detainees can be held for weeks, months, or even years in police facilities, including while serving their sentences.[22] Often, these police stations do not meet the minimum and "elementary material requirements" referred to by the European CPT. Such a situation was called by the European CPT following its visit to Switzerland. Although conditions in which detainees are held in police custody throughout the country are relatively good, it noted with concern the situation in the French-speaking part of Switzerland, particularly in two police stations. These stations were holding detainees in "intolerable conditions for longer than the legal limit of 24 hours provided for in the Code of Criminal Procedure, sometimes for more than thirty days."[23] That situation is unfortunately shared across continents.

An illustration of this situation is police detention in the province of Buenos Aires in Argentina. In 2017, following the death of seven persons detained in the police station of Pergamino, the Inter-American Commission on Human Rights (IACHR) voiced its concerns regarding police detention practices in the country. The IACHR denounced that "people are detained for months in police stations, which are designed as temporary holding facilities and are not equipped with the infrastructure and basic services to ensure decent conditions of detention; moreover, police personnel are not trained to serve as prison wardens."[24]

The IACHR's call remained unheard, as another tragedy took place a year later in another police station (Esteban Echeverría) where ten persons died. This highly problematic situation was one of the priority issues discussed by the newly established National Preventive Mechanism of Argentina, during the first National Assembly of the Argentinean Torture Prevention System. On that occasion, the

[21] Association for the Prevention of Torture (2018) Towards the Effective Protection of LGBTI Persons Deprived of their Liberty, a Monitoring Guide, p. 104.

[22] Association for the Prevention of Torture (2018) Towards the Effective Protection of LGBTI Persons Deprived of their Liberty, a Monitoring Guide, p. 105.

[23] European Committee for the prevention of Torture and inhuman or degrading treatment of punishment, Rapport au Conseil fédéral suisse relatif à la visite effectuée en Suisse par le Comité européen pour la prévention de la torture et des peines ou traitements inhumains ou dégradants (CPT) du 22 mars au 1 er avril 2021, para 39.

[24] Inter-American Commission on Human rights (2017) IACHR Laments Deaths in Fire at Police Jail in Buenos Aires, Argentina. https://www.oas.org/en/iachr/media_center/PReleases/2017/026.asp (accessed on 29 April 2023).

Assembly underscored the need to investigate and sanction those responsible, and to implement measures that guarantee the non-repetition of such incidents.[25]

8.3.2 Detention Practices

The 2018 annual report of the European CPT focuses on police custody and risks of torture and ill-treatment. It provides an overview of the main issues the European CPT had come across in the course of its monitoring of police detention for the past thirty years. The European CPT does recognise that in the "overwhelming majority of Council of Europe member states, most persons met by CPT visiting delegations who were, or had recently been, in police custody have not alleged to have suffered any kind of police abuse. Indeed, they considered that they had been treated correctly by the police officers who had apprehended them, escorted them to police establishments, kept them in custody, or interviewed them."[26] The CPT further emphasised that in some countries, "police reforms have led to significant improvements." However, cases of police ill-treatment still take place in a number of European countries. The European CPT particularly highlights the fact that "police ill-treatment mainly occurs during the high-risk period around the time of apprehension of persons suspected of having committed criminal or other offences." Abuses by the police can occur for many reasons, including—to name a few—excessive use of force during apprehension, abuse of power to extort information, existence of a culture of impunity where police abuses are unlikely to be sanctioned or even prosecuted,[27] and questionable practices in the use of restraints or during the conduct of searches. Such practices may have dreadful consequences: in England and Wales, there were 23 deaths in or following police custody in 2017/2018, the highest number recorded in over a decade.[28] Although police practices may not have necessarily contributed to the deaths, 11 of the deceased persons were subjected to force or restraint.[29] The CPT also mentioned in its 2018 annual report that

[25] Centro de Estudios Legales y Sociales (2018) Deaths in the Esteban Echeverría police station are a focus of the national system for the prevention of torture. https://www.cels.org.ar/web/en/2018/12/reunion-de-la-asamblea-anual-del-sistema-nacional-para-la-prevencion-de-la-tortura/ (accessed on 29 April 2023).

[26] European Committee for the prevention of Torture and inhuman or degrading treatment of punishment (2018) 28th general report on the CPT's Activities, para 62.

[27] Association for the Prevention of Torture (2013) Monitoring Police custody a practical guide, p. 10.

[28] United Kingdom's National Preventive Mechanism (2019) Ninth annual report https://s3-eu-west-2.amazonaws.com/npm-prod-storage-19n0nag2nk8xk/uploads/2019/01/6.5163_NPM_AR_2017-18_WEB.pdf, p. 17 (accessed 29 April 2023).

[29] Independent Office for Police Conduct (2018) Deaths during or following police contact: Statistics for England and Wales 2017/18, p. 14. https://www.policeconduct.gov.uk/sites/default/files/Documents/statistics/deaths_during_following_police_contact_201718.pdf (accessed on 29 April 2023).

ill-treatment "during or in the context of police interviews remains a very serious problem," which could even "be qualified as a torture in almost one-third of Council of Europe member states."[30] It further details the type of abuses committed against persons detained by the police, and expressed concerns regarding what they call the "deliberate nature of such treatment," which "was often applied by apprehending/operational officers in the initial period of custody and prior to a first formal police interview, for the purpose of obtaining a confession or other information."[31] The CPT calls attention to the trend, to favour practices which aim at circumventing the implementation of key legal and procedural safeguards, such as informal questioning of "persons of interest"[32] identified in some Council of Europe states. The European CPT thus welcomed the adoption of the Méndez Principles during its 105th plenary meeting in July 2021,[33] as well as the UN SPT which noted that they "provide guidance for police and others on obtaining accurate and reliable information in full respect of the human rights of the person being interviewed, including through the implementation of legal and procedural safeguards in the first hours of police custody."[34]

8.3.3 *Groups in Situation of Vulnerability*

The Méndez Principles are one of the very few frameworks that recognise the inherent situation of vulnerability of people in police custody. As such, one of the six Principles (Principle 3) is exclusively dedicated to this issue.

The Méndez Principles acknowledge that everyone is in a situation of vulnerability "due to the inherently unequal balance of power characterising such interactions with authorities."[35] However, the document emphasises that "some interviewees will experience a situation of heightened vulnerability when the interview intersects with certain other specific risk factors. In such circumstances, the interviewee will have additional needs and rights requiring attention from

---

[30] European Committee for the Prevention of Torture and inhuman or degrading treatment of punishment (2018) 28th general report on the CPT's Activities, para 65.

[31] Ibid.

[32] Ibid.

[33] See European Committee for the Prevention of Torture and inhuman or degrading treatment of punishment, News 2021, available at: https://www.coe.int/en/web/cpt/-/105th-plenary-meeting-of-the-european-committee-for-the-prevention-of-torture-and-inhuman-or-degrading-treatment-or-punishment-cpt- (last accessed on 28 July 2023).

[34] OHCHR Press Release, November 2021, available at: https://interviewingprinciples.com/.

[35] See Principles on Effective Interviewing for Investigations and Information Gathering, May 2021, para 132.

authorities."[36] The Méndez Principles reaffirm what other bodies and practice had concluded over the years:

Persons in situation of vulnerability—including women, juveniles, migrants, persons with psycho-social disabilities or lesbian, gay, bisexual, trans and intersex (LGBTI) persons—are at particular risks of suffering abuses while in police custody, and their situation can also be impacted by material and structural conditions of detention.

The guide published by the Association for the Prevention of Torture highlights the specific risks faced by LGBTI persons during police detention, depending on the size and configuration of police stations: in collective cells, LGBTI persons face a risk of violence from fellow detainees, even when custody is limited to 24 hours. Transwomen are particularly subjected to violence if they have to share a cell with men.[37] The European CPT has also observed that "certain categories of persons (such as persons with mental health problems and juveniles) could run a higher risk of ill-treatment during apprehension due to their specific vulnerabilities."[38]

8.4 Successes of NPMs: Bringing Transparency Into a Closed Environment

Almost two decades after its entry into force, the mere fact that 92 states in the world have joined the OPCAT and agreed to open their places of detention to external scrutiny is a success per se. Transparency and accountability of places of detention today is a global reality. On every continent, domestic bodies have strong powers and unfettered access to all places of detention, to all information and to all persons relevant to their torture prevention mandate, as well as the mandate to conduct unannounced visits and private interviews. Thanks to these powers, they are able to gather first-hand information on the treatment and conditions of detention, even in police custody, one of the most closed environments. Their powers also act as a strong deterrent factor against police abuse, as unannounced visits to police stations could, in principle, happen at any time and without any warning.

[36] See Principles on Effective Interviewing for Investigations and Information Gathering, May 2021, para 135.

[37] Association for the Prevention of Torture (2018) Towards the effective protection of LGBTI persons deprived of liberty: A monitoring guide, p. 104.

[38] European Committee for the prevention of Torture and inhuman or degrading treatment of punishment (2018) 28th general report on the CPT's Activities, para 64.

8.4.1 Access to Places of Detention Enshrined in Law: An OPCAT Success

One of the strongest powers NPMs have is their access to all places of detention, all information and all persons, as provided for by Article 20 of the OPCAT. This article mirrors Article 14 (1) of the international torture prevention convention, that provides similar powers to the UN Subcommittee on Prevention of Torture. Two differences shall be noted between the two OPCAT provisions:

- Article 14 (1) OPCAT provides for "unrestricted access" to the UN Subcommittee, whereas Article 20 (OPCAT) only refers to "access" for NPMs; and
- Article 14 (2) includes a limitation clause for the UN SPT, as states can object to a visit to a specific place of detention, provided "urgent and compelling grounds of national defence, public safety, natural disaster or serious disorder in the place to be visited that temporarily prevent the carrying out of such a visit." This limitation clause is not included for the NPM.

Article 20 of the OPCAT has been interpreted as granting similar powers to NPMs as the SPT, as "an unrestricted right of access of NPMs to all places of detention cannot be regarded as an absurd or unreasonable result of interpretation."[39] The majority of NPM founding legislations reflect the text of Article 20 of the OPCAT, and sometimes go beyond to include "unfettered" or "unrestricted." When they do not, the UN subcommittee has expressed its concerns on numerous occasions and encouraged amendments.

Unhindered access to all places where persons are detained, all information and all persons, is an absolute requirement for an NPM to be effective. Thanks to this power, they are in a unique position to obtain an objective picture of the situation in detention, check and triangulate the information collected to detect situations of risks of torture and ill-treatment. Access is a cornerstone of an NPM and one of their most powerful rights that equip them to detect situations of abuses and prevent them from happening. The sole fact that, almost two decades after its entry into force, 77 states are bound by the concept of transparency and agree, in principle, to grant unfettered access to all information, places and persons to an independent monitoring body is already a considerable success of the OPCAT. Bringing transparency and independent oversight to closed environments requires a strong commitment to openness and change.

[39] Nowak and McArthur (2008) The United Nations Convention against Torture, A Commentary (ed) Oxford Commentaries on International Law Article 20 Obligations of States Parties to Facilitate Visits, p. 1091, para 15.

8.4.2 Access to Places of Detention in Practice

Article 20(c) reaffirms the obligation, established by Article 1 of the OPCAT, for states parties to allow NPMs access to all places of detention as defined in Article 4. As mentioned in the previous section, its interpretation is clear insofar that NPMs should be given "the same powers as the SPT to conduct visits without interference by state authorities."[40] The SPT, in its practical guide addressed to NPMs, also reaffirms that NPMs "should have unrestricted access to all places."[41] The Méndez Principles recognise and further strengthen the important role of external oversight bodies and NPMs in monitoring police custody, in particular its Principle 5 on Accountability. They state that external oversight bodies should "have access to any facility in which a detained person is interviewed and information on the persons detained within."[42] The Méndez Principles thus operationalize the OPCAT provisions in relation to access in the context of policy custody.

In the context of police custody, the meaning of places of detention or places of deprivation of liberty shall not be restricted to police stations. Temporary holding facilities, police cars and detainee transport vehicles also fall within that definition.[43] NPMs monitoring powers thus cover these situations. In some countries, police cells or police transportation vehicles were not covered by any oversight institution prior to OPCAT's ratification. In a few states parties to the OPCAT—such as Georgia and the United Kingdom, police cells have not always been overseen by the institutions designated as NPMs. Therefore, some changes were required to bring them in line with the OPCAT. For instance, in the United Kingdom, the functions of Her Majesty's Inspectorate of Constabulary (HMIC) and Her Majesty's Inspectorate of Prisons (HMIP) were extended as the government recognised that police stations were not overseen by any monitoring mechanism.[44] When existing legislations are unclear, some NPMs have conducted some extensive interpretation of their mandate. For instance, in Chile, the General Auditor of the Republic (*Controlaría General de la República*), published an opinion[45] on the founding legislation of the National Human Rights Institution—also designated as NPM. It granted the power to the NHRI to have access to all "specifically limited places under the responsibility of public agents," although the NHRI law was unclear on the matter. Since then, the

[40] Association for the Prevention of Torture and Instituto Interamericano de Derechos Humanos (2010) Optional Protocol to the UN Convention against Torture Implementation Manual revised edition, Chapter II, Commentary on the Articles of the OPCAT, p. 96.

[41] Office of the United Nations High Commissioner for Human Rights (2018) Preventing torture: The role of national preventive mechanisms, a practical guide, p. 6.

[42] See Principles on Effective Interviewing for Investigations and Information Gathering, May 2021, para 188.

[43] UN Subcommittee on Prevention of Torture, Draft general comment No. 1 on places of deprivation of liberty (Article 4).

[44] Murray et al. (2011), p. 118.

[45] Contraloría General de la República (2012) Opinion N° 58.070.

Chilean NHRI has monitored conditions and treatment of persons detained in police vehicles, particularly in the context of public demonstrations. To be truly effective, the legal powers to have access to all places where persons are—or may be—deprived of their liberty should be coupled with the practical ability of NPMs to use that power. The UN SPT voiced specific concerns regarding the lack of access laid down in the law—or in practice—to places that fall under the jurisdiction of the police or states security services. In the case of Ukraine, the UN SPT voiced concerns regarding the Ukrainian NPM's inability, in practice, to "visit every place of deprivation of liberty given that it has limited access to State Security Service premises, where people may be held for investigative purposes."[46] They thus recommended that the NPM have "the legal authority and practical capacity to access any place (...)."[47] The UN SPT also expressed concerns regarding Article 13 of the Tunisian NPM law, which allowed authorities to "refuse requests for access to a place of detention by invoking national defence and security interests or the existence of a natural disaster or 'serious disorder' at the place of detention in question." It recommended amendments to be made, in particular to ensure "that the mechanism has unhindered access to all places of detention, including those under the jurisdiction of the Ministry of the Interior and the Ministry of National Defence."[48] The UN SPT reiterated in its Draft General Comment on Article 4 of the OPCAT that "It is crucial that States parties guarantee both the Subcommittee and national preventive mechanisms full access to places, facilities or settings in which individuals currently are, previously were or potentially may be deprived of their liberty. The length of time of the deprivation of liberty is irrelevant for the determination of such a place."[49]

Other NPMs have managed to circumvent limitations contained in their legislation through practice, and assert their powers in their internal rules and regulations. This is the case of the Italian NPM for instance. When the NPM legislation was adopted, unhindered access to police detention centres was uncertain as the law specified that the NPM (National Guarantor for the Rights of Persons Detained or Deprived of Liberty) shall be authorised by the police to gain access. However, in practice, the NPM has been able to conduct unannounced visits to police stations and did not face any obstacles in getting access. The NPM reiterated its powers to have access to all places, information and people, in particular with regard to police in its

[46] United Nations Subcommittee on Prevention of Torture and other cruel, inhuman or degrading treatment of punishment (2017) Report from visit to Ukraine undertaken from 19 to 25 May and from 5 to 9 September 2016: observations and recommendations addressed to the State party, CAT/OP/UKR/3, para 17.

[47] Ibid., para 20.

[48] United Nations Subcommittee on Prevention of Torture and other cruel, inhuman or degrading treatment of punishment (2017) Report from visit to Tunisia undertaken from 11 to 14 April 2016: Observations and recommendations addressed to the national preventive mechanism, CAT/OP/TUN/2, para 8.

[49] UN Subcommittee on Prevention of Torture, Draft general comment No. 1 on places of deprivation of liberty (Article 4), para 29.

internal regulation, as follows: “in full independence and without any condition, the National Guarantor (. . .) visits, on a regular basis and with no need of permissions: police forces detention cells, where admission to any place used for restrictive and security purposes shall take place without restriction.”[50]

8.4.3 The Power to Conduct Unannounced Visits

Access to all places of detention also includes the power to conduct unannounced visits. As stated by the UN SPT practical guide for NPMs, NPMs should therefore be able to “choose freely the places of deprivation of liberty in which visits are to be carried out, to determine whether the visits will be announced or unannounced, and have unrestricted access to all parts of the premises and facilities. The visits should be primarily unannounced in order to help ascertain the real situation of persons deprived of their liberty. They should also be carried out at various times of the day, including during the night.”[51] The latter is particularly relevant for police custody where risks of torture and ill-treatment are higher, as well as removal of detainees is possible. As police stations are often small with few detainees, the “surprise” effect is particularly powerful, as it also avoids the risks that detainees are being removed prior to the visit if it is announced.[52] The power of NPMs to conduct unannounced visits to places of detention is also reaffirmed by the Méndez Principles on Effective Interviewing.[53]

The majority of NPMs’ founding legislation have included the right to conduct “unannounced visits” to places of detention. When for some of the NPMs, prior notification is required by their founding legislation, the SPT has flagged their shortcomings with the OPCAT and its interpretation, and recommended specific amendments in that regard. For instance, the UN SPT expressed its concerns following its visit to Cyprus,[54] where the law of the Commissioner for Administration’s Act (which acts as the NPM) required “the Commissioner to provide prior written notification of the planned visit, as these conditions represent an obstacle to

[50] Self Regulatory Code of the National Guarantor for the Rights of the Persons Detained or Deprived of Liberty Article 3 d), resolution dated 31 May 2016. http://www.garantenazionaleprivatiliberta.it/gnpl/resources/cms/documents/cedf7d3991577af84cbb221ca5b21379.pdf (accessed on 29 April 2023).

[51] Office of the United Nations High Commissioner for Human Rights (2018) Preventing torture: The role of national preventive mechanisms, a practical guide, p. 21.

[52] Association for the Prevention of Torture (2013) Monitoring Police custody a practical guide, p. 14.

[53] See Principles on Effective Interviewing for Investigations and Information Gathering, May 2021, para 190.

[54] United Nations Subcommittee on Prevention of Torture and other cruel, inhuman or degrading treatment of punishment (2017) Report from visit to Cyprus undertaken from 25 to 29 January 2016: Observations and recommendations addressed to the state party, CAT/OP/CYP/1, para 87.

free access to places of detention." The SPT noted the lack of compliance of the Commissioner's law with some OPCAT provisions. It thus recommended Cyprus to "repeal, as a matter of urgency, subsections (2) and (3) of section 5 of Law No. 2 (III) of 2009 and ensure that the national preventive mechanism has the right, in practice, to visit all places of deprivation of liberty in Cyprus, without preconditions and in line with the Optional Protocol."[55] The ability to conduct unannounced visit is a powerful torture prevention measure, as demonstrated by the Carver & Handley research.[56]

8.4.4 Access to Information [Article 20 a) and b)]

Under the Article 20 a) and b) of the OPCAT, states should grant the NPMs the power to have access to all information relevant to their mandate, in particular: number and location of persons deprived of their liberty, number and location of places of deprivation of liberty; as well as information referring to the treatment and conditions of detention of persons deprived of their liberty. NPMs should thus "seek and be able to obtain prompt, regular and unhindered access to all information."[57] This power is also reaffirmed by the recent Méndez Principles on Effective Interviewing which emphasize that NPMs should be granted with access to "information and files."[58]

The range of information that NPMs can get access to is thus very broad and encompasses a wide range of documents, including: records; registers; files; internal rules; staff regulations; aggregated and individual medical records; schedules; suicide watch arrangements, and disciplinary records.[59] Some of the information the NPM will have access to could be confidential, such as individual records or medical reports. The NPM has to respect the confidentiality of such information, including by not disclosing any personal data without the expressed consent of the person concerned,[60] as provided for by Article 35 of the OPCAT. However, access to personal and sensitive information does not require the consent of the person concerned, and such access cannot be limited to only some members of the NPM, for instance members with a medical background. Such a restriction would

---

[55] Ibid., para 88.

[56] Carver and Handley (2016), p. 95.

[57] Office of the United Nations High Commissioner for Human Rights (2018) Preventing torture: The role of national preventive mechanisms, a practical guide, pp. 22–23.

[58] See Principles on Effective Interviewing for Investigations and Information Gathering, May 2021, para 190.

[59] Association for the Prevention of Torture and Instituto Interamericano de Derechos Humanos (2010) Optional Protocol to the UN Convention against Torture Implementation Manual revised edition, p. 95.

[60] Ibid.

contradict the spirit of the OPCAT.[61] The SPT made it clear that NPMs do have access to medical files. Following its visit to Germany, it recommended the NPM to seek "prompt, regular and unhindered access to information on detainees during its visits, including the incident registers and medical records which should be kept at every place of detention, in addition to the personal files of each detainee."[62]

A few NPMs have reported obstacles in accessing information. For instance, the UN SPT noted that the Uruguayan NPM faced difficulties to access data of NPM's interest from the Ministry of Interior. It thus recommended that the state should provide the NPM with all information on places of detention, persons deprived of their liberty and their treatment and the conditions of their detention, in conformity with Article 20 OPCAT.[63] The SPT expressed similar concerns regarding the practical obstacles faced by the NPM of Malta with regards to access to personal information of detainees, although unlimited access is provided for in the NPM founding legislation. The SPT thus urged Malta to "ensure that the NPMs are given full and unlimited access to all relevant information and to all places of deprivation of liberty in order to enable them to properly fulfil their mandate." [64]

8.4.5 Access to All Persons

NPMs have the power to conduct private interviews with all relevant persons according to their mandate, as provided for by Article 20 d) OPCAT and as reaffirmed by the Méndez Principles in its Principle 5: they have the "power to conduct interviews in private with persons deprived of liberty as well as with the staff."[65] These are the cornerstones of their visiting functions. Private interviews—in the absence of any witness, including authorities—enable detainees to talk freely to the NPM, and the NPM to gather first-hand information on treatment and conditions in detention. NPMs have the ability to choose whom to speak to, and to decide when,

---

[61] Office of the United Nations High Commissioner for Human Rights (2018) Preventing torture: The role of national preventive mechanisms, a practical guide, pp. 22–23.

[62] United Nations Subcommittee on Prevention of Torture and other cruel, inhuman or degrading treatment of punishment (2013) Report on the visit for the purpose of providing advisory assistance to the national preventive mechanism of the Federal Republic of Germany CAT/OP/DEU/2, para 41.

[63] United Nations Subcommittee on Prevention of Torture and other cruel, inhuman or degrading treatment of punishment (2019) Report on the visit undertaken from 4 to 15 March 2018 in Uruguay, CAT/OP/URY/1, para 7.

[64] United Nations Subcommittee on Prevention of Torture and other cruel, inhuman or degrading treatment of punishment (2017) Report on the visit for the purpose of providing advisory assistance to the national preventive mechanism of the Republic of Malta, CAT/OP/MLT/1, para 33 and 34.

[65] See Principles on Effective Interviewing for Investigations and Information Gathering, May 2021, para 190.

where, how long and how persons will be interviewed.[66] The power to conduct private interviews is often enshrined in NPM legislations, and is one of the added values brought by the OPCAT to existing oversight bodies.

The Carver and Handley research also confirmed that the NPMs' ability to conduct private interviews with detainees has a strong correlation with their capacity to prevent torture and ill-treatment from happening, as follows: "monitors' ability to conduct interviews with inmates of prisons and detention centres privately also has an impact on the incidence of torture. Again, this can presumably be understood as a measure of how far these institutions are able to conduct their activities unimpeded by the authorities."[67]

However, in practice, conducting private interviews in police stations could be very challenging as detainees could be reluctant to discuss freely with detention monitors for a wide range of reasons, as explained by APT's guide on monitoring police detention: intense stress due to the uncertainty of the detainees' cases and recentness of their arrest; fear to suffer physical or mental reprisals or be otherwise sanctioned by the police once monitors have left; fear that collaborating with monitors may negatively impact decisions regarding their release or the progress of their case; or even fear from being identified as the source of information, particularly if there are other persons present at the time of the interview[68]. Material conditions can also impact the possibility for NPMs to carry out private interviews with detainees, such as the lack of privacy. For these reasons, NPMs shall be able to assess the possibility to conduct private interviews in police stations, or whether they could gather information in other custodial settings.

8.5 Bridging the Gap Between Law and Practice in Police Custody: The Role of NPMs

Safeguards, especially at the very early stages of detention, are crucial to prevent police abuse, which could amount to ill-treatment or torture.[69] Amongst the most effective safeguards in terms of preventing torture are: the right of access to a lawyer, the right of access to a doctor and the right to have the fact of one's detention notified to a relative or another third party of one's choice. The Carver and Handley research demonstrated that, if applied in practice, detention safeguards have the highest torture prevention impact, followed by prosecution and independent monitoring mechanisms. However, although their obligations may be enshrined in national

[66] Office of the United Nations High Commissioner for Human Rights (2018) Preventing torture: The role of national preventive mechanisms, a practical guide, p. 22.

[67] Carver and Handley (2016), p. 96.

[68] Association for the Prevention of Torture (2013) Monitoring Police custody a practical guide, p. 13.

[69] Ibid., p. 6.

legislation, there often exists an important gap between law and practice.[70] NPMs have the unique mandate to bridge this gap.

8.5.1 *NPMs' Role and Practices in Monitoring the Implementation of Detention Safeguards*

The Carver and Handley research provides examples of the positive influence of different types of monitoring on detention practices, as illustrated by the case of Georgia: "The Public Defender's Office made very frequent visits from the end of 2004 until 2006. It visited every police station in Tbilisi every few days and monitoring groups regularly visited police stations in the regions. This intense programme, actively supported by the Ministry of Interior, had a very clear impact on police detention procedures."[71]

NPMs, due to their unique access to all places of deprivation of liberty and broad powers to monitor conditions and treatment in detention, are ideally placed to bridge this gap. They can propose concrete improvements in detention practices, through their regular monitoring, their advisory function regarding laws and policies, as well as their continued cooperation with the authorities ensuring, through their recommendations that detention practices are improved.[72] Their potential to contribute to significant change in police culture was also recognised by the European CPT in its 2018 Annual Report,[73] as well as by the Méndez Principles in its Principle 5 on Accountability.

In the context of police custody, NPMs have the power to monitor the situation and treatment of persons detained and deter potential abuses from happening. In New Zealand, the NPM is comprised of five bodies,[74] including the Independent Police Conduct Authority (IPCA). After five years of operations, the New Zealand NPMs reflected on its implementation and voiced that the "ultimate measure of its success is the impact it has on people who are detained." It then reflected upon the fact that there had been no deaths in police custody since 2007/8, the period since when the IPCA began monitoring police custody as NPM.[75]

---

[70] Association for the Prevention of Torture (2016) "Yes torture prevention works" Insights from a global research study on 30 years of torture prevention, p. 15.

[71] Carver and Handley (2016), p. 414.

[72] Association for the Prevention of Torture (2016), "Yes torture prevention works" Insights from a global research study on 30 years of torture prevention, p. 28.

[73] European Committee for the prevention of Torture and inhuman or degrading treatment of punishment (2018) 28th general report on the CPT's Activities, para 72.

[74] See Association for the Prevention of Torture's OPCAT Database for further information, last refer on 14 July 2019.

[75] Human Rights Commission of New Zealand (2013) A review of OPCAT implementation by New Zealand's National Preventive Mechanisms. https://www.hrc.co.nz/files/2214/2398/7100/Opcat-2013_web.pdf (accessed on 29 April 2023).

NPMs do also verify whether detainees had effective access to key detention safeguards. As stated by the UN SPT following its visit to Germany, "The mandate of the mechanism should not be limited to visiting and monitoring the material conditions of deprivation of liberty, but it should involve innovative solutions for the prevention of torture and other ill-treatment (...). The SPT also recommends to the NPM that it (...) (ii) considers the extent to which legal safeguards are observed in practice."[76] The SPT further elaborated on NPMs' role vis-à-vis the monitoring of implementation of detention safeguards upon its visit to the Former Yugoslav Republic of Macedonia, as follows "*The NPM (shall) direct additional focus to the development and effectiveness of preventive safeguards and the effective operation of protective procedures at those points of the detention process where there is a heightened risk of torture and ill-treatment, including in relation to medical care, with a particular focus on availability, records, medical screening and the reporting of injuries.*"[77]

Thanks to their powers, NPMs gain a unique and overall picture of the situation and treatment of persons detained throughout the chain of custody (and not restricted to police custody). This is one of the greatest added values of NPMs compared to other monitoring bodies which may only have access to one place of detention, or one institution.

For the past decade, NPMs have mostly focused their monitoring work on the treatment in detention and material conditions of police custody, although they are progressively including the element of monitoring the effective implementation of detention safeguards in their methodology. Around the world, NPMs have been able to use their unfettered access and their independence from authorities, to start questioning law enforcement practices. This is done with the aim to bridge the gap between what it stated in the law, and what happens on a daily basis in a police station. The French NPM (General Controller of Places of Deprivation of Liberty) is an institution established in 2007 with the sole and unique mandate to monitor all places of deprivation of liberty to prevent abuses from happening. Over the past twelve years, it conducted numerous visits to police stations and made recommendations on police treatment, material conditions in police custody, as well as on the implementation of key detention safeguards. In its latest annual report, it summarises the main conclusions stemming from the 31 police stations visited over the previous year, including the poor material conditions in which people are detained.[78] For

[76]United Nations Subcommittee on Prevention of Torture and other cruel, inhuman or degrading treatment of punishment (2013) Report on the visit for the purpose of providing advisory assistance to the national preventive mechanism of the Federal Republic of Germany, CAT/OP/DEU/2, para 23.

[77]United Nations Subcommittee on Prevention of Torture and other cruel, inhuman or degrading treatment of punishment (2013) Report on the visit to the former Yugoslav Republic of Macedonia undertaken from 23 to 29 April 2017: observations and recommendations addressed to the State party, CAT/OP/MKD/1, para 33.

[78]Contrôleur general des lieux de privation de liberté (2018), Annual Report 2018, pp. 70–71: "Hygiene kits, especially for women, are often lacking, blankets are poorly maintained, mattresses

instance, the French NPM noted that despite of what is provided for by law, the letter of rights is never left with the person detained in police custody. In some cases, "the notification of the rights itself is perfunctory, without explanation, and comes down to a simple signature which does not always seem to be collected at the beginning of the procedure. It is particularly unfortunate that, in at least one of the police stations visited, these practices have the support of the public prosecutor's office."[79]

In Norway, according to the law, detainees shall be informed as soon as possible about the grounds of their detention, and about their rights and duties. Both the European CPT and the Norwegian Parliamentary Ombudsman[80]—who acts as the NPM since 2013—recommended that "detainees be provided with both written and oral information about their rights, in a language they understand, as soon as possible after their detention," that this "should be documented in the custody log," and that "all detainees sign a declaration confirming that they have been informed about their rights in a language they understand." [81] The Norwegian authorities replied that they would follow up the recommendation. Following the visits made to six police custody facilities over two years (2014–2016), the NPM noted that none of them had procedures in places as recommended by both monitoring bodies.[82]

Other NPMs have used their powers to make recommendations, to influence directly the content of the standard operating procedures and training of the police (Paraguay[83] and the Former Yugoslav Republic of Macedonia[84]), or the content of police registers used on a day-to-day basis in police stations (Costa Rica).

NPMs have also been able to use their unique collaborative approach, to support inter-institutional dialogues, with the view of reaching the effective implementation of detention safeguards. For instance, in Paraguay, the NPM has initiated the establishment of inter-institutional roundtables to discuss the implementation of detention safeguards, in particular access to a lawyer. The NPM managed to bridge the dialogue gap between institutions, in particular the police and the public defenders' offices. Concrete proposals are being discussed to facilitate access to

---

are insufficient, showers can not be used for lack of towels, smelly odors permeate cells and toilets, even offices, the heating does not always work and is sometimes not even installed in the cells."

[79] Ibid.

[80] For further information on the role of the Parliamentary Ombudsman as National Preventive Mechanism, refer to: https://www.sivilombudsmannen.no/en/torturforebygging/ (accessed on 29 April 2023).

[81] Norwegian Parliamentary Ombudsman (2017) Article on the Right to Information.https://www.sivilombudsmannen.no/en/news/prevention-torture/the-right-to-information/ (accessed on 29 April 2023).

[82] Ibid.

[83] Paraguay National Commission for the Prevention of Torture (2019) 2018 Annual report, p. 11. http://www.mnp.gov.py/index.php/repository/informe-anual-de-gestion/Informe-anual-de-gesti%C3%B3n/Informe-Anual-de-Gesti%C3%B3n%2D%2D-A%C3%B1o-2018/ (accessed on 29 April 2023).

[84] Replies of the former Yugoslav Republic of Macedonia to the report of the Subcommittee on Prevention of Torture and Other Cruel, Inhuman or Degrading Treatment or Punishment on the visit undertaken from 23 to 29 April 2017 (2019), CAT/OP/MKD/1/Add.1, para 12.

public defenders for detainees coming from a disadvantaged socio-economic backgrounds.[85]

8.5.2 Challenges Related to the Monitoring of Implementation of Detention Safeguards

One of the main challenges related to the effective implementation of detention safeguards is their imprecision in the law. For instance, national laws often provide for access to a lawyer in a "prompt manner," or "immediately" as soon as the person is apprehended, or transferred to the relevant authorities. What does "prompt" or "immediate" mean in practice for a detainee? This is often neither defined in the law, nor in the standard operating procedures of the police or law enforcement officials. This imprecision leaves important margins of discretion in the decision-making by individual police officers, and thus opportunities for potential abuses. For instance, in Mexico, the law provides that the detainee must be transferred to the "Public Prosecutor's Office immediately after the police arrest." Therefore, it is often understood that detainees should be granted access to a lawyer once being held by the Public Prosecutor's Office. Nonetheless, the requirement of "immediacy" is not defined precisely: there is no definition of the maximum time limits for the transfer. In practice, some detainees could spend until 15 hours—and sometimes even longer—before seeing a lawyer, or even talking with their families, leaving them at risks of potential abuses, including ill-treatment and torture.[86]

NPMs have the powers to make recommendations on detention practices (Article 19b of the OPCAT), as well as on laws and policies relevant to their mandate (Article 19c of the OPCAT). In that capacity, they can propose to the authorities the adoption or revision of specific rules of procedures to include the most precise interpretation of these general standards. When the law is vague, NPMs can also encourage inter-institutional dialogues between interested parties, such as bar associations, legal aid systems, police authorities and public prosecutors' offices in order to guarantee equal treatment of detained persons.

A second challenge to effective implementation of detention safeguards is the risk of "superficial implementation," meaning that law enforcement officials comply with the requirement of the relevant laws and rules of procedures, but do it in a superficial manner, which may impede detainees to effectively exercise their rights. For instance, detainees are told about their rights upon arrest in a systematic manner

[85] Paraguay National Commission for the Prevention of Torture, 2018 Annual report, p. 49, http://www.mnp.gov.py/index.php/repository/informe-anual-de-gestion/Informe-anual-de-gesti%C3%B3n/Informe-Anual-de-Gesti%C3%B3n%2D%2D-A%C3%B1o-2018/ (accessed on 29 April 2023).

[86] Association for the Prevention of Torture (2019) Access to a lawyer during the first hours of custody in Mexico, a situation analysis.

by the detaining authorities, and the information is well registered in a dedicated register. However, the manner in which the rights are read or explained to detainees is absolutely key to make sure that detainees have well understood their rights, and that they are able to exercise them. In that sense, the manner in which the information is shared or transmitted between the law enforcement agent and the detainee is almost as important as the right itself. This was confirmed by a study, which looked into the rights of suspects at the investigative stage of the criminal process in nine European Union countries. It found that, whilst most countries have a standard letter of rights, they are "lengthy and complex, so that many suspected and accused persons, particularly those with vulnerabilities or those who have language difficulties, are unable to fully understand them." The same study also highlights that "oral information about procedural rights is often provided in a formalistic way, and in some countries the evidence suggests that the police discourage suspects from exercising their procedural rights, and in some cases, even prevent them from doing so."[87]

Thus, in their monitoring work, NPMs need to take this risk of superficial implementation into account when it comes to the effective implementation of detention safeguards. They need to check not only whether safeguards are in place, i.e. whether a letter of rights was read and handed out to detainees, but also *how* these safeguards were implemented, *when* they were implemented, and *why* there were implemented (or not) in such a way. NPMs' monitoring methodology may need to be adapted in order to be able to collect such information from a wide range of sources, inside and outside of police stations. Many NPMs have started to ask questions to detainees held in prisons or remand centres about their conditions and treatment in police detention—including about if and how they had access to the key detention safeguards.

8.6 Conclusion

For more than fifteen years, NPMs have monitored conditions and treatment of persons deprived of their liberty, including in police custody. The publication of the Méndez Principles represents a new opportunity for NPMs to embed their policing work into a new framework which is becoming the new international reference on the matter. Beyond their monitoring functions, NPMs are uniquely placed to initiate dialogue with relevant stakeholders to discuss how and if the Méndez Principles are being implemented at the national level, and if not, what measures should be taken to make them a reality. With the Principles, the NPM preventive mandate is heightened and strengthened. They can maximise all their powers of access to collect first-hand

[87] Irish Council for Civil Liberties and the Open Society Justice Initiative (2018) Inside Police Custody 2, An empirical study of suspects' rights at the investigative stage of the criminal process in nine EU countries, p. 5.

information that will inform a collective debate around policing. They will continue to foster changes at various levels: in detention practices; in laws and policies; and ultimately, changes in mindsets. Although changes take time to happen—particularly when it comes to institutional culture, mindset and practices—NPMs have now a unique, concrete and practical alternative to coercive interviewing that has demonstrated its potential for reducing torture and ill-treatment in the first moments of police custody. It will now be up to NPMs to seize this opportunity to encourage dialogue amongst all interested parties on the future of policing in their countries.

References

African Commission on Human and Peoples' Rights

African Commission on Human and Peoples' Rights Guidelines on the Conditions of Arrest, Police Custody and Pre-Trial Detention in Africa, also known as the Luanda Guidelines (2014)

African Commission on Human and Peoples' Rights - Resolution ACHPR/Res.545 (LXXIII) (2022)

Council of Europe

European Committee for the prevention of Torture and inhuman or degrading treatment of punishment (1992) 2nd General Report on the CPT's activities covering the period 1 January to 31 December 1991

European Committee for the prevention of Torture and inhuman or degrading treatment of punishment (2018) 28th general report on the CPT's Activities

European Committee for the prevention of Torture and inhuman or degrading treatment of punishment, Rapport au Conseil fédéral suisse relatif à la visite effectuée en Suisse par le Comité européen pour la prévention de la torture et des peines ou traitements inhumains ou dégradants (CPT) du 22 mars au 1 er avril 2021 (only available in French)

Inter-American Commission on Human Rights

Inter-American Commission on Human rights (2017) IACHR Laments Deaths in Fire at Police Jail in Buenos Aires, Argentina.https://www.oas.org/en/iachr/media_center/PReleases/2017/026.asp. Accessed on 29 April 2023

Legal Articles

Carver R, Handley L (2016) United Kingdom. In: Carver R, Handley L (eds) Does torture prevention work. Liverpool University Press

Centro de Estudios Legales y Sociales (2018) Deaths in the Esteban Echeverría police station are a focus of the national system for the prevention of torture. https://www.cels.org.ar/web/en/2018/12/reunion-de-la-asamblea-anual-del-sistema-nacional-para-la-prevencion-de-la-tortura/. Accessed on 29 April 2023

Murray R, Steinerte E, Evans M, de Wolf AH (2011) The role of NPMs. In: The optional protocol to the UN convention against torture. Oxford University Press

Nowak M, McArthur E (2008) The United Nations convention against torture, a commentary. Oxford commentaries on international law. Oxford University Press

National Preventive Mechanisms

Contraloría General de la República (2012) Opinion N° 58.070

Contrôleur général des lieux de privation de liberté (2018), Annual Report 2018

Human Rights Commission of New Zealand (2013) A review of OPCAT implementation by New Zealand's National Preventive Mechanisms. https://www.hrc.co.nz/files/2214/2398/7100/Opcat-2013_web.pdf. Accessed on 29 April 2023

Independent Office for Police Conduct (2018) Deaths during or following police contact: Statistics for England and Wales 2017/18. https://www.policeconduct.gov.uk/sites/default/files/Documents/statistics/deaths_during_following_police_contact_201718.pdf. Accessed on 29 April 2023

Norwegian Parliamentary Ombudsman (2017) Article on the Right to Information.https://www.sivilombudsmannen.no/en/news/prevention-torture/the-right-to-information/. Accessed on 29 April 2023

Paraguay National Commission for the Prevention of Torture (2019) 2018 Annual report. http://www.mnp.gov.py/index.php/repository/informe-anual-de-gestion/Informe-anual-de-gesti%C3%B3n/Informe-Anual-de-Gesti%C3%B3n%2D%2D-A%C3%B1o-2018/. Accessed on 29 April 2023

United Kingdom's National Preventive Mechanism (2019) Ninth annual report https://s3-eu-west-2.amazonaws.com/npm-prod-storage-19n0nag2nk8xk/uploads/2019/01/6.5163_NPM_AR_2017-18_WEB.pdf. Accessed on 29 April 2023

Non-Governmental Organizations

APT (2016) "Yes torture prevention works," Insights from a global research study on 30 years of torture prevention

Association for the Prevention of Torture (2013) Monitoring Police custody a practical guide

Association for the Prevention of Torture (2018) Towards the Effective Protection of LGBTI Persons Deprived of their Liberty, a Monitoring Guide

Association for the Prevention of Torture (2019) Access to a lawyer during the first hours of custody in Mexico, a situation analysis

Association for the Prevention of Torture and Instituto Interamericano de Derechos Humanos (2010) Optional Protocol to the UN Convention against Torture Implementation Manual revised edition

Irish Council for Civil Liberties and the Open Society Justice Initiative (2018) Inside Police Custody 2, An empirical study of suspects' rights at the investigative stage of the criminal process in nine EU countries

Submission of the Association for the Prevention of Torture to the Questionnaire of the OHCHR to members states, national human rights institutions, civil society and other relevant stakeholders on the role of prevention in the promotion and protection of human rights (2011)

United Nations

Office of the United Nations High Commissioner for Human Rights (2018) Preventing torture: The role of national preventive mechanisms, a practical guide

Replies of the former Yugoslav Republic of Macedonia to the report of the Subcommittee on Prevention of Torture and Other Cruel, Inhuman or Degrading Treatment or Punishment on the visit undertaken from 23 to 29 April 2017 (2019), CAT/OP/MKD/1/Add.1

UN Special Rapporteur on Torture and other cruel, inhuman or degrading treatment or punishment, Report to the 61st session of the UN General Assembly (2006), A/61/259

UN Special Rapporteur on Torture and other cruel, inhuman or degrading treatment or punishment, Report to the 71st session of the UN General Assembly (2016), UN A/71/298

UN Subcommittee on Prevention of Torture, Report on the Visit of the SPT to the Maldives, UN Doc. CAT/OP/MDV/1, 26 February 2009

UN Subcommittee on Prevention of Torture, Draft general comment No. 1 on places of deprivation of liberty (Article 4) (2023)

United Nations Convention against Torture and Other Cruel, Inhuman or Degrading Treatment or Punishment (1984)

United Nations General Assembly Third Committee - Resolution on Administration of Justice (2022), A/RES/77/219

United Nations General Assembly Third Committee - Resolution on Torture (2022), A/RES/77/209

United Nations Optional Protocol to the Convention against Torture (2002)

United Nations Subcommittee on Prevention of Torture and other cruel, inhuman or degrading treatment of punishment (2013a) Report on the visit for the purpose of providing advisory assistance to the national preventive mechanism of the Federal Republic of Germany, CAT/OP/DEU/2

United Nations Subcommittee on Prevention of Torture and other cruel, inhuman or degrading treatment of punishment (2013b) Report on the visit to the former Yugoslav Republic of Macedonia undertaken from 23 to 29 April 2017: observations and recommendations addressed to the State party, CAT/OP/MKD/1

United Nations Subcommittee on Prevention of Torture and other cruel, inhuman or degrading treatment of punishment (2017a) Report from visit to Ukraine undertaken from 19 to 25 May and from 5 to 9 September 2016: observations and recommendations addressed to the State party, CAT/OP/UKR/3

United Nations Subcommittee on Prevention of Torture and other cruel, inhuman or degrading treatment of punishment (2017b) Report from visit to Tunisia undertaken from 11 to 14 April 2016: Observations and recommendations addressed to the national preventive mechanism, CAT/OP/TUN/2

United Nations Subcommittee on Prevention of Torture and other cruel, inhuman or degrading treatment of punishment (2017c) Report on the visit for the purpose of providing advisory assistance to the national preventive mechanism of the Republic of Malta, CAT/OP/MLT/1

United Nations Subcommittee on Prevention of Torture and other cruel, inhuman or degrading treatment of punishment (2017d) Report from visit to Cyprus undertaken from 25 to 29 January 2016: Observations and recommendations addressed to the state party, CAT/OP/CYP/1

United Nations Subcommittee on Prevention of Torture and other cruel, inhuman or degrading treatment of punishment (2019) Report on the visit undertaken from 4 to 15 March 2018 in Uruguay, CAT/OP/URY/1

Others

Principles on Effective Interviewing for Investigations and Information Gathering, May 2021. Retrieved from: www.interviewingprinciples.com

Audrey Olivier Muralt (she/her) holds a 'master's degree in International Humanitarian and Human Rights Law from Aix Marseille University III (France) and an LLM in Political Sciences and Public Administration from Science Po Rennes (France). She is a published author on torture prevention and the Optional Protocol of the UN Convention against Torture (OPCAT), having co-authored two academic publications: OPCAT in Federal states: towards a better understanding of NPM models and challenges, published in the Australian Journal of Human Rights in May 2019; and OPCAT Challenges and The Way Forwards: the ratification and implementation of the Optional Protocol to the UN Convention against Torture, published in the Essex Human Rights Review in December 2009.

She has worked on torture prevention for more than a decade and held various leadership positions at the international torture prevention NGO, also known as the Association for the Prevention of Torture (APT, www.apt.ch). Until September 2023, she was the Deputy Secretary General at the APT, focusing on promoting better detention conditions through advocacy, policy and practices change. As the Deputy, she led a small team based in Geneva as well as in Asia, Latin America and Oceania. Her responsibilities included operations, communication, fundraising, representation, digital transformation and organisational change. She now supports social change and human rights organisations in crafting their strategies and developing their organisational model and is currently the Director of Operations at the Geneva International Film Festival (GIFF).

Chapter 9
The National Preventive Mechanism in Georgia: Experiences, Success Stories, and Challenges

Nika Kvaratskhelia

Contents

Abstract This article examines the role of the National Preventive Mechanism in torture prevention from a practical point of view. Relying on the firsthand experience of the National Preventive Mechanism of Georgia, it provides practical insight into the wide-ranging issues relevant to the objective of minimizing risks of torture and ill-treatment in police custody. It attempts to explore to what extent the National Preventive Mechanism of Georgia has succeeded in lessening the likelihood of torture and ill-treatment occurring. The text presents the concept of prevention of torture and the interpretation of the mandate of the National Preventive Mechanism, which are not always correctly understood. It highlights two parallel processes of the National Preventive Mechanism maturing and developments taking place in the field of protection against torture and ill-treatment in Georgia, trying to outline causal links between these processes. It also provides a brief overview of challenges and possible solutions.

N. Kvaratskhelia (✉)
Office of the Public Defender of Georgia, Tbilisi, Georgia
e-mail: nkvaratskhelia@ombudsman.ge

R. Alleweldt (ed.), *Fair Treatment of Persons in Police Custody*,
https://doi.org/10.1007/978-3-031-61737-9_9

9.1 Introduction

The present paper provides information on how the National Preventive Mechanism (NPM) of Georgia has come into being, what problems it faced at the very outset, what the situation in Georgia was at that moment, what steps were taken by the NPM, and whether or not it has contributed to the strengthening of protection against torture. It seeks to identify room for improvement in the working methodology of the NPM, putting a particular emphasis on the follow-up to NPM recommendations.

As a first step, the paper highlights the concept of prevention of torture and then provides an overview of the history and experience of the NPM of Georgia, the success stories, and the challenges to be tackled. In the course of preparation for this contribution, the reports of the NPM of Georgia have been surveyed and the jurisprudence of international treaty bodies consulted.

9.2 Concept of Torture Prevention

The objective of torture prevention has long been pursued around the world. Article 5 of the Universal Declaration of Human Rights (UDHR) stipulates that "no one shall be subjected to torture or to cruel, inhuman or degrading treatment or punishment."[1] This very simple sentence in the UDHR was further clarified and reinforced by the UN Convention Against Torture and Other Cruel, Inhuman or Degrading Treatment or Punishment (UNCAT) in 1984. UNCAT has established a clear definition of torture;[2] created the obligation of states parties to take effective legislative, administrative, judicial, or other measures to prevent acts of torture in any territory under its jurisdiction;[3] and reaffirmed the absolute nature of the prohibition of torture.[4]

[1] The prohibition of torture is also included in the International Covenant on Civil and Political Rights ('ICCPR'). According to Article 7, "no one shall be subjected to torture or to cruel, inhuman or degrading treatment or punishment. In particular, no one shall be subjected without his free consent to medical or scientific experimentation".

[2] For the purposes of this Convention, the term "torture" means any act by which severe pain or suffering, whether physical or mental, is intentionally inflicted on a person for such purposes as obtaining from him or a third person information or a confession, punishing him for an act he or a third person has committed or is suspected of having committed, or intimidating or coercing him or a third person, or for any reason based on discrimination of any kind, when such pain or suffering is inflicted by or at the instigation of or with the consent or acquiescence of a public official or other person acting in an official capacity. It does not include pain or suffering arising only from, inherent in or incidental to lawful sanctions. Article 1(1), UNCAT.

[3] Article 2(1), UNCAT.

[4] "No exceptional circumstances whatsoever, whether a state of war or a threat of war, internal political instability or any other public emergency, may be invoked as a justification of torture." Article 2(2), UNCAT.

After the entry into force of UNCAT, the idea of having regular visits to places of deprivation of liberty became topical again, and following intensive debates, the UN General Assembly adopted the Optional Protocol to the Convention Against Torture and Other Cruel, Inhuman or Degrading Treatment or Punishment (OPCAT) on December 18, 2002. Four years later, OPCAT entered into force after the 20th ratification, laying the foundation for a new, global torture prevention system.

OPCAT is a unique international treaty establishing both international and national visitation mechanisms. It was clearly mentioned in its preamble that "further measures are necessary to achieve the purposes of the Convention [...] and to strengthen the protection of persons deprived of their liberty against torture and other cruel, inhuman or degrading treatment or punishment." The preamble further reads as follows: "[...] efforts to eradicate torture should first and foremost be concentrated on prevention. [...] The protection of persons deprived of their liberty against torture and other cruel, inhuman or degrading treatment or punishment can be strengthened by non-judicial means of a preventive nature, based on regular visits to places of detention." Thus, clearly defining its objectives, OPCAT created the Subcommittee on Prevention of Torture (SPT),[5] an international treaty body, as well as NPMs,[6] to operate at the domestic level.

In 2010, in its twelfth session, the SPT adopted the concept of prevention of torture,[7] which has defined its approach to the obligation of states parties to UNCAT to prevent torture and other cruel, inhuman, or degrading treatment or punishment. The SPT is of the view that "whilst the obligation to prevent torture and ill-treatment buttresses the prohibition of torture, it also remains an obligation in its own right and a failure to take appropriate preventive measures which were within its power could engage the international responsibility of the State, should torture occur in circumstances where the State would not otherwise have been responsible."[8]

Relying on general comment No. 2[9] of the Committee Against Torture (CAT), citing that the duty to prevent is "wide-ranging" and is in the process of continual evolution, the SPT believes that "the prevention of torture and ill-treatment embraces—or should embrace—as many as possible of those things which in a given situation can contribute towards the lessening of the likelihood or risk of

---

[5]OPCAT, Article 2.

[6]OPCAT, Article 3.

[7]"The approach of the Subcommittee on Prevention of Torture to the concept of prevention of torture and other cruel, inhuman or degrading treatment or punishment under the Optional Protocol to the Convention against Torture and Other Cruel, Inhuman or Degrading Treatment or Punishment", Subcommittee on Prevention of Torture and Other Cruel, Inhuman or Degrading Treatment or Punishment, twelfth session, Geneva, 15-19 November 2010. https://tbinternet.ohchr.org/_layouts/treatybodyexternal/Download.aspx?symbolno=CAT/OP/12/6&Lang=en accessed on 29 April 2023.

[8]Ibid. para. 1.

[9]General Comment No.2, CAT/C/GC/2, 24 January 2008. https://tbinternet.ohchr.org/_layouts/treatybodyexternal/Download.aspx?symbolno=CAT%2fC%2fGC%2f2&Lang=en Accessed on 29 April 2023.

torture or ill-treatment occurring."[10] It also stresses the importance of taking into account the specific context existing in a particular state party. Thus, the SPT argues that "it is not possible to devise a comprehensive statement of what the obligation to prevent torture and ill-treatment entails in abstracto."[11] The SPT proceeds to suggest that the prevalence of torture and ill-treatment is preconditioned by a variety of factors, among others, by the general level of enjoyment of human rights and the rule of law, levels of poverty, social exclusion, corruption, discrimination, etc.[12] The SPT makes special emphasis on the necessity to engage with broader regulatory and policy frameworks. It must look at how these frameworks are implemented in practice,[13] that is, whether there is a wide variety of procedural safeguards set forth in the legislation and applied in practice for persons deprived of their liberty. Interestingly, the SPT believes that "since the purpose of such safeguards is to reduce the likelihood of torture or ill-treatment occurring, they are of relevance irrespective of whether there is any evidence of torture or ill-treatment actually taking place."[14]

The SPT recognizes the complexity of the objective of torture prevention and calls on states parties to employ a holistic approach. In the SPT's words, "prevention is a multifaceted and interdisciplinary endeavor." The SPT, in principle, acknowledges the fact that there is no logical limit to the range of issues that might have a preventive impact but remains pragmatic to focus on those issues that appear, in its view, to be most pressing, relevant, and realizable.[15]

The SPT underlines the importance of several issues in this paper concerning the concept of prevention of torture. Most importantly, it stresses that the prevention of torture and ill-treatment is feasible if the system of detention is open to scrutiny. "NPMs, together with national human rights institutions and ombudsman's offices, play a key role in ensuring that such scrutiny takes place," the SPT suggests. It also emphasizes the complementary role of judicial scrutiny and concludes that NPMs, civil society, and judicial oversight are essential and mutually reinforcing means of prevention.[16]

In light of the foregoing, it is evident that by elaborating the concept of prevention of torture, the SPT tries to reinforce the preventive approach and to define the mission of the oversight bodies created under OPCAT. Accordingly, the present paper will dwell on the key elements of this concept of the prevention of torture.

---

[10] The approach of the Subcommittee on Prevention of Torture to the concept of prevention of torture and other cruel, inhuman or degrading treatment or punishment under the Optional Protocol to the Convention against Torture and Other Cruel, Inhuman or Degrading Treatment or Punishment", para. 3.

[11] Ibid.

[12] Ibid. para. 5(a).

[13] Ibid. para. 5(b).

[14] Ibid. para. 5(c).

[15] Ibid. para. 5(f).

[16] Ibid. para. 5(h).

9.3 Experience Gained over the Decade

9.3.1 Torture and Ill-Treatment in Police Custody Before the Establishment of the NPM

For the purposes of having a broader picture of the context preceding the establishment of the NPM in Georgia, it is reasonable to look at major challenges concerning the prevention of torture and other forms of ill-treatment in police custody. This is important inasmuch as the existing context has ultimately influenced the working methods of the NPM of Georgia. Besides, it is also crucial to delineate the point of departure to assess the impact of the work of the NPM of Georgia over the decade.

According to the report of the US Department of State on Georgia, in 2008, the following was to be identified: "The main human rights abuses reported during the year included at least two suspected deaths due to excessive use of force by law enforcement officers, intimidation of suspects, abuse of prisoners, poor conditions in prisons and pretrial detention facilities, police impunity, lack of access for average citizens to defense attorneys, reports of politically motivated detentions, lack of due process in some cases, and reports of government pressure on the judiciary." Nevertheless, the report mentioned some positive aspects, such as the decrease in complaints against the police and the absence of complaints against the staff of temporary detention facilities.[17]

Earlier, in 2007, the conduct of law enforcement in Georgia was assessed by the European Committee for the Prevention of Torture and Inhuman or Degrading Treatment or Punishment (CPT), stating that "the situation as regards the treatment of persons detained by the police in Georgia had considerably improved since the Committee's second periodic visit. The great majority of persons interviewed during the 2007 visit, who were or had recently been in police custody, indicated that they had been treated in a correct manner." However, there were several isolated cases identified where police officers had allegedly physically ill-treated a detainee. The CPT outlined the significant decrease in the number of allegations of police ill-treatment.[18] It went on to say that this positive change was a result of a number of measures taken by the Georgian authorities, including the recruitment of new staff, the enactment of new selection and training procedures, the adoption of the Code of Ethics, the acquisition of modern technical means of inquiry, the restructuring of temporary detention facilities, the introduction of a new definition of torture, lessening reliance on confessions in criminal proceedings, etc. The CPT

[17] 2008 Country Reports on Human Rights Practices, Georgia, Bureau of Democracy, Human Rights, and Labor, US Department of State. https://www.state.gov/j/drl/rls/hrrpt/2008/eur/119080.htm. Accessed on 29 April 2023.

[18] Report to the Georgian Government on the visit to Georgia carried out by the European Committee for the Prevention of Torture and Inhuman or Degrading Treatment or Punishment (CPT) from 21 March to 2 April 2007, paras. 11: https://www.coe.int/en/web/cpt/georgia. Accessed on 29 April 2023.

specifically underlined the occurrence of regular monitoring of police establishments by the Public Defender's Office (PDO).[19]

It can be seen from the aforementioned that, indeed, the period before the establishment of the NPM in Georgia was marked by active reforms in the police system. Inarguably, there were efforts made to combat corruption, equip the police with necessary means, and build its capacity as a functional institution, but it would make an erroneous impression as to the situation concerning torture and other forms of ill-treatment if one neglected the situation existing in prisons, where remand prisoners awaited trials and the issue of effective investigation of cases of torture and ill-treatment remained unsolved. Apparently, the conditions of detention and the impunity were the Achilles' heel of the international reputation of Georgia, since the above cited reports had raised concerns in this regard.

9.3.2 *Establishment of the NPM*

Georgia ratified OPCAT in 2005, and it was only in 2009 that the NPM of Georgia was established. The Organic Law on Public Defender of Georgia[20] was amended to assign the function of the NPM to the Public Defender of Georgia.[21] According to Article 19^1 of the Organic Law, with a view to discharging the functions of the NPM, the Special Preventive Group was established with the Public Defender of Georgia. The Organic Law goes on to provide relevant provisions to enable the effective operation of the NPM. It defines key elements for the functioning of the NPM and leaves the structure and precise modus operandi for further interpretation. For example, it does not mention the NPM department within the office of the Public Defender of Georgia, which, in practice, is the core unit. It also omits to define that the mandate of the NPM is primarily preventive and should be based on system-oriented, proactive, and preventive visiting. Apparently, the legislator had opted not to go into details as the OPCAT system was emerging at that time and there could be some progressive interpretations following the first experience.

As the experience has shown, there was a confusion of mandates at the very outset within the Office of the Public Defender of Georgia. Clearly, there was a lack of understanding of the differences between the mandates of the Public Defender of Georgia as an Ombuds institution and the NPM. That was why, from the very beginning up until the end of 2014, the NPM of Georgia used to deal with individual complaints. While referring to a confusion of mandates, it would be fair to note that the establishment of the NPM coincided with a period of widespread torture and

[19] Ibid. para. 12.

[20] The Office of the Public Defender of Georgia is an "A" status holder National Human Rights Institution tasked with oversight of the protection of human rights in Georgia. The foundation of the institutions is laid down in Article 35 of the Constitution of Georgia.

[21] Article 31(1).

ill-treatment in the criminal justice system of Georgia. Due to this fact, the work of the NPM of Georgia initially was more reactive than proactive. It had to handle complaints of alleged torture and ill-treatment in the same way as the PDO had long handled them.

It is also fair to note that despite the workload caused by complaint handling, the Georgian NPM team conducted regular visits to places of deprivation of liberty. Only in 2009, it carried out 198 planned visits to different places of deprivation of liberty. It is also noteworthy here that, in addition to planned visits, there was a total of 323 ad hoc visits,[22] which goes to show again how the work of the NPM of Georgia was overwhelmed by complaint handling.

While it was important to follow up on individual complaints in the given context, the NPM of Georgia began to feel that the impact of its work was somewhat sporadic and needed enhancement. Bearing in mind the unique mandate of the NPM under the OPCAT system, the NPM team started to elaborate strategies to increase the effectiveness of its work. The first issue on the "to-do list" was to remove the reactive work and switch to more proactive and system-oriented work. Not to compromise the interests of complainants, it was decided that the function of complaint handling would be assigned to the Criminal Justice Department of the PDO in 2014. This created an opportunity to have more staff members of the PDO involved in complaint handling and enabled the NPM team to primarily focus on preventive work through regular visits to places of deprivation of liberty, reporting and engaging in dialogue with the relevant authorities. Following the aforementioned change in the working methodology, the NPM of Georgia began to produce reports following visits and to conduct thematic studies with complex methodologies.[23] Besides, the NPM team implemented several capacity-building projects and drafted precise instruments for visits to each type of places of deprivation of liberty. As a consequence, the NPM of Georgia started to produce more analytical and system-oriented annual reports.

Apart from the importance of the proper understanding of the NPM mandate, one of the major lessons learned over the decade is that there should be a sufficient level of cooperation between the NPM and the relevant authorities. As experience has shown, there will be very little progress without a truly constructive dialogue. That being acknowledged, the NPM of Georgia commenced to elaborate follow-up and advocacy strategies to bring about the implementation of its recommendations. With the generous support of the European Union, the NPM team started a project to this effect with the Association for the Prevention of Torture (APT). Within this project, several workshops were held to analyze the working methodology and elaborate guidelines for a proper follow-up to NPM recommendations. The efforts to revise

[22] Annual Report 2009, the NPM of Georgia, p. 5. https://www.ohchr.org/Documents/HRBodies/OPCAT/NPM/NPM_Georgia2009_AnnualReport.pdf. Accessed on 29 April 2023.

[23] For example, the recent Report on Impact of Prison Conditions on Prisoners' Health, 2018. https://www.ombudsman.ge/eng/190307075330spetsialuri-angarishebi/patimrobis-pirobebis-gavlena-patimarta-janmrtelobaze Accessed on 29 April 2023.

and update the working methodology of the NPM of Georgia are constantly kept up in the light of the views taken by the SPT.[24]

9.4 Success Stories

The first very important success story is the establishment of a system of regular, unannounced[25] visits conducted by the NPM of Georgia. This conveys a clear message that those behind closed doors will not be forgotten and left neither helpless nor hopeless. The expectation that NPM members may appear at any time at places of deprivation of liberty in itself can have a preventive effect, but certainly, this is not the limit. Most importantly, the NPM of Georgia is focused on the introduction of safeguards against torture and other forms of ill-treatment. It pursues the objective of lessening the likelihood of torture and ill-treatment occurring. This strategic approach is seen as a key to the prevention of torture.

The second success story relates to public awareness raising. Currently, through NPM reports, the public has been well informed of the situation in places of deprivation of liberty. The NPM holds regular public discussions and campaigns on the prevention of torture and in this way attempts to mobilize the community against torture. The media remains a trustful ally in this process.

The third success story is linked to the increase in the quality of cooperation between the NPM and the relevant authorities. While in the dynamic process of interactions some tensions[26] arise from time to time, generally the level of cooperation remains high. There are regular meetings held with relevant governmental agencies, and NPM recommendations are discussed in a constructive way. Importantly, in 2013, the Parliament of Georgia came forward with an initiative to have detailed deliberations on the parliamentary report of the Public Defender of Georgia, which includes the findings and recommendations of the NPM. Notably, this had been a rare case before as the reports of the Public Defender were mostly ignored. Interestingly, by doing so, the Parliament of Georgia delivered a clear message that it would exercise its parliamentary control over the implementation of the Public Defender's recommendations on a regular basis.[27]

---

[24] Guidelines on National Preventive Mechanisms, Subcommittee on Prevention of Torture and Other Cruel, Inhuman or Degrading Treatment or Punishment, twelfth session, Geneva, 15–19 November 2010, CAT/OP/12/5. https://tbinternet.ohchr.org/_layouts/treatybodyexternal/Download.aspx?symbolno=CAT/OP/12/5&Lang=en. Accessed on 29 April 2023.

[25] The visits of the NPM of Georgia are always unannounced.

[26] In the past, there were instances of physical and verbal attacks on the Public Defender and its staff. The most notorious case was the beating of the Public Defender, Mr. Sozar Subari, during the violent dispersal of the peaceful assembly on 7 November 2007.

[27] After the hearing in the Committee of Human Rights and Civil Integration of the Parliament of Georgia, the Public Defender of Georgia presents the parliamentary report at the plenary session. The Parliament of Georgia then adopts the resolution, which includes the list of the Public

The fourth success story relates to the fact that the NPM recommendations started to be reflected in the National Human Rights Action Plan and, importantly, in the separate interagency Action Plan on Combating Torture. The NPM of Georgia participates in discussions on draft action plans and keeps an eye on the implementation of those action plans.

The above-listed four topics considered as success stories are indeed preconditions for a greater positive impact of the Georgian NPM's work in pursuit of setting safeguards and lessening the likelihood of torture and ill-treatment happening. Now it is important to see whether the Georgian NPM's work has entailed the introduction of such safeguards. First, the key NPM recommendations since 2009 will be reviewed and then their implementation assessed. The NPM's annual report of 2009, the very first report of the NPM of Georgia, outlined several recommendations concerning the notification of injuries presumably inflicted by police officers; the improvement of material conditions in temporary detention facilities; the increase of personal living space, hygiene, and sanitation; access to nutritious food; and the construction of special detention facilities for administrative offenses.[28] The NPM's annual report of 2010, in addition to those mentioned above, included completely new or reformulated (revisited) recommendations, inter alia, on the effective investigation of cases of ill-treatment, the introduction of a unified system of injury records, the employment of medical staff in all temporary detention facilities, the conduct of training on the documentation of injuries, and the observance of medical confidentiality. The report also emphasized the importance of defining clear rules and procedures on the phone notification of detention to a third party.[29] In 2012, the NPM of Georgia further recommended the decrease of the maximum term of administrative detention (for administrative offenses) from 90 days to 15 days.[30] The NPM's annual report of 2014 introduced specific recommendations on the installation of CCTV cameras in all police stations and keeping the records of the CCTV system both in police stations and temporary detention facilities for a reasonable time period.[31] In its annual report of 2015, the NPM of Georgia further called for the video recording of the whole period from the moment of arrest until placement in a temporary detention facility. The NPM believed that this could be

---

Defender's recommendations (including those of the NPM of Georgia). By virtue of the adoption of the parliamentary resolutions, those recommendations become binding on the relevant governmental agencies and are subject to parliamentary control. Ultimately, the governmental agencies are requested to provide information on the implementation of the mentioned recommendations before the hearing of the next parliamentary report of the Public Defender of Georgia.

[28] NPM annual report of 2009, pp. 27–28.

[29] NPM annual report 2010, pp. 53–60. https://www.ohchr.org/Documents/HRBodies/OPCAT/NPM/2010MonitoringPenitentiaryInstitutionsTemporaryDetentionIsolators.pdf. Accessed 29 on April 2023.

[30] NPM annual report 2012, pp. 73–83. https://www.ohchr.org/Documents/HRBodies/OPCAT/NPM/NPMreport2012_Georgia.pdf. Accessed on 29 April 2023.

[31] NPM annual report 2014, pp. 154–166. https://www.ohchr.org/Documents/HRBodies/OPCAT/NPM/Georgian_NPM_annual_report2014.pdf. Accessed on 29 April 2023.

made possible by equipping police officers with body cameras and installing cameras in police vehicles and police stations.[32] It also stressed the importance of the maintenance of accurate custody records through an amendment of relevant regulations, staff training, and close supervision.[33] In the same report, the NPM of Georgia highlighted issues concerning the complaint mechanism and inspections. It recommended for a confidential complaint mechanism to be put in place in temporary detention facilities and for all detainees to be briefed about the procedure.[34]

In the latest annual report of 2017,[35] the NPM of Georgia made several new recommendations. Namely, it recommended the amendment of the Code of Criminal Procedure of Georgia to the effect that a detained person immediately be brought to a temporary detention facility.[36] Again, the importance of access to legal aid was outlined by recommending the increase of the operational capacity of free legal aid service. Furthermore, the NPM of Georgia recommended keeping appropriate records on access to a lawyer and notification of arrest to a third party. It also made recommendations concerning the working conditions of police officers. In particular, the NPM recommended the reconsideration of shifts to avoid the professional burnout of police officers and the increase of remuneration for the work carried out. The report also highlighted the need for police training to be guided by a human-rights-based approach.[37] Following the review of the NPM recommendations, it has to be noted that the Public Defender and the NPM of Georgia, bearing in mind the vital importance of the fight against impunity in preventing torture, revealing systemic shortcomings of the Prosecutor's Office of Georgia, have urged the state authorities for many years to establish an independent investigative body. Ultimately, after numerous advocacy efforts made at national and international levels concerning an independent investigative mechanism, in July 2018, the Law on the State Inspectorate was passed. According to the mentioned law, the State Inspectorate shall become operative in July 2019. It is indeed a step forward, and the NPM of Georgia hopes that a newly established investigative body will prove to be effective in the fight against impunity.

[32] NPM annual report 2015, p. 244. https://www.ohchr.org/Documents/HRBodies/OPCAT/NPM/NPM_Georgia_2015.pdf. Accessed on 29 April 2023.

[33] Ibid. pp. 250–251.

[34] Ibid. p. 255.

[35] In parallel to the drafting of the present paper the NPM of Georgia was working on the annual report of 2018.

[36] This recommendation echoed the position of the UN Special Rapporteur on Torture, Mr. Juan Mendez, who visited Georgia in 2015 and considered temporary detention facilities safer places for a detainee to be immediately brought. The report is available at: http://ap.ohchr.org/documents/dpage_e.aspx?si=A/HRC/31/57/Add.3. Accessed on 29 April 2023.

[37] NPM annual report 2017, pp. 29–30. https://www.ohchr.org/Documents/HRBodies/OPCAT/NPM/NPM_Georgia_2017.pdf. Accessed 29 on April 2023.

While it is widely recognized that the fight against impunity should be seen as a point of departure,[38] the NPM of Georgia believes that creating safeguards against torture and ill-treatment is equally important, as these safeguards aim at preventing the occurrence of acts of torture and ill-treatment. This being said, it is now interesting to see how the NPM of Georgia has succeeded in establishing those safeguards and in lessening the risks of torture and ill-treatment. The first very important achievement in this regard is creating a system of medical documentation of bodily injuries in temporary detention facilities and penitentiary establishments (including those designed for pretrial detention).[39] It is crucial in terms of the timely identification of cases of torture and ill-treatment even in the absence of a formal complaint and for securing medical evidence for investigative purposes. Currently, medical staff in temporary detention facilities and penitentiary establishments are required to conduct a medical examination of a detainee upon admission, document injuries in a predesigned medical form, take photographs of injuries, and report to investigative authorities in case there is a suspicion that a detainee may have been subjected to torture and ill-treatment.

Importantly, the NPM of Georgia welcomes the recent approval of the procedure introduced for sending complaints from temporary detention facilities and notes that a confidential complaint mechanism has been in place in penitentiary establishments since the Imprisonment Code of Georgia became effective in 2010.

Seen as a very important aspect in preventing arbitrary or incommunicado detention and torture, the NPM of Georgia has been looking closely at the issue of the appropriate keeping of custody records.[40] It is welcomed that in recent years,

[38]"By defining the offence of torture as distinct from common assault or other crimes, the Committee considers that States parties will directly advance the Convention's overarching aim of preventing torture and ill-treatment. Naming and defining this crime will promote the Convention's aim, inter alia, by alerting everyone, including perpetrators, victims, and the public, to the special gravity of the crime of torture. Codifying this crime will also (a) emphasize the need for appropriate punishment that takes into account the gravity of the offence, (b) strengthen the deterrent effect of the prohibition itself, (c) enhance the ability of responsible officials to track the specific crime of torture and (d) enable and empower the public to monitor and, when required, to challenge State action as well as State inaction that violates the Convention" - General Comment No.2, para. 11.

[39]The Istanbul Protocol—Manual on the Effective Investigation and Documentation of Torture and Other Cruel, Inhuman or Degrading Treatment or Punishment—was consulted in the process. The Istanbul protocol is available at: https://www.ohchr.org/en/publications/policy-and-methodological-publications/istanbul-protocol-manual-effective-0. Accessed 29 on April 2023.

[40]"The CPT considers that the fundamental safeguards granted to persons in police custody would be reinforced (and the work of police officers quite possibly facilitated) if a single and comprehensive custody record were to exist for each person detained, on which would be recorded all aspects of his custody and action taken regarding them (when deprived of liberty and reasons for that measure; when told of rights; signs of injury, mental illness, etc; when next of kin/consulate and lawyer contacted and when visited by them; when offered food; when interrogated; when transferred or released, etc.). For various matters (for example, items in the person's possession, the fact of being told of one's rights and of invoking or waiving them), the signature of the detainee should be obtained and, if necessary, the absence of a signature explained. Further, the detainee's lawyer

there has been significant improvement in this regard. Nevertheless, the NPM has a number of relevant recommendations aimed at the further improvement of custody recordkeeping.

Yet another success is linked to the fact that temporary detention facilities are becoming safer places for detainees. For the past few years, no allegations of torture and ill-treatment by the staff of temporary detention facilities have been received from detainees. While remaining subordinate to the Ministry of Internal Affairs of Georgia, the staff of these facilities have demonstrated their commitment to human rights. They have not shown any signs of corporate loyalty to police officers by authorizing or otherwise turning a blind eye to their wrongdoings. They clearly understand their mission to keep detainees safe until they are released or moved to penitentiary establishments.

Apparently, another example of the removal of risky practices is the decrease of the maximum term of detention for administrative offenses from 90 days to 15 days. The prolonged detention for administrative offenses without due process in appalling conditions was used against political opponents in the past.[41] Hence, the decrease in the number of days of detention was welcomed by the NPM of Georgia. At the same time, while acknowledging significant progress in improving detention conditions, the NPM continues to argue that these improved conditions are still substandard in the light of detention for up to 15 days for administrative offenses. The NPM's strategic approach to the issue is most likely to result either in special, well-designed detention facilities for administrative offenses or in the complete abolishment of detention for administrative offenses; the latter would be more desirable.[42]

The NPM of Georgia has long been recommending making use of modern technologies to make sure that police conduct is in line with human rights standards. One of the issues discussed relates to the use of CCTV cameras in police stations and police vehicles, as well as equipping police officers with body-worn cameras. According to the NPM recommendation, the number of CCTV cameras and areas covered by the CCTV system in police stations has been increasing every year. The ultimate goal is to cover all areas where detainees are kept in police stations.[43] Yet

should have access to such a custody record."—Extract from the 2nd General Report of the CPT, published in 1992, CPT/Inf(92)3-part1, para. 40.

[41] Administrative Error, Georgia's Flawed System for Administrative Detention, Human Rights Watch, 4 January 2012. https://www.hrw.org/report/2012/01/04/administrative-error/georgias-flawed-system-administrative-detention#. Accessed on 29 April 2023.

[42] Discussions among stakeholders are ongoing.

[43] In its concluding observation of 2018, the CAT recommended the Russian Federation to ensure that Video recordings of all interrogations are maintained and video surveillance installed in all areas of custody facilities where detainees may be present, except in cases where detainees' rights to privacy or to confidential communication with their lawyer or a doctor may be violated. Such recordings should be kept in secure facilities, for example in prosecutors' offices, and made available to investigators, detainees, and their lawyers. https://tbinternet.ohchr.org/_layouts/treatybodyexternal/Download.aspx?symbolno=CAT%2fC%2fRUS%2fCO%2f6&Lang=en. Accessed on 29 April 2023. Similarly, the CAT made the following recommendation to Spain: The

another issue linked to video surveillance is the recording of interviews. While the Code of Criminal Procedure of Georgia authorizes an investigator to make audio-video recordings of interviews,[44] this is done very rarely. This is why the NPM of Georgia is now considering recommending to make the recording of interviews a statutory obligation.

With regard to body-worn cameras, the NPM recommendation has only partly been implemented as only patrol police and some territorial units have been equipped with body-worn cameras. Obviously, this is a step forward to ensure that the detention is lawful and the use of force is necessary and proportionate. Regretfully, the NPM recommendation has not been fulfilled with respect to establishing a statutory obligation of recording certain types of police interaction with citizens and, most importantly, the process of arrest. The NPM of Georgia has intensive discussions of this issue with the Ministry of Internal Affairs and hopes that a positive outcome will be reached in the nearest future.

Another issue that can be considered a success story is related to the training of police officers. Although there are many problems in this field, the recent change in the strategy of the Academy of the Ministry of Internal Affairs of Georgia is a promising sign of progress. It is now expected that more resources will be invested in professional training and the education of police officers to ensure that the police system is provided with newly recruited human resources.[45] These newly recruited officers are hoped to foster a change of institutional culture to strengthen the fair treatment of detained persons and to exercise proper policing. The NPM of Georgia is convinced that it is important that police capacity-building endeavors are made in a way that best makes human rights operational in the daily activities of the police.

Last but not least, although the NPM of Georgia has never expressed recommendations on keeping statistical data relevant to torture prevention, the regular interaction and official request of disaggregated data from the Ministry of Internal Affairs of Georgia has made it possible to establish a methodological framework for keeping

---

State party should ensure the audiovisual recording of all procedures in police stations and places of detention involving persons deprived of their liberty, including those in incommunicado detention, except in cases where it might violate the right to privacy or detainees' right to confidential consultation with their lawyer or doctor. Such recordings should be kept in secure facilities and be made available to investigators, detainees, and their lawyers. https://tbinternet.ohchr.org/_layouts/treatybodyexternal/Download.aspx?symbolno=CAT%2fC%2fESP%2fCO%2f6&Lang=en. Accessed 29 on April 2023.

[44] [. . .] The code should also indicate the systematic audio and/or video recording of the time each interview begins and ends [. . .] interviews should be conducted in dedicated interview rooms which are suitably equipped and have the necessary audio/video equipment installed"—the CPT report on the visit to Serbia from 31 May to 7 June 2017, CPT/Inf (2018) 21. https://rm.coe.int/16808b5ee7. Accessed on 29 April 2023.

[45] For more information, please, consult the official webpage of the Academy of the Ministry of Internal Affairs of Georgia. https://police.ge/en/lepl/mia-police-academy. Accessed 29 April 2023.

statistical data.[46] Now it is crucial that this methodology is reviewed and relevant formal regulations are enacted in order to ensure the sustainability of the practice. It is expected that the well-established system of data collection and analysis will enable the tracking of dynamics in the field of policing and human rights.[47]

9.5 Challenges

The challenges faced by the NPM of Georgia can be divided into two groups. The first set of challenges is related to the working methodology of the NPM itself, whereas the second includes challenges linked to the objective of lessening the risks of torture and ill-treatment. That being said, the following two subsections will discuss these challenges separately with a focus on finding ways to address them.

9.5.1 Methodological Challenges

NPMs around the world are advised to constantly review their working methodology.[48] This advice stems from the complexity of the concept of torture prevention. It is also true that in emerging democracies, the rapidly changing course of events necessitates some degree of flexibility and ability to adapt to new realities. While not losing the focus on developments taking place in the field of torture prevention globally, the NPMs have to be mindful of their domestic context in order to select the most appropriate strategy for strengthening the protection against torture and ill-treatment.

The very fact that NPMs are expected more to engage in constructive dialogue with relevant state authorities and provide practical recommendations (solutions), rather than only condemning the flaws and malpractices identified, gives rise to the need for the diverse expertise of the respective NPMs. Furthermore, it is important

[46]The relevant statistical data are available at: https://info.police.ge/cat?id=88 Accessed on 29 April 2023.

[47]In its concluding observation of 2019, the CAT recommended Senegal to ensure that medical personnel inform an independent investigation body of any evidence of torture or ill-treatment confidentially and without risk of reprisals; the State party should compile statistical data on the number of cases identified through this mechanism, as well as detailed information on the outcome of investigations concerning these cases. https://tbinternet.ohchr.org/_layouts/treatybodyexternal/Download.aspx?symbolno=CAT%2fC%2fSEN%2fCO%2f4&Lang=en. Accessed 29 on April 2023.

[48]The SPT Guidelines on National Preventive Mechanisms, para. 31.

that NPM recommendations meet so-called "Double-SMART" criteria.[49] Contrary to this, as practice has shown, many of the NPM recommendations were of a general nature, creating communication problems with relevant authorities. In December 2016, the NPM of Georgia conducted an experiment during the training of prison governors to assess the level of understanding of NPM recommendations by the prison governors. It appeared that some of the NPM recommendations were not well understood by the latter. When the essence of these recommendations was explained in other words and more carefully, the governors started to comprehend these recommendations and expressed their willingness to implement them. The conclusion made following this experiment was that the NPM of Georgia had to review the way it communicated its recommendations and enhance the level of face-to-face discussions with relevant authorities.

In 2017, it was decided to implement a project concerning follow-up on NPM recommendations. After a series of workshops and discussions, as well as carefully examining the existing working methodology, the NPM of Georgia, with the active involvement of APT experts, drafted new guidelines on the follow-up to NPM recommendations. These guidelines, being an internal methodological reference document, deal with two major aspects. The first aspect relates to the methodology of drafting NPM recommendations in line with these "Double-SMART" criteria; the second one further goes on to explore the modalities of enhancing NPM's communication with relevant authorities and advocacy efforts. It also foresees systematization and, when needed, the reformulation of the NPM recommendations with a specially designed "tracking tool." Since the introduction of the guidelines on the follow-up, NPM recommendations have become more specific and result oriented; however, the process of NPM's self-reflection still continues.

The NPM of Georgia has recently started to look at the issue of the impact assessment of NPM recommendations. While the abovementioned guidelines provide comprehensive guidance on drafting "Double-SMART" recommendations as well as the follow-up and advocacy, it is silent with regard to the assessment of the impact of a particular or set of recommendations. While not always can one make a direct link between NPM recommendations and positive changes happening in the field, it is clear that the impact assessment should be attempted. It is not only academic inspiration that feeds the idea of having the methodology to assess the impact of NPM recommendations on the protection against torture and ill-treatment but two practical considerations—first, the aspiration for the NPM to be confident that its efforts have reached the target and will do so in the future and, second, if necessary, to modify its working methodology to increase the impact.

[49] Recommendations should meet these criteria: **S**pecific, **M**easurable, **A**chievable, **R**esult-oriented, **T**ime-bound, in addition, **S**olution-suggestive, **M**indful of prioritization, sequencing, and risks, **A**rgued, **R**oot-cause responsive, **T**argeted. Detention Monitoring Briefings, Briefing N1—Making Effective Recommendations, 2008. https://www.apt.ch/sites/default/files/publications/Briefing1_en.pdf. Accessed on 29 April 2023.

9.5.2 Challenges Concerning the Implementation of Safeguards

It follows from the review of the Georgian legislation that the fundamental safeguards[50] against torture are formally recognized in Georgia. However, it is the implementation of those safeguards that is currently problematic. Accordingly, the NPM of Georgia faces a major challenge of how to make sure that the safeguards enlisted in the legislation are actually implemented. In recent years, the NPM of Georgia has focused on the implementation of fundamental safeguards (particularly on "three rights").[51] It explored the practice concerning the notification of rights, access to a lawyer, access to a medical doctor, and the notification of arrest to a third party. It has provided important recommendations, such as keeping the records of a detainee exercising his/her right to a lawyer and to notification of arrest to a third party. Guided by the interest in lessening the possibility of abuse of power by police officers, the NPM specifically recommended that these records indicate the date and time of a detainee requesting to contact a lawyer, family,[52] and/or consulate; the name of the police officer acting on the request; and whether or not the police officer succeeded in communicating with a lawyer, family, and/or consulate. The records should be signed accordingly by the detainee and the police officer.[53] Regretfully, the Ministry of Internal Affairs still challenges this recommendation, arguing that

[50] Georgian legislation envisages such guarantees as maintaining an official register of detainees, the right of detainees to be informed of their rights, the right promptly to receive independent legal assistance, independent medical assistance, and to contact relatives, the impartial mechanisms for inspecting and visiting places of detention and confinement, and the availability to detainees and persons at risk of torture and ill-treatment of judicial and other remedies that will allow them to have their complaints promptly and impartially examined, to defend their rights, and to challenge the legality of their detention or treatment as set forth by the CAT in its General Comment No. 2, para. 13.

[51] According to the CPT, it "attaches particular importance to three rights for persons detained by the police: the right of the person concerned to have the fact of his detention notified to a third party of his choice (family member, friend, consulate), the right of access to a lawyer, and the right to request a medical examination by a doctor of his choice (in addition to any medical examination carried out by a doctor called by the police authorities). They are, in the CPT's opinion, three fundamental safeguards against the ill-treatment of detained persons which should apply as from the very outset of deprivation of liberty, regardless of how it may be described under the legal system concerned (apprehension, arrest, etc.)." https://rm.coe.int/16806cea2f. Accessed on 29 April 2023.

[52] Currently, there is no uniform approach to documentation of notification of arrest to family, so the practice varies from one police station to another. Nevertheless, since the NPM of Georgia has paid much attention to this issue, according to the NPM's study, the percentage of cases of notification of arrest within 3 hours (statutory time limit) has increased from 56% in 2016 to 71 % in 2017.

[53] In 2019, the CPT made the following recommendation with respect to Croatia: to ensure that all persons deprived of their liberty by the police, for whatever reason, be granted the right to notify a close relative or third party of their choice (as well as the relevant consular authorities in the case of foreign nationals) about their situation as from the very outset of the deprivation of liberty (that is, from the moment when they are obliged to remain with the police). Further, the police should record in writing in the relevant registers whether or not notification of custody has been carried out in each

there is no need[54] for the introduction of such records and that this would be burdensome for police officers. Discussions are still ongoing. With regard to the notification of rights, the NPM has recently come up[55] with a specific recommendation on the audio-video recording of the process of briefing a detainee on his/her rights. The NPM also recommends that police officers have clear instructions on how to inform detainees of their rights in the most appropriate way and that some additional materials, such as leaflets and posters, be available in police stations and temporary detention facilities.

Being greatly concerned about the implementation of the abovementioned rights, the NPM of Georgia has started to realize that there will be little progress and few durable solutions to the challenges related to strengthening the protection against torture unless the police culture changes progressively and ultimately. Accordingly, the NPM of Georgia finds it appropriate to clearly identify its role in facilitating the change of police culture to make it human rights based. It understands that it is necessary to deal with many overarching issues, ranging from proper selection, capacity building, training, and mentoring to the gender perspectives of the transformation of the police institutional culture. This, in its turn, requires more NPM resources, but evidently, this is where to invest as an abuse of power by police officers will most likely be prevented if they are trained well, confident, and sensitive to human rights protection.

9.6 Conclusion

The review of the experience of the NPM of Georgia shows that the impact of its work in the field of torture prevention cannot be easily identified for the following reasons: firstly, some major reforms, including the introduction of fundamental safeguards against torture in the legislation, had already been implemented before the establishment of the NPM in Georgia. Secondly, the NPM of Georgia failed to properly understand the NPM mandate from the very beginning, and it was not easy to establish an appropriate working methodology. It took time to get a sense of key issues with regard to police custody and to progressively alter the NPM recommendations to be more result oriented. Thirdly, it also took considerable time to increase the level of cooperation between the NPM and relevant state authorities. Despite this

individual case, with the indication of the exact time of notification and the identity of the person who has been contacted. https://rm.coe.int/16808e2a0e. Accessed on 29 April 2023.

[54]Notably, according to an NPM study (reports of 2016 and 2017), the percentage of lawyer involvement in criminal proceedings within 24 hours after arrest ranges from 15 to 17 percent. While a low ratio of lawyer involvement can be conditioned upon various factors, the NPM of Georgia has received credible information that detainees were denied having a lawyer on numerous occasions.

[55]This recommendation will be included in the NPM annual report of 2018 to be submitted to the Parliament of Georgia before 31 March 2019.

hard experience, it is obvious that the NPM of Georgia has made significant progress in terms of its own capacity building. It remains committed to self-reflection and the improvement of its own working methodology. Accordingly, the establishment of a system of regular, proactive, and preventive visits and the increase of public awareness on the issue of torture prevention have to be viewed as a major success.

Although there are challenges regarding the impact assessment of the work of the NPM, it is inarguable that there have been these two parallel processes of the NPM developing and measures to strengthen the protection against torture taken—these processes being interlinked to some degree. The present paper has identified some positive developments concerning the reflection of the NPM recommendations in the action plans, the enactment of the law on independent investigative body, improved conditions of detention and the humane treatment of detainees in temporary detention facilities, the decrease of the maximum term of detention for administrative offenses from 90 days to 15 days, the setting up of a system of medical documentation of bodily injuries in temporary detention facilities and penitentiary establishments, the approval of the procedure for lodging complaints from temporary detention facilities, improved custody recordkeeping, the installation of CCTV cameras in police stations, equipping police officers with body-worn cameras, and the introduction of a new approach to police training.

Bearing in mind the complexity of the concept of torture prevention and its practical challenges, it is not only academic inspiration that feeds the idea of drafting the methodology to assess the impact of NPM recommendations on the protection against torture and ill-treatment but two practical considerations—first, the need for the NPM to be confident that its efforts have reached the target and will do so in the future and, second, if necessary, a need to modify its working methodology to increase the impact.

References

- Universal Declaration of Human Rights: http://www.un.org/en/universal-declaration-human-rights/
- International Covenant on Civil and Political Rights: https://www.ohchr.org/en/professionalinterest/pages/ccpr.aspx
- Convention Against Torture and Other Cruel, Inhuman or Degrading Treatment or Punishment: https://www.ohchr.org/en/professionalinterest/pages/cat.aspx
- Optional Protocol to the Convention Against Torture and Other Cruel, Inhuman or Degrading Treatment or Punishment: https://www.ohchr.org/en/professionalinterest/pages/opcat.aspx
- "The approach of the Subcommittee on Prevention of Torture to the concept of prevention of torture and other cruel, inhuman or degrading treatment or punishment under the Optional Protocol to the Convention against Torture and Other Cruel, Inhuman or Degrading Treatment or Punishment," Subcommittee on Prevention of Torture and Other Cruel, Inhuman or Degrading Treatment or

Punishment, twelfth session, Geneva, 15-19 November 2010: https://tbinternet.ohchr.org/_layouts/treatybodyexternal/Download.aspx?symbolno=CAT/OP/12/6&Lang=en

- 2008 Country Reports on Human Rights Practices, Georgia, the Bureau of Democracy, Human Rights, and Labor, the US Department of State: https://www.state.gov/j/drl/rls/hrrpt/2008/eur/119080.htm
- Report to the Georgian Government on the visit to Georgia carried out by the European Committee for the Prevention of Torture and Inhuman or Degrading Treatment or Punishment (CPT) from 21 March to 2 April 2007: https://www.coe.int/en/web/cpt/georgia
- Constitution of Georgia: http://www.parliament.ge/files/68_1944_951190_CONSTIT_27_12.06.pdf
- Organic Law of Georgia on the Public Defender of Georgia: https://matsne.gov.ge/en/document/download/33034/14/en/pdf
- Annual Report 2009, NPM of Georgia: https://www.ohchr.org/Documents/HRBodies/OPCAT/NPM/NPM_Georgia2009_AnnualReport.pdf
- Annual report 2010, NPM of Georgia: https://www.ohchr.org/Documents/HRBodies/OPCAT/NPM/2010 MonitoringPenitentiaryInstitutionsTemporaryDetentionIsolators.pdf
- Annual report 2012, NPM of Georgia: https://www.ohchr.org/Documents/HRBodies/OPCAT/NPM/NPMreport2012_Georgia.pdf
- Annual report 2014, NPM of Georgia: https://www.ohchr.org/Documents/HRBodies/OPCAT/NPM/Georgian_NPM_annual_report2014.pdf
- Annual report 2015, NPM of Georgia: https://www.ohchr.org/Documents/HRBodies/OPCAT/NPM/NPM_Georgia_2015.pdf
- Annual report 2017, NPM of Georgia: https://www.ohchr.org/Documents/HRBodies/OPCAT/NPM/NPM_Georgia_2017.pdf
- Annual report 2020, NPM of Georgia: https://www.ombudsman.ge/eng/tsliuri-angarishebi/preventsiis-erovnuli-mekanizmis-2020-tslis-angarishi
- Annual report 2021, NPM of Georgia: https://www.ombudsman.ge/eng/tsliuri-angarishebi/preventsiis-erovnuli-mekanizmis-2021-tslis-angarishi
- Guidelines on National Preventive Mechanisms, Subcommittee on Prevention of Torture and Other Cruel, Inhuman or Degrading Treatment or Punishment, twelfth session, Geneva, 15–19 November 2010, CAT/OP/12/5: https://tbinternet.ohchr.org/_layouts/treatybodyexternal/Download.aspx?symbolno=CAT/OP/12/5&Lang=en
- Report of the Special Rapporteur on torture and other cruel, inhuman or degrading treatment or punishment on his mission to Georgia, Human Rights Council, thirty-first session, 1 December 2015: http://ap.ohchr.org/documents/dpage_e.aspx?si=A/HRC/31/57/Add.3
- The Istanbul Protocol - Manual on the Effective Investigation and Documentation of Torture and Other Cruel, Inhuman or Degrading Treatment or Punishment, PROFESSIONAL TRAINING SERIES No. 8/Rev.1, 2004: https://www.ohchr.org/Documents/Publications/training8rev1en.pdf

- Code of Criminal Procedure of Georgia: https://matsne.gov.ge/ka/document/download/90034/64/en/pdf
- Imprisonment Code of Georgia: https://matsne.gov.ge/en/document/download/91612/18/en/pdf
- Administrative Error, Georgia's Flawed System for Administrative Detention, Human Rights Watch, 4 January 2012: https://www.hrw.org/report/2012/01/04/administrative-error/georgias-flawed-system-administrative-detention#
- Concluding observations on the sixth periodic report of Spain, Committee against Torture, 29 May 2015, CAT/C/ESP/CO/6: https://tbinternet.ohchr.org/_layouts/treatybodyexternal/Download.aspx?symbolno=CAT%2fC%2fESP%2fCO%2f6&Lang=en
- Concluding observations on the sixth periodic report of the Russian Federation, Committee Against Torture, 28 August 2018, CAT/C/RUS/CO/6: https://tbinternet.ohchr.org/_layouts/treatybodyexternal/Download.aspx?symbolno=CAT%2fC%2fRUS%2fCO%2f6&Lang=en
- Concluding observations on the fourth periodic report of Senegal, Committee Against Torture, 30 January 2019, CAT/C/SEN/CO/4: https://tbinternet.ohchr.org/_layouts/treatybodyexternal/Download.aspx?symbolno=CAT%2fC%2fSEN%2fCO%2f4&Lang=en
- Detention Monitoring Briefings, Briefing N1 – Making Effective Recommendations, 2008: https://www.apt.ch/content/files_res/Briefing1_en.pdf
- Extract from the 2nd General Report of the CPT, published in 1992, CPT/Inf(92) 3-part1: https://rm.coe.int/16806cea2f
- Report to the Croatian Government on the visit to Croatia carried out by the European Committee for the Prevention of Torture and Inhuman or Degrading Treatment of Punishment (CPT) from 14 to 22 March 2017, CPT/Inf (2018) 44: https://rm.coe.int/16808e2a0e
- Report to the Serbian Government on the visit to Serbia carried out by the European Committee for the Prevention of Torture and Inhuman or Degrading Treatment of Punishment (CPT) from 31 May to 7 June 2017, CPT/Inf (2018) 21: https://rm.coe.int/16808b5ee7
- General Comment No.2, CAT/C/GC/2, 24 January 2008: https://tbinternet.ohchr.org/_layouts/treatybodyexternal/Download.aspx?symbolno=CAT%2fC%2fGC%2f2&Lang=en

Nika Kvaratskhelia holds a master's degree in international and European Law from Riga Graduate School of Law, Latvia. Since 2013, he has served as the head of the National Preventive Mechanism (NPM) Department at the Office of the Public Defender of Georgia organising regular preventive visits to places of deprivation of liberty, writing reports and leading advocacy campaign. He has also been acting as a member of the UN Subcommittee on Prevention of Torture (SPT) since 2019, where he coordinates the work of the SPT's Regional Team for Asia and the Pacific.

Prior to joining the NPM, as a member of local NGOs he had been involved in human rights strategic litigation before the national courts and the European Court of Human Rights. He has participated in various international conferences concerning the protection of human rights of persons deprived of their liberty. He conducts trainings on prevention of torture. The areas of his particular interest include law enforcement, penitentiary system and mental health care.

Chapter 10
A Systemic Approach to Building Capacity for the Prevention of Torture and Other Ill-Treatment While in Police Custody

Cristina Sganga

In memory of Anneke Osse
'The sad truth is that most evil is done by people who never make up their minds to be either good or evil.' (Arendt 1977, p. 180)

Contents

Abstract Considering the vast number of individuals under the custody of State officials or, in some cases, private organisations, how can we identify and develop sustainable approaches and programmes that safeguard the fair treatment of all persons deprived of their liberty? This article outlines some of the key steps to follow when designing and implementing robust torture and ill-treatment prevention capacity-building programmes aimed at law enforcement officials. The piece aims to

C. Sganga (✉)
London, UK
e-mail: csganga@gn.apc.org

R. Alleweldt (ed.), *Fair Treatment of Persons in Police Custody*,
https://doi.org/10.1007/978-3-031-61737-9_10

provide practical pointers on how to identify the most common pitfalls and what has been identified as good practices as well as serve as a rallying call for a deeper commitment to the reform of law enforcement services on the part of governments and donors.

10.1 Introduction

In this article, I examine the crucial steps to follow when designing and implementing robust torture and ill-treatment prevention capacity-building programmes aimed at law enforcement officials.[1]

I focus on the phases and approaches recommended when developing and implementing capacity-building programmes rather than look at the content of such programmes. What topics of human rights and policing to cover should always be chosen and delivered based on the results emerging from tailor-made training needs assessments of the local context.[2] However, it is important to underline that the content of capacity-building programmes aimed at preventing ill-treatment must be drawn from agreed international, regional and national human rights law and that at the core of any capacity-building programme there should be the recognition that fair treatment is when individuals are treated according to human rights standards, regardless of their background, nationality, place of residence, sex, national or ethnic or social origin, genetic features or skin colour, religion, language, belief, political or any other opinion, membership to a national minority, property, birth, disability, age or sexual orientation or any other status. The concept of fair treatment encapsulates the absence of discrimination, torture or cruel, inhuman and degrading treatment or punishment.

I discuss programmes aimed at law enforcement officials. However, much of what I present can also be applied in the development and implementation of capacity-building programmes aimed at other public or private agencies entrusted with the incarceration or confinement of individuals.

---

[1]In this article "The term 'law enforcement officials' includes all officers of the law, whether appointed or elected, who exercise police powers, especially the powers of arrest or detention." United Nations General Assembly resolution 34/169, "UN Code of Conduct for Law Enforcement Officials", 17 December 1979, http://www2.ohchr.org/english/law/codeofconduct.htm. The terms law enforcement officials and police will be used interchangeably.

[2]OSCD/ODIHR (2012).

10.2 The Background

The latest World Prison Population List (2021)[3] by the Institute for Crime & Justice Policy Research (ICPR) at Birkbeck, University of London, which hosts and maintains the World Prison Brief database and publishes the Prison Lists, estimates that, worldwide, 10.77 million people are held in penal institutions, including pre-trial detention. Additionally, an unknown number of people live behind locked doors in institutions such as psychiatric hospitals, immigration detention centres and refugee camps. It is in out-of-sight places that torture or other cruel, inhuman or degrading treatment or punishment has more chances of happening.

The reasons why unfair and violent treatment of detainees occurs are multiple. Often it is due to the failure of the judiciary to perform its role because it is too slow, too incompetent, too lenient, too corrupt, and/or too privileged and distant from the everyday realities of rural areas and the streets of towns and cities. In such instances, police officers may develop a belief that they are vested with the authority to deliver real and immediate justice (street justice) to preserve order and prevent crime.[4]

Officers may also consider that they have the right or even the mission to provide informal punishment to suspects of criminal acts or acts of defiance or non-conformity (i.e. expressions of sexual orientation different from heterosexuality, political dissent, religious adherence, etc.), or simply because that is what is believed to be expected from them, even by the suspects themselves.[5] In 1989, while in Venezuela freelancing for The Guardian newspaper and the BBC Latin American Service, I interviewed survivors of torture after *El Caracazo*.[6] It became apparent that those being interviewed only considered to have been submitted to torture if electricity or other extreme forms of inducing pain had been used. They would not report beatings, slapping and kicking as part of the torture they experienced as they interpreted these to be part and parcel of any encounter with the police. They expected such ill-treatment and did not think worth mentioning it until having been prompted with careful supplementary questions about their treatment during their detention.

In societies with high levels of violence—domestic violence, political violence, intolerance for those who are different and do not conform, etc.—police brutality is commonly tolerated by the general public and overlooked by the criminal justice system. In these instances, most probably the violent treatment of suspects is not based on the law but is acquiesced by State organs. The use of violence by the police

---

[3] See https://duckduckgo.com/?q=The+latest+World+Prison+Population+List&t=newext&atb=v287-1&ia=web.

[4] Chan (2001); Carver and Handley (2016).

[5] Chan (2001).

[6] *El Caracazo* was a wave of protests and riots that began in Caracas on 27 February 1989 in response to the government's economic restructuring and the resulting increase in the price of gasoline and public transport. The week-long clashes resulted in mass arrests, the widespread use of torture and the deaths of thousands of people at the hands of security forces.

can be construed to be a 'moral' expression on their part to attempt to control crime, punish the perceived guilty or perverts or assert authority to fill a vacuum left open by a non-functioning criminal system or a 'too liberal' criminal judiciary.[7]

It is also relevant to consider the mental health of officers who live in violent environments with limited or no institutional oversights to restraint their worse impulses. It would not be surprising that officers working and living in such brutal contexts would suffer from post-traumatic stress disorder (PTSD). Consequently, due to work-related stresses and trauma, they may develop tendencies for strong feelings of suspicion towards the 'perceived' enemy and justification for the use of aggression and excessive force. This mental frame can transpire in behaviours such as lack of empathy or remorse when placed in potentially perceived as dangerous or emotionally charged situations.[8]

It is well possible that the stresses experienced by officers may increase the likelihood of them engaging in the use of excessive force; however, this complex working conditions and its potential mental health implications cannot be used to excuse the use of torture by law enforcement officers.[9]

When facing extreme and everyday forms of police brutality which have government acquiescence, it is legitimate to marvel at the idea of starting to develop a capacity-building and reform programme that can credibly bring change and stop these abuses.

10.3 Engaging with the Police

To diminish and prevent the use of torture and ill-treatment while in custody, it will be inevitable to have to engage and work with police officers who have committed human rights violations and with other government officials who are complicit and condone such acts. However, in some circumstances where there are no signs of a real wish to reform, it might not be possible to establish a dialogue, and other steps should be taken, such as campaigning for legal reform, lobbying, public awareness programmes, international pressure, etc.

Nevertheless, when there is enough evidence of the possibility to generate alternatives towards and improvements in the prevention of ill-treatment, it is imperative to talk to police officers, even if they are perpetrators of human rights violations. I concur with Zaira Drammis when she states that such engagement allows us to develop important insights about how they view themselves and how we can best influence them. Moreover, as they are to be the ones to change their

[7]Chan (2001).

[8]Falkenbach et al. (2018), pp. 420–428.

[9]Understanding What Police Brutality Is and Why It Occurs, Arlin Cuncic, January 28, 2023.

perceptions of their role, learn to do their work differently and embrace human-rights-based values, they need to be active participants in this transformation.[10]

Engaging with the police is not a synonym for condoning their behaviour. Any relationship/collaboration with any police force or service, even in more stable and democratic contexts, requires a clear memorandum of understanding, a risks assessment and an exit strategy in case things go wrong and human rights or development organisations consider that they no longer can associate with the authorities and, in particular, the police.

Some key questions to consider when establishing a working relationship with a police force include the following:

- How to build trust?
- What are the aims and activities of the partnership?
- What is the nature of the partnership (rules of engagement)?
- At what level in the police, ministry of interior and the non-governmental organisation does the engagement take place?
- What are the communication mechanisms?
- What are the decision-making mechanisms?
- How is the engagement monitored to ensure progress is being made?
- How is the wider community consulted and invited to participate (when relevant)?
- What is the level of resources required to achieve the aims of the collaboration?
- Is there a long-term capacity to maintain the engagement long enough in order to produce long-lasting changes in operational practices and value-based frameworks (culture)?[11]

10.4 Unravelling How Capacity Building Can Go Wrong

Let us start from the beginning by developing an understanding of what capacity building is not! In my 30+ years career in the field of human rights education, I can no longer count the times when I have come across projects where capacity building was equated with the simple provision of training.

Moreover, in the realm of capacity building for law enforcement officials, somehow, training normally implies teaching about human rights norms, what I describe as the over-legalisation of human rights practice. This often translates into abstract lectures about international standards and mechanisms prohibiting torture and ill-treatment, sprinkled with references to national norms, if they exist, and a few examples from real life.

---

[10] Drammis (2015).

[11] Adapted from Police and NGOs: Why and how human rights NGOs and police services can and should work together, European Platform for Policing and Human Rights (EPPHR) (2004).

Per se, such lectures are not a problem; the difficulties arise when the expectation is that officers will change their practices and refrain from using violence the moment they hear that the right not to be tortured or ill-treated is absolute. We cannot be sure about that, even if the lecture is practice oriented and provides real-life examples—for example, it explains that a public authority can never use lack of resources as justification against an accusation that it has treated someone in an inhuman or degrading manner. If the officers attending the lecture exercise their duties in a context where torture is endemic and where resources are so scarce that their salary does not allow them a dignified existence, hearing about the absolute prohibition will not produce the desired outcomes. Similarly, Carver and Handley concluded through the quantitative analysis carried out as a result of their study in 16 countries that overall training aimed at improving skills is more effective in preventing torture and ill-treatment than training aimed at teaching legal norms.[12] More complex and multi-layered interventions are necessitated in order to break vicious circles of violence and to address issues related to under-resourced facilities, poorly trained and remunerated officers, corruption in the judiciary, etc.

Capacity building, in this field as in all others, must be approached from a holistic perspective, which considers the complexity of the multiple reasons why torture and ill-treatment continue to be pervasive.[13]

Knowledge of the law is not enough; skills, infrastructure and working conditions must be placed in a journey towards change and improvement, along with other key agencies in the criminal justice system, the political paradigm and monitoring mechanisms. For example, concurrently to enhancing the capacity of law enforcement agencies and their officers, it is crucial to liaise with those involved in supporting and strengthening the capacity of monitoring mechanisms by ensuring they can activate prompt safeguards, for instance visits and access to independent lawyers, doctors, etc.

Officers need to develop skills to do things differently, but more importantly, there needs to be the political and institutional will to undergo transformation and to face the choppy waters and tension that change brings—those who demand more and faster transformation and those who are vested in the status quo. In the case of the police, the ultimate decision, legal infrastructure and resources will need to come from the political masters, thus the need for a systemic approach, which engages them throughout the change process.

A recent and promising example of the adoption of a holistic approach is the work of the Council on Criminal Justice (USA) through the Task Force on Policing launched in November 2020 by the Council on Criminal Justice. Its mission is to identify the policies and practices most likely to reduce violent encounters between officers and the public and improve the fairness and effectiveness of American policing.[14] Concurrently, its Task Force on Long Sentences convened in February

---

[12] Carver and Handley (2016), p. 632.

[13] Celermajer (2017).

[14] https://counciloncj.foleon.com/policing/assessing-the-evidence/policy-assessments.

2022 to assess drivers of growth in the number of people sentenced to 10 years or more behind bars, the effectiveness of long sentences in preventing and deterring crime and their effects on incarcerated people and their families, crime victims and survivors, communities, and correctional staff.[15]

10.5 Assembling How Capacity Building May Work

Before I go any further, I want to table a definition of what I have come to understand capacity building to be. This understanding emerges from my work on four continents in the past three decades.

Capacity building for the attainment of human rights and development is a multi-layered process by which individuals, groups, communities, public and private institutions and international entities gain, retain and improve knowledge, skills, practices and attitudes.

It comprises:

- The implementation of a multi-layered systemic analysis of the roles and motivations of the key institutions and players involved
- Multidisciplinary, collaborative and participatory development of a blueprint of the desired outcomes
- The development and management of a monitoring and evaluation mechanism to regularly review the progress obtained and adjust problems encountered throughout the capacity-building programme process
- The acquisition of new knowledge, skills, practices and attitudes by the diverse players involved (at all levels—senior and junior/managerial and operational).
- The development of new tools, equipment and other physical means necessary to do the job (in our case policing) to an increasing level of efficiency and effectiveness—in accordance with international, regional and national human rights standards striving towards a sustainable way of dignified private and professional life
- The recognition of the mental health sequels of endemic violence and the development of long-term programmes to tackle these by supporting individuals and teams/units in overcoming the harm caused by perpetrating and experiencing sustained levels of aggression and brutality over many years, if not decades.
- A transition period where proficiency in the new competencies is consolidated
- A follow-up period where technical support is available and further consolidation is secured
- Oversight from robust independent bodies
- Monitoring from civil society organisations

[15] https://counciloncj.foleon.com/tfls/long-sentences-final-report/about-the-task-force.

- Public awareness campaigns to change the perspective of what the function of the police is, what the rights of community members are and how policing and the judiciary relate—including training for media and other social influencers

In other words, capacity building is the development and implementation of a finely orchestrated progression of multifaceted activities and interventions through which individuals, institutions and communities develop competencies, individually and collectively, to peacefully (without the use of force or violence) solve problems, perform their duties and claim their rights while considering the greater good of the larger community in harmony with the rights of the minorities existing within it.

10.5.1 Understanding the Many Layers of the Context

When starting the conceptualisation of a capacity-building programme aimed at the prevention of torture and ill-treatment, it is indispensable to carry out a systemic analysis of the locally existing architecture aimed at preventing torture and ill-treatment. The organisers of the capacity-building programme, collectively, should hold an in-depth grasp of how sociocultural-political events and developments have played a role in influencing the use of torture and ill-treatment and, concurrently, of the struggles against these practices. Who have been the main players? What are their motivations, gains and losses? What are the links with historical events and cultural forms that apply violence as a norm? Examples are past conflicts, race relations, treatment of minorities, use of mob justice or lynching, slavery, practices that mutilate the body, etc. What challenges do individual officers face in their professional and private spheres?

If the capacity-building initiative stems from an international organisation, particularly if based abroad, it needs to secure the active involvement of local actors from the inception of the programme.

Capacity building requires that when analysing the context and the diverse players, the obstacles that inhibit and the opportunities that enhance the abilities of individuals, institutions and communities are identified and all its minutiae examined. My experience and that of others have taught us that to develop effective and sustainable capacity-building programmes we need to investigate the root causes that bring about ill-treatment.[16]

Since this crucial preparatory step requires time, expertise and **resources**, it is often omitted or only partially carried out, resulting in programmes that mostly limit themselves to one component of the overall problem, thus lacking the capacity to make linkages and maximising synergies to stimulate sustainable changes in how detainees are treated, how information is gathered from suspects (interviews vs. interrogations), how investigations are carried out (evidence-based

[16] OMCT (2008); Celemajer (2018).

policing vs. reactive policing), how detention conditions are managed, the supervision and career development of officers, etc. For example, as previously mentioned, the sole focus of many projects is on training low-ranking police officers rather than developing a more comprehensive and multi-layered programme of work that will secure longer-lasting benefits. A low-ranking group of officers trained in isolation will most probably not be able to affect change in a system and cultural framework that permits or relies upon torture and ill-treatment for conducting police investigations and other tasks.

A systemic analysis of the local architecture should examine the functioning and connexions amongst bodies and measures which should contribute to the prevention of torture and ill-treatment.[17]

This analysis should take account of:

- **The political context** (effective separation of powers, the government's and political parties' commitment to the rule of law and to stop and prevent the use of torture and ill-treatment, etc.)
- **The cultural climate** (the proliferation of violence as a means of expression at the domestic and community levels etc.)
- **The legal and policy framework** (legal and procedural developments, arrest and interviewing procedures, investigation of allegations, training of law enforcement personnel and other relevant public officials, etc.)
- **Control mechanisms** (cooperation with international and regional mechanisms, monitoring places of detention, national independent complaint mechanisms, etc.)
- **Public awareness and education programmes** (including the professional training of medical personnel, journalists and law students, as well as programmes for the general public to facilitate access to assistance and remedies, etc.).[18]

Additionally, it should include a review of the application or absence of fundamental safeguards during detention:

- Freedom from unlawful use and the application of physical restraints
- Freedom from physical and psychological abuse by staff or other detainees
- Freedom from bullying, threats and disrespectful treatment by staff or other detainees
- Freedom from neglect by staff
- Risk assessments by a qualified practitioner as soon as reasonably practicable after initial detention and continuous review of the risk assessment thereafter
- Distribution of the risk assessments to relevant professionals (medical staff, social services, etc.);

[17] Carver and Handley (2016).

[18] Adapted from: Preventing Torture: An Operational Guide for National Human Rights Institutions, OHCHR, APT and APF (2010).

- Access to timely and appropriate medical and mental health care, including treatment for drug, alcohol or other addictions
- Access to family contact
- Information and advice in an appropriate format on how to access legal or other support

What is more, the analysis should involve an assessment of the reasons why safeguards are not enforced—for example due to omission, lack of training, resources, discrimination against specific detainees belonging to specific minorities or vulnerable groups, etc.

Moreover, the systemic examination of the context must cover a substantive analysis of the training curricula of all the personnel involved in the custody procedure, including the methodological approaches used to develop their skills and reinforce human-rights-compliant attitudes.

This preparatory research phase must be implemented with the full involvement and active participation of a variety of public officials who have decision-making powers and relevant practical and theoretical expertise and who will directly benefit from the programme's activities (civil servants and high- and low-ranking police officers), along with representatives from civil society and torture survivors' groups. Mixed working groups must contribute to the development of the preparatory fact-finding and analysis framework upon which the capacity-building programme will be developed, reviewed, implemented and evaluated. A fundamental element, when aiming to build engagement and commitment to change, is ownership by the recipients and beneficiaries of the process, from its inception.

This approach accentuates the rule of law and the long-term development of the justice system, rather than the immediate provision of order, and it incorporates human rights as an intrinsic component within institutional development. After all, we would want any capacity-building programme for the prevention of torture and ill-treatment to imbue a human-rights-based approach.

It is essential that the organisers of the programme (and the funders) grasp the importance of the systemic analytical phase as a critical stepping stone towards building 1) trust and openness towards breaking down prejudices and stimulating open, collaborative working relations and 2) forging 'emotional' and 'intellectual' commitment to change. Any long-term developmental perspective involves fostering intellectual and emotional commitment on the part of the officials involved, as well as the wider community. Normally, individuals grasp reasonably fast the implications of change at a cognitive level; however, they need more time to form the required emotional tie.[19]

This blurred dual allegiance usually produces ambiguous signals and gives the sensation of a two step forwards, one step backwards mode of travel. The organisers are required to have the capacity and flexibility to manage this intellectual and emotional whirlpool, which is an integral part of groups of people developing new

[19] Witting (2012); Conner (2011).

skills and most importantly developing new values frameworks in which to base their judgements and decision-making. The more extreme the violations committed in the past are, the slower and confusing the change process will be and, what is more, the longer term the capacity-building programme will need to be before sustainable impacts start to emerge and consolidate.

10.5.2 Knowing What We Mean When We Speak About the Police

Frequently, it is assumed or taken as a given that those involved in torture prevention have the same conception about what the police are and are for. The police and its functions are often discussed in the media, by governments, by non-governmental organisations (NGOs) and, sometimes, even by the police itself without having a shared understanding of the meaning.

As part of developing a capacity-building programme, the organisers, in close collaboration with police officers (high and low ranking) and other relevant agencies of the criminal justice system and government agencies, must identify what at present makes a police force or service tick, and function the way it does, including the main elements making up the internal means of communicating and how officers relate to each other: what the different internal 'cultural' patterns are.[20]

I hesitate to instead use the terms 'institutional culture' and 'organisational culture' as these are often oversimplified and there is not a clear 'thing' about 'police culture'. Thus, in examining how a law enforcement agency functions, I prefer to first identify the markers that, when put together, may compose cultural patterns that provide cohesion to the group or entity, in our case a police team, a department or a regional force.[21]

Similarly, it is a mistake to assume that all police officers act, think and are the same as it would be an error to suppose that all departments within a police force share the same modus operandi (McCulloch 2001), as well as to forget that police culture and structure 'are a direct reflection of the power structures of societies policed'.[22]

Once more, I advocate for the use of a systemic approach that considers the complexity of the multiple layers that make up the police, policing and the outcomes and consequences emerging from its performance. Theorising about policing requires exploring the key dimensions involved in the police and policing (Reiner 2012, p. 16).

The following dimensions of policing could be explored (Table 10.1):

[20]Reiner (2012).

[21]Chan (1997); Cockcroft (2014).

[22]Reiner (2012) p. 132.

Table 10.1 Dimensions of policing

Present dimensions[a]	Description of the dimension
1. What is society's prevalent concept of police?	
2. What are the police for?	
3. What is policing understood to be by the government, the police and the public?	
4. What do the police do?	
5. What motivates people to join the police?	
6. What motivates police officers to remain in the police?	
7. What social functions do the police have, and how do they perform them?	
8. What are the means and powers of the police?	
9. How are the police structured and organised?	
10. How do the police relate to the government?	
11. How do the police relate to the rest of the criminal justice system?	
12. How do the police impact different social groups, particularly vulnerable groups, including minorities?	
13. How does the mistrust or even hate from the side of the public influence the police?	
14. Who polices the police? How and to what effect?	

[a]This set of questions unravelling the police and policing main dimensions was adapted from R. Reiner and further elaborated by Cristina Sganga and Laura Fine as part of developing the Resource Centre for Human Rights-Based Policing, London, 2018

It is essential to analyse and understand the root causes of why the police, in a specific country, violate human rights, particularly in their use of force—what conditions are present that encourage or condone the use of torture and ill-treatment? As Celemajer concludes, 'to change behaviour, we need to address the factors that influence the individual—peer group(s), cultural values, community norms, public policy, law, how the organisation she works in operate, her place in the economy and so on—rather than just changing the individual'[23] or providing them with knowledge about human rights.

Genuine change is often found to be difficult, and it is almost impossible if we do not know exactly what we want and what we are proposing and, in our case, if we do not work hand in hand with the police and other relevant agencies.

Clarity on what the police are for is an essential element of any capacity-building programme aimed at preventing torture and ill-treatment. The initial analysis of the context helps to understand what has happened and what exists in the present; however, in order to construct a better future, it is necessary to develop a collective well-defined description of what we expect from the police, what would need to be its functions and its structure and what needs to change. The overarching question of how the police must change should be framed in terms of what would make police

[23]Celemajer (2015), p. 11.

Table 10.2 Evidence-based policing

What are the present dimensions of police and policing?	What is needed to make policing more evidence based?

work more evidence based rather than violence/force based. In theorising about policing and setting up a capacity-building programme to generate long-term change, it is necessary to generate a vision of the desired police and policing. Thus, having gathered the answers to questions in the table above, one has to identify the desired police dimensions in order to prevent torture and ill-treatment (Table 10.2).

Without a shared and relatively detailed understanding of what we need the police and policing to be and what needs to be carried out to affect change, it is unrealistic to expect a capacity-building programme to result in sustainable changes in the performance of police officers, particularly in the prevention of torture and ill-treatment.

10.5.3 Building the Theory of Change and Guiding the Transformation

Another component in capacity-building programmes is that there are frequently theories of changes that are inadequately developed and only partially followed up. In my experience, there is a tendency to design theories of change that are too complex and focused on the macro-level, disregarding the complexity of the linkages between the micro-levels. A macro-level theory is necessary, but this needs to be accompanied by supplementary models that look at the micro-levels and help guide the actual transformation.

There are numerous theories of change models, presenting different advantages and drawbacks. More importantly, it is to be realised that not one model will be a perfect fit for all situations. Successful change initiatives adapt aspects of various models to suit the needs of the organisation/agency and the context in which change is to be encouraged. Regardless of the change model(s) to be adopted, all require leadership:

(a) To create and sustain emotional and intellectual commitment and purpose
(b) To manage activities and mechanisms for planning and monitoring change and
(c) To ensure that the outcomes are those desired and are sustainable long-term

I find William Bridges' thinking on change extremely helpful as he invites us to see change as a process within which there are many moments of transition that are key in accompanying the consolidation of new practices, new ways of thinking and new ways of feeling about what individuals do, in our case officers and civilians

Table 10.3 Schematic representation of Bridges' transition[a]

Ending and letting go	The neutral zone	The new beginning
A time to understand why change is not only necessary but also desirable, a moment to commit to stop/end what used to be—this moment also includes identifying who is losing what, acknowledging the loss, communicating what is changing and why and stating the gains and advantages.	While the new way of doing things settles, individuals might feel confused and demotivated. Leadership should offer a clear direction and objectives, encouraging dialogue and participation to increase ownership and commitment.	A time for acceptance, when individuals adopt the new ways of thinking and doing, embracing the changes; they are consolidating the new knowledge, understanding, skills, values and attitudes. They are seeing gains and advantages of doing things differently.

[a]See Bridges (1991)

working for the police, as well as other relevant agencies in the government and the criminal justice system. He focuses on transition, not change.[24] His three-phase process of transition helps explain what happens in people's minds as they are guided through change. Bridges argues that change is situational, and it is about the different policies, practices or structures that are being changed, whereas transition describes the psychological reorientation that people must go through before the change can be embraced into regular daily work practice. He argues that until people successfully transition from the old way to the new way of thinking, doing and feeling things, the change will not succeed (Table 10.3).[25]

In this approach, it is essential to engage people at all stages, including getting them involved in setting up the criteria to measure change and defining expectations and the expected gradual timetable for achieving milestones. The theory of change emerging from the initial analysis of the local context and of policing must incorporate this dual perception of change and transition.

10.5.4 The Preferred Approach to Apply in Capacity-Building Programmes

As indicated throughout this article, the approach has to be one of inclusion and ownership on the part of as many as possible police officers in the services involved in the programme, as well as relevant government officials, organised civil society, torture survivors' groups and National Preventive Mechanisms. The initiators or organisers of the capacity-building programme have to play the role of well-informed **facilitators**, calling in diverse expertise but mostly fully involving those who are expected to transform their practices—the individual police officers (high and low ranking), police teams and departments.

[24]Bridges (1991).

[25]Ibid.

If we want law enforcement officers to refrain from using torture and ill-treatment, they will need to learn how to do their jobs differently. As I mentioned earlier, to achieve this shift, it is not enough to just provide them training about human rights. They will need to become accustomed to different (new) ways of viewing their role, relating to the public, suspects and victims, and the policing structure etc. To establish these changes, it is needed to:

- Set a cooperative climate in the workplace with decision-makers and operational staff and in settings where learning new police tactics and perspectives on policing will be acquired (this could be a classroom, but could also be on the street or meetings with the community, or when handling the use of new equipment etc.)
- Assess the police officers' specific needs and interests and whether these are reflected in the planned interventions (the officers must see their needs reflected in the format and content)
- Develop desired outcomes based on the police officers' needs, interests and skill levels needed to achieve the desired outcomes
- Design logical sequential and in-progression sets of activities to achieve the desired outcomes
- Select methods, materials and resources for instruction which reflect the needs and skill sets of police officers
- Monitor and assess the quality of the reform experience and adjust, as necessary.

Remember that adults need to understand why they are being asked to do something differently or something new. They need to see what is in it for them that is going to motivate them to undertake the complicated journey towards change. Police officers and their superiors are the ones who need to change their opinion about the role of law enforcement, rejecting torture and ill-treatment as means of extracting information and imparting punishment. If they are to embrace human-rights-based values, they need to be active participants in this transformation. Public opinion, international pressure and changes in the law can spur them towards a transformative path, but ultimately, it will be them who affect the transformation.

10.6 The Chicken or Egg Question

Having explored how to determine and best execute the key components of a capacity-building programme for the prevention of torture and ill-treatment while in police custody, it remains to discuss the hardest problem that somehow we are yet to find a solution to. The prior analysis, the multi-layer systemic approach, the collaborative participant-centred methodology, the monitoring and the follow-up all require time. We all know that reforming the police, and with it needing to also improve the performance of the criminal justice system,[26] is going to take many years, possibly decades. However, we continue to disburse resources in a piecemeal approach, setting three- to five-year projects that only cover partial aspects of the overall problem.

The funding question—in a post-Covid world plagued by austerity and ever-diminishing budgets for human rights and development work—remains a very tough nut to crack. It is difficult to envisage in-depth, well-thought-out, long-term capacity-building programmes being initiated or going longer than three or five years, even though we know that the present efforts fall short of what is required. By stating this, I do not want to undermine the excellent work being done by many organisations; at the same time, if we did not continue to ask for better funding strategies, we would do injustice to all of those who regularly find themselves having to compromise the integrity of their work due to the dictates of short-sighted, often ideologically plagued, approaches of the world of international development aid.

In 1997, well before the financial collapse of 2008, while presenting a paper on human rights education during a conference organised by the OECD in Paris, in the question and answer session, I was told by a representative of an Oxford (UK) based think-tank that my advocacy for long-term commitments (at least 10 years but ideally 15 to 20 year) was totally out of step. In 2019, with the experiences gathered from South Africa, Kenya, Nigeria and many other countries, perhaps we may be closer to finding a luminary funding agency or government to call for an international conference to help set up the mechanisms to develop a systemic approach for the creation of capacity-building programmes that will help us get closer to the prevention of the use of torture and ill-treatment in custodial procedures and in all other moments in policing.

In the words of George Soros, 'To others, being wrong is a source of shame; to me, recognising my mistakes is a source of pride. Once we realize that imperfect understanding is the human condition, there's no shame in being wrong, only in failing to correct our mistakes'.[27] Capacity-building programmes that achieve the reform of law enforcement agencies that substantially diminish and ideally permanently abolish the systematic use of torture and ill-treatment will only become widespread when the necessary funding and time are made available, of course, with all the required monitoring, learning and evaluation systems to ensure accountability and the best possible use of resources.

[26] Carver and Handley (2016).

[27] Soros (1995), p. 11.

10.7 Conclusions

A growing sector of the human rights training/education community is recognising the need for long-term police participatory reality-centred capacity-building programmes for the elimination and prevention of torture and ill-treatment.

As national governments initiate reforms to curb the use of torture, the international aid community should be able to step up and offer sufficient ongoing financial support and expertise for carrying out in-depth systemic participatory analysis in order to implement finely orchestrated progression of multifaceted activities and interventions through which individuals, institutions and communities develop competencies, individually and collectively, to prevent the use of torture and ill-treatment.

Capacity-building programmes must give emphasis on the duty of the police to do their job with full respect for human rights; thus, the interventions must be practical and relevant for the police to see the benefits derived from the changes proposed.

The development and analysis phase is crucial if we are to successfully kindle commitment on the part of the police to abandon the use of torture. If this is not done well, utilising the necessary time to forge an understanding on the side of the police and government officials of why torture and ill-treatment not only are morally wrong and illegal but also damage those involved and stunts the development of countries; we may be achieving little and, in some cases, doing harm. When talking with police officers 'benefiting' from a capacity-building project in the early 2000s in Venezuela, I asked them why they were so keen to attend. Their reply did not come as a surprise but just confirmed what I feared: they wanted to understand better how to use torture so that they would not be found out and would know how to build their defence if they were brought in front of a judge. Needless to say, I emphatically recommended the project to stop immediately. I had just been engaged as one of a team of training consultants. So as not to find us in situations like the one I described above, those invested in developing and delivering capacity-building programmes for the police need to embrace the reality that this work needs time, sincere engagement and shared ownership. All engaged require the time to understand the history of violence. There is also a need to sustain motivation and buy-in, trust and develop reflection with the purpose of transforming mindsets—a challenging task! Building capacity does not initiate at the first training. It starts when, jointly with law enforcement officials and relevant authorities, one embarks on drafting and agreeing on the terms of reference for the analysis and carrying it out jointly, examining the findings and developing the programme of activities together.

It is only with a long-term vision that we can aspire to develop an effective strategy on how the fair treatment of all persons in police custody may be ensured globally. National prevention mechanisms play a crucial role in building this perspective. However, without viable and effective capacity-building programmes, fair treatment may be a long way away in most corners of the world where individuals are held behind closed doors.

References

APT (2010) Preventing torture: an operational guide for national human rights institutions, OHCHR, APT and APF, Geneva
Arendt H (1977) The life of the mind. Harcourt Inc., New York
Arlin Cuncic (2023) Understanding what police brutality is and why it occurs, verywellmind.com, updated January 28, 2023
Balash J, Falkenbach D (2018) The ends justify the meanness: an investigation of psychopathic traits and utilitarian moral endorsement, personality and individual differences, vol. 127. Science Direct Elsevier, pp 127–132
Bridges W (1991) Managing transitions: making the most of change, 3rd edn. Da Capo Press, Philadelphia
Carver R, Handley L (2016) Does torture prevention work? Liverpool University Press
Celemajer D (2015) Issues paper 2: exploring the root causes of torture. University of Melbourne, Melbourne
Celemajer D (2018) The prevention of torture: an ecological approach. Cambridge University Press
Celermajer D (2017) The ritualization of human rights education and training: the fallacy of the potency of knowing. Journal of Human Rights, Routledge
Chan J (1997) Changing police culture: policing in a multicultural society. Cambridge University Press, Cambridge
Chan J (2001) Backstage punishment: police violence, occupational culture and criminal justice. In: Coady T et al (ed) Violence and police culture. Melbourne University Press
Cockcroft TW (2014) Police culture and transformational leadership: outlining the contours of a troubled relationship. Policing J Policy Pract 8(1):5–13
Conner D (2011) Lessons learned about building commitment to change, blog
Council of Europe (2004) European platform for policing and Human Rights (EPPHR). Police and NGOs: Why and how human rights NGOs and police services can and should work together
Council on Criminal Justice (CCJ) Task Force on Long Sentences (2023). https://counciloncj.foleon.com/tfls/long-sentences-final-report/about-the-task-force
Council on Criminal Justice (CCJ) Task Force on Policing (2023) Policy Assessments. https://counciloncj.foleon.com/policing/assessing-the-evidence/policy-assessments
Drammis Z (2015) Evaluating human rights campaigns: talking to "the enemy", Open Democracy. https://www.opendemocracy.net/openglobalrights/zaira-drammis/evaluating-human-rights-campaigns-talking-to-enemy
European Platform for Policing and Human Rights (EPPHR) (2004) Police and NGOs: why and how human rights NGOs and police services can and should work together. Council of Europe
Fair H, Walmsley R (2021) Thirteenth edition of the world prison population list, Institute for Crime and Policy Research, Birkbeck University, London
Falkenbach D, Balash J, Tsoukalas M, Stern S, Lilienfeld SO (2018) From theoretical to empirical: considering reflections of psychopathy across the thin blue line. Personal Disord Theor Res Treat 9(5):420–428. https://doi.org/10.1037/per0000270
McCulloch J (2001) Keeping the peace and making war: the police and military – rhetoric and reality. In: Coady T et al (eds) Violence and police culture. Melbourne University Press, Melbourne
OMCT (2008) Addressing the economic, social and cultural causes of torture in Kenya
OSCD/ODIHR (2012) Guidelines on human rights education for law enforcement officials. ODIHR, Warsaw
Reiner R (2012) The politics of the police. Oxford University Press, Oxford
Sganga C (2006) Human rights education - as a tool for the reform of the police. JSSE 5(1)
Soros G with Wien B, Koenen K (1995) Soros on soros: staying ahead of the curve. John Wiley & Sons, New York
Witting C (2012) Employees reactions to organizational change. OD Pract 44(2)

Cristina Sganga born in Colombia, Italian citizen, is a Human Rights Promotion Specialist. She graduated with honours from New York University (B.A. in History and Anthropology) and holds an M.A. in Social Sciences with honours from the University of Amsterdam, The Netherlands.

She has worked in the human rights field since 1985 with the specific focus of promoting a better understanding and use of human rights standards to enhance the capacity of States to fulfil their obligations and promote the participation of industry and civil society in the protection and promotion of rights. For most of the 1990s, Cristina established and led Amnesty International's Human Rights Education worldwide programme. She is a co-founder of Human Rights Education Associates.

Since 2010, Cristina has worked as a freelance resource person, developing, and delivering in-person and virtual courses aimed at human rights monitors and human rights educators. She has also focused on the design of learning programmes for the development of human rights compliant law enforcement officials such as police, migration services, nature conservation organisations (park rangers) and counter-terrorism units. Cristina has regularly worked amongst others for Amnesty International, Equitas, the OSCE/ODIHR, the UN OHCHR, ICMPD, IRF and various community-based organisations and governments.

Chapter 11
International Peace Missions and the Prevention of Ill-Treatment: Legal Aspects of UN Policing and Detention

Judith Thorn

Contents

Abstract This article gives an overview of UN policing and the prevention of ill-treatment. Detailing the tasks performed by UN Police in peacekeeping, the article shows levels where the prevention of ill-treatment may have an effect. In difficult post-war situations, the UN and its personnel may be challenged to adhere to the standards of international human rights law, especially related to the prohibition of torture and ill-treatment. For example, UN peacekeepers have detained civilians since the beginning of the success story of their operations. However, not all legal problems concerning detention in peace missions have been solved to date. This article highlights the legal backgrounds: Which law must be followed? Which human rights standards must be taken into account during UN operations? Primarily, the following components are being discussed: the preconditions for detention as such, the minimum conditions for detention (the treatment of detainees) as well as the procedural rights of detainees. Furthermore, the article focuses on the UN Standard Operation Procedure on Detention in UN Peacekeeping Operations. Finally, accountability as well as conduct and disciplinary measures are examined briefly.

J. Thorn (✉)
Giessen, Germany
e-mail: judith.thorn@recht.uni-giessen.de

R. Alleweldt (ed.), *Fair Treatment of Persons in Police Custody*,
https://doi.org/10.1007/978-3-031-61737-9_11

11.1 Introduction

International peace missions are a well-known concept in the field of peace and security and fulfil a crucial task: they keep the peace in challenging surroundings and war-torn areas. The core idea of peacekeeping is to support a host state in its path from conflict to peace.[1] Very rarely do the United Nations (UN) peacekeepers therefore take on the role of peace enforcement on their own.[2] Respecting the sovereignty of the host state, which is one of the fundamental principles of peacekeeping,[3] law enforcement still lies in the hands of the host state. Linking UN peacekeeping and the topic of ill-treatment therefore seems surprising at first glance.

Even though policing and the maintenance of security usually are not core responsibilities of the UN Police but remain the task of the host state and its security forces, the UN may take on a supportive role in these situations. Nevertheless, the UN and especially the UN Police may, with the consent of the state and the specific mandate of the Security Council, also take on an executive role and therefore be challenged to adhere to the standards of international human rights specifically related to the prohibition of torture and ill-treatment. It may be surprising, but United Nations peacekeepers from the beginning of their missions' success story have detained civilians for several reasons, e.g. security or criminal reasons.[4] Some operations even are explicitly mandated to detain.[5] This is, however, not so well known in the public sphere. This paper will not be able to cover all the legal issues related to "International peace missions and the prevention of ill-treatment". It will not be focused on the very rarely granted executive mandates of the UN, like in Kosovo and Timor Leste, where the UN has had full executive powers.[6] It will, however, focus on the more common types of peacekeeping mandates, which usually do not grant the UN such a broad set of powers. Furthermore, it will only cover UN-led operations. Operations authorized by the UN and led by single states or so-called coalitions of the willing will not be addressed. Therefore, law enforcement operations by individual states or other international organizations in the field of counter-piracy or counter-terrorism operations will not be the focus of this analysis. Last but not least, this article will focus not on UN soldiers but on the not-so-well-known UN police component. When looking at detention in UN peacekeeping operations, specific challenges arise. Commonly, peacekeepers are

[1]For the basic idea of UN Peacekeeping see the UN homepage on Peacekeeping, https://peacekeeping.un.org/en/what-is-peacekeeping, Accessed: 29 April 2023.

[2]For the conceptualisation of peacekeeping, peacemaking, peacebuilding and peace enforcement see among others: Bellamy and Williams (2010), 14 et seqq. and Labuda (2015), para. 1 et seqq. and Bothe (2016).

[3]Bothe (2016), para. 41; and for the core principles of peacekeeping see amongst others: Labuda (2015), para. 3.

[4]Oswald (2011), p. 120; Kessing (2012), p. 273.

[5]See below.

[6]Grenfell (2016), p. 347.

deployed during a somehow unclear, blurred situation, which could neither be clearly defined as a war-time nor a peace-time situation.[7] Peacekeepers (soldiers as well as police) from different states and therefore coming from different legal and cultural backgrounds act together on the basis of an often vague and imprecise mandate from the UN Security Council.[8] The core question is, which law must be followed? Does the situation escalate to an armed conflict, and is the International Humanitarian Law (IHL) therefore applicable?[9] Or does International Human Rights Law (IHRL) apply? This evaluation, if taken seriously, must be made by every peacekeeper in each and every single situation. However, this is a very challenging task, and it must be questioned whether this is a realistic approach.[10] However, this article will not focus on the soldiers but rather the UN Police, which might make this highly complex task slightly easier, which may be noted a little later.

11.2 UN Police and Its Tasks in the Prevention of Torture

The specific tasks of a UN peace operation are mandated by the UN Security Council in the resolution establishing the UN Mission for each and every single mission.[11] The resolution is one of the focal points concerning the rights and obligations of a mission.[12] Another crucial legal pillar is the consent of the host state.[13] Specific legal frameworks apply to executive mandates such as Kosovo and East Timor, which will not be addressed here.[14] The mandate of the Security Council, together with the consent of the host state, therefore builds the legal basis for the actions of peace-keepers in the respective state, also vis-à-vis the population of the host state.[15] But which tasks may be taken on by the UN Police in relation to the prevention of torture and ill-treatment? To answer this question, we need to look at the tasks performed by the UN Police in the mission area. In general, the UN outlines the role of the police very broadly:

> Depending on the mandate given by the United Nations Security Council, United Nations police build and support, or, where mandated, act as a substitute or partial substitute for,

[7] Also Kessing (2012), p. 272.

[8] Kessing (2012), p. 292.

[9] For details see Kessing (2012), pp. 274 et seqq. and Gill et al. (2017), p. 91 ff.

[10] Kessing (2012), p. 292.

[11] On the historical development of the tasks taken on by UN Police see Thorn (2018), pp. 247 et seq. with further references.

[12] Bothe (2016), para 27 et seqq.

[13] Labuda (2015), para. 3, 21; Grenfell (2016), p. 347.

[14] For details, please see Grenfell (2016), p. 347 et seq.

[15] Grenfell (2016), p. 347.

> host-state police capacity to prevent and detect crime, protect life and property and maintain public order and safety in adherence to the rule of law and international human rights law.[16]

More specifically, the UN policy "United Nations Police in Peacekeeping Operations and Special Political Missions"[17] defines the two core functions of the UN Police:

> a. Operational support/interim executive policing and other law enforcement: Operational support for and – when mandated – delivery of effective prevention, detection and investigation of crime, protection of life and property, and the maintenance of public order;
> and
> b. Support for the reform, restructuring and rebuilding of host state police: Support for the development of effective host state police capacity to provide representative, responsive and accountable police service of the highest possible professional standard.

The UN Police in missions thus perform the following tasks:

- Reform, restructuring and rebuilding
- Training and lectures
- Monitoring, mentoring and advising (e.g. joint patrols)
- Capacity building and development
- Material support
- Developing the organizational infrastructure and management system within the host state police
- Strengthening governance, accountability and integrity and
- Operational support/policing (specially formed police units)[18]

These tasks are taken on by different "parts" of the UN Police component. The UN Police consists mainly of individual police officers (IPOs) and formed police units (FPUs).[19] The formed police units (FPUs) are comparable to riot police units and take on robust functions within the missions, like "public order management, protection of United Nations personnel and facilities and support to such police operations that require a concerted response but do not respond to military threats (e.g. protection of civilians)".[20] However, they do not engage in situations of public disorder of a military nature.[21] They are not meant to act in situations "where there is

[16] United Nations, United Nations Police, The Mission of UN Police, https://police.un.org/en/node/8008, last Accessed: 29 April 2023.

[17] DPKO/DFS, Policy, United Nations Police in Peacekeeping Operations and Special Political Missions, 01.02.2014, Ref. 2014.01, D7, No. 53.

[18] The tasks are laid down in the DPKO/DFS Policy, United Nations Police in Peacekeeping Operations and Special Political Missions, Ref. 2014.01, 01.02.2014 and the revised Policy, Formed Police Units in United Nations Peacekeeping Operations, Ref. 2016.10, 01.01.2017.

[19] For further details see Thorn (2018), p. 248 et seqq.

[20] UN DPKO/DFS, Policy (Revised), Formed Police Units in United Nations Peacekeeping Operations, Ref. 2016.10, No. 13.

[21] The UN defines the term as such: "Situations of public disorder of a military nature: This generally refers to situations of public disorder where there is sustained and large-scale use of firearms or military weaponry. In such circumstances, units of the military component should have

sustained and large-scale use of firearms or military weaponry".[22] This important fact affects the legal basis of police peacekeeping. This means that the UN Police, from the conception of the UN and according to the idea behind the separation between military and police, should under normal circumstances act not based on the law of armed conflict but on the basis of international human rights law. Therefore, the law of armed conflict (IHL) will not be addressed further in this article.[23] The broad range of tasks taken on by the UN Police in peacekeeping missions today[24] and the conception of a peacekeeping operation provide the opportunity to look at the prevention of torture and ill-treatment from different angles. The UN does not have its own police force but is dependent upon the member states to contribute personnel to the UN missions. We have to keep in mind that this leads to several layers on which the prevention of the prohibition of torture and ill-treatment may have effects: the host state, the sending state and the UN mission and its personnel as such. The prevention of torture may influence the mission on every layer and in the end lead to a better treatment of civilians, especially in detention.

The sending states, for example, are responsible for the pre-deployment training of the Police.[25] The Police personnel therefore have a specific national background, and they are acting according to the law of the sending states, also concerning criminal procedures. As has already been seen, the host state is responsible for law and order in the state. Naturally, local police forces have a specific cultural and legal background as well as national training, which may differ enormously from the police of the sending states. The UN, furthermore, sets specific rules for the UN missions concerning the applicable law and the behaviour of its personnel. It also has specific requirements for possible candidates and tries to ensure specific common standards of the UN Police and personnel, e.g. via human rights screening.[26]

---

primacy in addressing such situations in support of or in cooperation with the relevant host-state agencies, as applicable.", Policy (Revised), Formed Police Units in United Nations Peacekeeping Operations, Ref. 2016.10, 01.01.2017, para. 52.

[22] UN DPKO/DFS, Policy (Revised), Formed Police Units in United Nations Peacekeeping Operations, Ref. 2016.10, No. 52.

[23] For an overview of IHL, see Kessing (2012) and Naert (2006), pp. 53 et seqq.

[24] For the evolution of tasks and functions of the Police in Peacekeeping: Kihara-Hunt (2017), pp. 16 et seqq. and Schmidl (1998), pp. 19 et seqq.

[25] The UN gives further information and training material on its homepage: https://police.un.org/en/un-police-training-materials-ipos. Accessed: 29 April 2023.

[26] UN Police, Information for Candidates, https://police.un.org/en/information-candidates. Accessed: 29 April 2023.

11.3 UN Police and Detention—Relevant Law

The aforementioned leads us to the question of applicable law. The law is a mix of domestic law of the sending state, the host state's law and international law.[27] To summarize, the legal bases for detention by the UN Police can principally be found in the following sources:

- Human rights law
- The mandate of the Security Council
- Treaties between the UN host state (so-called Status of Forces/Missions Agreements (SOFA/SOMA)[28]) as well as the UN and the sending states (so-called Memorandums of Understanding (MoUs)[29])[30]
- The law of the sending state and the host state, as well as
- Internal regulations and policies of the UN[31]

Human rights law plays an important role concerning the prevention of torture and ill-treatment. The UN is not a member of human rights treaties like the International Covenant on Civil and Political Rights (ICCPR)[32] or the Convention Against Torture and Other Cruel, Inhuman or Degrading Treatment or Punishment (UNCAT);[33] however, it is not seriously disputed that the UN is at least bound by international customary law.[34] The legal dispute concerning the reasons why and how the UN is bound to human rights law must not be addressed here in detail.[35] The UN itself stipulates in its principles and guidelines for UN peacekeeping that international human rights law is an "integral part of the normative framework for UN peace-keeping operations".[36] The recently adopted "Guidelines on Police Operations in United Nations Peacekeeping Operations and Special Political Missions"[37] specifically address the implications of international human rights law for the police component:

[27] See also Naert (2006), p. 53.

[28] For details see Gill et al. (2017), p. 120 ff.; Fleck (2015), para 6.06 et seqq; Oswald et al. (2011), pp. 34 et seqq.

[29] For details see Gill et al. (2017), p. 139 et seqq.; Oswald et al. (2011), pp. 51 et seqq.

[30] See also Foley (2017), p. 233 et seqq.

[31] See also Hessbruegge (2022), p. 96 et seq.

[32] UNTS vol. 999, p. 171 and vol. 1057, p. 407, entry into force: 23 March 1976.

[33] UNTS vol. 1465, p. 85, entry into force: 26 June 1987.

[34] See Thorn (2018), p. 263 with further references. See also Hessbruegge (2022), p. 94 and 98 with several further references.

[35] See Thorn (2018), p. 262 et seqq. with further references.

[36] UN DPKO/DFS, United Nations Principles and Guidelines, "Capestone Doctrin", 2008, https://www.un.org/ruleoflaw/files/Capstone_Doctrine_ENG.pdf. See also Grenfell (2016), p. 348.

[37] UN DPKO/DFS, Guidelines, Police Operations in United Nations Peacekeeping Operations and Special Political Missions, 01 January 2016, Ref. 2015.15.

> 11. All United Nations police operations (...) shall be guided by the obligation to respect and protect human rights, norms, ethics and standards in crime prevention and criminal justice and international human rights and humanitarian law. In all aspects of their operations, United Nations personnel shall ensure their compliance with human rights standards, shall promptly record and share allegations of violations with the human rights component, and shall be prepared to intervene, including through the use of force where mandated, to stop ongoing human rights violations and to protect civilians[38]

The most relevant human rights documents concerning the prohibition of torture and ill-treatment are the Universal Declaration of Human Rights (UDHR);[39] the International Covenant on Civil and Political Rights (ICCPR);[40] the Convention Against Torture and Other Cruel, Inhuman or Degrading Treatment or Punishment (UNCAT);[41] regional human rights treaties (e.g. the European Convention on Human Rights (ECHR)[42]);[43] and the UN Body of Principles for the Protection of All Persons Under Any Form of Detention or Imprisonment (Body of Principles).[44] The prohibition of torture is also a part of customary international law.[45] The Body of Principles is an important soft law instrument and gives guidance on the definitions and general principles concerning the treatment of prisoners and detainees. This article will not look at the details of international human rights law. However, the minimum standards, which must be taken into account by the UN operations, will be highlighted.

11.3.1 Legal Basis

The mandate given by the Security Council is one of the fundamental legal bases for detention by peacekeepers in UN missions. By authorizing the mission to use "all necessary measures/means", the Security Council does also include the power of detention as a lesser means of the use of deadly force.[46] Sometimes the Council also decides to explicitly mandate the detention in its resolutions.[47] However, before looking into detail and the minimum standards, which must be applied by peacekeepers, we should think about the term "detention". What is the definition of

[38] UN DPKO/DFS, Guidelines, Police Operations in United Nations Peacekeeping Operations and Special Political Missions, 01 January 2016, Ref. 2015.15, para. 11.

[39] UN General Assembly, UN Doc. A/RES/3/217A, 10 December 1948.

[40] UNTS vol. 999, p. 171, entry into force: 13.03.1976.

[41] UNTS vol. 1465, p. 85, entry into force: 26 June 1987, General Assembly resolution 39/46 of 10 December 1984.

[42] UNTS vol. 213, p. 221, entry into force: 3 September 1953.

[43] See also Naert (2006), p. 53.

[44] General Assembly, UN Doc. A/Res/43/173, 9 December 1988.

[45] Kretzmer (2022), para. 6.

[46] Kessing (2012), p. 294.

[47] See below.

detention? The Body of Principles, which was adopted by the General Assembly in resolution 43/173 of 9 December 1988, gives basic principles on the treatment of all persons subjected to any form of detention or imprisonment. It defines a detained person as "any person deprived of personal liberty except as a result of conviction for an offence".[48] "Detention" thereby means the condition of detained persons.[49] Detention in this article is to be understood as a general term for any deprivation of liberty of a person by personnel of a peace operation against the will of this person.[50] It should be made clear that the term arrest is slightly more specific and, even though sometimes used interchangeably with detention, is used for situations where a person's liberty has been deprived in the context of police enforcement of criminal law.[51] Even though it is common practice of the UN to detain civilians during UN-led peace operations,[52] the legal justification for this practice remains unclear.[53] This is a problem, especially concerning the protection of civilians from arbitrary detention.[54] Furthermore, the UN Police has to adhere to the minimum legal standards, which are laid down in international human rights law, namely the restrictions to a person's liberty.[55] The human right to liberty obliges the states[56] and also the UN[57] to set up substantive preconditions and procedural requirements for detention.[58] The deprivation of a person's liberty must not be arbitrary.[59] The internationally accepted standard for deprivations of liberty consists mainly of the following three components: the preconditions for detention as such, the minimum conditions for detention (the treatment of detainees) and the procedural rights of

---

[48] Body of Principles for the Protection of All Persons under Any Form of Detention or Imprisonment, General Assembly, UN Doc. A/Res/43/173, 9 December 1988, Scope of the Body of Principles, (b).

[49] Body of Principles for the Protection of All Persons under Any Form of Detention or Imprisonment, General Assembly, UN Doc. A/Res/43/173, 9 December 1988, Scope of the Body of Principles, (d).

[50] Oswald (2011), p. 135; Dörr (2021), para. 1.

[51] Oswald (2011), p. 135; Dörr (2021), para. 1.

[52] For an overview Oswald (2011), p. 123 et seqq. and International Committee of the Red Cross (2015).

[53] Kessing (2012), p. 273; Larsen (2012), p. 393.

[54] Kessing (2012), p. 273.

[55] Larsen (2012), p. 393 ff.; Dörr (2021), para. 1.

[56] The extraterritorial application of the Human Rights obligation of member states is assumed in this article. However, this is sometimes contested by states: see Naert (2006), p. 56. For details concerning the extraterritorial application see Thorn (2018), p. 256 et seqq.

[57] The UN is not a member of the ICCPR but is bound at least by customary law. For details if and how the UN is bound to Human Rights Law, see Thorn (2018), pp. 262 et seqq.; The right to personal liberty is also part of customary international law: Dörr (2021), para. 11. This assumption is also taken by Naert (2006), p. 56.

[58] Dörr (2021), para. 3.

[59] See Art. 9 (1) ICCPR; Larsen (2012), p. 393.

detainees.[60] If the circumstances that justify detention cease to exist, the person must be released.[61]

11.3.1.1 Legality of Detention

First of all, the main precondition for a lawful detention is that it must have a legal basis.[62] Detention thus can only be justified on a limited number of grounds.[63] The grounds for detention as well as the procedure must be laid down in a general binding norm of law before the detention occurs.[64] The norm must be sufficiently specific and precise to allow the persons concerned to foresee the consequences of their actions.[65]

Furthermore, the detention must be in conformity with the law. The deprivation of liberty must comply with the procedure prescribed and all substantive requirements.[66] Therefore, it must also be in conformity with international law.[67] The detention must have a substantive reason recognized by the applicable international human rights norm, even though most norms do not set specific reasons themselves but refer to domestic law.[68] Concerning the deprivation of liberty of persons by the UN Police and also UN peacekeepers in general, one problem arises. Do the UN Security Council resolutions provide a sufficient legal basis for detention? This subject is discussed in a controversial way. The UN Security Council explicitly authorized detention in peacekeeping only in very few cases. An explicit mandate,

[60] Dörr (2021), para. 11.

[61] Gill et al. (2017), pp. 163 et seq.

[62] Art. 9 ICCPR: 1. Everyone has the right to liberty and security of person. No one shall be subjected to arbitrary arrest or detention. No one shall be deprived of his liberty except on such grounds and in accordance with such procedures as are established by law.

2. Anyone who is arrested shall be informed, at the time of arrest, of the reasons for his arrest and shall be promptly informed of any charges against him.

3. Anyone arrested or detained on a criminal charge shall be brought promptly before a judge or other officer authorized by law to exercise judicial power and shall be entitled to trial within a reasonable time or to release. It shall not be the general rule that persons awaiting trial shall be detained in custody, but release may be subject to guarantees to appear for trial, at any other stage of the judicial proceedings, and, should occasion arise, for execution of the judgement.

4. Anyone who is deprived of his liberty by arrest or detention shall be entitled to take proceedings before a court, in order that that court may decide without delay on the lawfulness of his detention and order his release if the detention is not lawful.

5. Anyone who has been the victim of unlawful arrest or detention shall have an enforceable right to compensation.

[63] Gill et al. (2017), pp. 159 et seqq.

[64] Dörr (2021), para. 12.

[65] Dörr (2021), para. 12; Gill et al. (2017), p. 159.

[66] Dörr (2021), para. 13.

[67] Dörr (2021), para. 14.

[68] Dörr (2021), para. 15.

for example, was given in Congo 1961 (ONUC),[69] in Somalia 1993 (UNOSOM II)[70] and in Liberia 2006 (UNMIL).[71,72] More commonly, however, the power to detain is implied, and the Council may authorize the peacekeeping mission to take "all necessary measures/means".[73] Concerning the legality of detention, it is primarily problematic that the mandates of the Security Council are phrased in a broad language and, therefore, detention may not be based on legitimate grounds.[74] Resolutions are the outcome of a political compromise between states with different interests. Therefore, the wording of a resolution is open for interpretation, whether it includes the authorization of detention or whether it does not include the power to detain.[75] It is disputed if the resolutions of the Security Council are clear and specific enough to fulfil the requirements of the legality of detention.[76] Even though it is common practice to mandate a mission to take "all necessary measures/means", this may hardly be seen to be sufficiently precise and specific to provide a legal basis for detention.[77] This dilemma between legal requirements and practical necessity is not solved in a satisfying manner.

Furthermore, the UN Security Council, even though mandating a mission and also probably the use of force, including detention,[78] does not stipulate any details on the treatment of detainees, the procedure for detention or the judicial safeguards in its resolutions.[79]

Also, the applicable international agreements or the treaties between the host state and the UN (SOFAs/SOMAs) could include rules on detention and the transfer of detainees,[80] yet they do not necessarily include a sufficiently clear legal basis. The

---

[69] The Security Council authorised the UN Operation in the Congo (ONUC) to detain 'pending legal action [. . .] all foreign military and para-military personnel and political advisers not under United Nations command, and mercenaries'. See SC Res. 169, 24 November 1961, para. 4.

[70] The Security Council concerning Somalia authorised the Secretary-General to take all measures necessary to arrest and detain those responsible for carrying out the armed attacks against the UN military personnel serving with UNOSOM II. See SC Res. 837, 6 June 1993, para. 5.

[71] Concerning UNMIL the Security Council authorized to 'apprehend and detain former President Charles Taylor in the event of a return to Liberia'. See SC Res. 1638, 11 November 2005, para. 1.

[72] See Oswald (2013), p. 714.

[73] Oswald (2013), p. 714 with case examples; Kessing (2012), p. 294; Larsen (2012), p. 393 f.

[74] Larsen (2012), p. 394 concerning rulings on the ECHR and the ICCPR.

[75] Oswald (2013), p. 716; Naert (2006), p. 60.

[76] Oswald (2013), p. 716; Larsen (2012), p. 394.

[77] *Kleffner* puts it as follows: "[I]t may hardly be assumed that a Security Council mandate 'to use all necessary means' could provide a legal basis for operational detention that would not be clearly available under other rules of law.", Kleffner (2015), para. 26.03; Especially problematic is this for Member States of the ECHR. On the ruling of the ECtHR please see for further details in: Oswald (2013), p. 716; Larsen (2012), p. 394.

[78] Kleffner (2015), para. 26.03.

[79] Oswald (2013), p. 717.

[80] Kleffner (2015), para. 26.03; Grenfell (2016), p. 347 et seq.

peacekeepers may also be able to rely on host state law[81] or the right to personal self-defence.[82] Other internal documents (e.g. the Standard Operating Procedures on Detention in UN Peace Operations[83] and mission-specific guidance like Rules of Engagement and Directives on the Use of Force)[84] provide guidance concerning the "how" of detention but do not give an authorization to detain. Therefore, even the existence of a clear, sufficiently specific and precise norm for the detention by UN peacekeepers is questionable. The fact that there is a practical need to detain in certain situations is less debatable. As *Oswald* puts it: "The answer remains unsettled for those seeking to find an acceptable legal basis that achieves a balance between state practice and a specific positivist legal justification."[85]

11.3.1.2 Treatment of Detainees

The treatment of detainees is governed by the rules on the prevention of torture and degrading treatment, detailed in Art. 7 ICCPR and also Art. 10 ICCPR.[86] Furthermore, the Convention on the Prohibition of Torture (UNCAT)[87] is a crucial legal basis. Detainees therefore must be treated with humanity and with respect for their dignity. In several UN documents, the humane treatment of detainees is addressed. Especially, the Standard Operating Procedures on Detention in UN Peace Operations[88] should be mentioned. Furthermore, the Body of Principles for the Protection of All Persons Under Any Form of Detention or Imprisonment,[89] the Basic Principles for the Treatment of Prisoners,[90] the Standard Minimum Rules for the Treatment of Prisoners,[91] the Basic Principles on the Use of Force and Firearms by Law Enforcement Officials[92] and the Code of Conduct for Law Enforcement Officials[93] are to be considered relevant. Moreover, in October 2012, a group of states led by the

---

[81] Kleffner (2015), para. 26.02; Oswald (2011), p. 136.

[82] Kleffner (2015), para. 26.03.

[83] UN DPKO/DFS, Interim Standard Operating Procedures, Detention in UN Peace Operations, Ref. 2010.6, 25 January 2010.

[84] See also Grenfell (2016), p. 349.

[85] Oswald (2013), p. 707.

[86] Dörr (2021), para. 17 et seq.

[87] See above note 40.

[88] See above note 83.

[89] See above note 43.

[90] UN General Assembly, UN Doc A/RES/45/111, 14 December 1990.

[91] So-called Mandela Rules, General Assembly, UN Doc. A/C.3/70/L.3, 29. September 2015.

[92] Adopted by the Eighth United Nations Congress on the Prevention of Crime and the Treatment of Offenders, Havana, Cuba, 27 August to 7 September 1990, https://www.ohchr.org/en/instruments-mechanisms/instruments/basic-principles-use-force-and-firearms-law-enforcement. Last accessed: 29 April 2023.

[93] UNTS Vol. 1465 p. 85, entry into force 26 June 1987, UN General Assembly, UN Doc. A/RES/34/169, 17 December 1979.

Danish government adopted a set of principles and guidelines on detention, which are non-binding, called the "Copenhagen Principles".[94,95]

11.3.1.3 Rights of Detained Persons

The rights of detained persons are mainly procedural safeguards and are laid down in Art. 9 (2)–(5) ICCPR. They form a crucial backbone for the legal framework for lawful detention.[96]

First, the detainee has got the right to information, which contains the right to be informed on the reasons for the detention and of any charges brought against the person.[97] This includes the right to be informed in a way that the person concerned is able to understand the essential legal and factual grounds for their arrest.[98] Furthermore, anyone detained has got the right to challenge the lawfulness of the detention via a prompt judicial control mechanism.[99] *Dörr* emphasizes this as "an important safeguard against incommunicado detention and also against ill-treatment of the individual taken into custody".[100]

Concerning the rights of detained persons in peacekeeping operations, three problems stand out: 1) the length of detention in UN peacekeeping operations, 2) the judicial review process and the requirement of an effective remedy and 3) the transfer of detainees (non-refoulement principle).

The "length of detention" as well as the "judicial review process" are covered by the UN in its internal policies and guidance. However, concerning the transfer of detainees, the UN is faced with huge challenges in practice. What should the UN do if there is a real risk in the host state that the detainee will be subject to torture? What should the UN do if the state is unwilling to take over the detainee? Concerning the non-refoulement principle, there is a general agreement that "where there is a substantial belief that a detainee may be tortured by local authorities, the multinational force that has effective control of the detainee is prohibited from transferring the detainee to those authorities".[101] Therefore, situations where the host state has a poor human rights record or does not have a fully functioning state system (especially the law enforcement and the judicial system) are difficult.[102] Even if the

---

[94] The Copenhagen Process Principles and Guidelines on the Handling of Detainees in International Military Operations, 20 October 2012, https://2009-2017.state.gov/documents/organization/211975.pdf. Last Accessed: 29 April 2023.

[95] On the Copenhagen Principles see Oswald (2013) and Foley (2017), pp. 238 et seq.

[96] On the procedural safeguards see also Gill et al. (2017), pp. 164 et seqq.

[97] Dörr (2021), para. 22.

[98] Dörr (2021), para. 22; Gill et al. (2017), pp. 165 ff.

[99] Gill et al. (2017), pp. 164 et seq.; Dörr (2021), para. 24.

[100] Dörr (2021), para. 24.

[101] Oswald (2013), p. 718; see also Gill et al. (2017), pp. 171 et seqq.

[102] Gill et al. (2017), p. 173.

decision to transfer a person is taken, the question remains whether post-transfer monitoring must be conducted.[103] A general international rule on post-transfer monitoring does not exist.[104] However, the UN in its SOP does address monitoring after the handover of a detainee.[105]

For the UN, practical problems arise if they are not able to transfer the detainee to the host state due to the principle of non-refoulement or if the host state is unwilling to take the detainee into custody. The UN needs to provide adequate detention facilities, which usually are not planned for in peacekeeping operations. Furthermore, the UN does not have a judicial system to put potential criminals on trial.[106] How should the UN deal with people who are security risks?[107] Can they be held by the UN for a longer period of time because their release may be inappropriate?[108] Further practical problems could be added. Hence, in practical terms, there are still a lot of challenges concerning detention on the part of the UN.

11.3.2 Standard Operation Procedure on Detention in UN Peacekeeping Operations (SOP)

The "Standard Operation Procedure on Detention in UN Peacekeeping Operations"[109] is an internal document that focuses on the detention procedure in UN peacekeeping operations.[110] The guidelines shall ensure that people detained by the UN are handled humanely and in accordance with international human rights law.[111] However, the SOP does not give the right to detain. It solely covers the procedure in cases where the mandate gives the mission such power.[112]

The SOP is based on general principles.[113] Only two of those are relevant to the police component: first, any person detained by the UN shall be released or handed over to national law enforcement officials or other national authorities as soon as possible. Second, detention should not be arbitrary or unlawful, and detainees should

[103] Oswald (2013), p. 718.

[104] Oswald (2013), p. 718.

[105] See below.

[106] Naert (2006), p. 62.

[107] On the categories of detainees and persons posing a security threat in Peace Operations see Naert (2006), p. 59 et seqq.

[108] Naert (2006), p. 62.

[109] See above note 83.

[110] On the SOP see also Grenfell (2016) and Foley (2017), pp. 236 et seq.

[111] UN DPKO/DFS, Interim Standard Operation Procedures, Detention in United Nations Peacekeeping Operations, Ref. 2010.6, 25 January 2010, A. Purpose.

[112] Grenfell (2016), p. 350.

[113] UN DPKO and DFS, Interim Standard Operation Procedures, Detention in United Nations Peacekeeping Operations, Ref. 2010.6, 25 January 2010, para. 7 and 8.

be treated in a humane manner and with respect to the inherent dignity of the human person.

Besides, the SOP covers the following topics: taking and handling of detained persons, release and handover, and implementation measures. The rules on the handling of detained persons built the main part of the SOP. Here, only the most crucial parts of the SOP will be mentioned. However, it can be shown that the UN, by its internal guidance for peacekeepers, covers the procedural safeguards for detained persons.

First of all, a statement of the grounds for detention must be given to a detainee.[114] The person must be informed (in a language that they understand) about the reasons and factual basis for their detention.[115] At the earliest possible time, the detainee should receive a so-called Statement of Detention, which informs the person about their rights.[116] A further safeguard is the information of important mission personnel and also the International Committee of the Red Cross (ICRC): within 36 hours after taking the detainee into custody, the Detention Focal Point, the Chief of the Human Rights component, the Head of Mission as well as the ICRC must be informed about the intake.[117]

The SOP also regulates the right of the detainee to inform a designated person and (if the detainee is a foreigner) their embassy.[118] The internal rules further cover the humane treatment of a detainee. The SOP includes the prohibition of discrimination; the prohibition of torture and cruel, inhuman or degrading treatment or punishment; and issues concerning the detention facilities, like the provision of food and water, health and hygiene, privacy and accommodation, medical services and medical screenings. The UN personnel are, according to the SOP, responsible for the safety of a detained person.[119]

Furthermore, the use of force and physical restraint shall be strictly in accordance with international standards.[120] For the UN Police in particular, specific directives on the use of force exist, which specify the rules concerning the use of force. The SOP,

[114] UN DPKO and DFS, Interim Standard Operation Procedures, Detention in United Nations Peacekeeping Operations, Ref. 2010.6, 25 January 2010, para. 10.

[115] UN DPKO and DFS, Interim Standard Operation Procedures, Detention in United Nations Peacekeeping Operations, UN Doc. Ref. 2010.6, paras. 10.

[116] UN DPKO and DFS, Interim Standard Operation Procedures, Detention in United Nations Peacekeeping Operations, UN Doc. Ref. 2010.6, paras. 10.

[117] UN DPKO and DFS, Interim Standard Operation Procedures, Detention in United Nations Peacekeeping Operations, Ref. 2010.6, 25 January 2010, para. 11–13.

[118] UN DPKO and DFS, Interim Standard Operation Procedures, Detention in United Nations Peacekeeping Operations, Ref. 2010.6, 25 January 2010, para. 16 and 56.

[119] UN DPKO and DFS, Interim Standard Operation Procedures, Detention in United Nations Peacekeeping Operations, Ref. 2010.6, 25 January 2010, para. 22.

[120] UN DPKO and DFS, Interim Standard Operation Procedures, Detention in United Nations Peacekeeping Operations, Ref. 2010.6, 25 January 2010, para. 26–29.

though, also includes guidance on the questioning and search of detained persons.[121]

It is important to mention that the UN set up a register system for each detainee. Thus, a record is available, which may serve the detainee in the complaints procedure, which is implemented by the SOP. Detained persons have the right to complain about their treatment or the condition of detention.[122] All complaints are recorded in a detained person complaint register and reported immediately to the Detention Focal Point. The complaints shall be investigated in a timely manner. The UN also determines the length of detention. A detained person thereby shall not be held by UN personnel for more than 48 hours, before being 1) released or 2) handed over to the national authorities. In specific transit cases, the detainee may be held for up to 72 hours.[123] However, the SOP also provides an exception, whereby persons can be held longer than 72 hours in UN custody if 1) the host state officially requests the UN to detain the person on behalf of the state, 2) the mission has got a mandate to assist national law enforcement authorities in the apprehension and detention of alleged criminals and 3) the Head of Mission considers such detention to be reasonable.[124] If these conditions apply, the person may be detained up to the maximum period permitted under national law or otherwise specified in the mission mandate.

Otherwise, a person shall be released.[125] If they are not released, a person shall be handed over to the national authorities.[126] In the treaties between the UN and the host state (SOFA/SOMA), specific arrangements shall be concluded to protect the rights of a detainee and ensure their humane treatment. Even though the handover of detainees to national authorities is the priority of the UN, a handover cannot take place if there exists a real risk that a detained person will be tortured or ill-treated. In this case, the person shall be released. This also applies if a state is unwilling to accept the handover.

The UN, all in all, took a lot of implementation measures and set up: a detention register, a reporting mechanism as well as an internal evaluation mechanism. The UN furthermore stipulates a monitoring system by the ICRC and the Human Rights component. Even if a person is handed over, access to the person should be granted

[121] UN DPKO and DFS, Interim Standard Operation Procedures, Detention in United Nations Peacekeeping Operations, Ref. 2010.6, 25 January 2010, para. 41–51.

[122] UN DPKO and DFS, Interim Standard Operation Procedures, Detention in United Nations Peacekeeping Operations, Ref. 2010.6, 25 January 2010, para. 70–72.

[123] UN DPKO and DFS, Interim Standard Operation Procedures, Detention in United Nations Peacekeeping Operations, Ref. 2010.6, 25 January 2010, para. 73–74.

[124] UN DPKO and DFS, Interim Standard Operation Procedures, Detention in United Nations Peacekeeping Operations, Ref. 2010.6, 25 January 2010, para. 75.

[125] UN DPKO and DFS, Interim Standard Operation Procedures, Detention in United Nations Peacekeeping Operations, Ref. 2010.6, 25 January 2010, para. 76–79.

[126] UN DPKO and DFS, Interim Standard Operation Procedures, Detention in United Nations Peacekeeping Operations, Ref. 2010.6, 25 January 2010, para. 80–88.

to the UN and the ICRC.[127] The Human Rights component of the mission shall monitor the detention conditions in the host state.

11.4 Accountability and Conduct

However, the issues concerning an effective legal remedy are not solved. The SOP provides a complaint mechanism; however, this is not a judicial remedy. Judicial procedures against the UN or members of the UN Police are difficult or more or less impossible. Here, no detailed analyses shall be given. In short, the UN has absolute immunity in national courts and therefore is not subject to legal review.[128] The UN Police personnel have so-called functional immunity, which means the immunity applies only to official acts.[129]

The "Directives for Disciplinary Matters Involving Civilian Police Officers and Military Observers"[130] state:

> 8. Civilian police officers and military observers enjoy the status of 'experts performing missions' for the United Nations, under Article VI of the 1946 Convention on the Privileges and Immunities of the United Nations. In accordance with that status, they enjoy inter alia immunity for the purposes of the official acts they perform. These privileges and immunities are granted in the interests of the United Nations and not for the personal benefit of the individuals themselves. The Secretary-General has the right and the duty to waive the immunity of any individual in any case where, in the Secretary-General's opinion, the immunity would impede the course of justice. Such a waiver shall be without prejudice to the interests of the United Nations. Civilian police officers and military observers are, however, subject to the jurisdiction of the host country/territory in respect of any criminal offences that may be committed by them in the host country and any disputes/claims of a civil nature not related to the performance of their official functions.

Even though the Secretary General may waive the immunity, this rarely occurs.[131]

The UN additionally established an internal system of conduct and discipline. The Conduct and Discipline Units are charged with receiving and handling complaints, while the Office of Internal Oversight Services will take charge of serious criminal allegations.[132]

---

[127] UN DPKO and DFS, Interim Standard Operation Procedures, Detention in United Nations Peacekeeping Operations, Ref. 2010.6, 25 January 2010, para. 95–97.

[128] Kihara-Hunt (2017), pp. 231 et seq; Larsen (2012), p. 393.

[129] For the details, see Kihara-Hunt (2017), pp. 230 et seqq. and Thorn (2018), pp. 264 et seqq.

[130] UN Doc. DPKO/CPD/DDCPO/2003/001, DPKO/MD/03/00994, https://police.un.org/sites/default/files/directives_for_disciplinary_matters_involving_civilian_police_officers.pdf. Last Accessed: 29 April 2023.

[131] For details see Kihara-Hunt (2017), pp. 272 et seqq.

[132] Sweetser (2008), p. 1650.

So what does the UN internally do in cases of allegations? The procedure is laid down in the "Directives for Disciplinary Matters Involving Civilian Police Officers and Military Observers",[133] and the steps can be summarized as follows:

1. A report shall be submitted to the Head of Mission or Personnel Conduct Officer, who shall bring it to the attention of the Head of Mission.
2. A preliminary investigation shall be conducted to establish the facts of the case.
3. A mission headquarters Board of Inquiry shall convene to establish the facts of the case/determine cause and responsibility in the incident under review/recommendations. This, however, does not cover questions of compensation or legal liability.
4. The final report of the Board of Inquiry shall be submitted to the UN Headquarters in New York, along with the decision of the Head of Mission.
5. The Recommendations of the Board of Inquiry, together with any comments thereon by the Head of Mission and his/her final decision, shall be communicated to the commanders or other supervisors responsible for the maintenance of discipline.
6. The commander or other supervisor responsible for the maintenance of discipline shall take appropriate administrative and/or disciplinary action.

The possible measures the UN may take in cases of misconduct are removal from the position of command; redeployment to another position/area after retraining, if necessary; removal of benefits and concessions provided to United Nations personnel; suspension of leave/compensatory time off; full or partial recovery from Mission Subsistence Allowance, in cases of financial loss to the organization; recommendation to repatriate; or a written censure or reprimand, including a possible recommendation for non-eligibility for future assignment with the United Nations.

11.5 Conclusion

Human rights are a crucial part of peacekeeping by the UN Police today. The UN Police must adhere to international human rights law. Therefore, the prevention of torture also influences the mission. Especially in cases in which the UN Police has executive powers, like the power to detain, specific challenges concerning the humane treatment of detained persons arise. Due to the different legal and cultural backgrounds of the UN Police personnel, this is a challenging task. But the UN has done a lot to implement basic principles in its internal policies. The minimum standards are clear. Especially, the SOP on Detention in UN Peacekeeping

[133] UN Doc. DPKO/CPD/DDCPO/2003/001, DPKO/MD/03/00994, https://police.un.org/sites/default/files/directives_for_disciplinary_matters_involving_civilian_police_officers.pdf. Last Accessed: 29 April 2023.

Operations does provide useful guidance. However, not all issues are resolved, and there is still a need to carefully balance the practical necessities and the legal requirements.

References

Bellamy AJ, Williams PD (2010) Understanding peacekeeping. Polity Press, Cambridge

Bothe M (2016) Peacekeeping forces. In: Max Planck Encyclopedia of Public International Law [MPEPIL], online edition, last updated: August 2016. Accessed 27 June 2023

Dörr O (2021) Detention, Arbitrary. In: Max Planck Encyclopedia of Public International Law [MPEPIL], online edition, last updated: June 2021. Accessed 27 June 2023

Fleck D (2015) Status of forces in peace operations. In: Gill TD, Fleck D (eds) The handbook of international law of military operations, 2nd edn. Oxford University Press, Oxford

Foley C (2017) UN peacekeeping operations and the protection of civilians, saving succeeding generations. Cambridge University Press, Cambridge

Gill TD, Fleck D, Boothby WH, Vanheusen A (2017) Leuven manual on the international law applicable to peace operations. Cambridge University Press, Cambridge

Grenfell K (2016) Detention in United Nations Peace Operations. In: Rose G, Oswald B (eds) Detention of non-state actors engaged in hostilities. Brill Nijhoff, Leiden

Hessbruegge JA (2022) Human Rights Obligations of United Nations Peacekeepers: implementation through the UN's own policies and remaining challenges. J Int Peacekeeping 25(2022): 91–118

International Committee of the Red Cross (2015) Peacekeeping Operations: ICRC Statement to the United Nations, 6 November 2015. https://www.icrc.org/en/document/general-debate-comprehensive-review-whole-question-peacekeeping-operations-all-their. Accessed 29 April 2023

Kessing (2012) Security detention in UN peace operations. In: Larsen KM, Guldahl Cooper C, Nystuen G (eds) Searching for a 'Principle of Humanity' in International Humanitarian Law. Cambridge University Press, pp 272–303

Kihara-Hunt A (2017) Holding UNPOL to account. Brill Nijhoff, Leiden

Kleffner JK (2015) Operational detention. In: Gill TD, Fleck D (eds) The handbook of international law of military operations, 2nd edn. Oxford University Press, Oxford

Kretzmer D (2022) Torture, Prohibition of. In: Max Planck Encyclopedia of Public International Law [MPEPIL], online edition, last updated: May 2022. Accessed 27 June 2023

Labuda PI (2015) Peacekeeping and Peace Enforcement. In: Max Planck Encyclopedia of Public International Law [MPEPIL], online edition, last updated: September 2015. Accessed 27 June 2023

Larsen KM (2012) The human rights obligations of peacekeepers. Cambridge University Press, Cambridge

Naert F (2006) Detention in peace operations: the legal framework and main categories of detainees. Mil Law Law War Rev 45:51–78

Oswald B (2011) Detention by United Nations Peacekeepers: searching for definition and categorisation. J Int Peacekeeping 15(1–2):119–151

Oswald B (2013) Some controversies of detention in multinational operations and the contributions of the Copenhagen Principles. Int Rev Red Cross 95(891/892):707–726

Oswald B, Durham H, Bates A (2011) Documents on the law of peacekeeping operations. Oxford University Press, Oxford

Schmidl EA (1998) Police functions in peace operations: an historical overview. In: Oakley RB, Dziedzic MJ, Goldberg EM (eds) Policing the new world disorder. National Defence University Press, Washington, DC

Sweetser (2008) Providing effective remedies to victims of abuse by peacekeeping personnel. N Y Univ Law Rev 83(5):1643–1677

Thorn J (2018) United Nations Police Missions and Human Rights. In: Alleweldt R, Fickenscher G (eds) The police and international human rights law. Springer, Cham, pp 245–278

Judith Thorn born in 1985, studied law at the Justus Liebig University (JLU) Giessen (Germany) and the University of Nottingham (United Kingdom). Since graduation in 2011 she has been employed as research assistant at the Chair of Public Law and International Law (Prof. Dr. Thilo Marauhn, M.Phil.) at the JLU Giessen. She was also a member of the research group 'UN Policing—Legal Basis, Status and Directives on the Use of Force'. This project was funded by the German Foundation for Peace Research and implemented by the Chair of Public Law and International Law at the JLU in cooperation with the Peace Research Institute Frankfurt (PRIF). Since 2020 she works as a judge in the field of social law. Besides social law and constitutional law, her research interests also include Public International Law and especially the United Nations, Peacekeeping and UN Policing.

Chapter 12
International Peace Missions and the Prevention of Ill-Treatment: Practical Challenges and Proposed New Approaches

William G. O'Neill

Contents

Abstract The challenges connected with preventing ill-treatment in detention facing United Nations' (UN's) peace operations cannot be understood without analyzing the broader context of why the rule of law is so weak in the host country. The chapter examines how the UN has traditionally approached the rule of law programming and identifies several key flaws in its analysis of the problem, the execution of its programs, and the identification of priorities, including in the approach to preventing ill-treatment. Several proposals are made to fix this, with the central theme being that the UN needs to change the way it is doing business in the realm of peace operations.

W. G. O'Neill (✉)
New York, NY, USA

R. Alleweldt (ed.), *Fair Treatment of Persons in Police Custody*,
https://doi.org/10.1007/978-3-031-61737-9_12

12.1 Introduction

I always begin my presentation on the rule of law in the UN course for senior mission leadership showing a picture of a collapsed building in Haiti.

The rubble shown below the desperate rescuers was a school. The building collapsed one fine November morning in 2008. No rain, no hurricane, no earthquake. Why? The government had no building code governing construction so that the materials used for this school were diluted cement and weak wire rods. No government official ever inspected the construction site to make sure it was safe. The state had no land-use planning either; the school was built on a steep incline unsuitable for building, especially for a school. No health inspectors ever came to make sure the school was clean and safe, and no one from the Ministry of Education checked for overcrowding, the qualifications of the teachers, accessibility to clean water and toilets, or anything else that any other school would have to show in a country where there are minimum rules that must be followed. The school was a private one, not a state school. The owner's primary goal was to make money, not to educate children. Why does this matter for the UN and its peace operations and political missions? It is because the Haitian government had no rescue equipment and no bulldozers or other earth-moving equipment that could negotiate the narrow and harsh incline of the "street"; UN peacekeepers from the UN Support Mission in Haiti (MINUSTAH), including a three-star general from Brazil, joined frantic parents and neighbors with crowbars, shovels, or anything to hand to try to reach the victims. Haitian private citizens and UN peacekeeping personnel provided the only assistance that day. Even worse, the President of Haiti, when rushed to the site, stated that this was a tragedy and, unfortunately, there were many other buildings like this one in Haiti that were poorly constructed and were constructed where they never should have been built. The chief executive of the state essentially was admitting that he and his government, who had sworn to uphold the laws and the Constitution of Haiti, had abdicated their responsibility. The Haitian state was completely incapable or unwilling to protect its citizens yet feared no punitive consequences for their betrayal. Over 80 children were killed that day in a school, where they were supposed to be safe and learning. Neither happened. As mentioned, the school was a private school but totally unregulated by the Haitian state. This provided more compelling evidence of the absence of the rule of law. One half of Haitian children on any given school day are not in school. Of the half in school, 80% are in private schools, who enjoy a regulation-free environment. Anyone can start a school. This one with the cruelly ironic name of l'Ecole de la Promesse was a moneymaking enterprise for the owner, as are most Haitian private schools. The owners' only goal is to maximize profit, not to educate children. Keep expenses low, hence the cheap construction and the poorly paid and barely literate teachers, and revenues high: cram as many fee-paying kids in as many rooms as possible. The difference is profit. The owner of l'Ecole de La Promesse never was held accountable for these deaths, which constitute at least reckless homicides since it was entirely predictable that a disaster was bound to happen. In January 2010, when a

7.0-magnitude quake struck Haiti, thousands of buildings collapsed. A similar quake in California or Japan would cause hardly any damage. Why? It is because these countries have building codes, inspections with trained and well-equipped building inspectors, zoning laws and land-use policies that are enforced, and severe penalties for those who violate the laws and regulations. None of this was true in Haiti, and so over 250,000 people were killed and more than one million rendered homeless for many years. Most of this death and destruction was most preventable, yet the Haitian state failed its people because it did not have a rule of law culture and arguably never had one. Haiti serves as an example for illustrating just how vital the rule of law is. One could substitute Liberia, Sierra Leone, Burundi, South Sudan, Afghanistan, Timor Leste, Kosovo, Guatemala, Nepal, El Salvador, Rwanda, Libya, the Central African Republic, Mali, South Sudan, or any number of other places where UN peace operations or large political mission where the rule of law has been minimal to absent. The Haiti case also demonstrates that the "rule of law" is not some dry, abstract theoretical concept debated and analyzed in UN conference rooms in New York and Geneva but is rather literally a life or death matter for millions of people every day around the world. Arguably, more people die from the absence of the rule of law than they do from death squads, land mines, or brutal police and military forces in any given year in countries with UN peace operations.

12.2 Rule of Law Deficits and Preventing Ill-Treatment in Detention

Weak rule of law affects the issues that are the subject of this study and of the conference that was held in Berlin in October 2018: preventing ill-treatment in prisons, jails, and police lockups. The failure of the state to provide humane and decent conditions of detention has led to countless deaths, rampant disease, torture, and other forms of cruel, inhuman, and degrading treatment or punishment. Overcrowding is common, inadequate food and medical care are the rule, and unclean water, few and filthy toilets and showers, and corrupt and brutal guards have predominated in countries where UN peace operations have been present. Similar conditions also exist in many other states plagued by authoritarian governments. This has been documented by the former UN Special Rapporteur on Torture Manfred Nowak, inter alia, during official visits to Nigeria and Sri Lanka; his reports (see list of references) contain some photographs that illustrate the problems much more vividly than mere words could ever do.

12.3 The Traditional UN Approach to Rule of Law Reform Efforts

How does the UN address the rule of law vacuums that plague so many states? How can systemic weaknesses, lack of accountability, inadequate resources, and prevailing values lead to such results as are seen in the above photographs, whose contents could be replicated right now in dozens of other countries? What programs and approaches work best, and how do we know that? These are questions that have not been asked nearly enough. It is long past time for the UN to take a hard look at its work on prisons in particular and the broader rule of law issues in general in peace operations and admit its failings and try to identify a new and better approach. A good start would be to acknowledge that a huge dose of humility is required. The rule of law, broadly understood, is complex and highly sensitive, tied intimately to national politics and sovereignty. It is unrealistic to think that the UN can "create" the rule of law in such broken societies during the short presence of a peacekeeping or special political mission. The following charts from the World Bank Annual Report of 2011 on development in post-conflict countries make the point in the starkest possible terms (Table 12.1):

So two generations on average is relatively rapid for significant institutional reform in the rule of law. Even the very best examples of change are sobering (Table 12.2).

Table 12.1 Average timelines for institutional change

Historical average timelines for institutional change: years to develop at the pace of the fastest 20 states	
Bureaucratic quality	20 years
Corruption	27
Military out of politics	17
Government effectiveness	36
Control of corruption	27
Rule of law	41

Source: World Bank Annual Report (2011): "Conflict, Security and Development"

Table 12.2 Fastest-transforming states

Fastest states over threshold (minimum times for transformation)	
Bureaucratic quality	12 years
Corruption	14
Military out of politics	10
Government effectiveness	12
Control of corruption	16
Rule of law	17

Source: World Bank Annual Report (2011): "Conflict Security and Development"

12.4 Analyzing the Goals of Traditional UN Rule of Law Projects

Since the effort takes so long, what can the UN realistically hope to accomplish in a much shorter time frame? What types of interventions, programs, and policies might accelerate the pace of change and be best placed to hand off as quickly as possible to local national counterparts (governmental and nongovernmental) and/or to UN agencies in the UN Country Teams that tend to stay in a country for longer? Research into the effectiveness of different types of rule-of-law programs yields some interesting insights (Fig. 12.1).

The above diagram is based on research done by Serge Rumin, a highly experienced former UN human rights field officer and a former colleague in the UN Mission in Rwanda (1996–1997). Rumin analyzed a range of UN rule of law projects and other initiatives by regional and bilateral actors. He broke down the projects based on the nature of their activities and objectives, and as the image shows, each program falls into one of four categories:

- Operating/managing: projects designed to help police, courts, and prisons to function; creating policies and procedures; and offering many training programs

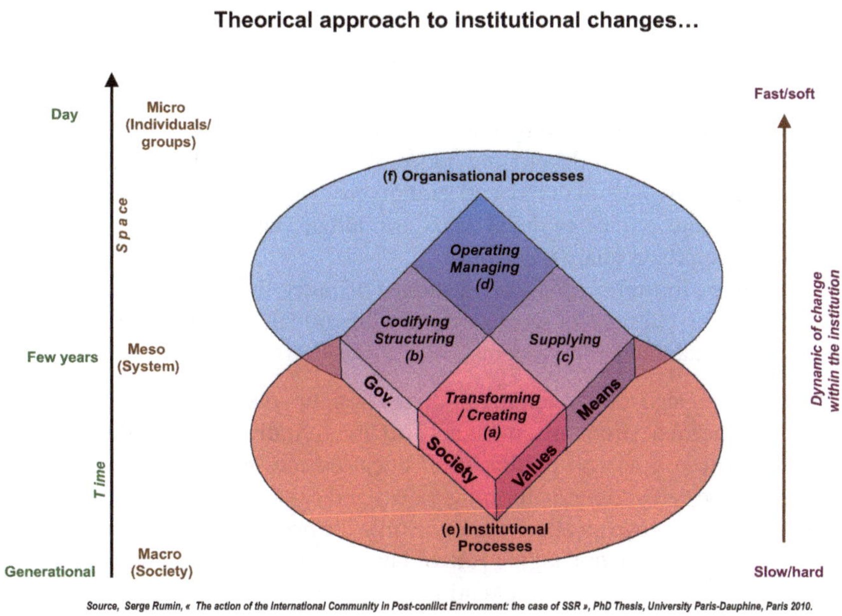

Source: Serge Rumin, L'action de la communauté internationale dans les situations de post-conflit: les réformes institutionelles. Thèse de doctorat. Université Paris Dauphine - Paris 9, 2010

Fig. 12.1 Theoretical approach to institutional changes. *Source*: Rumin (2010)

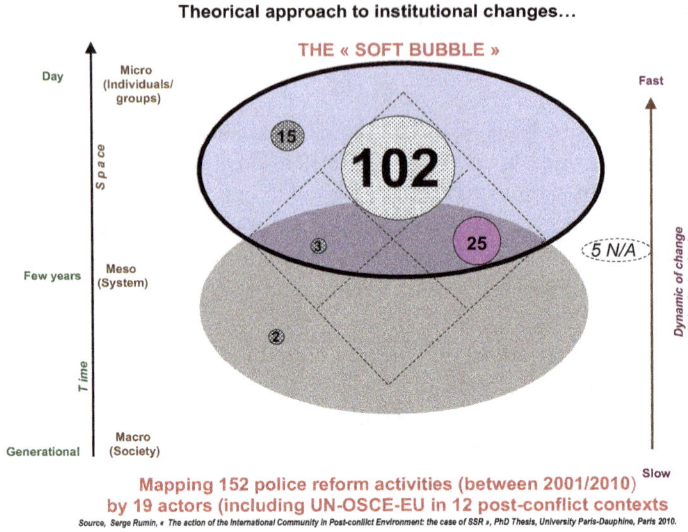

Source: Serge Rumin, L'action de la communauté internationale dans les situations de post-conflit: les réformes institutionelles. Thèse de doctorat. Université Paris Dauphine - Paris 9, 2010

Fig. 12.2 Theoretical approach to institutional changes: the "soft bubble". *Source*: Rumin (2010)

for various rule of law personnel, management, administrative/financial/logistical skills and knowledge

- Codifying/structuring: drafting new laws and constitutions, staffing tables for rule of law institutions, and developing codes of conduct and other rules/regulations
- Supplying: providing material and equipment such as vehicles for the police, courtrooms and copies of legal texts for judges and uniforms, and supplies and tools for prison guards; and
- Creating/transforming: programs designed to alter the incentives, values, and organizational cultures of previously dysfunctional, corrupt, and often brutal police, judicial, and penal systems

The diagram also has a temporal dimension on the right and the scope of participation needed (from macro/society to micro/individual) on the left of the "quadrant." These time and participation lines indicate that the lowest quarter of the quadrant, the "creating/transforming values and culture" efforts, takes the longest and must include a broad swath of society, while the upper three quarters, (codifying, supplying, and operating/managing rule of law reform projects) take less time while involving a narrower set of the population, often a self-selected group of specialists. So keeping this quadrant structure, the time line, and the extent to which the programs need to involve from narrow to broad bands of society in mind, how has the UN usually designed its rule of law programming? (Fig. 12.2)

Serge Rumin proceeded to map 140 police reform projects across 12 post-conflicts over 10 years, and he found that the overwhelming majority focused on what he calls the “Soft Bubble” or the upper three quadrants of codifying, supplying, and managing. There was not a single project that took on the most difficult and the most important quadrant: addressing values, incentives, and organizational culture in the judiciary, police, and prison systems. This diagram captures powerfully the reality of what have been the nature and goals of most rule of law projects in UN peace operations (and also the EU, the Organization for Security and Co-operation in Europe (OSCE), the AU, and bilateral projects) and demonstrates why so many have failed even to begin to construct a rule of law culture in post-conflict countries.

There are many reasons, some good, some bad, why the upper three quadrants receive all the attention and funds. One key reason arises from the demands made by the donors to these programs: they want fast, concrete, and demonstrable results, which one is more likely to achieve if the implementers, for example, focus on training judges, providing cars for the police, and drafting new prison administration laws and codes of conduct for prison guards. This is all fairly easy both to deliver and to measure, and then report back to the donors and check various boxes. The risk, however, is that this approach fails to include any elements that will address the bottom quadrant—the values/incentive/organizational culture—which in turn requires that the program consult with and involve a wide section of society and will take years, as indicated by the 2011 World Bank study cited above. Donors often do not have the patience to wait so long. Yet like a house built on a weak foundation, rule of law programs that ignore this vital foundational set of issues will also collapse quickly and completely once the peace operation leaves the country and all the money and effort is wasted. The UN is not alone in this approach. The United States Agency for International Development (USAID), EU, Department for International Development (DFID), Swedish International Development Cooperation Agency (SIDA), Canadian International Development Agency (CIDA), and OSCE, among others, also go for the relatively quick and easily quantifiable results from training, supplying logistics, and drafting laws and regulations. What can be done about this? How can UN rule of law programming, especially given the short-term nature of most peace operations and special political missions, incorporate in their projects some elements that begin to address the long-term task of changing values and attitudes within and toward core institutions like the police, courts, and prisons?

12.5 Some Proposals for a New Approach to Rule of Law Programming

Fortunately, another former colleague and experienced human rights and security sector reform practitioner, Alexander Mayer-Rieckh, has designed an approach that helps mitigate the now almost automatic tendency to focus on logistics, management, and technical training. In the diagram above, he identifies an important principle rarely seen on paper or in practice in UN rule of law programming:

integrity. Meyer-Rieckh stresses the importance of identifying, supporting, and rewarding integrity for both individuals in the rule of law sector and also building the overall integrity of the institution itself (judiciary, police, and prisons). Moreover, he identifies the crucial principles of accountability and transparency as part of an institution's integrity. Every rule of law initiative that was remotely successful often hinged on whether there was a price to be paid for misconduct or abuse of power (especially for those in charge who give the orders and/or fail to take action when abuses occur such as ill-treatment in detention) and whether good performance was recognized and rewarded. The main challenge for the UN is how to include elements from Rumin's bottom quadrant in programming (values, incentives, and organizational culture) with Meyer-Rieckh's emphasis on integrity and accountability in all UN rule of law projects, most of which probably will continue to fall into the other three quadrants (managing, supplying, and codifying). In other words, it is unlikely for a UN Peace Operation or Special Political Mission to announce and implement a project to change the organizational culture of the Central African Republic police or the prison administration system in Mali. But how, for example, in a project that trains judges, equips prison guards, or installs a case management system for the courts, can the UN ensure that these programs reinforce individual and institutional integrity and accountability whose impact will help change the values and culture of these institutions? One possible model is a fascinating new approach to training by the US Institute for Peace (USIP) in a course for police, judges, prosecutors, lawyers, civil society representatives, and government officials from the Middle East. Titled "People, Power and Politics: A New Approach to Rule of Law Training," the participants "explore how a strengthened rule-of-law culture can assist countries to better protect the state and society against modern-day justice and security challenges." There is that word again: "culture." (Fig. 12.3)

USIP states that "the 'culture' part of the course is important." It is not just another training in the rule of law. In fact, the course "challenges the traditional technical, law-led, state-focused approach to promoting the rule of law. Many professionals who specialize in helping develop the rule of law will be the first to admit that decades of effort and billions of dollars spent on reforming justice systems in transitional societies to uphold and promote the concept have produced unimpressive results. It seems clear that something has been missing from the traditional approach." What has been missing is an explicit focus on changing the prevailing culture as it relates to the rule of law. This USIP training incorporates the key values/culture component in Rumin's analysis, along with Mayer-Rieckh's emphasis on integrity and accountability. USIP notes: "At the heart of this change is not a new courthouse, but a newly conceived belief . . . that a society based on the rule of law is, in fact, possible." Everyone working on these issues needs to be much smarter and more aware of how to design and implement programs that help build a rule of law culture and not only buildings, laws, and technical expertise. While the latter are necessary, they are not sufficient.

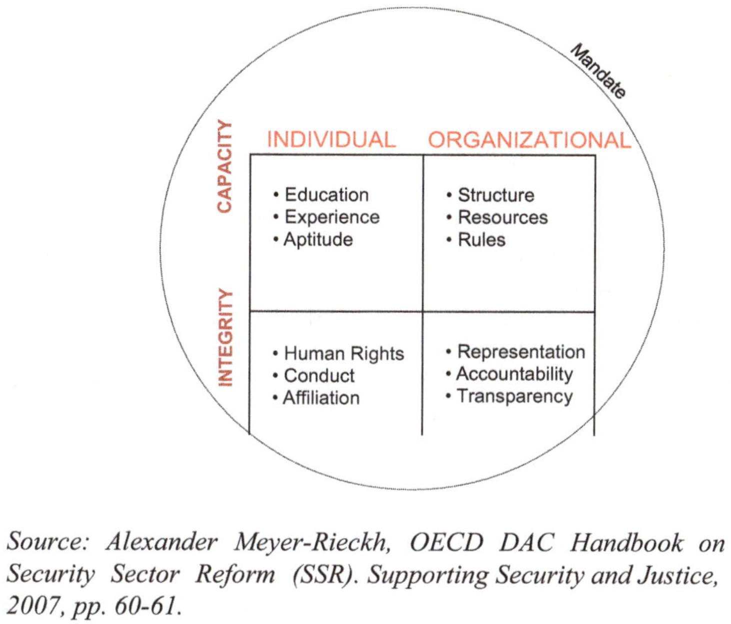

Fig. 12.3 Two principles of rule of law reform. *Source*: Meyer-Rieckh (2007), pp. 60–61

12.6 Increasing the Focus on the Beneficiaries of the Rule of Law: The People

A second element that helps explain the high failure rate of rule of law reform has been the failure to pay attention and listen to the demands of the population that rule of law institutions are supposed to serve and protect. Much rule of law programming has emphasized the "supply" side of the equation: all the training and courses, buildings and supplies, laws and procedures. Very little attention has been given to what the citizens want and need, the "demand" side of the equation. Much more programming is needed that helps citizens formulate and make demands on their public servants (a very important word) working in the police, courts, and penal sector. Putting constant pressure on these officials to do their jobs is a sound way to change attitudes, values, and beliefs, especially when this is combined with effective oversight bodies that can and do discipline or even fire and prosecute police officers, judges, and prison guards who fail to fulfill their duties. A police officer in training in Haiti once told me that firing and prosecuting one officer for abuse of power or malfeasance is "worth ten courses on human rights."

12.7 Reality Bites

Even if the UN and other multilateral and bilateral programming make these necessary changes, however, progress is not guaranteed. Why? The sad truth is that many of those in the elite groups in these countries oppose having the rule of law prevail or, as they would see it, imposed on them. They are quite happy to have things continue as they always have. They benefit from the absence of a rule of law culture. They benefit from being able to get their relatives, however unqualified, into the police or the courts or to intimidate or bribe judges to rule in their favor. The rule of law actually threatens them, and they will do everything they can to manipulate the efforts and see that the UN fails. No less a judge of human nature than Machiavelli got it right 500 years ago when he said: "There is nothing more difficult to take in hand, more perilous to conduct, or more uncertain in its success, than to take the lead in the introduction of a new order of things. Because the innovator has for enemies all those who have done well under the old conditions, and lukewarm defenders in those who may do well under the new." Another example from Haiti provides a perfect example of the role of local spoilers in thwarting rule of law reform all in the interest of preserving power and status. Haiti's prisons have been overcrowded for years. According to the premier Haitian human rights organization that monitors the prisons, the Reseau National des Droits des Haitiens, conditions are abysmal with inadequate food, water, sanitary facilities, and access to the most basic health care. Some prisoners have even died of starvation.

This overcrowding results from a dysfunctional judicial system, which fails to give those arrested a constitutionally mandated hearing on the legality of the arrest within 24 hours. Some detainees wait days, weeks, and even months before they have such a hearing, and if detained, they can wait years for a trial, even those accused of petty offenses. Yet Haitian judges spend on average only one hour per day in court. It is no wonder then that 82% of those in Haitian prisons have never been convicted of a crime. A recent visit by a group of mayors to the Women's Prison in Cabaret, according to the Haitian daily Le Nouvelliste, showed that only 35 of 252 women in prison had been convicted of any crime. This has been known and documented by numerous international and national investigations for at least 30 years now. Yet almost nothing has ever been done, no one held accountable, and no judge fired for incompetence or for not showing up for work. Even worse, powerful actors have prevented efforts to relieve the overcrowding and improve conditions. Turning back to Haiti, this is exactly what happened. A new prison was being built in the city of Hinche in central Haiti. It was supposed to meet international standards and help relieve overcrowding in prisons around the country. Yet construction stalled because no door could be built into the surrounding wall. Why? There was a UN military engineering battalion right across the road that could have helped install the door. The problem was that an influential businessman who won the contract to complete the installation of the door had a dispute and insisted on more money. He had influence inside the Ministry of Justice, which is responsible for the prisons. Despite several interventions by the Secretary-General's Special Representative in Haiti, the situation remained frozen for months, and Haiti's prisons remained overcrowded.

12.8 How to Measure Impact?

Finally, assuming the UN adopts this new approach that recognizes the importance of the values/incentives/culture in successful rule of law programming and addressing the demand side, how will the UN know it is making a difference? As one wise management consultant said, "you can't improve what you can't measure." Up until very recently, however, the UN and most other outside actors had either few or inadequate measures to assess the impact of their work. For example, toting up the number of police receiving human rights training or the quantity of beds provided to the prisons or copies of the penal code provided to judges tells you something but not what you really need to know about any change or progress in creating a rule of law culture. The good news is that the UN, after an extensive study and drafting exercise largely directed by the highly regarded Vera Institute on Criminal Justice, unveiled "Rule of Law Indicators" in 2012 (http://www.un.org/en/peacekeeping/publications/un_rule_of_law_indicators.pdf). Taking into account various legal systems (common law, civil law, Islamic, customary practice, etc.), the expert drafters identified a series of indicators for each main sector (police, prisons, and courts).

The indicators within each sector are then broken down into "baskets" assessing the performance of the institution, its integrity, the treatment of vulnerable groups, and capacity. Used wisely and adapted to local conditions and priorities, these indicators will show the impact of specific projects that include integrity, accountability, values, and incentive structures.

Some examples of indicators include the following:

- "To what extent do you agree that alleged incidents of police corruption or misconduct are seriously investigated and, when required by law, prosecuted?"
- "How often does it happen that people can avoid a conviction or receive a less severe punishment by paying a bribe to a judge, a prosecutor or other court personnel?"
- "To what extent do you think that corrections officers use excessive force (e.g., use of excessive physical force, use of restraints as punishment) against prisoners?"

For the first time, the UN will be able to measure any improvements or deterioration and identify the reasons for change. Real data (quantitative and qualitative), previously missing from most of the rule of law world, will be generated and used to assess and plan. Developing national capacity to manage data on police, courts, and crime is potentially a crucial by-product of this exercise that changes the culture. And merely by asking a wide number of people questions like the ones above could help change attitudes, values, and behavior and will certainly involve a greater segment of the population in the reform effort, a critical element identified by

Serge Rumin for change in the values/culture quadrant. The bad news, however, is that there has been reluctance and even resistance on the part of some in the UN to actually use the indicators. Why? After spending two years and over $2 million to develop the indicators, some fear that the UN does not want to be held accountable itself for failing to achieve results.

12.9 Conclusion

To move forward and to start the long process of building a rule of law culture, the following should be the guiding principles:

- Recognize up front that rule of law reform is complex, takes a very long time, and requires substantial effort to insure that whatever is begun by a UN peace operation or a special political mission will have to be taken up by others (national and international).
- Strive to ensure that every UN rule of law program reinforces integrity and accountability whatever its stated content or goal.
- Stress that the objective is to help set the foundation for a rule of law culture which requires a different approach that focuses on the demand side and on enhancing the capacity of the population to make demands and insist on accountability while not fixating on the traditional emphasis on supplies, buildings, new laws, and technical training.
- Insist on the UN's own accountability for achieving results and thus embrace the Rule of Law Indicators, don't let the perfect defeat the very good here.
- Recognize that powerful political actors (local and some external) will oppose efforts to support the rule of law and that equally powerful allies (also local and domestic) will be needed to win the fight.
- Understand that the rule of law is too important to be left to the legal, police, and penal experts alone: the UN Secretary-General, the Special Representatives of the Secretary-General in countries with peace operations, and even at times the Security Council will need to support those working on the ground. The issues are intensely political and need consistent and cohesive political support.

References

Cadelo V: The Méndez Principles: a step forward for preventing torture and ill-treatment worldwide. Penal Reform International Blog, 13 October 2022. https://www.penalreform.org/blog/the-mendez-principles-a-step-forward/#. Accessed 28 July 2023

Le Nouvelliste, "Seulement 35 des 252 femmes de la prison de Cabaret sont condamnees", 8 March 2019. https://lenouvelliste.com/article/198964/seulement-35-des-252-femmes-de-la-prison-de-cabaret-sont-condamnees-lamoh-monte-au-creneau

Macchiavelli N, Top Ten Quotes, www.brainyquote.com

Meyer-Rieckh A (2007) OECD DAC Handbook on Security Sector Reform (SSR). Supporting Security and Justice, pp 60–61

Reseau National des Droits des Haitiens, "Prison Civile de Port-au-Prince: des Conditions de detention inhumaine, January 2017. Available at www.rnddh.org/prison-civile-de-Port-au-Princedes-conditions-de-detention-inhumaine

Rumin S, L'action de la communauté internationale dans les situations de post-conflit: les réformes institutionelles. Thèse de doctorat. Université Paris Dauphine - Paris 9, 2010 (unpublished)

UN Department of Peace Operations et al., Standard Operating Procedure: The Handling of Detention in United Nations Peacekeeping Operations and Special Political Missions. Effective 1 January 2021. https://peacekeeping.un.org/sites/default/files/dpo-2021-00276_revised_sop_on_detention_jan_2021_for_attachment.pdf. Accessed 28 July 2023

UN Office on the rule of law and security institutions, OROLSI, Rule of law indicators, http://www.un.org/en/peacekeeping/publications/un_rule_of_law_indicators.pdf

UN Volunteers et al.: Upholding the dignity and rights of persons in detention. https://www.unv.org/Success-stories/upholding-dignity-and-rights-persons-detention. Accessed 28 July 2023

United States Institute of Peace, Introduction to Rule of Law Practice, training course

World Bank, 2011 Annual Report, "Conflict, Security and Development"

William G. O'Neill is a lawyer specialising in humanitarian, human rights and refugee law. He is the United Nations Designated Expert on Human Rights in Haiti. He was Senior Advisor on Human Rights in the UN Mission in Kosovo, Chief of the UN Human Rights Field Operation in Rwanda and led the Legal Department of the UN/OAS Mission in Haiti. He has worked on judicial, police and prison reform in Burundi, Liberia, Sierra Leone, South Sudan, Timor Leste, Tunisia, Nepal and Bosnia-Herzegovina. He investigated mass killings in Afghanistan for the UN High Commissioner for Human Rights. He also conducted an assessment of the human rights situation in Darfur and trained the UN's human rights monitors stationed there.

Chapter 13
Strategies for Ensuring the Fair Treatment of Persons in Police Custody: Past, Present and Future

Wolfgang S. Heinz

Contents

Abstract The contribution looks at strategies for ensuring fair treatment in police custody in four different contexts. It starts with a discussion of the recent research regarding instruments and practical steps for the prevention of ill-treatment in police custody. Key institutional issues such as the roles and competencies of police officers, impunity, interrogation and corruption are the subject of the following section. The political country context is often highlighted as a main variable as it has a strong impact on opening or limiting corridors for reform. In sub-chapters

W. S. Heinz (✉)
Free University Berlin, Berlin, Germany
e-mail: wolfgang.heinz@fu-berlin.de

R. Alleweldt (ed.), *Fair Treatment of Persons in Police Custody*,
https://doi.org/10.1007/978-3-031-61737-9_13

3 and 4, some general issues and specific experiences of three important countries are being explored (Brazil, India and the Russian Federation), including research on the self-image and reasoning of police actors acting in the field. After a short discussion on research regarding the effectiveness of measures to prevent ill-treatment, key results are presented in the concluding chapter. Among other points, the argument is emphasised that especially in more difficult country situations, research should focus on the internal organisation of police institutions (recruitment, training, informal rules and values, etc.). This is crucial to better understand police institutions and thereby develop better strategies for change management. In the face of considerable resistance against changes often met in reform processes, a good knowledge of inside police processes is of paramount importance.

Abbreviations

ACAT	Action by Christians for the Abolition of Torture
CPT	European Committee for the Prevention of Torture and Inhuman or Degrading Treatment or Punishment (Council of Europe)
CTI	Convention Against Torture Initiative
EU	European Union
UN CAT	Committee against Torture
UN SPT	Subcommittee on Prevention of Torture and Other Cruel, Inhuman or Degrading Treatment or Punishment
UN	United Nations

13.1 Introduction

Police ill-treatment in detention happens in a large number of countries, sometimes as an exception to a generally functioning rule of law system, more often in countries with a weak police and judicial system and a long history of disproportionate violence against detainees. It can also be a problem in democratic countries, though more on the level of (sometimes severe) ill-treatment and disproportionate use of violence in the setting of a demonstration or an arrest.[1] A large number of conventions and recommendations address standards for people arrested and imprisoned on the international, regional and national levels, as well as monitoring instruments,

[1] In a number of European countries, there is also a growing experience of violence against police officers in different settings which have resulted in heavier penalties.

with the UN Convention against Torture, with its definition of torture in Article 1, serving as an important point of departure.[2]

In Germany, police violence has been discussed in the context of political demonstrations and arrests. Major issues, some for decades, were that officers should be identifiable by the public (Töpfer and von Normann 2014; Deutsches Institut für Menschenrechte 2018). Identification by a sign system has been introduced now in twelve of 16 states. The UN Human Rights Committee, the expert body under the UN International Covenant on Civil and Political Rights, and the UN Committee against Torture (CAT) had, for a long time, requested national statistics on complaints against the police in regard to ill-treatment, but this was rejected by the German government. Finally, this proposal was taken up. Also, "racial profiling" is under discussion (Cremer 2013).

Police complaint bodies, with different institutional arrangements, were resisted by the states for quite some time but exist now in twelve out of 16 states in Germany.[3] Looking more in detail into obstacles to investigating allegations and punishing culprits, experts have stressed internal organisation flaws within the police to deal with errors and mistakes committed by officers (e.g. Schicht 2007) and the strong influence of an internal worldview with its own informal rules—entitled cop culture (e.g. Behr 2008; for the United Kingdom, Reiner 2010). Behr, himself a police officer for 15 years who became a sociologist, offers in his first book extensive materials of his interviews with police officers in Hesse state, Frankfurt am Main. He describes in detail the case of police ill-treatment as narrated by a police officer observing the incident and the difficulty for that officer to step forward and report fellow officers.[4] Last but not least, the issues of structural obstacles to investigate promptly and effectively police abuses within the judicial system are now being discussed in greater detail, thanks to more research (Singelnstein 2014; Abdul-Rahman et al. 2023).

Right from the beginning, I would like to clarify that I do not suggest that there is a simple tableau to be followed to abolish, or more realistically to diminish, torture and ill-treatment practices (the "one-size-fits-all approach"). Rather, it is my thesis that, apart from mainstream legal standards and organisational reform approaches, internal organisational culture and country framework conditions do play a

[2]To mention some examples, see the UN Code of Conduct for Law Enforcement Officials (UN General Assembly resolution 34/169 of 17 December 1979), UN Convention against Torture (1984), OPCAT (1992), UN Basic Principles on the Use of Force and Firearms by Law Enforcement Officials (1990) (for a proposal on implementation guidelines see Amnesty International Dutch section 2015), The European Code of Police Ethics (Recommendation Rec(2001)10 adopted by the Committee of Ministers of the Council of Europe on 19 September 2001 and explanatory memorandum), European Court of Human Rights (2022), CPT (2019a) and Guidelines on the Conditions of Arrest, Police Custody and Pre-Trial Detention in Africa (African Commission on Human and Peoples' Rights 2017). On monitoring of police stations see APT (2013).

[3]Information received from Eric Töpfer, German Institute for Human Rights, Berlin (11.06.2024). On complaint commissions in four European countries, see Töpfer and Tobias (2017).

[4]Ibid., 140ff.

considerable role in facilitating or inhibiting prevention strategies. Therefore, I argue for the importance of understanding better these two dimensions—difficult as it may be to move forward on these issues on the practical level.

For obvious reasons, it will not be possible to engage in this book chapter in a discussion on all possible measures to prevent torture by the police in the past, the present and the future. In the first section, I will address key steps and instruments for effective prevention against ill-treatment and torture in police custody without aspiring to cover every possible aspect. This is followed in the second section by a discussion of institutional dimensions featuring the roles and competencies of police officers, police interrogation, impunity and corruption. Then to illustrate some structural problems, I discuss the broader political context within which a police organisation has to work, starting with a heuristic typology of country situations, followed by three country sketches on Brazil, India and the Russian Federation. The focus will be on internal organisational issues and, in two cases, the moral universe of police officers. The concluding section brings together key findings of this contribution.

13.2 Past and Present: Key Steps and Instruments for Effective Prevention Against Ill-Treatment and Torture in Police Custody

I start with a brief review of the key instruments for effective prevention work based mainly on a comprehensive paper by Julia Kozma, former Austrian member of the European Committee for the Prevention of Torture and Inhuman or Degrading Treatment or Punishment (CPT), and Asbjørn Rachlew, detective superintendent at Oslo Police district. They look mainly at the CPT and UN experience (Kozma and Rachlew 2018) and have European countries as their focus. Authors recall that the CPT chiefly distinguishes between excessive use of force that amounts to inhuman or degrading treatment at the time of apprehension, ill-treatment during transport to police stations and in police custody, and ill-treatment, including torture as its most severe form, in the context of police questioning in criminal investigations, with the aim of extracting a confession or information.[5]

Methods identified by the CPT included:

> extensive beatings with hard objects such as a wooden bat, truncheon blows on the soles of the feet (i.e. the so-called falaka), handcuffing of detained persons in stress positions for hours on end and suspension/hyperextension by handcuffs, the infliction of electric shocks using electrical discharge weapons, mock executions with a pistol pointed at the temple or with the barrel of a pistol inserted into the mouth, old car tyres placed around the heads and shoulders while being forced to squat, burning a person's arm with a cigarette, infliction of burns to the genitals, asphyxiation with a plastic bag or a gas mask, or placing a plastic bag

[5] Kozma and Rachlew (2018), p. 3f.

over the head and spraying teargas inside, as well as combinations of the various methods mentioned above.[6]

13.2.1 General Safeguards

Regarding detention practice, the three CPT standards used in country visits continue to be of crucial importance. These are immediate access to a lawyer after detention by the police, notification of a trusted person and unhindered access to a medical doctor of choice by the detained person. It is of course very important that such safeguards are known, disseminated,[7] trained and respected in institutions of detention, which should include effective complaint mechanisms with relevant powers and autonomy of evaluation from the bureaucratic hierarchy of the institution concerned. Staff applying safeguards should not be punished for this.

13.2.2 Detention Standards

One key element is the meticulous registration of all arrested and detained persons.[8] Information rights include the right of persons detained by the police to be verbally informed of their rights upon apprehension and given an information sheet in a language they understand. Such information sheets should be supplemented by posters containing all the rights in places accessible to detainees, e.g. in waiting areas and on the inside of custody cell doors. Detainees should be presented before a judicial authority within a short time after their apprehension, the time limit stipulated in the Code of Criminal Procedure. Judges should take on the responsibility for detention, including the handling of complaints regarding the ill-treatment of a more serious type, apart from the complaint system in the detention institution. Following a decision to remand a person, he/she should be transferred to a pretrial detention facility. Specific safeguards for vulnerable groups, such as women, juveniles, persons suffering from a mental disorder, drug addicts or foreigners (language problems, access to the country's diplomatic representation), should be observed.

[6] Ibid., 4.

[7] Regarding dissemination of international safeguards/standards local actors (detention institutions, ministries, NGOs etc.) and international actors such as UN, regional international organisations, governments and NGOs have been active. See, for example, APT (2023). Regarding Central Asia and the Asia Pacific see Council of Europe (2023) and Asia Pacific Forum (2023) (APF consists of National Human Rights Institutions).

[8] Kozma and Rachlew (2018), Ibid, 5.

CCTVs, body- and helmet cameras, and audio- and video recordings of interviews are mentioned as offering additional possibilities for preventing police ill-treatment.[9]

13.2.3 Immediate Access to a Lawyer of Choice After Detention by the Police

The immediate access by a detainee to a lawyer of his or her choice is of central importance. As the experience of human rights organisations shows, the danger of ill-treatment is very high during the first few hours and days after apprehension. "The right of access to a lawyer must be enjoyed early on, by anyone who is under a legal obligation to attend—and stay at—a police establishment, irrespective of his/her precise legal status (i.e. whether formally declared a suspect or not), as from the outset of the deprivation of liberty."[10] It has also been learned that administrative detention and summonses of persons for so-called informative talks in certain countries "are regularly abused for bypassing safeguards that would usually apply to persons who are officially declared suspects".[11] Indigent persons are identified as more likely to be vulnerable to police ill-treatment compared to persons who choose their own lawyer.

To serve the preventative purpose of this right, several criteria are emphasised: lawyers should be able "to see their clients in person at the police station, and detainees should be able to speak in private with their lawyer, before they get questioned; lawyers should be able to be present during questioning, including preliminary or informal questioning; and persons who do not have the means to pay for their own lawyer should be provided with effective legal aid".[12]

13.2.4 Notification of a Trusted Person

Legal provisions regarding the notification of custody foresee that this should be done immediately after arrest, usually with some exceptions. However, in practice, the authors note that family members or other third persons were often only notified after considerable delays, during or after the first official interview with an investigator, when a statement had been drawn up, or even only upon arrival in a pretrial detention facility. Reasons for delays could be that "the officers effectuating arrests and/or custody do either genuinely not feel responsible for ensuring that detainees

[9] Ibid.

[10] Ibid.

[11] Ibid., 11.

[12] Ibid.

can inform somebody of their arrest, or that they experience insecurities as to whether this information might jeopardise the investigation and therefore rather leave it to the investigators working on the case".[13]

As to the limitations in many countries with reference to the protection of the legitimate interests of the police investigation, such exceptions "should be clearly defined in law and strictly limited in time, and resort to them should be accompanied by appropriate safeguards, such as recording any delay in writing with the reasons therefore, and the approval of a senior police officer unconnected with the case or a prosecutor".[14]

EU Directive 2013/48/EU on the right of access to a lawyer in criminal proceedings mentions the limitations of the right to notify a third person in exceptional circumstances:

> In limited, exceptional circumstances, however, it should be possible to derogate temporarily from that right when this is justified, in the light of the particular circumstances of the case, by a compelling reason as specified in this Directive. When the competent authorities envisage making such a temporary derogation in respect of a specific third person, they should firstly consider whether another third person, nominated by the suspect or accused person, could be informed of the deprivation of liberty (EU Directive 2013).

13.2.5 Access to a Medical Doctor of Choice by the Detained

Regarding access to a medical doctor, Kozma and Rachlew note that a number of Council of Europe member states have introduced systematic medical examinations of all persons who are deprived of their liberty by the police, before or during police custody. "These routine examinations are usually carried out by doctors, nurses or paramedics who are directly working at the respective police facility, by visiting doctors, or in public hospitals, where apprehended persons are brought before entering custody."[15]

The authors clarify that the right to a doctor includes the right "to be seen by a doctor upon request, without limitations or possibilities for denial or discretion on the part of the police to make an assessment whether medical care is indeed needed. The laws and regulations of some, but not all, Council of Europe Member States explicitly provide for this right, including the entitlement to see a doctor of one's choice at one's own expense. In practice, detainees in many States frequently report that the police denied their request to see a doctor."[16]

Practical shortcomings noted by the CPT in many countries are, among other points, a complete lack of medical confidentiality; i.e., police officers are routinely

[13] Ibid., 10.

[14] Ibid., 11.

[15] Ibid., 13.

[16] Ibid., 12.

present during medical examinations, and examinations are frequently "done in a cursory manner, detected injuries are not documented properly; and medical staff do not report indications or explicit allegations of ill-treatment to a competent authority. These problems appear to arise regardless of whether the medical professionals are private doctors visiting police stations, are employed by the police, or are working in public hospitals."[17]

In April 2019, the CPT published its General Report for 2018 with a thematic chapter on Preventing police torture and other forms of ill-treatment—reflections on good practices and emerging approaches, which discusses professional policing, investigative interviewing and centralised police detention and designated custody officers.[18]

13.3 Selected Institutional Issues

13.3.1 Roles of Police Officers in Detention Procedures

In most countries, police officers may have to fulfil dual or even triple roles of (a) operative officers responsible for the arrest of persons; (b) *de facto* custody officers who guard those who have been taken into custody—an arrest that might have involved the use of coercion, violent encounters and injuries; and (c) criminal investigators who have to question these persons in relation to a crime. It is obvious that officers might find it personally challenging to assume all of these roles simultaneously in a professional manner, especially if they are not clearly separated. There are clearly different logic and objectives at work. In a number of countries, police custody officers were introduced. Detainees have to be seen by them as the first step to arriving at the police station.

13.3.2 Police Interrogation

Ill-treatment is known to most likely take place during arrest, during transport to the police establishment and in the context of interrogation. During interrogation, the objective is usually to get information about the crime, details on other criminal suspects and, most importantly, a confession in order to bring charges. Ill-treatment could happen during the interrogation with only police officers present; it might happen after the interrogation when officers are not satisfied with the results or wish to punish the detainee in the hope of getting more information or a confession during the next round of interrogation (intimidation). During the last years, a discussion has

---

[17] Ibid., 13.

[18] https://www.coe.int/en/web/cpt/annual-reports.

started about developing a (more) effective and better police interrogation. Kozma and Rachlew emphasise that "it is important to address the distinction between the terms interrogation and investigative interviewing. The historic literature around interrogation refers to a heuristic approach, including coercive and/or manipulative techniques, designed to obtain a confession. Investigative interviewing—as defined by the United Kingdom Home Office in 1992, developed and refined by pioneering scholars in close cooperation with the police—is an evidence based approach, designed to gather and test accurate and reliable information from victims, witnesses and suspects of crime."[19]

They see "confession-oriented interrogation techniques and torture are only different means to the same end, administrated by the police to confirm their belief of guilt. Although manipulative confession-oriented techniques are less brutal than torture, the mindset of interrogating detectives is none the less the same: the police are trying to solve their (sometimes complex) tasks with a methodology designed to confirm their presumption of guilt."[20]

UN Special Rapporteur on Torture Juan Méndez pointed out to the UN General Assembly in his 2016 report:

> As a matter of best practice, interviewers are encouraged to proceed, when necessary, with probing questions designed to elicit information that will test all possible alternative explanations identified during the preparation of the interview. Strategic probing and disclosure of potential evidence allows officers to explore the interviewee's account in depth before proceeding to the next topic, helping to ensure that the presumption of innocence is respected while strengthening the case against a guilty suspect by preventing the subsequent fabrication of an alibi.[21]

He called for the development of a universal protocol identifying a set of standards for non-coercive interviewing methods and procedural safeguards.[22] In 2021, the document Principles on Effective Interviewing for Investigations and Information Gathering was adopted by a Steering Committee of Experts with the support of the Anti-Torture Initiative, the Association for the Prevention of Torture and the Norwegian Centre for Human Rights (APT et al. 2021).

13.3.3 Impunity

Impunity is a difficult topic for governments and states because it implies that there might be a structural problem in the investigation of crimes by state agents and their punishment rather than a few flaws or "bad apples" in the system. Especially, the

[19] Ibid., note 29, 14. They refer to Williamson (1993) and Walsh (2015).

[20] Ibid., 14f.

[21] United Nations Special Rapporteur on Torture, interim report, fn. 13, para. 54. See the training tool CTI (2017).

[22] UN Special Rapporteur on Torture (2016), UN Human Rights Council (2017), paras. 19ff.

Council of Europe has been active in addressing issues of impunity—a topic perhaps not so well known in the international discussion. The most important documents are the Guidelines adopted by the Committee of Ministers on 30 March 2011 on Eradicating impunity for serious human rights violations, which bring together recommendations and criteria for effective work against impunity (Council of Europe 2011).

Box: Council of Europe, Eradicating impunity for serious human rights violations, 2011[23]
III. General measures for the prevention of impunity

1. In order to avoid loopholes or legal gaps contributing to impunity,
   - States should take all necessary measures to comply with their obligations under the Convention. [European Convention on Human Rights—WSH] to adopt criminal law provisions to effectively punish serious human rights violations through adequate penalties. These provisions should be applied by the appropriate executive and judicial authorities in a coherent and non-discriminatory manner
   - States should provide for the possibility of disciplinary proceedings against state officials.
   - In the same manner, states should provide a mechanism involving criminal and disciplinary measures in order to sanction behaviour and practice within state authorities which lead to impunity for serious human rights violations.
2. States—including their officials and representatives—should publicly condemn serious human rights violations.
3. States should elaborate policies and take practical measures to prevent and combat an institutional culture within their authorities which promotes impunity. Such measures should include:
   - promoting a culture of respect for human rights and systematic work for the implementation of human rights at the national level;
   - establishing or reinforcing appropriate training and control mechanisms;
   - introducing anti-corruption policies;
   - making the relevant authorities aware of their obligations, including taking necessary measures, with regard to preventing impunity, and establishing appropriate sanctions for the failure to uphold those obligations;
   - conducting a policy of zero-tolerance of serious human rights violations;

(continued)

[23] Council of Europe (2011), p. 8f.

- providing information to the public concerning violations and the authorities' response to these violations;
- preserving archives and facilitating appropriate access to them through applicable mechanisms.

4. States should establish and publicise clear procedures for reporting allegations of serious human rights violations, both within their authorities and for the general public. States should ensure that such reports are received and effectively dealt with by the competent authorities.
5. States should take measures to encourage reporting by those who are aware of serious human rights violations. They should, where appropriate, take measures to ensure that those who report such violations are protected from any harassment and reprisals.
6. States should establish plans and policies to counter discrimination that may lead to serious human rights violations and to impunity for such acts and their recurrence.
7. States should also establish mechanisms to ensure the integrity and accountability of their agents. States should remove from office individuals who have been found, by a competent authority, to be responsible for serious human rights violations or for furthering or tolerating impunity, or adopt other appropriate disciplinary measures. States should notably develop and institutionalise codes of conduct.

The Guidelines refer to the basic rights of detained people, which have already been discussed earlier. They require states to investigate cases of serious human rights violations, a duty of "an absolute character".[24] Reference is made to the right to life (Article 2 of ECHR), the prohibition of torture and inhuman or degrading treatment or punishment (Article 3), the prohibition of slavery and forced labour (Article 4), the right to liberty and security (Article 5) and the right to respect for private and family life (Article 8). Where an arguable claim is made or the authorities have reasonable grounds to suspect that a serious human rights violation has occurred, the authorities must commence an investigation on their own initiative. "The fact that the victim wishes not to lodge an official complaint, later withdraws such a complaint or decides to discontinue the proceedings does not absolve the authorities from their obligation to carry out an effective investigation, if there are reasons to believe that a serious human rights violation has occurred."[25] The decision either to refuse to initiate or to terminate investigations should be taken only by an independent and competent authority in accordance with the criteria of an effective investigation as set out in section VI. They should be duly reasoned. The

[24] Council of Europe (2011), section V, 1.

[25] Ibid., under section The right to respect for private and family life (Article 8 ECHR), No. 3.

criteria for an effective investigation include adequacy, thoroughness, impartiality and independence, promptness and public scrutiny. The involvement of victims in the investigation is important, and specific measures are recommended to ensure participation (section VII). Decisions to refuse to initiate or to terminate investigations must be subject to appropriate scrutiny and be generally challengeable by means of a judicial process.

An important international law instrument enlisting standards for states is the Istanbul Protocol, the Manual on the Effective Investigation and Documentation of Torture and Other Cruel, Inhuman or Degrading Treatment or Punishment (Istanbul Protocol 2022). More recently, the UN Special Rapporteur on Torture gave a comprehensive overview of good practices in national criminalisation, investigation, prosecution and sentencing for offences of torture (UN Special Rapporteur on Torture 2023).

13.3.4 Corruption

In 2019, the UN Special Rapporteur on Torture, Nils Melzer, took up the issue of corruption as a facilitating context for ill-treatment and torture. His point of departure was a "growing awareness of the pervasive, incapacitating impact of corruption on the effective, transparent and accountable functioning of public institutions . . . including the protection of human rights. Corruption not only hinders the effective implementation of human rights obligation, but also creates an environment conducive to human rights abuses, including torture and ill-treatment."[26]

Referring to two academic authors, for him, corruption and torture or ill-treatment "are rarely isolated in a few 'bad apples' but, figuratively speaking, almost always extend to 'rotten branches', or even 'rotten orchards', and therefore are predominantly structural and systemic phenomena". They can be understood as "concurrent effects of the same original cause, namely a failure of the relevant governance system to prevent the abuse of unchecked power".[27]

He favoured the wider understanding of corruption used by the UN Subcommittee on Prevention of Torture (SPT, in its report focusing on the context of deprivation of liberty) as "the dishonest misuse or abuse of a position of power to secure undue personal gain or advantage, or to secure undue gain or advantage for a third party".[28]

He sees and elaborates on six patterns of interaction:

(a) Demanding "undue advantages" that per se amount to torture or ill-treatment
(b) Instrumentalising torture or ill-treatment for "undue advantages"
(c) Instrumentalising "undue advantages" for torture or ill-treatment

[26] UN Special Rapporteur on Torture (2019), para 7.
[27] Ibid., para 21.
[28] UN CAT (2014), para. 73.

(d) Exploiting exposure to torture or ill-treatment for "undue advantages"
(e) Torture or ill-treatment as a foreseeable "side effect" of corruption
(f) Torture or ill-treatment and corruption as foreseeable "side effects" of other policies and practices[29]

He emphasised what he calls systemic governance failures conducive to corruption and torture or ill-treatment and identifies six central dimensions:

(a) Systemic tolerance for unchecked power
(b) Normative and institutional shortcomings
(c) Unchecked power of corporate actors
(d) Inadequately resourced public services and institutions
(e) Socio-economic marginalisation and discrimination
(f) Excessive incarceration and involuntary institutionalisation[30]

In conclusion, Melzer suggests, inter alia, to adopt and/or ratify, without reservations, apart from the relevant UN human rights treaties, the United Nations Convention Against Corruption; to adopt and implement strict policies of zero tolerance for both corruption and torture or ill-treatment throughout all branches and levels of public authority, not only through strict enforcement at the level of individual officials, services and processes but also through decisive corrective action that may be required at the systemic level; and to proactively integrate their anti-torture and anti-corruption policies and practices, including through mutual mainstreaming. He proposes to establish and maintain accessible, well-resourced and fully independent monitoring, oversight and accountability mechanisms for the prevention of corruption and of torture or ill-treatment.[31]

13.4 Political Context(s)

There are probably rarely country situations where police organisations could act completely autonomously and independently from specific economic or political interests—which of course would be the "ideal type". Channels of influence will often go in both directions, from politics and business to the police and vice versa, and sometimes this means involvement in clearly illegal action. Political framework conditions differ considerably from one country to the other. In general terms, I believe it makes sense to distinguish between four rough categories of countries, within which the police needs to find its role, in normative terms of a law-based police controlled by the state and by democratic institutions as well as the judicial

[29] UN Special Rapporteur on Torture (2019), paras 28–47.
[30] Ibid., paras 64, 66.
[31] Ibid., paras 69–72.

system, because different context variables facilitate or constrain conditions for moving forward or blocking efforts to prevent ill-treatment and torture.[32]

In the first place, there is a large number of countries that can be considered more or less to be fragile democracies, sometimes with authoritarian tendencies, in which there is often no well-established policing system. Whatever the legal norms say, what happens on the ground depends a lot on the approach chosen by local commanders/officers in contact and influenced by higher police levels and local power brokers such as politicians, political parties and other relevant groups. Depending on the country, there may be stronger political control or institutionally imposed self-restriction of the police when its action affects the established interests of politicians or business or foreign interests. A second group of countries has established a more or less rule-based policing system—mostly democracies. Generally, police action is controlled by democratic institutions and the judicial system, but occasionally, there is interference or an attempt to interfere with the police by political or economic elites. Moreover, there may be some problem areas such as the control of demonstrations, the fight against organised crime, the fight against terrorism, etc.

A third, small group of governments has to be considered as outright dictatorships. The police enjoy almost no autonomy of action because the government believes it needs centralised control from the presidential palace down to the local police station—at least, this is what it attempts to do. There is no tangible division of power between the government, an effective parliament and the judicial system (North Korea and Syria under Assad, for example, would fall into this category). In highly authoritarian and "full" dictatorships, the police, together with the military and intelligence services, are mainly used for regime survival, which makes meaningful reform difficult or even impossible. In the fourth category, one could group countries or parts within countries where there has been extremely limited government control, sometimes with the consequence that non-state actors such as warlords, armed groups, etc. take over certain parts of a country. The following country sketches should help illustrate the importance of the political context as well as bring us closer to the "moral universe" of police officers, i.e. to practice and organisational processes.

13.5 Some Country Sketches

Many countries could have been selected for a brief sketch. In the following sections, we present sketches of three countries that are known for decade-long ill-treatment and torture by the police as a long-standing structural problem. Such treatment occurs in the fight against crime, during political persecution and/or in the fight

[32] For a model of factors affecting the incidence of torture focusing on law, practice and training see Carver and Handley (2016), p. 48f.

against political violence/terrorism. Despite some reform approaches and progress, because of limited time, the problem so far persists.

Reports about human rights violations have been widely published, dealing with cases, testimony, etc., so there is no need to repeat this material here. I will focus on institutional issues and on the "the other side", i.e. how military officers (in a police role) and police officers see their own professional role. The intention here is not to evaluate whether their statements are right or wrong, justifications or lies, but to explore the moral universe of those officers, a term used in Huggins et al. (2002) and Wahl (2017).[33] By this term we understand, as Huggins proposed, "how violence workers explained, justified and excused their own and others' violence". She identified four strategies on how "violence workers" explain and excuse their practice. These were "diffusing responsibility, blaming individuals—whether victims or perpetrators—[,] citing a just cause, and asserting that professionalism had correctly guided their and other' s violence".[34] There is no claim as to statistical significance in the sense that opinions of interviewees express a representative tendency for the police force to which they belong.

13.5.1 Brazil

Torture existed before, during and after the military dictatorship from 1964 to 1985. Comments from the United Nations on Brazil capture well the basic patterns of ill-treatment in Brazil. They will help get a first picture of the situation prevailing for a long time.

Already in 2001, the UN Committee against Torture had expressed concern about:

> (a) [t]he persistence of a culture that accepts abuses by public officials, the numerous allegations of acts of torture and cruel, inhuman or degrading treatment—in police stations, prisons and facilities belonging to the armed forces—and the de facto impunity enjoyed by the perpetrators of those acts, ...
>
> (e) The competence of the police to conduct enquiries following reports of crimes of torture committed by members of police forces without effective control in practice by the Public Prosecutor's office, with the result that immediate and impartial inquiries are prevented, which contributes to the impunity enjoyed by the perpetrators of these acts (UN CAT 2001, p. 50, para 119).

In response to the last state report of Brazil, the UN Human Rights Committee, the expert treaty body under the UN Covenant on Civil and Political Rights, stated in 2005 that it was:

---

[33] Huggins and Wahl address the challenges for the researcher in such interviews (Huggins et al. 2002, pp. 22–44; Wahl 2017, pp. 6f., 12–15). In this sub-chapter, I will only refer to Huggins because she conducted the interviews in Brazil.

[34] Huggins, 192.

> concerned about the widespread use of excessive force by law enforcement officials, the use of torture to extract confessions from suspects, the ill-treatment of detainees in police custody, and extrajudicial execution of suspects. It is concerned that such gross human rights violations committed by law enforcement officials are not investigated properly and that compensation to victims has not been provided, thus creating a climate of impunity ... (UN Human Rights Committee 2005, para 12).

The UN Subcommittee on Prevention of Torture and Other Cruel, Inhuman or Degrading Treatment or Punishment visited Brazil in 2012[35] and observed, inter alia, that:

> 79. The SPT received from interviewees repeated and consistent accounts of torture and ill-treatment committed by, in particular, the military and civil police. Allegations included threats, kicks and punches to the head and body, and blows with truncheons. Such beatings took place in police custody, but also on the street, inside private homes, or in secluded outdoor areas, at the moment of arrest. The torture and ill-treatment was described as gratuitous violence, as a form of punishment, to extract confessions, and as a means of extortion.
>
> 80. The SPT also received numerous and consistent allegations from children and adolescents of torture and ill-treatment suffered upon arrest and during police custody. Children and adolescents alleged that the torture and ill-treatment committed by the military police took place upon arrest and the methods included slaps, kicking and boxing on all parts of the body. A female prisoner reported that she had been raped by two police officers while in police custody (UN SPT 2012).

13.5.1.1 Some Structural Factors

During the military government, torture was widely used mainly against suspects from the guerrilla and the political left, in addition to the traditional ill-treatment criminal suspects often had to face. A doctrine of national security emphasised threats against the state and a state-focused understanding of security dominating all other possible concerns for state obligations such as the rule of law, human rights, independent oversight over state action and political participation.

In practical terms, the armed forces worked hand in hand with the state police and specialist units (DOI/CODI[36]), in a police role. All these agencies were involved in the torture of political prisoners.

There have been a number of works on the role of military and police officers during the military dictatorship. After Brazil transitioned towards democracy in 1985, traditional forms of policing and problems have often survived. This research, especially when it includes interviews with officers, can be helpful in determining how officers thought and think about such practices.

---

[35] UN-detailed public comments on a country human rights situation often result from states submitting reports on a treaty they have ratified or a visit by a special rapporteur to the country—if he/she is permitted to visit.

[36] Departamento de Operações de Informações/Centro de Operações de Defesa Interna (Department for Information Operations/Center of Internal Defense Operations departments).

13.5.1.2 Institutional Issues and the Moral Universe of Police Officers

Drawing on my own work on gross human rights violations in Argentina, Brazil, Chile and Uruguay in 1960–1990 (Heinz and Frühling 1999), I will now refer to some interviews I undertook in Brazil in 1990, five years after the transition to democracy. Important here is the role of military officers in a police role to support and indeed lead state repression during the dictatorship; the opposition then was conceived as an internal enemy rather than citizens suspected to have committed a crime. The suggestion here is to look at how the military explains, reasons about and rationalises what they considered to be necessary in the fight against the "subversives" during the military dictatorship. As mentioned earlier, the intention here is not to judge whether the statements are right or wrong, or justifications or lies. Various arguments quoted in the following sections have been discussed in the public discourse of the country. Former Brazilian President Jair Bolsonaro, for example, publicly expressed his support for the military dictatorship and for torture.[37]

Opinions held in the interviews take obviously very different positions from contributions from the human rights community, important civil society voices as well as democracy-oriented politicians.

Former army colonel Carlos Brilhante Ustra, later a state deputy in São Paulo, mentioned in his book that in the fight against the guerrilla, the interrogator would ask essentially four questions at the beginning of the interrogation of the detainee:

- "What is your next contact point?
- Where is your aparelho (place where he stayed)?
- What is your real name?
- What is your code name?"

Starting from these four questions, he asserts, a real struggle against time began. On the one hand, the interrogator urgently needed the responses to the questions he formulated. The "terrorist", on the other hand, tried at any cost to lie and to give wrong addresses, "cold points" and "police points". He was bitter about criticisms of military action, commenting: "Are (human rights) only valid for terrorists, subversives and agitators? What about those who fought against them, who remained invalids or were assassinated, don't they have also human rights?"[38]

Another army colonel, Erasmo Dias, talked to me about the fight against a Maoist guerrilla group of the Partido Comunista do Brasil in the Araguaia region of Pará state. Around 60 guerrilla fighters were killed by the Brazilian Army and "disappeared". He emphasised:

[37] New York Times (2018), Jair Bolsonaro Wins Brazil's Presidency, in a Shift to the Far Right, 18.10.2018, https://www.nytimes.com/2018/10/28/world/americas/jair-bolsonaro-brazil-election.html.

[38] Brilhante Ustra (1987), 160, 181, translated by the author (all quotes in this section are taken from Heinz 1993).

> It was important not to divulge any information about what happened, not to in any way to aid in stimulating the guerrilla. The journalists needed more time to arrive in that area where operations took place. The guerrilla did not have a rational doctrine. They were fanatic terrorists. We had to use the same methods they used.[39]

So what he probably wanted to say is that ordinary law could not be used in such a situation, while he did not openly suggest the use of torture.

A former experienced police commissioner told former torture victim and journalist Antonio Carlos Fon:

> In an interrogation, the important thing is to break the morale of the spirit of resistance of the interrogated person. You will pressure him until the moment when he breaks down and starts to talk... For an honest citizen who committed a small slip, it is enough to talk more loudly, to scream at him or to make faces. The marginal needs a bit stronger rough treatment because he is conscious that he broke the law, and, in a certain ways, he expects to be punished. ...
>
> It is always the most difficult thing to interrogate a subversive. Since the subversive does not accept the authority of the state, it is critical to show him that the state has the means to force him in an effective way. ... The interrogated person risks, as an accident, being subjected to too much pressure or not really having the information you need... The interrogator risks letting the moment pass where the resistance of the interrogated persons is broken, where he finally recognises the authority of the state but ... he does not talk [A second risk is that the interrogate gets emotionally involved. He then] "starts to pressure out of hate, and no longer to reach a predetermined goal (Fon 1979, p. 64).

The big problem according to this officer is the struggle against the clock:

> If you have no problems of time it would not be necessary to resort to violence. You tell the person that you have all the time in the world but both of you know that this is not true. It is necessary to get the information now because from now on to the future it might be too late. And to save time everything is valid (Fon 1979, p. 64).

In another interview, army general Carlos de Meira Mattos—a supporter of the military government—reflected on human rights in this way:

> There was torture. This was never the responsibility of the revolutionary government.[40] These were locally responsible officers. One has to take into account the size of Brazil and the fact that there were no more than a total of about 200 people who died or disappeared. There were cases where prisoners could not resist torture. This is very different from what happened in Argentina.[41]

13.5.1.3 Policing Under the Military Dictatorship and Democracy

US sociologist Martha K. Huggins has worked intensively on torture in Brazil, first on the "US connection", focusing on the US training of the Brazilian police during

[39] Interview by the author with Colonel (ret.) Erasmo Dias, São Paulo, November 1990. Dias was commander of the DOI/CODI of the Second Army in São Paulo between 1970–74.

[40] "Revolutionary government" is a term used by the military government for itself. The 1964 coup d'ètat against the democratically-elected government was called a "revolution".

[41] Interview by the author with General (ret.) Carlos de Meira Mattos, Rio de Janeiro, December 1990.

the military dictatorship (Huggins 1998). In her second book, Huggins presents the results of her interviews with 23 police officers, 14 of whom were categorised as violence workers (Huggins et al. 2002) because they were involved in torture and murder, spanning three generations. A first group joined the police between the late 1950s and early 1960s, a second group carried out their police careers almost exclusively during the military government and then two officers did after the military government. Officers were members of the military police (this is not the military police as it is known in Western countries but uniformed police in the street), Federal police and civilian police—the investigative state police force. Chapters 10 and 11 of her book, entitled *Secret and Insular Worlds of Serial Torturers and Executioners* and *Moral Universes of Torturers and Murderers*, are of particular interest. In the following section, I will focus on some of her interviews and her conclusions.

One officer with long experience in police and intelligence stated that he himself did not torture, but men he trained were invited to join internal security organisations such as the Department of Information Operations/Center for Internal Defense Operations (DOI/CODI); he described them as "all very hard-nosed". The extreme violence they meted out further "bestialized" them.[42] Operating in a context in which torture was taking place, this officer would argue that excess violence might have been avoided had there been better police training.

Huggins et al. present a table with the title "Moral Reckoning About Torture", with the categories "acceptable", "not wholly acceptable but understandable" and "unacceptable" (horizontal dimension). The vertical sections under the title "Casual Evaluation" cover (1) "perpetrators' described characteristics", (2) "assumed proximate causal influence" and (3) "assumed larger motivation conditions". Torture was seen as *acceptable* if (1) the officer was professionally trained and controlled and (2) was psychologically cunning and intelligent and (3) there was a just cause to get information, a belief that only violence will succeed and the victim was uncooperative. In the second category, *not wholly acceptable but understandable*, officers described perpetrators' characteristics as youthful, aggressive, stupid and ignorant; lacking in training; and temporally out of control. Larger motivating conditions were that he acted under brutalising social conditions and had to be actively present but not actively participating. Torture was *unacceptable* when perpetrators could be described as sadistic, irrational, cruel and cold-bloodedly vicious. Assumed proximate causal influence would be out-of-control character disorder and judgement impaired by drugs and alcohol. Assumed larger motivating conditions were named hedonistic satisfaction and economic greed.[43] Four de facto explanations accepting or denying personal responsibility were denials, justifications, excuses and confessions.[44]

[42]Huggins et al. (2002), p. 194.

[43]Ibid., 197.

[44]Ibid., 196.

Huggins et al. conclude the analysis of acceptable and unacceptable violence in these terms:

> All [officers interviewed, WSH] had remarkable similar criteria for assigning past violence to one or another moral category. Each interviewee's moral calculus was sufficiently flexible to make violence acceptable in one situation, excusable in another, and totally inacceptable in a third. Finally, the status of perpetrator, victim, or hero shifted according to sociopolitical context so construed. Only subtle nuances in Portuguese separated one moral classification from another.

And she mentioned as an "interesting foundation for most interviewee's moral calculus" that "torture had to be kept operationally distinct from murder: torturer who did their jobs properly should not kill, and killers should not dirty themselves with torture".[45]

13.5.2 *India*

In India, the use of torture and ill-treatment has been a widespread problem for decades. United Nations expert bodies, international and local human rights NGOs as well as academia[46] have published data and analysis on the subject. The UN Human Rights Committee wrote in its conclusions in 1997:

> The Committee expresses concern at allegations that police and other security forces do not always respect the rule of law and that, in particular, court orders for habeas corpus are not always complied with, particularly in disturbed areas. It also expresses concern about the incidence of custodial deaths, rape and torture, and at the failure of the Government of India to receive the United Nations Special Rapporteur on the question of torture and other cruel, inhuman or degrading treatment or punishment.[47]

Twenty-five years later, the Indian government insisted in its report to the UN Human Rights Committee:

> The Constitution of India and laws made thereunder provide adequate recourse including the writ of habeas corpus that secure liberty of every individual in India. Other modes of redressals are also available under criminal laws of India. ... India maintains an inviolable stand on torture, rape or sexual violence by the state actors including security forces. There are provisions under the IPC on certain aggravated forms of rape which includes rape by a member of the armed forces.[48]

---

[45] Ibid., 205.

[46] E.g. Hoenig and Singh (2015), with a section with cases of torture, extrajudicial executions and disappearances which mentioned in some accounts of cases responses to allegations from the Indian government, and Lokaneeta and Jesani (2016), with a comprehensive overview of political and legal issues, statistics etc.

[47] UN Human Rights Committee (1997).

[48] Government of India (2022), para 85.

An important legal impediment for complaints is that civilians have only a very limited possibility to challenge public officials in court in the states. According to the Criminal Procedure Code, Section 197(1), this can only happen with the permission of the central government. The state, however, is unwilling to give such a permission, shielding thereby its officers.[49]

Until June 2023, India has not ratified, but only signed the UN Convention on Torture (1984) in 1997 and ratified the International Covenant on Civil and Political Rights (1966) in 1979, which prohibits torture and cruel, inhuman or degrading treatment or punishment in Article 7.

13.5.2.1 Institutional Issues and the Moral Universe of Police Officers

Rachel Wahl published a book in 2017 entitled *Just Violence. Torture and Human Rights in the Eyes of the Police*, in which she, as a reviewer put it, "provides a systematic framework to bridge the divide between human rights groups and the police in India over how they understand violence and why the police—and at times the public—tend to view torture as a necessary means of upholding security and justice" (Monshipouri 2018, p. 488). She conducted 60 in-depth interviews with 33 police officers participating in a distance learning course, awarding them a master's degree in human rights; other course participants and interviewees were human rights activists, educators and civil servants. Wahl's objective is to illuminate the "moral universe inhabited by law enforcers who support or use torture, and the implications for how they respond to activism and education to protect human rights" (Wahl 2017, p. 19). She gives a vivid description of how police officers see their role in policing in a difficult society in which crime is a major problem and quotes extensively from her interviews, which is helpful for an understanding of officers' perceptions and how she develops her analysis. Her book does not claim to present a statistical survey but offers interesting insights into the reasoning of police officers from North India.[50] The book contains chapters inter alia on police beliefs and the moral imaginary of violence and police responses to human rights activists. Specific aspects discussed, inter alia, are officers' conceptions of justice versus human rights, political interference, judicial inefficiency, insufficient resources and legal protection.[51] I will present some key aspects without aspiring to be inclusive of her findings. According to Wahl, police officers tend to consider torture as integral to preserving a just society, especially in view of the weaknesses and material conditions as well as defective political and legal systems in India.[52] Wahl starts by presenting a real criminal case to police officers in which a wife disappeared and

[49] Lokaneeta and Jesani (2016), p. 535ff.

[50] From Delhi, Punjab, Haryana, Uttar Pradesh, Jammu and Kashmir, Assam.

[51] Wahl (2017), p. 65ff.

[52] Ibid., 13, 75–85.

her family would request the police to look for her whereabouts. The police undertook interviews and brutally tortured the husband to give information about his wife. She asked various interviewees for opinions on this course of action. Officers tended to justify the torture of the husband. A high-ranking police officer commented that the police and the parents of the girl suspected the husband ("May be the husband is trying to play smart. . . ."). Probably her parents had turned to the police asking them to act against the husband. A low-ranking officer from Haryana argued, "Using torture doesn't mean the police are violating human rights. They are also trying to deliver justice to someone."[53]

13.5.2.2 Explanations and Justifications

Generally, officers saw human rights as compatible with the religion and tradition of the country. They tended to use a utilitarian approach in their reasoning. They made distinctions as to who could and should be tortured. The use of torture was justified against "hardened criminals", "militants" and "terrorists" but not for regular criminals. In a few cases, an officer would justify this practice against any criminal, meaning a criminal suspect.[54] One officer proposed that a classification of criminals should be established to allow for different levels of human rights protection depending on the category of the criminal.

The officers interviewed did not defend *all* police behaviour. To use violence in response to bribes by interested people was not acceptable. However, looking at reports about corruption in the Indian media, at sources from civil society organisations and even the government, the use of violence is often driven by the motivation to obtain a bribe.

Wahl mentions that "(o)fficers would often negotiate by framing torture as something that can be done morally or immorally, rather than as an inherent wrong".[55] She quotes from an interview with a high-ranking officer from Punjab: "It is wrong to torture if someone is inflicting pain in an irresponsible manner for small information . . . but if it is beneficial, then it is positive. . . . Responsibility is very important. For human rights, dignity is very important. Maintain the dignity and be responsible."[56]

Torture and the Justice System

In the perception of officers, the intention to act in accordance with (informal) police standards was important in how officers assessed action by their colleagues. What

[53] Ibid., 1ff.

[54] Ibid., 52–55, 74–75, 86ff.

[55] Ibid., 137.

[56] Ibid.

was very important was whether the acting officer believed that the suspect is guilty. Officers who tortured and killed for the public good should not be punished, whereas torture for personal gain was condemned.[57]

Officers reinterpreted the evident tension between their action and legal norms, referring to law provisions depriving the accused of their rights such as the loss of liberty. In their perception, the use of torture would not violate the principles of law but just be adapted and extended to exceptional people. A mid-ranking officer from Rajasthan suggested to Wahl that in the case of a member of organised crime, one should have a certain code of conduct for these people, like 20 shots to the lower back, then stop for medical examination, and then 20 more shots. In other words, criminals should be dealt with according to their crime.[58] This assertion implies that the police would know that those persons were guilty of a crime before the trial had taken place.

Pressure from the Public

A high-ranking police officer from the Police Research and Development institution emphasised the influence of public pressure when he worked as a police officer. "The public wants us to beat the criminal."[59] While not himself arguing in favour of the use of torture, this practice was presented as a result of public pressure.

In conclusion, in Wahl's analysis, officers generally neither simply follow orders against their better judgement nor act for personal gain. Rather, they hold "moral beliefs, that help them understand violence as right and good and enable them to deflect criticism".[60] She also notes that despite officers having to face diverse influences, such as religious, cultural, law and order, human rights training and public pressure to punish criminals officers, they showed a strong, separate identity to be a police officer.[61]

13.5.3 The Russian Federation

The Russian Federation has a long history of police ill-treatment/torture in general and particularly in the Chechen Republic. Information is being published by local human rights NGOs, which are increasingly restricted in their work.[62] International

---

[57] Ibid., 57.

[58] Ibid., 58f.

[59] More examples at ibid., 62–65.

[60] Ibid., 19.

[61] Ibid., 144.

[62] One Russian NGO, the Committee for the Prevention of Torture reported for example that it represented torture victims in court and in front of investigative bodies. It also provided assistance on issues pertaining to obtaining compensation for medical rehabilitation. As some of its

human rights NGOs, UN bodies (UN Human Rights Committee (CCPR) and CAT treaty bodies), media and the Council of Europe's CPT until 2022 report about the situation. Little serious investigation takes place, fostering impunity.

The Russian Federation submits reports to the UN treaty bodies and receives concluding observations on these reports that are in the public domain.

The UN Human Rights Committee observed in 2015 that:

> (w)hile noting that acts that may constitute torture or ill-treatment can be prosecuted under several articles of the Criminal Code, the Committee remains concerned about reports that torture and ill-treatment, including for the purpose of eliciting confessions, are still widely practised, and notes with concern recent allegations that Zaur Dadaev and other suspects had confessed to the killing of opposition leader Boris Nemtsov under torture (arts. 2, 7 and 14) (UN Human Rights Committee 2015, para 14).

In 2018, the UN Committee against Torture urged once again the Russian Federation to criminalise torture as an independent crime. And it was:

> . . .deeply concerned at numerous reliable reports of the practice of torture and ill-treatment in the State party, including as a means to extract confessions, and at many recent reports documenting cases of torture, such as the deaths of Valery Pshenichny in 2018 and Ruslan Sayfutdinov in 2017. The Committee is also concerned at reports that allegations of torture rarely resulted in criminal prosecutions and that, even when prosecuted, the perpetrators were charged with simple assault or abuse of authority. In the light of its previous recommendation the Committee regrets the absence of a public statement by the State party's high-level authorities reaffirming the absolute prohibition of torture (arts. 2, 4, 12 and 16) (UN CAT 2018, paras 9, 12).

Until 2022, the only international body with regular access to police stations and prisons under an international treaty was the CPT (after its invasion of Ukraine, Russia was expelled from the Council of Europe). It visited the country 30 times between 1998 and 2021, including many times the Chechen Republic.[63] The Russian government has only permitted the publication of four CPT visit reports to date.[64] In 2007 and in 2019, the Committee decided under its powers under the European Convention on the Prevention of Torture (ECPT) to issue a Public Statement on the Russian Federation, Chechen Republic.[65] Attached to the statement were 23 pages of examples from unpublished CPT reports (CPT 2007).

---

achievements, it reported in 2017 that it has been successful in cancelling 793 unlawful decisions and getting a conviction for 127 perpetrators. It also secured 51 million rubles in compensation for a number of torture victims through court hearings (People in Need 2017). See also international reporting by Amnesty International, Human Rights Watch and ACAT (2013).

[63] Regular visits should take place every four years in every country of the Council of Europe. The CPT can decide on additional ad-hoc visits if required by conditions in that country.

[64] According to the European Convention on the Prevention of Torture and Inhuman or Degrading Treatment or Punishment the publication of visit reports is subject to the invitation of the state visited. The publication includes a response to the CPT report by that state (ECPT, Article 11 para 2).

[65] "If a Party to the Convention fails to cooperate or refuses to improve the situation in the light of the Committee's recommendations, the Committee may decide, after the Party has had an

13.5.3.1 Institutional Aspects

Criminal investigations are in the hands of the Investigative Committee of the Russian Federation, with branches at different administrative levels. This powerful body has been operating since 2011, when the investigation functions of the office of the Prosecutor General were separated and the federal Investigative Committee was set up.[66] It is answerable to the President. CPT has been meeting increasingly with representatives of this body during its visits in 2016, 2017 and 2018. In a 2017 news flash, CPT stated that it wanted "to examine the effectiveness of investigations into allegations of ill-treatment of detained persons by law enforcement officials".[67]

In March 2019, the CPT issued its fourth Public Statement on the Russian Federation, stating: "it is clear from the information gathered by the Committee in the course of ... visits that resort to torture and other forms of ill-treatment by members of law enforcement agencies in the Chechen Republic remains widespread, as does the related practice of unlawful detentions which inevitably heightens significantly the risk of resort to ill-treatment, in particular due to the denial of fundamental safeguards. Further, it remains deeply worrying that, in their responses to the CPT's visit reports, the Russian authorities have failed to acknowledge the gravity of the situation" (CPT 2019b, p. 2). The CPT's ongoing dialogue with the Russian authorities was reported to have reached an impasse. Regarding investigations into allegations, the Committee noted that:

> the precise nature of the obligations of a Party to the Convention under Article 8(2)(d) has been re-emphasised during several face-to-face meetings between CPT delegations and senior representatives of the Investigative Committee of the Russian Federation and of the Investigative Committee's Investigative Departments for the North Caucasian Federal District and for the Chechen Republic. The Russian authorities have not complied with their obligation to demonstrate that effective investigations have taken place. The CPT must stress that nothing can justify an outright refusal to grant access to information of this nature, which is necessary for the Committee to carry out its task, or providing access on conditions which would be tantamount to a refusal (CPT 2019b, p. 3).

13.5.3.2 Police Reform Efforts and the Role of Police Officers

In 2011, a major reform effort of the Russian police was undertaken to improve the public image of police officers and increase their general efficiency. The institution was renamed from militia in Soviet times to police (for an interesting overview, see contributions in *Russlandanalysen* 2011). According to Semukhina, positive steps were to do away with the issue of bad police and increase the levels of job

---

opportunity to make known its views, by a majority of two-thirds of its members to make a public statement on the matter". (ECPT, article 10 para 2).

[66] English portal: https://en.sledcom.ru.

[67] See news flash on visits at https://www.coe.int/en/web/cpt/russian-federation. More general on the CPT methods of work: Heinz (2018).

satisfaction among police officers. In the process, the lack of a coherent plan became visible to reform the police. New measures tended to be just reactive. In the public discussion, a deep division became visible about the role and function of the police and whether authority should be further expanded or curtailed under a new law (Semukhina 2014, p. 4).

At the time, there was a national police force of around one million employees under the Ministry of Interior. Many work on the local level in approximately 2000 local departments. Key structural factors are strict hierarchical subordination and the quality-based performance assessment system, which has a strong impact on career advancement and take-home pay (McCarthy 2014, p. 5f; for an evaluation of interviews with police officers, see Gladarev 2012). According to McCarthy, there is multiple accountability in the quantitatively based performance system requirements. The strict hierarchical subordination policy makes officers dependent on superiors who have a strong influence on promoting low-ranking officers and deciding who gets bonuses.

The performance assessment system is based on three key indicators, the number of cases cleared (the suspect has been identified and charged), the number of cases investigated within the time limits set by the Criminal Procedure Code and the comparison of case activities to the previous reporting period. The police, the author argues, might use violence and other coercive tactics in order to get suspects to confess to crimes so that cases can be registered as cleared. She also noted that there is a strict code of silence not to report on the behaviour within the force: "If the bosses are corrupt and someone needs to benefit from the corruption whistleblowing becomes even less likely since everyone benefits just enough to keep the corrupt practices going."[68]

Many of these incentive structures are also located in other parts of the criminal justice system, such as investigators, prosecutors and judges. She sees a strong conviction bias in the criminal justice system and a bias towards prosecuting people on the margins of society who do not have the resources or connections to defend themselves.[69] In her view, important long-term challenges in improving the low ratings of the police by citizens are to create incentive structures for officers that would align with citizens' expectations. Another way to help increase public trust is to devolve control to subordinate officers that would align with citizen priorities.[70]

[68] McCarthy (2014), p. 6.

[69] Ibid., 7.

[70] Ibid.

13.6 Effectiveness of Measures for Torture Prevention

Empirical research is a difficult venture, given that torture usually takes place in a shadowy world. There usually do not exist solid data on the scope, frequency and severity of torture, given that almost everyone involved realises that these are crimes to be kept secret. While a lot has been written about torture, especially on methods, legal norms and work of institutions, more specific studies on policies and practical measures to reduce torture incidents are not so frequent. A rare comprehensive example is the study by Richard Carver and Lisa Handley, "Does Torture Prevention Work?" (2016). It examines the effectiveness of more than 60 different measures for the prevention of torture, to be more precise, whether measures actually reduced the risk of torture.[71] Authors developed their own score with three separate elements—frequency, geographical spread and severity—basing their score on the definition of torture in Article 1 of the UN Convention against Torture (CAT) (Carver-Handley Torture Score (CHATS)). Their point of departure is the definition of a victim as someone "in the official or unofficial, prolonged or temporary custody of the perpetrator".[72] Researchers contributed 14 country studies, looking at torture and prevention mechanisms over a 30-year period (1984–2014). Prevention measures were grouped into four main categories, countries that saw consistent and sustained improvement (United Kingdom, Chile), countries where positive developments have stalled after initial success (Hungary, Indonesia, Israel, Peru, South Africa), countries that have made recent dramatic improvements which may or may not be sustained (Georgia, Tunisia, Turkey) and countries where there has been no discernible sustained improvement over the 30-year period (Ethiopia, India, Kyrgyzstan and the Philippines).[73] Sixty-six independent variables were identified on the basis of legal obligations in relevant international and regional conventions and were recommended by human rights mechanisms, which are divided into four main categories: detention, prosecution, monitoring and complaints, with each cluster further subdivided into law and practice. A variable about the training received by personnel in each of the groups of categories was added: training is believed to be an important feature of torture prevention. To a modest degree, this belief turned out to be correct.[74]

Authors emphasise that the considerable gap between law and practice was often determined by various factors, of which the political environment was a particularly important one, which can have direct positive and negative effects as well as indirect ones. They refer to constitutional and procedural guarantees compared to a conflict or emergency situation. However, their work is more focused on law and the practice of prevention measures.[75] The overall conclusion of the study is that torture

[71] Carver and Handley (2016), p. 36.

[72] Ibid., 38ff.

[73] Ibid., 5ff.

[74] Ibid., 34f., 98f.

[75] Ibid., 47ff.

prevention works. In terms of effectiveness, detention practice comes first,[76] prosecution and monitoring practices being also relevant.[77] External complaint mechanisms are reported to have a lesser impact on the prevention of torture. They are strongest when findings of torture are directly referred to prosecution authorities.[78] Regarding the investigation and punishment of torturers, the gap between law and practice was found to be vast. Country chapters consistently report that states failed to investigate and prosecute torturers. Effective investigations and prosecutions were considered by the authors as particularly effective in reducing torture.[79]

13.7 Conclusion

As mentioned in the introduction, there is no one-size-fits-all solution to the problem of torture. However, from the discussion, certain key dimensions have emerged for a broader, structural approach for countries with major problems.

Strategic Elements of Effective Prevention or the Classic Approach: Legislative, Institutional and Behavioural Changes

To develop serious reform efforts, there is a need to pay particular attention to the dimensions of detention practice, prosecution, monitoring and complaints, even if in the latter case Handley and Carver found less evidence about its effectiveness in their 2016 study. Clear legal norms regarding the prohibition of torture and ill-treatment and a serious, independent implementation in the area of criminal procedure and criminal law are key instruments, though by no means generally accepted and/or functioning in many countries. Another dimension variable on the national, regional and local levels of police is the gap in training when young police officers after a modern initial training often follow old habits at their workplace propagated by his or her superiors (official and de facto role models). While this might be called the mainstream approach in many teaching kits, recommendations, and laws, these are still important framework conditions for a comprehensive approach—assuming that there is some basic political will to reform, usually absent in a "full" dictatorship. Political will must be present at the government, Ministry of the Interior, police leadership (national, intermediate) and especially superiors' levels. That said, these steps are often not enough.

Necessity to Move Beyond the Mainstream Approaches in Situations of More Frequent Abuse and Ill-Treatment

Depending on the political context—especially the nature of crimes and threats in the work of the police, the quality of government and management of the police, the approaches selected, the resources available, etc.—there is a clear need to look more

[76] Ibid., 66ff.

[77] Ibid., 81ff., 93ff.

[78] Ibid., 92.

[79] Ibid., 82, 84.

in depth into the internal organisational structure, both formal and informal, and the belief system to identify structural and other factors that might have led to an internal culture of tolerating arbitrary violence within the police, such as esprit de corps, individual understandings of whether and to what degree officers feel they have to protect other officers when there is a complaint, forms of misplaced loyalty, corruption and other factors.

In addition to the formal legal code, one needs to look at *de facto* norms and informal rules for behaviour, the emergence of subcultures that basically allow for more violence and coercion than the legal codes permit. Such violence is often directed against certain categories of criminal suspects typified by officers, depending on their country, as hardened criminals, people who are on the verge of society (poor, destitute, marginalised), terrorists, subversives and the like.

I am thinking of an internal organisational culture in the sense that officers decide, relatively independent from the law, who should be treated in which way, who should be punished in some way and who cannot really expect to be treated according to the "book" (= legal norms). Officers sometimes invent categories of people who might—or even should—be ill-treated because superiors and/or the public would look away or even "request" such action for public safety. An exaggerated belief in the power of legal norms to engender reform neglects the organisational-attitudinal side and is simply misplaced. This is an important conclusion for an organisation endowed with the state monopoly of legal coercion and that is always in need to project the image of always acting following the laws of the country.

There are two additional factors for which to watch out. Subcultures appear to emerge more likely in certain specialised police units dealing, for example, with organised crime, terrorism and drug trafficking, in other words the "tough units" or elite units, which are often separated from the normal police work and are more confronted with violence in their daily work. Moreover, in some countries, there is a strong influence from old and new military codes/practices; the police is essentially militarised and lacks the concept of dealing with a citizen, who is only a suspect, as opposed to a concept that it fights an (internal) "enemy".

Observing Organisational Processes and Police Practice from Within

Here, it can be helpful to go beyond traditional approaches (law, political science) and explore a social science or anthropological approach in the sense of seeking to understand what is being thought, felt and practised within police institutions, i.e. recruitment, training, informal rules and values, etc. and, in a broader sense, the internal security sector architecture. As has been demonstrated, there have been a number of interesting contributions in observing and interviewing officers in countries with problematic police work. Moreover, interaction with other state institutions is another important topic to look at, e.g. the judicial system, parliament, ombudsman institutions, police complaint bodies, national human rights institutions with powers to receive complaints and civil society/NGO work on police and human rights, some of which might work on complaints by citizens. (To be clear, at least for state institutions, it is not suggested here to set up a complicated complaint structure. Rather, it would be helpful to have a small number of complaint bodies with a clearly delineated division of labour—powers to investigate—and that are sufficiently trained and financed.) In any reform effort, it is helpful to learn from those who experience first-hand the police system. For this, it is crucial to have systems of information, communication and complaints where complainants are protected against retaliation and complaints are followed up systematically and in a transparent way. Of course, there can be cases of vague, confused complaints, sometimes trying to blame certain officers to put undue pressure on them. Nevertheless, in reform projects, systematic statistics on complaints (charges filed, trial outcome) should be set up to verify the impact on the beneficiaries. For this, it is important to be able to swiftly verify by qualified impartial observers what really happened. For this, you need investigators, but not necessarily all must be police investigators because also lawyers with experience in criminal law are in a good position to undertake these investigations.[80] Another important dimension is the way police interrogations are carried out and the role of confessions for convictions in the criminal system. Standards for non-coercive interviewing methods and procedural safeguards have been developed and should be used.

Finally, one has to keep in mind that the tightening of certain procedural safeguards can lead in practice to the emergence of other unwanted behaviour, such as the questioning of suspects in unofficial places outside of police stations and remand prisons. Human rights violations sometimes might shift from one type of violation to other forms, from ill-treatment on the way to or at the police institution to ill-treatment in private "safe houses" where no one is formally registered, and from such houses to extrajudicial executions and disappearances. Hence, a holistic strategy should be developed with a view to minimising the risks of such shifts (internal and external monitoring mechanisms). While loopholes will always be sought out by some officers, care should be taken to adopt a comprehensive approach that makes shifts to new forms of human rights violations as difficult as possible.

Possible prospects towards reform will obviously differ depending on political and legal framework conditions in a given country. International cooperation agencies are well advised to explore in depth these framework conditions to assess realistically right from the beginning what should—and could be—feasible objectives under prevailing conditions. The fundamental challenge is whether some sort of real reform is envisioned (political will and appropriate planning) or superficial projects are undertaken, purporting to show other countries and international organisations that the government is committed to human rights, without any real political will.

[80] In Norway for example both lawyers and police investigators work on complaints against the police (Norway: https://ipcan.org/members/the-norwegian-bureau-for-the-investigation-of-police-affairs).

References

Abdul-Rahman L, Espín Grau H, Singelnstein T (2023) Kernbefunde des DFG-Forschungsprojekts "Körperverletzung im Amt durch Polizeibeamt*innen" (KviAPol), May 2023. https://kviapol.uni-frankfurt.de/images/pdf/Zusammenfassung Gewalt im Amt.pdf

ACAT (2013) The multiple faces of torture – a study of the phenomenon of torture in Russia. https://www.acatfrance.fr/public/acat_russia_en.pdf

African Commission on Human and Peoples' Rights (2017) Guidelines on the Conditions of Arrest, Police Custody and Pre-Trial Detention in Africa (Luanda Guidelines). https://apcof.org/wp-content/uploads/2017/03/conditions-of-arrestpolice-custody-and- pre-trial-detention-in-africa-luanda-guidelines-trainee-manual.pdf

Amnesty International Dutch section (2015) Use of force. Guidelines for implementation of the UN Basic principles on the use of force and firearms by law enforcement officials. Short version, Amsterdam. https://www.amnesty.nl/content/uploads/2017/07/guidelines_use_of_force_eng.pdf?x43474

APT (Association for the Prevention of Torture) (2013) Monitoring police custody. A practical guide, Geneva. https://www.apt.ch/en/resources/publications/monitoring-police-custody-practical-guide-2013

APT et al (2021) Principles on Effective Interviewing for Investigations and Information Gathering. https://www.apt.ch/sites/default/files/inline-files/apt_PoEI_EN_08.pdf

APT (2023) APT's Strategic Plan 2020-2023: our roadmap for torture prevention. https://www.apt.ch/en/what-we-do/strategic-plan-2020-2023

Asia Pacific Forum (APF) (2023) Preventing torture in places of detention. https://www.asiapacificforum.net/support/human-rights/preventing-torture/

Behr R (2008) Cop Culture. Der Alltag des Gewaltmonopols: Männlichkeit, Handlungsmuster und Kultur in der Polizei, Wiesbaden

Brilhante Ustra CA (1987) Rompendo o Silêncio, Brasília

Carver R, Handley L (2016) Does torture prevention work? Liverpool University Press, Liverpool

Council of Europe (2001) The European Code of Police Ethics (Recommendation Rec(2001)10 adopted by the Committee of Ministers of the Council of Europe on 19 September 2001. https://rm.coe.int/16805e297e

Council of Europe (2011) Eradicating impunity for serious human rights violations, guidelines and reference texts, Strasbourg. https://rm.coe.int/1680695d6e

Council of Europe (2023) European standards of prevention of torture and ill-treatment: focus of high-level conference in Kazakhstan - Director Claus Neukirch visits Almaty. https://www.coe.int/en/web/programmes/-/european-standards-of-prevention-of-torture-and-ill-treatment-focus-of-high-level-conference-in-kazakhstan-director-claus-neukirch-visits-almaty-on-20-april-2023

CPT (2007) Public statement concerning the Chechen Republic of the Russian Federation. https://rm.coe.int/1680697bd0

CPT (European Committee for the Prevention of Torture and Inhuman or Degrading Treatment or Punishment) (2019a) Standards regarding Police. https://www.coe.int/en/web/cpt/standards

CPT (2019b) Public statement on the Russian Federation concerning the Chechen Republic and other republics of the North Caucasian region (made on 11 March 2019), Strasbourg. https://rm.coe.int/168093710ee

Cremer H (2013) "Racial Profiling" – Menschenrechtswidrige Personenkontrollen nach § 22 Abs. 1 a Bundespolizeigesetz. Empfehlungen an den Gesetzgeber, Gerichte und Polizei, Berlin: Institut für Menschenrechte. https://www.institut-fuer-menschenrechte.de/publikationen/detail/racial-profiling-menschenrechtswidrige-personenkontrollen-nach-22-abs-1-a-bundespolizeigesetz

CTI (Convention against Torture Initiative) (2017) Investigative interviewing for criminal cases. CTI training tools 1/2017. https://cti2024.org/content/docs/CTI-Training_Tool_1-Final.pdf

Deutsches Institut für Menschenrechte (2018) Stellungnahme. Zur individuellen Kennzeichnungspflicht für Polizeibeamt_innen bei geschlossenen Einsätzen. Öffentliche

AnhÖrung des Innenausschusses der Bürgerschaft der Freien und Hansestadt Hamburg am 15. Juni 2018, Berlin: Deutsches Institut für Menschenrechte. https://www.institut-fuer-menschenrechte.de/fileadmin/user_upload/Publikationen/Stellungnahmen/DIMR_Stellungnahme_Kennzeichnung_Polizei_HH.pdf

EU 2013 Directive 2013/48/EU of the European Parliament and of the Council of 22 October 2013 on the right of access to a lawyer in criminal proceedings and in European arrest warrant proceedings, and on the right to have a third party informed upon deprivation of liberty and to communicate with third persons and with consular authorities while deprived of liberty. https://eur-lex.europa.eu/LexUriServ/LexUriServ.do?uri=OJ:L:2013:294:0001:0012:En:PDF

European Court of Human Rights (2022) Fact sheet Police arrest and assistance of a lawyer, Strasbourg. https://www.echr.coe.int/Pages/home.aspx?p=press/factsheets&c=

Fon CA (1979) Descendo aos poroes, *Veja*, 21.02.1979

Gladarev B (2012) Russian police before the 2010-2011 reform: a police officer's perspective, The Journal of Power Institutions in Post-Soviet Societies [Online], Issue 13 | 2012, Online since 20 November 2012, connection on 13 October 2018. http://journals.openedition.org/pipss/3978

Government of India (2022) Fourth periodic report submitted by India under article 40 of the Covenant pursuant to the optional reporting procedure, due in 2020, UN doc. CCPR/C/IND/4, 31.10.2022. https://digitallibrary.un.org/record/3975403

Heinz WS (1993) The military, torture and human rights. Experiences from Argentina, Brazil, Chile and Uruguay. In: Crelinsten RD, Schmid AP (eds) The politics of pain. Torturers and their masters. Leiden, pp 72–108

Heinz WS (2018) The European Committee for the Prevention of Torture (CPT) and its work with the police. In: Alleweldt R, Fickenscher G (eds) The police and international human rights law. Springer Verlag, Berlin, pp 305–319

Heinz WS, Frühling H (1999) Determinants of gross human rights violations by state and state-sponsored actors in Brazil, Uruguay, Chile, and Argentina. 1960-1990. Kluwer Publishers, Den Haag

Hoenig P, Singh N (2015) Landscapes of fear: understanding impunity in India. Zubaan Books, New Delhi

Huggins MK (1998) Political policing: The United States and Latin America. Duke University Press Books, Durham, N.C.

Huggins MK, Haritos-Fatouros M, Zimbardo PG (2002) Violence workers. Police torturers and murderers reconstruct Brazilian atrocities. University of California Press, Berkeley: Los Angeles. https://www.amazon.de/Violence-Workers-Torturers-Reconstruct-Atrocities/dp/0520234472

Istanbul Protocol (2022) Manual on the Effective Investigation and Documentation of Torture and Other Cruel, Inhuman or Degrading Treatment or Punishment, New York/Geneva. https://www.ohchr.org/sites/default/files/documents/publications/2022-06-29/Istanbul-Protocol_Rev2_EN.pdf

Kozma J, Rachlew A (2018) Combating torture during police custody and pre-trial detention. Discussion Paper prepared in cooperation with DIGNITY – Danish Institute against Torture Conference hosted by the Danish Chairmanship of the Committee of Ministers of the Council of Europe, 22-23 March 2018 Copenhagen, Denmark. https://rm.coe.int/1680797130

Lokaneeta J, Jesani A (2016) India. In: Carver R, Handley L (eds) Does torture prevention work? Liverpool, pp 501–547

McCarthy LA (2014) The day-to-day work of the Russian police. In: Russian Analytical Digest No. 151, 30 June 2014, pp 5–8. https://css.ethz.ch/content/dam/ethz/special-interest/gess/cis/center-for-securities-studies/pdfs/RAD-151-5-8.pdf

Monshipouri M (2018) Book review: Wahl, Rachel 2017 just violence, torture and human rights in the eyes of the police, Stanford: Stanford University Press. Hum Rights Q 40:489–494

New York Times (2018) Jair Bolsonaro Wins Brazil's Presidency, in a Shift to the Far Right, 18.10.2018. https://www.nytimes.com/2018/10/28/world/americas/jair-bolsonaro-brazil-election.html

People in Need (2017) No matter who you are you never be safe from torture in Russia. https://www.clovekvtisni.cz/en/no-matter-who-you-are-you-will-never-be-safe-from-torture-in-russia-3920gp

Reiner R (2010) The politics of the police, 4th edn. Oxford: University Press, Oxford

Russlandanalysen (2011) Polizeireform. http://www.laender-analysen.de/russland/pdf/Russlandanalysen219.pdf

Schicht G (2007) Menschenrechtsbildung für die Polizei. Deutsches Institut für Menschenrechte, Berlin. https://www.institut-fuer-menschenrechte.de/fileadmin/_migrated/tx_commerce/studie_menschenrechtsbildung_fuer_die_polizei.pdf

Semukhina O (2014) From Militia to Police: the path of Russian law enforcement reforms. In: Russian Analytical Digest No. 151, 30 June 2014, pp 1–7. http://www.css.ethz.ch/content/dam/ethz/special-interest/gess/cis/center-for-securities-studies/pdfs/RAD-151-5-8.pdf

Singelnstein T (2014) Körperverletzung im Amt durch Polizisten und die Erledigungspraxis der Staatsanwaltschaften – aus empirischer und strafprozessualer Sicht. Neue Kriminalpolitik (NK) 2014:15–27. https://www.nk.nomos.de/fileadmin/nk/doc/Aufsatz_NK_14_01.pdf

Töpfer E, Tobias P (2017) Unabhängige Polizeibeschwerdestellen. Was kann Deutschland von anderen europäischen Staaten lernen? Deutsches Institut für Menschenrechte, Berlin. https://www.institut-fuer-menschenrechte.de/fileadmin/user_upload/Publikationen/ANALYSE/Analyse_Unabhaengige_Polizeibeschwerdestellen.pdf

Töpfer E, von Normann J (2014) Unabhängige Polizei-Beschwerdestellen. Eckpunkte für ihre Ausgestaltung. Deutsches Institut für Menschenrechte, Berlin. https://www.institut-fuer-menschenrechte.de/fileadmin/_migrated/tx_commerce/Unabhaengige_Polizei_Beschwerdestellen.pdf

UN Body of Principles for the Protection of All Persons under Any Form of Detention or Imprisonment, General Assembly resolution 43/173 of 9 December 1988. https://digitallibrary.un.org/record/53865

UN CAT (Committee against Torture) (2014) Seventh annual report of the Subcommittee on Prevention of Torture and Other Cruel, Inhuman or Degrading Treatment or Punishment, UN doc. CAT/C/52/2, 20 March 2014

UN CAT (2018) Concluding observations on the sixth periodic report of the Russian Federation, CAT/C/RUS/CO/6, 28 August 2018

UN Code of Conduct for Law Enforcement Officials, General Assembly resolution 34/169 of 17 December 1979

UN General Assembly (2001) Official Records 56th Supplement number 4 (A56/44) Report of the Committee against Torture, UN General Assembly 25th session, 26th session, New York

UN Human Rights Committee (1997) Consideration of reports submitted by states parties under article 40 of the covenant, UN doc. CCPR/C/79/Add.81, 4 August 1997. https://tbinternet.ohchr.org/_layouts/treatybodyexternal/Download.aspx?symbolno=CCPR/C/79/Add.81&Lang=En

UN Human Rights Committee (2015) Concluding observations on the seventh periodic report of the Russian Federation, 28 April 2015; UN doc. CCPR/C/RUS/CO/7. https://tbinternet.ohchr.org/_layouts/treatybodyexternal/Download.aspx?symbolno=CCPR/C/RUS/CO/7&Lang=En

UN Human Rights Council (2017) Summary of the discussions held during the seminar entitled "Exchanging national experiences and practices on the implementation of effective safeguards to prevent torture and other cruel, inhuman or degrading treatment or punishment during police custody and pretrial detention". Report of the United Nations High Commissioner for Human Rights, UN doc. A/HRC/37/27, 26 December 2017. https://digitallibrary.un.org/record/1466828/files/A_HRC_37_27-EN.pdf

UN Special Rapporteur on Torture (2016) Interim report of the Special Rapporteur on torture and other cruel, inhuman or degrading treatment or punishment, UN doc A/71/298, 5 August 2016. https://undocs.org/A/71/298

UN Special Rapporteur on Torture (2019) Torture and other cruel, inhuman or degrading treatment or punishment. Report of the Special Rapporteur. UN doc. A/HRC/40/59, 16.01.2019. https://undocs.org/A/HRC/40/59

UN Special Rapporteur on Torture (2023) Good practices in national criminalization, investigation, prosecution and sentencing for offences of torture, UN doc. A/HRC/52/30, 16.02.2023. https://www.ohchr.org/en/calls-for-input/2022/good-practices-national-criminalization-investigation-prosecution-and

UN SPT (Subcommittee on Prevention of Torture and Other Cruel, Inhuman or Degrading Treatment or Punishment) (2012) Report on the visit of the Subcommittee on Prevention of Torture and Other Cruel, Inhuman or Degrading Treatment or Punishment to Brazil, UN doc. CAT/OP/BRA/1, 5 July 2012. http://acnudh.org/wp-content/uploads/2012/09/OPCAT-Brazil.pdf

Wahl R (2017) Just violence, torture and human rights in the eyes of the police. Stanford University Press, Stanford

Walsh D et al (eds) (2015) International developments and practices in investigative interviewing and interrogation, volume 2: suspects, Routledge Frontiers of Criminal Justice

Williamson TM (1993) From interrogation to investigative interviewing: strategic trends in police questioning. J Community Appl Soc Psychol 3(2):89–99

Wolfgang S. Heinz studied Political Science and Psychology at Free University of Berlin. Until 2019, he worked as Senior Policy Adviser at the German Institute for Human Rights, responsible for international security policies and the United Nations human rights system. Among a broad variety of professional experiences, he served as Vice President of the Council of Europe's Committee for the Prevention of Torture (CPT), as chair of the UN Human Rights Council Advisory Committee and of the UN Working Group on Communications dealing with complaints regarding Gross Human Rights Violations.

Wolfgang S. Heinz teaches Political Science at the Free University of Berlin with a focus on international relations and international peace and security issues. Among his many publications in English are: German Unification, in: David P. Forsythe (ed.), Encyclopedia of Human Rights, vol. 2: Democracy Promotion, Oxford 2009, pp. 305–311; Germany. State Responses to Terrorist Challenges and Human Rights, in: Brysk, Alison/ Shafir, Gershon, (eds.), National Insecurity and Human Rights. Democracies debate Counterterrorism, Berkeley 2007, pp. 157–176; The Military, Torture and Human Rights. Experiences from Argentina, Brazil, Chile and Uruguay, in: Ronald D. Crelinsten/Alex P. Schmid (eds.), The Politics of Pain. Torturers and their Masters, Boulder, Col. 1995, pp. 66 ff.; Prevention of Torture and Ill-Treatment. Experiences from the work of the CPT, in: ACAT (ed.), A World of Torture, Paris, pp. 181–190. In German, his last book edited together with Sarah Jäger deals with International law traditions of UN Security Council member states and Germany (Frieden durch Recht. Rechtstraditionen und Verortungen, Wiesbaden 2020).

Chapter 14
Protecting Human Rights in Police Custody: Findings and Proposals

Ralf Alleweldt

Contents

Abstract In this concluding chapter, drawing on the insights of the authors of this book, I will highlight two areas that appear to be particularly important for ensuring the humane treatment of persons in police custody. First, fundamental safeguards against mistreatment must be in place and actually observed, and these safeguards should be as effective as possible. I am proposing, in particular, that an arrested person be brought before a judicial authority within hours of arrest, wherever feasible, for maximum preventive effect. Second, there is a link between the quality of professional police work and the appropriate treatment of detained persons. This is particularly true with respect to the conducting of police questioning. I will again emphasise that the investigative interviewing approach is an important instrument for improving the effectiveness of police work and, at the same time, enhancing

R. Alleweldt (✉)
Brandenburg State Police University, Oranienburg, Germany
e-mail: ralf.alleweldt@hpolbb.de

R. Alleweldt (ed.), *Fair Treatment of Persons in Police Custody*,
https://doi.org/10.1007/978-3-031-61737-9_14

respect for the human rights of persons in police custody. A brief outlook will conclude this chapter and the book.

Many problems are easier to identify than solve. As I said in the introduction to this book, the rule is very simple: all persons deprived of their liberty must be treated with humanity and with respect for their inherent dignity, and no one must be subjected to torture or cruel, inhuman, or degrading treatment or punishment.[1] It is apparently a much more complex task, from a worldwide perspective, to ensure that very powerful institutions like police forces respect and implement these rules in each and every case.[2]

As the contributions in this volume show, many activities of great diversity are necessary or useful to achieve this aim. Put together briefly, we need the right rules, we need adequate safeguards and procedures,[3] we need the police to apply good working methods[4] and to use appropriate equipment,[5] and we need police officers with a humane attitude[6] in police organisations with a human-rights-friendly culture.[7]

In this concluding chapter, drawing on the insights of the authors of this book, I would like to highlight two areas that appear particularly important for ensuring the humane treatment of persons in police custody. First, fundamental safeguards against mistreatment must be in place and actually observed, and these safeguards should be as effective as possible. Second, there is an important link between the quality of professional police work and the appropriate treatment of detained persons. This is particularly clear with respect to the conduct of police questioning.

[1] As laid down in Articles 7 and 10 of the International Covenant on Civil and Political Rights.

[2] "A multifaceted and interdisciplinary endeavour"; cf. Sub-Committee on the Prevention of Torture (SPT), The approach of the Subcommittee on Prevention of Torture to the concept of prevention of torture and other cruel, inhuman or degrading treatment or punishment under the Optional Protocol, UN-Doc. CAT/OP/12/6, 30 December 2010, para. 5 (i).

[3] See the contributions of Richard Carver, Krassimir Kanev, Christina Hof, Audrey Olivier Muralt, Nika Kvaratskhelia, and Wolfgang S. Heinz (Chapters 2, 3, 4, 8, 9, 13).

[4] See above, Asbjørn Rachlew, Chapter 5; Frances Surmon-Böhr, Laurence Alison and Emily Alison, Chapter 6.

[5] See above, Richard Carver, Chapter 2; Cristina Sganga, Chapter 10.

[6] See above, Walter Suntinger and Moritz Birk, Chapter 7; Wolfgang S. Heinz, Chapter 13.

[7] See above, Walter Suntinger and Moritz Birk, Chapter 7; Audrey Olivier Muralt, Section 8.4.1; Nika Kvaratskhelia, Section 9.5.2; William O'Neill, Section 12.3; Wolfgang S. Heinz, Chapter 13.

14.1 Fundamental Safeguards and Procedures

Many proposals to ensure fair treatment of persons in police custody—and to prevent their torture and ill-treatment—concern the introduction and implementation of procedures and safeguards.[8] Typically, such safeguards have their place in situations where a specific risk exists that the law will be violated.

Police custody inherently entails such a risk. It is undoubtedly necessary, in order to protect society against crime, that police forces have the power to arrest persons involved in criminal activities. The problem is that once persons are arrested, they are entirely in the control of the police, without the possibility, at least for a certain time, to have contact with and to receive support from the outside. This is, by nature, a risky situation; arrested persons are particularly vulnerable, and it has long been common ground that whenever there is a risk that torture and ill-treatment occur, it is most likely to happen in the first hours after arrest.[9] Uncontrolled power may always be abused, and police forces are very powerful institutions.

Accordingly, an obvious measure to prevent any form of abuse is to reduce the opportunities for it to occur by reducing the periods during which arrested persons are in the sole power of the police, i.e. by introducing safeguards providing them with access to the outside world.

Such risks associated with police custody have been recognised long ago. According to international human rights law and, usually, also national law, the police, on their own authority, can only detain persons for a relatively short period until the intervention of a judge is necessary.

14.1.1 The Right of the Detained Person to Be Brought Promptly Before a Judge

This right is one of the most important safeguards for protecting persons in police custody. It is laid down, for example, in Article 5 para. 3 of the European Convention on Human Rights: all persons arrested by the police because they may have committed, or should be prevented from committing, a criminal offence have to be brought promptly before a judge. In the context of Article 5, this rule aims to ensure that the lawfulness of detention is reviewed as soon as possible by an independent and competent authority. In addition, this rule provides a safeguard that the arrested person is adequately treated.[10]

---

[8] See above, Richard Carver, Section 2.2: "torture is a crime of opportunity" (citing Nigel Rodley).

[9] See, for example, CPT, Preventing police torture and other forms of ill-treatment – reflection on good practices and emerging approaches, extract from the 28th General Report, CPT/Inf (2019) 9, para. 66.

[10] For more details, see above, Richard Carver, Section 2.3.

The term "promptly" is interpreted by the European Court of Human Rights to be, in any case, not longer than four days.[11] The European Committee for the Prevention of Torture (CPT) recommends that police custody should in no case (whether the person is suspected of a criminal offence or not) exceed 72 hours and that authorities ensure that such rules are respected in reality.[12] The judge should have the right, and duty, to order an appropriate investigation and other measures if a person complains about ill-treatment or if other evidence of ill-treatment, like visible injuries, comes to light.[13]

This is a strong and well-established safeguard. However, it seems that this safeguard may be strengthened by further reducing the duration of police custody, i.e. well below the duration of 72 or 96 hours. National governments wishing to ensure the fair treatment of persons in police custody with maximum effectiveness may reduce police custody to the absolutely necessary period. Such a development could be supported by a reinterpretation of the term "promptly" in Article 5 para. 3 of the European Convention on Human Rights. I will come back to this issue below in Section 14.2.

14.1.2 Fundamental Safeguards During Police Custody

During police custody, additional safeguards can and should be put in place. Any contact with the outside world or other persons not belonging to the police forces contributes to preserving the physical and psychological integrity of persons in custody. Accordingly, the CPT and other preventive mechanisms recommend to governments, as described by Krassimir Kanev, Wolfgang Heinz, and Richard Carver in this book,[14] to adopt three fundamental safeguards against ill-treatment: the right of detainees, from the very beginning of custody, to inform a family member or friend about their detention; the right to access to a lawyer; and the right to request a medical examination by a doctor. All detainees should be expressly informed about these rights. Any possibility for authorities to delay the exercise of one of these rights should be clearly defined in law, limited in time, and accompanied by appropriate safeguards.[15]

---

[11] See European Court of Human Rights, Case of Brogan v. United Kingdom (1988), para. 62; Case of McKay v. United Kingdom (2006), para. 47.

[12] Cf., for example, CPT, Report on the visit to Bulgaria in 2010, CPT/Inf (2012) 9, paras. 10–11; Report on the visit to Ukraine in 2009, CPT/Inf (2011) 29, paras. 9–11; Report on the visit to Georgia in 2010, CPT/Inf (2010) 27, para. 10.

[13] CPT, 12th General Report, CPT/Inf (2002) 15, para. 45; 14th General Report, CPT/Inf (2004) 28, para. 28.

[14] See above, Richard Carver, Section 2.2; Krassimir Kanev, Section 3.2; Wolfgang S. Heinz, Section 13.2.

[15] See, for example, CPT, Police Custody, Extract of the 2nd General Report, 1992, CPT/Inf (92) 3, paras. 36–37; CPT, Developments concerning CPT standards in respect of police custody, Extract of the 12th General Report, 2002, CPT/Inf (2002) 15, paras. 40–44.

14.1.3 Notification of Custody to Family Members or Other Persons

As the CPT stated as early as 1992, the right of detained persons to have their detention notified to a third party is one of the fundamental safeguards against ill-treatment.[16] This right has also been recognised by the member states of the Council of Europe in Rule 57 of the European Code of Police Ethics.[17]

The right to notification reduces the isolation of the person in custody. Family members or friends, once notified, may contact a lawyer or take other steps to ensure the well-being of the detained person. They may monitor the person's treatment and, if necessary, take steps to complain about such treatment.[18] Notification ends incommunicado detention and "reduces the risk that a person will be disappeared".[19]

14.1.4 The Right to Access to a Lawyer

This right is undoubtedly a key safeguard for ensuring that persons are adequately treated in police custody. It is unlikely that a person will be ill-treated in the presence of a lawyer, and in cases where ill-treatment occurs, a lawyer will be in a position to take appropriate action, e.g. by lodging a complaint.[20]

This right should apply from the moment of arrest, i.e. from the minute the person is obliged to stay with the police, with no regard to whether the person is considered to be a suspect or a witness or just held for "informative talks".[21] The right should be enjoyed by all persons deprived of their liberty. Sometimes state legislation provides for exceptions with regard to persons suspected of minor (e.g. administrative) or serious (e.g. terrorist) offences; such rules create "loopholes", which can lead to high-risk situations.[22]

The right of access to a lawyer must include the right to meet him in private. Apart from fair trial considerations, detained persons must be in a position to tell their lawyer about any possible ill-treatment, which is much easier and safer for the person

[16] CPT, Police Custody, Extract of the 2nd General Report, 1992, CPT/Inf (92) 3, para. 36.

[17] Council of Europe, Committee of Ministers, Recommendation Rec (2001) 10 of the Committee of Ministers to member states on the European Code of Police Ethics, 19 September 2001, Appendix.

[18] Association for the Prevention of Torture (APT), 2017 Symposium on Procedural Safeguards in the first hours of police custody. Outcome Report, p. 16.

[19] Convention against Torture Initiative (CTI), Safeguards in the first hours of police detention, 2017, p. 5.

[20] CPT, Developments concerning CPT standards in respect of police custody, Extract of the 12th General Report, 2002, CPT/Inf (2002) 15, para. 41.

[21] CPT, Access to a lawyer as a means of preventing ill-treatment, Extract from the 21st General Report, CPT/Inf (2011) 28, para. 19.

[22] Ibid., para. 20–21.

if the conversation takes place in private.[23] Detained persons should have the right to have their lawyer present during any questioning conducted by the police, and the lawyer should be able to intervene in the course of the questioning. This would exclude the possibility that the police use improper methods, e.g., for obtaining a confession.

In addition, the CPT recommends that "appropriate provision should be made (...) for persons who are not in a position to pay for a lawyer".[24] Indeed, this is a practical problem of great importance. In many countries, legal aid schemes are underfunded, so not enough lawyers are able or willing to take up legal aid cases. This "leaves many of the poorest and most vulnerable detainees without even basic legal assistance".[25] States should seriously consider the possibility of introducing free legal assistance to all persons deprived of their liberty by the police, as proposed, inter alia, by the National Preventive Mechanism (NPM) of Georgia[26], or even assign lawyers to every police station, like in the English "duty solicitor" scheme.[27]

The right to access to a lawyer has been included in the European Code of Police Ethics;[28] it is also recommended by the UN Human Rights Council[29] and the Special Rapporteur on Torture.[30] It has been the subject of extensive discussion in the context of the Association for the Prevention of Torture (APT)[31] and the Convention Against Torture Initiative (CTI).[32]

[23] Ibid., para. 23.

[24] Ibid., para. 20.

[25] APT, 2017 Symposium on Procedural Safeguards in the first hours of police custody. Outcome Report, p. 11.

[26] See above, Nika Kvaratskhelia, Section 9.4.

[27] See above, Richard Carver, Section 2.3.

[28] European Code of Police Ethics, Article 57. See Council of Europe, Committee of Ministers, Recommendation Rec (2001) 10 of the Committee of Ministers to member states on the European Code of Police Ethics, 19 September 2001, Appendix.

[29] Human Rights Council, Torture and other cruel, inhuman or degrading treatment or punishment: Safeguards to prevent torture during police custody and pretrial detention, A/HRC/31/L.26 rev.1, 23 March 2016, No. 5, 7.

[30] Juan E. Méndez, Interim Report of the Special Rapporteur on torture and other cruel, inhuman or degrading treatment or punishment, 5 August 2016, UN-Doc. A/71/298, paras. 68–75.

[31] APT, 2017 Symposium on Procedural Safeguards in the first hours of police custody. Outcome Report.

[32] CTI, Safeguards in the first hours of police detention, 2017.

14.1.5 Electronic Recordings

The CPT has long recommended the electronic (audio or video) recording of police interviews as an effective measure to prevent ill-treatment during questioning,[33] and many countries have introduced it during the last few decades.[34] Electronic recording facilitates the investigation of any allegations of ill-treatment as well as the investigation of the (possible) crime that is the subject of the interview. Such recordings may provide clarity as to whether the suspect actually made a certain statement and how it might be interpreted.[35] Recordings may protect interviewers against cognitive overload or false accusations.[36] They preserve the evidence in its original form, which may be used for training purposes and, as such, for developing and improving the interviewing skills of police officers.[37] The video surveillance of interviews and police stations, in general, is considered an important safeguard by the Georgian NPM, as Nika Kvaratskhelia points out.[38] Indeed, as Richard Carver and his team found out during their in-depth research, if used as a routine procedure, the electronic recording of interviews is highly effective in ensuring that the interviewed persons are adequately treated.[39]

14.1.6 Making Detention Safeguards a Reality

It may be a long way from the idea, or recommendation, to introduce safeguards ensuring the fair treatment of detainees to their realisation in practice. First, governments have to accept their responsibility to introduce such safeguards. Second, a clear legal basis for them must be created in laws or regulations.[40] Third, although such rules are necessary, they are by no means sufficient for ensuring that safeguards work in reality. As Cristina Sganga points out, it is not enough that police officers know the rules,[41] and in the apt and disillusioning words of Wolfgang Heinz: "An exaggerated belief in the power of legal norms . . . is simply misplaced."[42]

---

[33] CPT, Developments concerning CPT standards in respect of police custody, Extract of the 12th General Report, 2002, CPT/Inf (2002) 15, para. 36.

[34] See above, Asbjrn Rachlew, Section 5.10.

[35] Cf. CPT, Developments concerning CPT standards in respect of police custody, Extract of the 12th General Report, 2002, CPT/Inf(2002)15, para. 36.

[36] See above, Asbjrn Rachlew, Section 5.10.

[37] See above, Asbjrn Rachlew, Section 5.10.

[38] See above, Nika Kvaratskhelia, Section 9.4.

[39] See above, Richard Carver, Section 2.3.

[40] A case in point is the EU "Roadmap" directives described by Krassimir Kanev, above, Section 3.2.

[41] See above, Cristina Sganga, Section 10.4.

[42] See above, Wolfgang S. Heinz, Section 13.7.

As Richard Carver and his colleagues found in their research, the mere legal entitlement to prompt access to a lawyer does not seem to influence the incidence of torture.[43] In contrast, creating such an entitlement and implementing it, i.e. granting access to a lawyer in reality, goes hand in hand with reducing torture and ill-treatment. It is safe to say that such implementation has a high preventive impact.[44] In many countries, there still seems to exist a considerable gap between law and practice as far as detention safeguards are concerned.[45]

Accordingly, in order to make detention safeguards an everyday reality, monitoring mechanisms, in particular NPMs, will have to reiterate and refine their recommendations to exercise some friendly pressure, as it happened in Georgia, where it appears, as Audrey Olivier Muralt reports, that with the support of the Ministry of Interior, during certain periods, every police station in the capital city was visited by an NPM delegation every few days, and all police stations in the regions regularly as well.[46]

It is one of the important tasks of the National Preventive Mechanisms around the world to insist that detention safeguards are respected in reality.[47] Very importantly, detainees must be informed in a comprehensive and well-understandable way, at best both orally and in writing, about their rights so that they can make use of them in a meaningful manner. Competent government authorities, particularly senior officers, may instruct all police officers to inform detainees properly about their rights and, in general, to implement all rules concerning detention safeguards to the letter. In addition, governments should consider providing human rights organisations with access to places of detention and permit them to conduct monitoring activities.[48]

Of course, safeguards will work most efficiently if police officers implement them because they are convinced themselves that this is the right thing to do. In those countries where the use of investigative interviewing methods will be introduced or strengthened (see below Section 14.3.2), greater respect may be expected for the rights of persons in custody, including their rights concerning detention safeguards.

In addition, though not technically a fundamental safeguard, complaints about ill-treatment by the police must be investigated effectively, in particular by an independent authority. Such investigations deal with past events, but they also certainly have a preventive effect. This important requirement has been discussed in some detail in another volume.[49]

---

[43] See above, Richard Carver, Section 2.3.

[44] See above, Audrey Olivier Muralt, Section 8.4.

[45] See above, Richard Carver, Section 2.2; Nika Kvaratskhelia, Section 9.5.2.

[46] See above, Audrey Olivier Muralt, Section 8.4.1; Jikia and Shalikashvili (2016), pp. 395, 414.

[47] See above, Audrey Olivier Muralt, Section 8.4.

[48] See above, Krassimir Kanev, Section 3.5.

[49] See Smith (2018), pp. 83–101.

14.2 Duration of Police Custody—Considering a Reinterpretation of the Right to Be Brought "Promptly" Before a Judge

As mentioned above, international human rights law prescribes that every criminal suspect shall be brought "promptly" before a judge, as required by Article 5 para 3 of the European Convention on Human Rights. This principle is universally recognised.[50]

Judicial involvement in such cases serves (at least) two purposes. On the one hand, the decision as to whether the narrow, exceptional legal conditions for a deprivation of liberty are fulfilled should be made by an authority that is both legally particularly competent and independent from the executive force. On the other, the risk of ill-treatment is highest as long as a person is under the full and exclusive control of just one state institution, namely the police. In the words of the European Court of Human Rights:

> [T]he Court's case-law establishes that there must be protection of an individual arrested or detained on suspicion of having committed a criminal offence through judicial control. Such control serves to provide effective safeguards against the risk of ill-treatment, which is at its greatest in this early stage of detention, and against the abuse of powers bestowed on law enforcement officers or other authorities for what should be narrowly restricted purposes and exercisable strictly in accordance with prescribed procedures. (. . .) The judicial control on the first appearance of an arrested individual must, above all, be prompt to allow detection of any ill-treatment and to keep to a minimum any unjustified interference with individual liberty. The strict time constraint imposed by this requirement leaves little flexibility in interpretation, otherwise, there would be a serious weakening of a procedural guarantee to the detriment of the individual and the risk of impairing the very essence of the right protected by this provision.[51]

Thus, there is an obvious connection between a person's right to liberty (Article 5 of the Convention) and the prohibition of torture and other ill-treatment (Article 3).

The Court's argument seems reasonable and convincing, and it certainly justifies its position that the maximum period of police custody should be as short as possible. One may doubt, however, whether a maximum period of two, three, or even four days—as accepted in the case law of the Court—is adequate for the purposes of effective human rights protection. In cases where a person is subjected to severe ill-treatment from the moment of arrest, four days of police custody without judicial intervention will obviously be felt to be a very long time. Although the Court commits itself to "little flexibility in interpretation", it is submitted that the four-day period is much too long and flexible for ensuring both the lawfulness of detention and the effective prevention of ill-treatment in police custody.

---

[50] See International Covenant on Civil and Political Rights, Article 9 para. 3; American Convention on Human Rights, Article 7, para. 5; Arab Charter on Human Rights (revised 2004), Article 14, para. 5.

[51] European Court of Human Rights, *McKay v. United Kingdom* (2006), paras. 32, 33.

The legitimate interests of conducting criminal prosecutions can be preserved effectively even if a person is brought before a judge within a much shorter period than four days. It will be recalled that a person may be arrested under Article 5 (1) c of the European Convention on Human Rights "for the purpose of bringing him before the competent legal authority", and this may happen only "on reasonable suspicion of having committed an offence". Accordingly, the apparent purpose of this provision is to obtain a decision by an independent, legally educated authority as to whether there is indeed a reasonable suspicion of a criminal offence against the person concerned.

The object of questioning during police detention may indeed be "to further the criminal investigation by confirming or dispelling the concrete suspicion grounding the arrest".[52] It is also true, as the Court has stated repeatedly, that "facts which raise a suspicion need not be of the same level as those necessary to justify a conviction or even the bringing of a charge, which comes at the next stage of the process of a criminal investigation".[53] In this sense, it is also correct that "a certain period between the arrest and the prompt appearance before the judge may be necessary for the investigating authorities to obtain evidence to substantiate that there are reasons to justify the detention".[54]

However, although the duration of police custody may and should certainly be used for additional investigatory activities, the purpose of police custody cannot be to gain time for finding the evidence on which an *initial* reasonable suspicion can be based. Such evidence must already exist *before* an arrest is carried out. It is not (lawfully) possible to arrest a person first and only afterwards find the evidence justifying the arrest. This view is actually confirmed by a judgment of the European Court in another case, according to which its findings accepting periods of police custody of two or three days "are not designed to afford the authorities the opportunity to intensify their investigations and to collect the substantial and consistent evidence required for the applicants to be placed under formal investigation by the investigating judge, for example, because they have contested the charges".[55] Accordingly, the competent legal authority is in a position immediately after arrest to verify whether grounds for (initial) arrest exist. There is no reason to delay judicial intervention. The decisions of whether criminal charges should be brought and whether detention pending trial should be ordered may be taken at a later stage, if necessary, during a separate hearing, e.g. one or two days later. They need not be taken at the first intervention.

Consequently, in the light of the necessity to avoid arbitrary arrests and ill-treatment in the most effective way, the words "promptly"/"aussitôt" in Article 5 para. 3 of the Convention should be interpreted very narrowly, so bringing the person before the judge should be, as a rule, a matter of hours, not days.

---

[52] European Court of Human Rights, *Murray v. United Kingdom* (1994), para. 55.

[53] European Court of Human Rights, *Erdagöz v. Turkey* (1997), para. 51.

[54] European Court of Human Rights, *S., V. and A. v. Denmark* (2018), para. 132.

[55] European Court of Human Rights, *Vassis v. France* (2013), para. 61.

Such a rule has indeed been established by the Court, but only for preventive detention because "the facts constituting the risk of committing an offence must already be established at the time when the person is detained in order to prevent his or her committing an offence".[56] I want to submit respectfully that the facts constituting the "reasonable suspicion of having committed an offence" must equally be established at the moment of arrest. The distinction made by the Court allowing a longer period of police custody without judicial intervention if the person is suspected of having already committed an offence is not convincing.

If necessary, the judge could extend detention and the time for police questioning by a reasonable period, e.g. 12 or 24 hours. But there are normally no legitimate reasons why a person arrested by the police should be under exclusive police control for more than a few hours. Longer delays in judicial intervention should only be considered acceptable if they cannot be avoided for objective reasons, such as when the arrest occurs in remote rural areas[57] or on the high seas.[58] The purposes of Article 5 para. 3—namely avoiding all forms of arbitrary detention as well as preventing ill-treatment effectively—can only be achieved if the judicial authority intervenes as soon after arrest as possible.

This proposal is supported by considerations of proportionality. In various contexts, the Court has interpreted Article 5 of the Convention to the effect that deprivation of liberty must be in line with the principles of necessity and proportionality.[59] The proportionality principle may today be considered a general principle of (national and) international human rights law. Unnecessary interferences usually violate human rights.

Accordingly, proportionality must also limit the duration of police custody. If persons are not brought before the judge as soon as possible, they are kept in police custody longer than necessary. This means unnecessarily increasing the risk of unlawful detention as well as the risk of ill-treatment. If it is true, as the Court has recognised (above), that police custody without judicial intervention is a particularly serious and risky interference with human rights, then the compelling conclusion is that such interference should not be more intense, and thus should not last longer, than necessary.

Thus, bringing an arrested person before the judge should be a matter of hours unless there are special circumstances justifying a delay. Such a practice would be most effective in terms of ensuring the fair treatment of detainees, and it would not harm the criminal investigation.

---

[56] Ibid., paras. 133, 134.

[57] Cf. the decision of the German Constitutional Court (Bundesverfassungsgericht) of 15 May 2002, 2 BvR 2292/00, para. 27: "Not avoidable are, for example, the delays caused by the length of the route, difficulties in transportation, the necessary registration and logging, a recalcitrant behaviour of the arrested person or comparable circumstances." (Author's translation)

[58] European Court of Human Rights, *Medvedyev v. France* (2010), paras. 131, 132.

[59] See, for example, European Court of Human Rights, *Gatt v. Malta* (2010), paras. 36–51; *James, Wells and Lee v. United Kingdom* (2012), para. 195.

How could this be achieved? First, it is proposed that the European Court of Human Rights might reconsider its interpretation of the word "promptly"/"aussitôt" in Article 5 para. 3 of the Convention to the effect that it should cover periods that normally are not longer than, say, six or nine hours and that any delay extending these periods must be of an exceptional character. Second, at the same time, and independently from the course the Court's case law may take, the CPT, other international bodies or the National Preventive Mechanisms may propose governments to reduce the period of police custody as much as possible. Third, national governments and legislatures may decide for themselves, in the interest of enhanced human rights protection, to introduce short maximum periods of police custody into their national law.

14.3 Effective Policing

14.3.1 General Requirements

Ensuring the fair treatment of persons in police custody is an important requirement of ethics and the law. In addition, it is also an issue of effective policing and professional competence. In other words, professional policing and the fair treatment of persons in custody go hand in hand. A lack of professional behaviour—or a lack of possibility to act professionally—increases the likelihood of ill-treatment during police custody.

Various authors of this volume emphasise that the inappropriate treatment of persons in police custody often occurs in countries where the criminal justice system does not work properly and relies too heavily on confession evidence.[60] Accordingly, each measure improving police work, and making the criminal justice system more functional, may help the police find and evaluate other kinds of evidence, thus contributing to ensuring the proper treatment of persons in their custody.

Proposals made in this book include improving the equipment and the infrastructure of police institutions.[61] Where necessary, capacity-building projects may support police forces in this respect.

Police officers fulfil a task that is very important for protecting society, a task that may be challenging and sometimes difficult. Society should recognise this, and working conditions should be as good as possible.[62] If it is true, as Richard Carver states, that police are "typically under-resourced, poorly trained, badly paid, have a low status in society",[63] this has to change. In particular, performance assessment systems should not set false incentives. Police officers should be required to follow

[60] See above, Richard Carver, Section 2.3; Wolfgang S. Heinz, Section 13.4.

[61] See above, Cristina Sganga, Section 10.5.

[62] See above, Cristina Sganga, Section 10.5; Nika Kvaratskhelia, Section 9.4.

[63] See above, Richard Carver, Section 2.3.

the facts, wherever they may lead them. They should be rewarded for solving cases correctly, not for securing convictions.[64]

As Walter Suntinger and Moritz Birk point out, the typical qualities of police officers are courage, determination, empathy, a firm sense of humanity, professionalism, negotiation, and communication skills.[65] Indeed, many police officers choose their job because they want to protect the human rights of individual persons.[66] These positive qualities and positive objectives of police officers should be taken into account and used when taking steps to improve the human rights performance of police forces.

During capacity-building or peacekeeping activities, for example, it may at times be necessary, as Cristina Sganga points out, to engage with professionals who may be responsible for human rights violations.[67] In such a situation, if we want to achieve change, it is not sufficient to criticise the situation and to organise training about the rules. We also have to take into account that law enforcement officers, although not following the applicable legal rules, may be living in their own moral universe.[68] Many of them may consider that they are doing the right thing and that even illegal action may be justified by "higher" objectives. If we want these officers to refrain from ill-treating persons in custody, it will be greatly helpful if we are able to show them other effective ways to do their job professionally, for example with regard to the conducting of interviews.

14.3.2 Investigative Interviewing

Questioning suspects and witnesses is an indispensable tool of the police for establishing the facts of a case and for finding out the truth about whether and how a crime has been committed and who committed it.[69] There still seems to be a widespread belief that coercive questioning methods, exercising pressure on the interviewed person, are suitable for finding and punishing the guilty.[70] Of course, not each and every questioning method, not each form of exercising pressure on a suspect, amounts to ill-treatment or even torture, but ill-treatment and torture are certainly particularly serious forms of exercising pressure.

---

[64] See above, Richard Carver, Section 2.3.

[65] See above, Walter Suntinger and Moritz Birk, Section 7.3.12.

[66] Ibid., Section 7.3.11.

[67] See above, Cristina Sganga, Section 10.3.

[68] See above, Wolfgang S. Heinz, Sections 13.5.1, 13.5.2.

[69] See above, Asbjrn Rachlew, Section 5.1.

[70] See above, Frances Surmon-Böhr, Laurence Alison and Emily Alison, Section 6.1; and also Juan E. Méndez, Interim Report of the Special Rapporteur on torture and other cruel, inhuman or degrading treatment or punishment, 5 August 2016, UN-Doc. A/71/298, para. 9.

In this sense, although torture and ill-treatment *are never justified*, torturers may sometimes *feel justified* because they are acting to solve a crime, i.e. for a good cause protecting society and potential victims and possibly deterring a criminal from committing more crimes. Indeed, as several authors of this volume point out, the public may sometimes even expect such behaviour from police officers, particularly in countries where the criminal justice system is not functioning properly.[71]

The assumption underlying coercive questioning is that it is particularly effective for solving crimes. The *investigative interviewing* approach, as described in this volume by Asbjrn Rachlew as well as by Frances Surmon-Böhr, Laurence Alison, and Emily Alison, shows that this assumption is fundamentally flawed. Investigative interviewing is more effective and, at the same time, much more conducive to respecting human rights.

Investigative interviewing means that the interview takes place in a non-coercive setting and an atmosphere of open communication. As Asbjrn Rachlew describes, the objective of the interviewing process is to obtain detailed, reliable, and complete information about the events under investigation.[72] The interviewed persons (suspects, victims, or witnesses) are informed about their rights and asked to give a complete, uninterrupted account of the events at issue as they memorise them. Once they have finished their account, the interviewer may ask for further details. If their account conflicts with other evidence already obtained, they are informed at some point about this conflict and asked to provide an explanation. The whole interviewing process takes place in an open, communicative atmosphere, leaving the interviewed persons with all the possibilities to put forward their view of the matter.[73]

The difference between coercive and investigative questioning is that, at the beginning of the interview, a confession-oriented interviewer is more or less convinced already that the suspect is guilty and just a confession is needed. The investigative interviewer, in contrast, recognises that the evidence may point to the suspect's guilt but more information is needed to get a complete picture. Logically, and typically, in the beginning, interviewers *do not yet have all relevant information*; i.e., they do not know everything about the case. Otherwise, there would be hardly any point in conducting an interview at all; at least, there would be no need to obtain a statement from the interviewed person.

Actually, it should be obvious that the only legitimate reason to conduct interviews is to obtain accurate and complete information about the events in the issue. As Asbjrn Rachlew points out and as research shows, at the beginning of the police interview, many suspects have not yet decided whether to make a statement or even make a confession.[74] Coercive, dominant questioning methods may trigger their

[71] See above, Richard Carver, Section 2.3; Christina Sganga, Section 10.2; Wolfgang S. Heinz, Section 13.5.

[72] See above, Asbjrn Rachlew, Section 5.1.

[73] See, in detail, Asbjørn Rachlew, Chapter 5.

[74] See above, Asbjrn Rachlew, Section 5.1.4.

resistance and block them from providing information, whereas fair and cooperative interviewing is likely to make suspects cooperate with the police.[75] This has been proven to be true even in cases of persons suspected of terrorist crimes.[76] The evidence shows that investigative interviewing leads to much more reliable results with regard to the investigation and solving of crimes and even to more efficient prevention of acts of terrorism.

In addition, and in particular, as Frances Surmon-Böhr, Laurence Alison and Emily Alison describe in this volume, physical ill-treatment and torture may impair the capacity of the human brain to recall perceived information accurately.[77] As was said by Cesare Beccaria as long ago as 1764, torture may make anyone confess to any crime, be they guilty or innocent.[78] False confessions lead to false convictions.[79]

Each time an innocent is convicted, this is a tragedy and a grave injustice towards the affected person. That is bad enough. But additionally, at the same time, the guilty person will go free to commit more crimes. Thus, in cases where coercive questioning leads to false confessions and convictions, this will not contribute to our safety but may create additional unsafety for society. So investigative interviewing methods are not only a requirement of respect for human rights but also a tool for fighting crime more effectively.

The decision to use investigative interviewing methods is supported by strong legal considerations. Confession-oriented questioning starts from the assumption that the suspect is guilty. Such an approach is not in line with the presumption of innocence, which lies at the basis of each and every fair trial.[80] Even if there is strong evidence against a particular person, he or she must be given the opportunity to give an uninterrupted account of the event and to prove that he or she is innocent or, at least, that the evidence is not as overwhelming as it seems.[81]

Thus, it turns out that investigative interviewing is ethical and effective. It is a win-win method of questioning suspects by the police. In line with the presumption of innocence, the interviewer starts with an open mind about whether or not the suspect is guilty. In line with the proportionality principle, investigative interviewing is the least intrusive method of questioning. The human dignity of the interviewed

---

[75] See above, Asbjrn Rachlew, Section 5.2.4.

[76] See, for example, Leslie (2017).

[77] See above, Frances Surmon-Böhr, Laurence Alison and Emily Alison, Section 6.2.3.

[78] "The result of torture, then, is a matter of calculation, and depends on the constitution, which differs in every individual, and is in proportion to his strength and sensibility; so that to discover truth by this method, is a problem which may be better resolved by a mathematician than a judge, and may be thus stated: *The force of the muscles, and the sensibility of the nerves of an innocent person being given, it is required to find the degree of pain necessary to make him confess himself guilty of a given crime.*" Cesare Beccaria, An essay on crimes and punishments, 1764, Chapter XVI: Of Torture.

[79] See above, Frances Surmon-Böhr, Laurence Alison and Emily Alison, Section 6.2.4.

[80] See above, Asbjrn Rachlew, Section 5.1.1; Frances Surmon-Böhr, Laurence Alison and Emily Alison, Section 6.2.2.

[81] See above, Asbjrn Rachlew, Section 5.7.2.

person is respected in the best possible way. At the same time, investigative interviewing contributes to solving crimes more effectively than any method involving pressure or coercion. It is a necessary element of effective policing and professional competence.

Since investigative interviewing serves the interests of the affected person as well as the interests of the police, its dissemination and its introduction are undoubtedly key elements in ensuring the fair treatment of persons in police custody and abolishing all kinds of abuse, ill-treatment, and torture in the future. The former Special Rapporteur of the United Nations Against Torture, Juan A. Méndez, has advocated to introduce a universal protocol for interviews in his 2016 report.[82] The European Committee for the Prevention of Torture (CPT) has endorsed these efforts.[83] Since then, a group of experts from many countries and various professional backgrounds have elaborated the "Principles on Effective Interviewing for Investigations and Information Gathering" (the "Méndez Principles").[84] These principles were published in May 2021; they may be considered to be a big step towards preserving human dignity and solving crimes effectively all over the world.

14.4 Concluding Remarks and Outlook

As described in the Introduction, persons in police custody are not always treated in accordance with their human rights.[85] There is still too much suffering in (the detention cells of) the world. However, this is only a part of the truth. There has never been a time when so many governments, so many intergovernmental and non-governmental organisations, and so many smart and engaged people are joining their efforts to ensure that persons in police custody are treated fairly everywhere.

Since Amnesty International shocked the world with its report on torture 50 years ago,[86] the international community has come a long way towards effective human rights protection. In 1976, the international human rights covenants entered into force. In 1984, governments agreed on the Convention Against Torture. In 1990, the European Committee for the Prevention of Torture (CPT) took up its activities, and in 2007, the UN Subcommittee on Prevention of Torture (SPT) followed suit with worldwide reach and perspective. Governments throughout the world have decided

[82] Juan E. Méndez, Interim Report of the Special Rapporteur on torture and other cruel, inhuman or degrading treatment or punishment, 5 August 2016, UN-Doc. A/71/298.

[83] See CPT, Preventing police torture and other forms of ill-treatment – reflections on good practices and emerging approaches, 28th General Report, 2019, CPT/Inf (2019) 9, para. 73–80.

[84] Principles on Effective Interviewing for Investigations and Information Gathering, available at https://interviewingprinciples.com.

[85] See above, Section 1.3.

[86] Amnesty International (1973).

to open all places of detention for international monitoring bodies in order to improve the treatment of detained persons.

Based on the Optional Protocol to the Convention Against Torture (OPCAT), National Preventive Mechanisms (NPMs) have been created in the last 15 years. Under the supervision of the SPT, they are monitoring places of detention, including police stations. While fully preserving the sovereignty of states, the NPMs indicate ways to preserve the human rights of detained persons and improve their treatment to their governments, without prejudice to any legitimate security considerations. And given their relatively short history, their impact has only just started to materialise.

Yet not all governments are already making use of this option. While 173 states are party to the Convention Against Torture, only 91 have agreed to be bound by OPCAT so far.[87] For governments with a genuine will to improve the human rights situation of detained persons, including those in police custody, ratifying the OPCAT and creating a National Preventive Mechanism should be a very serious consideration.

We are not yet where we would like to be, and progress in human rights has so far often been achieved at a slower pace than might be desirable. At the same time, there is no reason to give up on the struggle. In many ways, the world is moving in the right direction, although there is still some way to go in ensuring, globally, the fair treatment of persons in police custody.

References

Amnesty International (1973) Report on Torture. Duckworth, London

Association for the Prevention of Torture (APT): Symposium on Procedural Safeguards in the first hours of police custody. Outcome Report, 2017

Beccaria C (1764) An essay on crimes and punishments. Available at: https://oll.libertyfund.org/title/voltaire-an-essay-on-crimes-and-punishments

Convention Against Torture Initiative (CTI), Safeguards in the first hours of police detention, 2017

Council of Europe, Committee of Ministers: Recommendation Rec (2001) 10 of the Committee of Ministers to member states on the European Code of Police Ethics, 19 September 2001

European Committee for the Prevention of Torture and Inhuman or Degrading Treatment or Punishment (CPT): Police Custody, Extract of the 2nd General Report, 1992, CPT/Inf (92) 3

European Committee for the Prevention of Torture and Inhuman or Degrading Treatment or Punishment (CPT): Developments concerning CPT standards in respect of police custody, Extract of the 12th General Report, 2002, CPT/Inf (2002) 15

European Committee for the Prevention of Torture and Inhuman or Degrading Treatment or Punishment (CPT): Report on the visit to Georgia in 2010, CPT/Inf (2010) 27

European Committee for the Prevention of Torture and Inhuman or Degrading Treatment or Punishment (CPT): Access to a lawyer as a means of preventing ill-treatment, Extract from the 21st General Report, CPT/Inf (2011) 28

[87] United Nations Treaty Collection, Multilateral Treaties Deposited with the Secretary-General, Chapter IV: Human Rights, Nr. 9, 9b, at: https://treaties.un.org/Pages/Treaties.aspx?id=4&subid=A&clang=_en.

European Committee for the Prevention of Torture and Inhuman or Degrading Treatment or Punishment (CPT): Report on the visit to Ukraine in 2009, CPT/Inf (2011) 29

European Committee for the Prevention of Torture and Inhuman or Degrading Treatment or Punishment (CPT): Report on the visit to Bulgaria in 2010, CPT/Inf (2012) 9

European Committee for the Prevention of Torture and Inhuman or Degrading Treatment or Punishment (CPT): Preventing police torture and other forms of ill-treatment—reflections on good practices and emerging approaches, 28th General Report, 2019, CPT/Inf (2019) 9, paras. 61–85

Jikia B, Shalikashvili M (2016) Georgia. In: Carver R, Handley L (eds) Does torture prevention work? Liverpool University Press, Liverpool, pp 395–417

Leslie I (2017) The scientists persuading terrorists to spill their secrets, The Guardian, 13 October 2017

Méndez JE (2016) Interim Report of the Special Rapporteur on torture and other cruel, inhuman or degrading treatment or punishment, 5 August 2016, UN-Doc. A/71/298

Principles on Effective Interviewing for Investigations and Information Gathering, available at https://interviewingprinciples.com

Smith G (2018) Effective investigation into alleged police human rights abuse: combating impunity. In: Alleweldt R, Fickenscher G (eds) The police and international human rights law, pp 83–101

Sub-Committee on Prevention of Torture and other Cruel, Inhuman or Degrading Treatment or Punishment (SPT): The approach of the Subcommittee on Prevention of Torture to the concept of prevention of torture and other cruel, inhuman or degrading treatment or punishment under the Optional Protocol, UN-Doc. CAT/OP/12/6, 30 December 2010

United Nations, Human Rights Council: Torture and other cruel, inhuman or degrading treatment or punishment: Safeguards to prevent torture during police custody and pretrial detention, UN Doc. A/HRC/31/L.26 rev.1, 23 March 2016

Ralf Alleweldt teaches constitutional law, EU law and international human rights law at the Brandenburg State Police University in Oranienburg. He holds an LLM from the European University Institute and a PhD from the University of Heidelberg. Since 2005 he has worked as a law teacher at the Yeditepe University Istanbul and the Universities of Constance, Potsdam and Munich as well as at the Catholic University of Eichstätt-Ingolstadt. He was also involved in long-term projects of the Council of Europe and the European Union dealing with justice reform in Ukraine and the legal education in EU law in Armenia. He has participated in human rights training and consulting activities in Eastern Europe and West Africa. From 2007 to 2012, he was an international scholar in the Academic Fellowship Program of the Open Society Institute.

His research interests include constitutional justice, refugee law and European human rights law including the prevention of torture. Important publications: Preamble to the 1951 Convention Relating to the Status of Refugees. In: Andreas Zimmermann (ed.), 1951 Convention Relating to the Status of Refugees and its 1967 Protocol (2nd ed. 2024); Avoiding another Brexit: the subsidiarity principle, the European Convention on Human Rights and the United Kingdom. Commonwealth and Comparative Studies 57 (2019), pp. 223–241; The police and international human rights law (ed., with Guido Fickenscher) (2018); Prevention of torture in the Black Sea region: progress or stagnation? In: Ralf Alleweldt, Raphaël Callsen, Jeanne Dupendant (eds.), Human rights abuses in the contemporary world (2012), pp. 27–45; Bundesverfassungsgericht und Fachgerichtsbarkeit (2006).

www.ingramcontent.com/pod-product-compliance
Lightning Source LLC
Chambersburg PA
CBHW070249260926
51849CB00001BA/89

* 9 7 8 3 0 3 1 6 1 7 3 6 2 *